IN MEMORIAM
Professor Michael Foley, University of Wales, Aberystwyth
Scholar, Educator, Thinker
Who contributed to this in so many ways.

DANGEROUS DIPLOMACY

Dangerous Diplomacy

Bureaucracy, Power Politics, and the Role of the UN Secretariat in Rwanda

HERMAN T. SALTON

OXFORD
UNIVERSITY PRESS

OXFORD

UNIVERSITY PRESS

Great Clarendon Street, Oxford, OX2 6DP,
United Kingdom

Oxford University Press is a department of the University of Oxford.
It furthers the University's objective of excellence in research, scholarship,
and education by publishing worldwide. Oxford is a registered trade mark of
Oxford University Press in the UK and in certain other countries

© Herman T. Salton 2017

The moral rights of the author have been asserted

First Edition published in 2017

Impression: 1

Published in the United States of America by Oxford University Press
198 Madison Avenue, New York, NY 10016, United States of America

British Library Cataloguing in Publication Data
Data available

Library of Congress Control Number: 2017935256

ISBN 978-0-19-873359-1

Printed in Great Britain by
CPI Group (UK) Ltd, Croydon, CR0 4YY

PER VEHIA
La mia Rosa di Tahiti
Che mi ha accompagnato in questo viaggio
Come nella vita

Foreword

This book reassesses the role of the United Nations (UN) Secretariat during what is arguably the worst atrocity since the Holocaust: the Rwandan genocide. As such, it deals with two tragedies: the human tragedy that engulfed Rwanda from April to July 1994, and the institutional tragedy that hit the Secretariat as it tried to manage that crisis. Although these two sets of events are obviously linked, the latter is broader in scope, is rooted in UN institutional history, and transcends Rwanda. The genocide resulted from a toxic mix of ethnic hatred, European colonialism, and racist propaganda, whereas the responses of the UN Secretariat to that event emerged from policy choices, bureaucratic competition, and power struggles in New York. This book connects these two tragedies by showing how the latter contributed to the former.

My interest in Rwanda and the UN goes back two decades. As an undergraduate in the early 1990s, I held a naïve view of the human condition and lofty expectations about the role of the UN. At that time it was the first tragedy—the human tragedy of Rwanda—that struck me, particularly the difficulty of comprehending why an entire population turned against itself. The more I read about the genocide and the conditions that led to it, the more motivated I became to understand what pushed ordinary people to kill their neighbours, priests to decapitate their parishioners, and mayors to organize death squads. All norms of civilized behaviour seemed to have collapsed in Rwanda, a reminder of Bertold Brecht's 'dark times' when 'there was only wrong and no outrage'.[1] As I moved to law school, I found the second tragedy—the institutional one involving the UN—even harder to grasp. One question stood out: why did the international organization which had *inter alia* been established to avert—and had a legal obligation to prevent—another Holocaust remain idle in the face of genocide? Grotius's *jus gentium*, at least as presented to me in international law classes, seemed as far removed from those events as possible. The 'gentle civilizer of nations' had failed, and so had the body set up to enforce it.[2] Though traumatized by the UN's role in Bosnia, Sergio Vieira de Mello described the Rwandan genocide as 'the gravest single act of betrayal ever committed by the United Nations'.[3]

---

[1] Hannah Arendt, *Men in Dark Times* (New York: Harcourt Brace, 1968), p.viii.

[2] Jens David Ohlin, *The Assault on International Law* (Oxford: Oxford University Press, 2015).

[3] Samantha Power, *Chasing the Flame* (London: Allen Lane, 2008), p.200.

As a cosmopolitan with an aversion to borders and serious misgivings about the idea of nation-state, my explanation for 1994 was parsimonious as well as dangerously circular: states—greedy, selfish, and cynical—had prevented the UN Secretariat from carrying out its mission. Partly because international law had failed to address my early questions about global affairs, my interest then turned to the broader field of international relations, which nevertheless cemented my negative outlook on states. The idea that international organizations may have faults as well as strengths of their own, that both could exist independently of states, and that they may have positive as well as negative implications for international affairs, only crossed my mind when I was exposed to the constructivist and bureaucratic literatures as a graduate student in Oxford.[4] Together with my interest in the UN, those works encouraged me to learn more about the UN institutional history, especially the link between the Secretary-General, 'his' or 'her' bureaucracy, and states. Although New York is supposedly home to some key fault lines in international relations and global ethics—internationalism and statism, cosmopolitanism and relativism, as well as 'global' and domestic interests—little research exists on the institution where such fault lines intersect: the UN bureaucracy.

Given the gulf that separates the theory and the practice of international affairs—or, to use E. H. Carr's distinction, the 'Intellectual' and the 'Bureaucrat'—this should not surprise. Academics think along broad lines, whereas practitioners do so empirically; the former tend to make practice conform to theory and see their work as influencing practitioners, whereas bureaucrats perceive themselves as experts handling specific problems on their merit. Curiously, however, both professions regard themselves as *au-dessus de la mêlée*, or dispassionate, if not neutral, towards a given problem—intellectuals by virtue of their scholarly outlook, bureaucrats by way of their technocratic expertise. As Carr noted, 'When a bureaucrat wishes to damn a proposal, he calls it "academic". Practice, not theory, bureaucratic training, not intellectual brilliance, is the school of political wisdom.'[5]

Carr's distinction struck a chord with me in 2008, when I briefly worked at the Office of the Under-Secretary-General for Political Affairs (DPA) in New York. Having been given the task of attempting to conceptualize the DPA's preventive diplomacy efforts and enhancing their visibility, I also experienced the effects of institutional pathology—especially of an inter-departmental kind—from close up. My interest in the links between the UN bureaucracy and member states was further reinforced in 2011 when I was given exclusive

---

[4] Michael Barnett and Martha Finnemore, 'The Politics, Power, and Pathologies of International Organizations', *International Organization*, Vol.53, No.4 (1999), p.710; Michael Barnett, *Rules for the World* (Ithaca: Cornell University Press, 2004); Michael Barnett, *Eyewitness to a Genocide* (Ithaca: Cornell University Press, 2002).

[5] Edward H. Carr, *The Twenty Years' Crisis, 1919–1939* (Basingstoke: Palgrave Macmillan, 2001), p.16.

and unrestricted access to the papers of the late Sir Marrack Goulding—an Under-Secretary-General from 1986 to 1997—in view of their publication. This is the point where my academic interest *in* the UN began to overlap with my professional experience *of* the UN—and where my Oxford research became *Dangerous Diplomacy*. What follows reflects that fascinating but difficult process of interaction between academic analysis, policy debates, and archival research.

Acknowledgements

Writing a book is a lonely enterprise, but conceiving of one is a collaborative process. During both phases I contracted many debts with numerous people on several continents.

In Oxford, Exeter College and the Department of Politics and International Relations were instrumental in encouraging me to develop this research. I am especially grateful to Jonathan Wright, Professor Emeritus at Christ Church, who read an early version of this project and provided comments and criticism; *Dangerous Diplomacy* was born out of our discussions in his picturesque office overlooking the Christ Church cathedral. Anne Deighton, Rosemary Foot, Mishana Hosseinioun, Neil MacFarlane, Milos Martinov, Victoria Petitjean, Salim Rachid, Avi Shlaim, and two anonymous examiners offered invaluable feedback. The Academic Council on the United Nations System (ACUNS) supported an earlier version through their Dissertation Award. I am very grateful to them all.

In London, my heartfelt thanks go to the Goulding family, especially Henry Goulding and Susan d'Albiac, who entrusted me with confidential documents and sensitive information. They handed over an archive that was unknown to them and that turned out to contain highly personal—at times uncomfortably personal—details to somebody who was then a perfect stranger. I have enormous respect for the dignity they have shown in coming to terms with some of the most unpalatable aspects of those papers. I also greatly appreciate the complete independence they have granted me, which of course includes the freedom to come to my own assessments about people and events. Henry, in particular, has been a source of inspiration throughout his medical ordeals. David Hannay and Mark Malloch Brown generously gave their time to discuss some of the concepts behind this book.

In New York, I incurred more debts than I can acknowledge. Tom Weiss, through his encyclopaedic knowledge of the UN and good humour, made my research leave at the Graduate Centre of the City University of New York possible, productive, and pleasurable. Also in New York, James Jonah, Álvaro de Soto, and several former UN colleagues gave me useful advice and much food for thought. I am indebted to Steven Siqueira for discussing with me some of the issues underlying this book with his usual candour, and to Joan Felli for always making me feel at home at the UN.

In Wales, Simon Rushton offered excellent feedback, constructive criticism, and much encouragement, while the late Mike Foley provided exceptionally detailed and helpful feedback throughout the life of this project. Mike's integrity, thoroughness, and kindness remain a source of inspiration and will be sorely missed. Ian Clark, Alistair Finlan, Milja Kurki, Laura Lima, Andrew Linklater, Jenny Mathers, Linda Melvern, Justin Morris, Richard Rathbone, Len Scott, and Hidemi Suganami were generous with their suggestions, as was Ayla Göl, who also provided a good deal of friendship. I have greatly benefited from the intellectual and practical support of the remarkable group of scholars who call Aberystwyth their home.

In Asia, Faiz Ahmad, Meherun Ahmed, Rosie Bateson, Joanne Bretzer, Varuni Ganepola, Sharmistha Ghosh, Bhupinder Gupta, Nirmala Rao, Sangita Rayamajhi, John Stanlake, and Sarah Shehabuddin provided me with a 'home away from home', while Ezaz Afzal, Fahima Aziz, Geneviève Gamache, Jinnie Garrett, Andrea Phillott, and all of my students were exposed—far more than they deserved—to the joys and sorrows that accompanied this book. My outstanding teaching assistants—Rebecca Dawson, Emily Eckardt, Janeen Mantin, and Katarina O'Regan—protected me from some of the demands of teaching, while my research assistants—Anshu Adhikari, Latifa Ayazi, Tshering Denkar, Thuy Huynhle, Maliha Khan, Deki Peldon, Mercy Rezaun Nahid, and Farihah Tasneem—were both professional and friendly. I am especially grateful to my editorial assistant, Erina Mahmud, for her diligence, speed, and hard work in preparing this manuscript for submission.

In Italy, my family and especially my parents, Giuseppe and Graziella Salton, showed great forbearance and offered tremendous support, alongside the best writing retreat one could hope for. Words cannot convey my gratitude to them; they are the two persons I most admire in life and they will always be my main source of inspiration. I am also indebted to my sister Manuela and my brother-in-law Paolo Manera, without whom I would not have been able to go to Oxford. Their generous support has been unstinting.

At Oxford University Press—a 'City upon a Hill'—Dominic Byatt has my profound gratitude for his kindness, professionalism, and enthusiasm. This project was accompanied by a health condition that made it difficult, and at times impossible, to meet deadlines. My thanks go to Dominic and to all those at OUP—including Kim Allen, Lisa Eaton, Ela Kotkowska, Sarah Parker, and Olivia Wells—who responded with patience and compassion to my enforced delays. Michael Barnett and OUP's three anonymous reviewers also provided outstanding feedback. Any remaining error is of course mine alone.

Last but not least, in Tahiti, Vehia La Neve has remained a constant source of love and support. I dedicate this book to her, *ma rose tahitienne*.

Herman Tutehau Salton

Yangon, Myanmar
October 2016

Contents

Dramatis Personae Maiores

Albright, Madeleine	US Permanent Representative to the UN, 1993–96; US Secretary of State, 1997–2001
Annan, Kofi	Under-Secretary-General for Peacekeeping, 1993–96; UN Secretary-General, 1997–2006
Baril, Maurice	DPKO's Military Adviser, 1992–95
Beardsley, Brent	UNAMIR's Military Attaché, 1993–94
Bolton, John	US Assistant Secretary of State for International Organization, 1989–93; US Permanent Representative to the UN, 2005–06
Booh Booh, Jacques-Roger	Special Representative of the Secretary-General in Rwanda, 1993–94
Boutros-Ghali, Boutros	UN Secretary-General, 1992–96
Christopher, Warren	US Secretary of State, 1993–97
Clinton, Bill	President of the United States, 1993–2001
Dallaire, Roméo	UNAMIR's Force Commander, 1993–94
De Soto, Álvaro	Special Political Adviser to the Secretary-General, 1982–94; Assistant Secretary-General for Political Affairs, 1995–99
Gambari, Ibrahim	Nigerian Permanent Representative to the UN, 1990–99
Gharekhan, Chinmaya	Special Representative of the Secretary-General to the Security Council, 1993–96
Goulding, Marrack	Under-Secretary-General for Special Political Affairs, 1986–91; Under-Secretary-General for Peacekeeping, 1992–93; Under-Secretary-General for Political Affairs, 1993–96
Habyarimana, Juvénal	President of Rwanda, 1978–94
Hannay, David	UK Permanent Representative to the UN, 1990–95
Jonah, James	Assistant Secretary-General for Special Political Questions, 1991–92; Under-Secretary-General for Political Affairs, 1992–94
Kagame, Paul	Leader of Rwandan Patriotic Front; President of Rwanda, 1994–current

Mitterrand, François	President of France, 1981–95
Mubarak, Hosni	President of Egypt, 1981–2011
Pérez de Cuéllar, Javier	UN Secretary-General, 1982–91
Riza, Iqbal	Assistant Secretary-General for Peacekeeping, 1993–96; Chief of Staff to the Secretary-General, 1997–2006

Abbreviations

ASG	Assistant Secretary-General
DPA	Department of Political Affairs
DPKO	Department of Peacekeeping Operations
EOSG	Executive Office of the Secretary-General
E-10	Ten Elected Members of the Security Council
IL	International law
IO	International organization
IR	International relations
LMRGA	Linda Melvern Rwanda Genocide Archive
MIG-MD	Marrack Irvine Goulding—Meeting Diary
MIG-PA	Marrack Irvine Goulding—Personal Archive
MIG-PD	Marrack Irvine Goulding—Personal Diary
MIG-TD	Marrack Irvine Goulding—Travelling Diary
MIPR	Mission d'Information Parlementaire sur le Rwanda
NATO	North Atlantic Treaty Organization
NGO	Non-governmental organization
OIOS	Office of Internal Oversight Services
ORCI	Office for the Research and Collection of Information
OSPA	Office for Special Political Affairs
P-5	Five Permanent Members of the Security Council
PBC	Peacebuilding Commission
R2P	Responsibility to Protect
RDP	Rwanda Documents Project
RGF	Rwandan Government Forces
ROE	Rules of Engagement
RPF	Rwandan Patriotic Front
SC	Security Council
SG	Secretary-General
SITREPS	Situation reports
SRSG	Special Representative of the Secretary-General
UN	United Nations
UNAMIR	United Nations Assistance Mission for Rwanda
UNOMUR	United Nations Observer Mission to Uganda–Rwanda
UNOSOM	United Nations Operation in Somalia
USG	Under-Secretary-General

Introduction

Bureaucracy, Power, and Tragedy in Rwanda

The year 2014 marked the twentieth anniversary of the Rwandan genocide. Although much has been written about it by journalists, academics, and officials, the role of the United Nations (UN) Secretariat during this horrific event has attracted comparatively little attention. The New York bureaucracy has been criticized for a number of shortcomings, but the consensus remains that it could do little against the powerful members of the Security Council (SC).[1] It was Washington, London, and Paris—not New York—that sealed the fate of Rwanda, where non-intervention was the fault of self-interested states. While international relations (IR) scholars will find this statist view familiar, most UN officials would also endorse it. My early outlook mirrored Lord Caradon's remark according to which there is nothing wrong with the UN that is not attributable to its members.

A growing body of literature has questioned this approach and has suggested that, like most bureaucracies, the UN Secretariat projects as well as reflects power[2]—that it does more than states wish (and mandate) it to do.[3] This book aims to contribute to that debate by carrying out an in-depth reassessment of the role of the UN Secretariat during the Rwandan genocide, focusing specifically on the decision-making processes in New York. Perhaps unsurprisingly

---

[1] David Ambrosetti, *La France au Rwanda* (Paris: Karthala, 2000); Colette Braeckman, *Rwanda* (Paris: Fayard, 1993); Gérard Prunier, *Rwanda 1959–1996* (Paris: Éditions Dagorno, 1997).

[2] Samuel Barkin, *International Organization* (Basingstoke: Palgrave Macmillan, 2013); Michael Barnett and Raymond Duvall, eds, *Power in Global Governance* (Cambridge: Cambridge University Press, 2004).

[3] Thomas Weiss and Rorden Wilkinson, eds, *International Organization and Global Governance* (Abingdon: Routledge, 2013); Kenneth Abbott et al., *International Organizations as Orchestrators* (Cambridge: Cambridge University Press, 2015); Joel Oestreich, ed., *International Organizations as Self-Directed Actors* (Abingdon: Routledge, 2012); Guglielmo Verdirame, *The UN and Human Rights* (Cambridge: Cambridge University Press, 2011); Silke Weinlich, *The UN Secretariat's Influence over the Evolution of Peacekeeping* (Basingstoke: Palgrave Macmillan, 2014).

since the UN is more often associated with the mighty SC than with the self-effacing Secretariat, books on the former greatly outnumber those on the latter. Even the few that do focus on the UN bureaucracy tend to treat it as a coherent body and assume a pyramidal system where decisions at the top are executed by those at the bottom.[4] Inis Claude's influential distinction between 'the two UNs'—one made up of states and the other of international civil servants—reflects the widespread perception that Secretary-General (SG) and Secretariat form a coherent unit. It certainly reinforced my early prejudices about 'good' Secretariat officials working for the benefit of humankind *vis-à-vis* 'bad' national diplomats defending the narrow interests of their governments.[5] Although a 'third UN'—made up of experts and non-governmental organizations (NGOs)—has helpfully been added to Claude's classification,[6] it does not fundamentally alter the image of a monolithic Secretariat upon which such classification rests. As I soon discovered, in New York my IR and international law (IL) toolkits proved useful and burdensome in equal measure—useful as they allowed me to see links and draw parallels, burdensome as they blinded me to others.

Recently declassified documents, the Goulding Archive, and my own experience paint a more idiosyncratic decision-making process whereby different parts of the UN Secretariat are often at odds with each other—and with the SG. To bring into focus this neglected factor, Part I considers the roles played by each of the key UN units involved in Rwanda: the Department of Peacekeeping Operations (DPKO), the Department of Political Affairs (DPA), the United Nations Assistance Mission for Rwanda (UNAMIR), the SG's office, and the SC. Only by looking at the contribution of—and interactions among—all of the Secretariat's players can we hope to trace the complex web of decisions reached in New York during the Rwandan crisis. Among other findings, this in-depth analysis shows a fragmented Secretariat composed of semi-autonomous entities that disagreed over the best course of action, failed to cooperate, and concealed important information from each other. While competition is hardly unusual in large organizations, in 1994 intra-UN strife was so serious that the Secretariat did not—and could not—speak with one voice. Conflict in New York preceded and influenced conflict in Rwanda, a situation that affected UN peacekeeping there and elsewhere.

---

[4] Leon Gordenker, *The UN Secretary-General and the Maintenance of Peace* (New York: Columbia University Press, 1967); Leon Gordenker, *The UN Secretary-General and Secretariat* (Abingdon: Routledge, 2010); Thant Myint-U and Amy Scott, *The UN Secretariat* (New York: International Peace Academy, 2007).

[5] Inis Claude, *Swords into Plowshares* (New York: Random House, 1971).

[6] Thomas Weiss et al., 'The "Third" United Nations', *Global Governance*, Vol.15 (2009), pp.123–42.

ARGUMENTS

Having found that the UN Secretariat lacked a coherent policy in the run-up to the Rwandan genocide and that different departments and officials adopted different positions, Part II identifies three explanations for this fragmentation. The first is bureaucratic and comes down to the competition existing before, during, and after the genocide between the two most important parts of the UN Secretariat, DPKO and DPA. While the existing literature focuses almost exclusively on DPKO and ignores DPA's role in both Rwanda and New York, this book takes a different approach. It suggests that while DPA worked behind the scenes in 1994, it did so tirelessly and was instrumental in shaping the contours of the Rwanda operation, carrying out—though not necessarily sharing—assessments of the local situation while also conducting the peace negotiations that preceded, accompanied, and followed the genocide. The 'political' department and its leaders were also tasked with limiting the influence of DPKO, a unit that the SG saw as under direct US control. Although Goulding likened the roles of DPA and DPKO to having two referees in one ring, the often different agendas of DPA and DPKO, coupled with their respective supporters, meant that neither department could be a truly impartial referee in Rwanda. DPA's broad mission, proximity to the SG, and neglect by the UN literature makes it an especially intriguing object of study.

The second explanation for the Secretariat's fragmentation in Rwanda is linked to the bureaucratic confrontation between DPA and DPKO, but has a significant power-political dimension to it. The fact that these two departments were clashing in 1994 is hardly surprising, since at the time of the Rwandan genocide DPA saw itself—and, importantly, was perceived by Boutros-Ghali—as the 'eyes and ears' of the SG and as his prime tool to balance the rising influence of the Washington-backed DPKO ('the blue-eyed boy of member states',[7] as a senior UN official described it to me). As a result, in 1994 competition between these two departments was more than a clash of personalities or a struggle for bureaucratic influence within the Secretariat. It was also a fight to assert the independence of the SG *vis-à-vis* the UN membership in general and the USA in particular, especially after the trauma of Somalia. UNAMIR was set up in this toxic environment and paid a steep price for this power struggle in New York.

The third rationale for the DPA–DPKO confrontation involves the conceptual difficulty of separating peacebuilding and peacekeeping. Until the early 1990s this remained a largely abstract question to the extent that the Cold War had paralysed the organization and these two tasks had been centrally managed by the SG via his Executive Office (EOSG). Following the collapse of

---

[7] My interview with Álvaro de Soto, 20 July 2011, New York, USA (and via email on 4 June 2016).

the Soviet Union and the renewed optimism for the UN, however, in 1992 responsibility for peacebuilding and peacekeeping was split and two new departments created, with DPA supposedly in charge of 'political' negotiations while DPKO was to be responsible for the 'operational' aspects of peacekeeping. As this book shows, however, this separation worsened the friction in New York, a friction that also percolated to Rwanda. While the issue of the so-called 'political' functions of the SG has been confronting the UN since its founding, it gained prominence in mid-1993, precisely when UNAMIR was set up. Then, the conceptual confusion between peacekeeping and peacebuilding fuelled long-held doubts about the roles of DPA and DPKO, both of which claimed the right to carry out 'political' functions that nevertheless remained largely undefined. If Aristotle was right that man is by nature a 'political animal' (ζῷον πολιτικόν, or *zōon politikón*),[8] then most human endeavours are also 'political'—an argument that DPA and DPKO used to expand their functions.

Twenty years on, why does all this matter? *Dangerous Diplomacy* suggests that the Secretariat of 1994 was split by internal rivalries and competing agendas that negatively affected the Rwanda operation. Although the constructivist and principal–agent theories of IR have advanced our knowledge of international organizations (IOs) in important ways, the former has stopped short of 'deconstructing' the UN Secretariat of 1994 into its constituent units, whereas the latter has underestimated the possibility that different parts of the same bureaucracy (such as DPA and DPKO) may be used by different IR actors (such as SGs and member states) to promote different interests and to push for divergent policy outcomes (such as intervention and nonintervention). In their quest for generally applicable patterns, these excellent theories also neglect a circumstance that seems to be more familiar to historians than to IR scholars: consequences are often unintended and policies—including UN policies—depend on individuals as much as on structures and processes. While DPA and DPKO are part of the same bureaucracy and share a number of bureaucratic pathologies, they differ from their closest comparators (such as a Ministry of Foreign Affairs and a Ministry of Defence) in several ways. As we shall see, factors that affected their 'behaviour' in 1994 included their closeness to the SG and to the UN membership, their bureaucratic 'cultures', events on the ground, and the personal views and professional ambitions of their leaders. In Rwanda, the UN Secretariat was neither an autonomous body nor an appendix of states. It was in some way not a unified actor at all, but a collection of departments and individuals with a range of interests, supporters, and agendas.

Far from being a sterile bureaucratic hub, this book comes to the conclusion that the UN Secretariat can be an arena where different departments and

---

[8] Hannah Arendt, *The Human Condition* (Chicago: University of Chicago Press, 1998), p.27.

leaders—in addition to SGs and states—vie for influence and power. Internal Secretariat politics is never really 'internal' but always to some extent international, and looking at the fluctuating fortunes of DPA and DPKO provides fascinating clues not only about the pathologies of the Secretariat, but also about the degree of independence sought by SGs *vis-à-vis* states—another reason why studying the UN bureaucracy is both useful and exciting. At least with reference to UN Headquarters, Susan Strange's characterization of IOs as the 'Great Yawn'[9] thus appears misplaced.

SOURCES

The prevailing view of the SG as 'powerless' is not the only reason for the dearth of academic scrutiny of the UN bureaucracy. Reconstructing the institutional history of the Secretariat through primary sources is labour-intensive and requires first-hand materials that are often difficult—if not impossible—to find. This is particularly true at Headquarters, a place that has retained some of its Cold War secrecy.[10] Against this background, the emergence of new sources—including the personal diaries and private papers of the head of DPA during the Rwandan crisis, new French and UN materials, several interviews with key players, as well as the minutes of the Council's secret meetings on Rwanda—is noteworthy.

The archive of the late Sir Marrack Goulding and the opportunities and challenges it presents require a dedicated explanation. As Under-Secretary-General (USG) for Peacekeeping (1992–93) and Political Affairs (1993–97), and as Boutros-Ghali's most trusted adviser (1992–96), in 1994 Goulding was effectively the highest-ranking UN official after the SG. Although he died in 2010, Goulding kept meticulous diaries throughout his career, along with a significant quantity of private papers. In 2011 his family granted me exclusive and unrestricted access to all of his diaries and papers, and asked me to work towards their publication (they will be deposited, albeit in embargoed form, with Oxford's Bodleian Library). Goulding rode the crest of the UN wave—including the 'Golden Age' of peacekeeping, which in 1988 won him the Nobel Peace Prize with the Blue Helmets[11]—and is especially well placed to record its crash against the rocks of the early 1990s.

---

[9] See Susan Strange, *The Retreat of the State* (Cambridge: Cambridge University Press, 1997).
[10] Because of confidentiality clauses, this book does not of course use any document or any information I was privy to during my time in New York.
[11] 'U.N. Peacekeeping Forces Named Winner of the Nobel Peace Prize', *The New York Times*, 30 September 1988. UN peacekeepers are often referred to as 'Blue Helmets'.

For a book on bureaucratic pathology, Goulding matters on another level. Having been given the role of UN chief peacekeeper at the end of the Cold War—a job that had only been held by Count Bernadotte, Ralph Bunche, and Brian Urquhart, the three 'founding fathers' of the UN—Goulding 'inherited' UN peacekeeping in the late 1980s, single-handedly managed it until 1991, oversaw the creation of DPA and DPKO in 1992, and went on to lead both departments. Bureaucratically, therefore, Goulding cannot easily be pigeon-holed, an infrequent occurrence in Boutros-Ghali's factionalized Secretariat. Partly as a result of his split allegiances, Goulding also often disagreed with his DPA colleagues and, to Boutros-Ghali's chagrin, sided with Kofi Annan and DPKO on a number of issues. Despite being frustrated by what he called the 'trench warfare' between DPA and DPKO that had become so pervasive in the early 1990s, Goulding also failed to contain it. Few UN diplomats were thus more knowledgeable about—and had more professional exposure to—the issues discussed in this book than Goulding. Although in 2002 he published his memoirs, *Peacemonger* covers Goulding's earlier time in charge of peacekeeping (1986–92) but is largely silent about his stint at DPA and his post-1992 roles, including in Rwanda.[12] '[T]he vineyards in which I laboured were no longer missions in the field but committees in New York',[13] a thwarted Goulding wrote of his later assignments. As this book will suggest, however, those vineyards were hardly infertile and institutional historians are unlikely to find them tedious either.

INTERNAL BIAS

None of the above makes Goulding's archive less challenging to use. Like all private papers, Goulding's raise the issue of internal bias, that is, the possibility that he may have had an agenda. His diaries regularly mix the very private—hence his family's decision to embargo them—with the professional, thus suggesting that they were not meant for publication (unlike letter-writing, diary-keeping is rarely a performative act).[14] Yet they are still diaries and are inevitably one-sided, something that this book tries to balance through a wealth of other materials and by highlighting the points where (and the reasons why) Goulding may have been being self-serving. While many of Goulding's thoughts were in my view prescient, I disagree with some of his positions and I suspect that the Briton would have likewise dissented from some of the arguments put forward in this book. The fact that his frankness in

[12] Marrack Goulding, *Peacemonger* (London: John Murray, 2002).
[13] Goulding, *Peacemonger*, p.333.
[14] See John Searle, *Expression and Meaning* (Cambridge: Cambridge University Press, 1976).

life is more than matched by his outspoken papers will not come as a surprise; Goulding had strong views on a range of subjects and individuals, and while this makes for fascinating reading, it also makes it prudent to approach his archive with the same vigilance that E. H. Carr urged in relation to the Stresemann papers: 'These documents do not tell us what happened, but only what Gustav Stresemann thought had happened, or what he wanted others to think, or perhaps what he wanted himself to think had happened.... What really happened would still have to be reconstructed in the mind of the historian.'[15]

Therein lies another difficulty, albeit a familiar one to historians. In a book published in 1989, Arlette Farge described the mix of exhilaration and exhaustion, of promises and perils, that archival research produces. Archives are intriguing, important, and thrilling, but also intimidating, unnerving, and daunting. They can even be dangerous because they offer a 'torrent of singularities'[16]—or the appearance of ordered and logical patterns—in a context where exceptions abound, should one have the skills and time to find them. 'Just as archives provide evidence for arguments, they undo them; for as soon as a pattern seems to emerge from one set of boxes, it is displaced by a contradictory configuration from the next set.'[17] Depressingly, a complete absence of contradictions is more alarming still: even the towering Tocqueville overstated the centralizing tendencies of the French monarchy because he limited his scrutiny to a set of boxes which contained the correspondence between royal officials and Versailles, thus giving the false impression that Paris controlled everything. Nevertheless, 'traces of the soul'[18] are arguably more likely to be found in archives than in other historical materials, which is why for Farge they are an acquired taste, as the title of her book (*Le Goût de l'Archive*) evocatively suggests.

Farge's comments have resonated throughout this project. There is disproportion between the Goulding archive—one of the largest private collections of UN-related documents—and the paucity of primary sources on the inner workings of the UN, a gap that often makes it impossible to corroborate Goulding's statements. This is especially so since the British official adopted a peculiar approach to diary-keeping, seeing it as his duty to record events and discussions, rather than commenting on them. This obsession with what he saw as factual accuracy led him to keep as many as three daily diaries throughout his forty-year career: meeting, travelling, and personal diaries.

---

[15] Edward H. Carr, *What is History?* (Basingstoke: Palgrave Macmillan, 2001), p.13.
[16] Arlette Farge, *Le Goût de l'Archive* (Paris: Éditions du Seuil, 1989). Unless otherwise stated, all translations are mine. See also Jacques Derrida, *Archive Fever* (Chicago: University of Chicago Press, 1988); Carolyn Steedman, *Dust* (Manchester: Manchester University Press, 2001).
[17] Robert Darnton, 'The Good Way to Do History', *The New York Review of Books*, 9 January 2014, p.54.
[18] Darnton, p.55.

Consequently, his entries were often scribbled 'on the go' in pocket notebooks which he carried everywhere and that record his meetings, field trips, and on-the-spot reactions—more like a reporter's notes than diaries. While this creates problems in terms of information overload and consistency of assessments, the historian will find much of interest in Goulding's attempt to contribute to the historical record by minuting confidential meetings and by recounting little-known events. Although Goulding had a reputation for frankness,[19] his diaries are not 'neutral' and when he fails to be balanced, he fails spectacularly. Yet they are unusually candid, including—indeed, especially—about his (and the UN's) failures. As one of Goulding's obituaries noted, 'His subtitle was "Win some, lose some", and although his years were the most successful of any in UN peacekeeping, he was more inclined to accept blame for the failures than credit for the successes.'[20]

EXTERNAL BIAS

Since it is easier to recognize somebody else's partiality than our own, the risk of external bias—that is, of me unduly relying on Goulding's materials—is potentially even more problematic than the partiality of those papers.[21] Though I never met Goulding and my interest in him is purely scholarly, the nature of my access to his archive increases that risk exponentially, particularly since I share Goulding's support for the UN and his preference for multilateralism as a way of solving international disputes. Some scholars are also understandably uncomfortable with the idea of 'exclusive' access to primary sources, for this amplifies the risk of uncritical exposure to (and unchecked overreliance on) those materials. The fact that, like Goulding, I briefly worked for DPA creates additional problems, though two of the most sophisticated accounts of the role of the UN Secretariat in Rwanda were written by former practitioners who, like me, found that the IR literature did not prepare them for their policy experiences in IOs.[22]

Biases are best controlled when an author is aware of them and when the reader is told about them, hence this introduction's personal touch. In this

---

[19] See Ingvild Bode, *Individual Agency and Policy Change at the UN* (Abingdon: Routledge, 2015), p.162.

[20] United Nations Association Oxford, quoted in Bode, p.162.

[21] Carr, *What is History?*, p.24; Pierre Renouvin and Jean-Baptiste Duroselle, *Introduction à l'Histoire des Relations Internationales* (Paris: Armand Colin, 2007); Ennio Di Nolfo, *Prima Lezione di Storia delle Relazioni Internazionali* (Rome: Laterza, 2006).

[22] Barnett and Finnemore, *Rules for the World*, p.vii. See also Michael Barnett, 'The UN Security Council, Indifference, and Genocide in Rwanda', *Cultural Anthropology*, Vol.12, No.4 (1997), pp.551–78.

respect, it should soon become clear that this book is hardly a hagiography of Goulding, DPA, or the UN, although it is certainly committed to treating them fairly. Yet biases are also inevitable when the subject is a misunderstood and inherently ambiguous organization the functions of which can be seen through several lenses. My conclusions are a case in point: the Secretariat of 1994 emerges from this book as a place where different bureaucratic units competed with each other, where the influence of certain states over some of those units was considerable, and where the choices of the SG were often frustrated by his own bureaucratic machinery. That SGs cannot fully rely on their 'cabinets'—USG posts being 'vetted' and often chosen by influential capitals in what is referred to as 'institutional power'—is well known.[23] Less recognized is the fact that the UN bureaucracy can itself, under certain circumstances, become a playground between member states and SGs, and that the head of the UN Secretariat has far less control over his bureaucracy than is assumed. Whether this situation is regrettable or desirable, however, depends entirely upon one's outlook of the UN and international politics. Sensitivities over the independence of the international civil service, in particular, reflect a legitimate split between those who perceive the UN Secretariat as an inter-*governmental* body that should do nothing more than its members want, on the one hand; and those who see it as the duty of SGs and their officials to push states to implement the provisions of the UN Charter, on the other. This fault line in turn reflects the historically ambiguous relations between the statist and the cosmopolitan streams of the UN founding document, an ambiguity that reverberates throughout this book. The 'alchemic' qualities attached by the Charter to the UN and to DPA—both of which are supposed to turn the 'metal' of conflict into the 'gold' of peace—are examples of that ambiguity. The latter is deepened by the fact that the UN Secretariat is often and 'by default' assumed to be cosmopolitan and to pursue the larger interests of humanity, rather than those of the UN members. Yet the UN is as much an expression of nationalism as internationalism, and it is hardly uncommon for different parts of the Secretariat to support whichever approach bureaucratically benefits them the most.

All this to note that this project's challenges are considerable. They consist in handling a large quantity of new sources that are necessarily subjective and were produced across several decades, with the need to situate them within the Rwandan, UN, and IR contexts—while also coming to a balanced assessment of departments and individuals that became entangled in what can only be described as horrific events. E. H. Carr defined history as 'a continuous process

---

[23] Claude, p.192. See also Marrack Goulding, Letter to N.B., 28 May 2001, Marrack Irvine Goulding Personal Archive (hereinafter, MIG-PA).

of interaction between the historian and his facts, an unending dialogue between the past and the present'.[24] This book aims to contribute to that dialogue.

FOCUS

A further peril involves the intentionally narrow focus of this book. Concentrating on the Secretariat rather than the UN organization as a whole may seem eccentric and, seen from New York, also largely unfair, given the influential nations (the USA, France, Egypt) and the complex issues (colonialism, ethnic conflict, border disputes) involved in the events of 1994. While touching upon concurrent crises in Somalia, Bosnia, and Haiti, this book focuses on Rwanda, a choice that prioritizes depth over breadth but that necessarily constrains its explanatory value. My use of the word 'tragedy' can also be said to overstate the role of the Secretariat in those events: if an *institutional* tragedy existed in 1994, surely it affected the UN organization as a whole— especially the SC—rather than a part of it?

As a former practitioner of international affairs, I am sympathetic to the claim that the SG and Secretariat are routinely censured for faults that lie elsewhere. The most visible IO also attracts the criticism of those who simply see the Secretariat as another bureaucracy—bloated, unaccountable, and un-representative,[25] 'a Remington typewriter in a smartphone world',[26] as a former Assistant Secretary-General defined it. In 2015, a *Guardian* report on the UN's 70th anniversary unceremoniously dismissed the organization as 'a byzantine, unaccountable, inscrutable, alphabet soupocracy of 85,000 people that has spent half a trillion dollars over the past 70 years, a significant portion of it on its own bureaucratic needs'.[27] On the other side of the fence, its human losses mean that Rwanda remains an emotionally charged subject at the UN— an organization, to borrow James Baldwin's description of the USA *vis-à-vis* race relations, 'suffering from a pain so profound that it cannot be discussed openly'.[28] Being accused of contributing to an event—genocide at that—over which one felt little control is unfair. Given my past connection to the UN and DPA, it may even be seen as an act of defiance, if not betrayal.

The reverse is true. In a letter to his publisher, Goulding noted that his frankness in *Peacemonger* may damage his friendships and upset some of his

[24] Carr, *What is History?*, p.30.
[25] James Wilson, *Bureaucracy* (New York: Basic Books, 1991).
[26] Anthony Banbury, 'I Love the UN, But it is Failing', *The New York Times*, 18 March 2016.
[27] Mark Rice-Oxley, 'Happy 70th Birthday, United Nations', *The Guardian*, 8 September 2015.
[28] Nathaniel Rich, 'James Baldwin & the Fear of a Nation', *The New York Review of Books*, 12 May 2016.

UN colleagues. 'But', he continued, 'I am now convinced that if the book is to have any historical value (and I would like it to do so), it cannot be silent about the weaknesses of individuals, including the author, where these affected the UN's performance.'[29] This is precisely what this project aims to do—without fear or favour—with Goulding as well as with the UN Secretariat, namely, refrain from gratuitous criticism while not shying away from reviewing uncomfortable episodes that are within the public interest, given the tragic events of 1994. The issues discussed in this book clearly transcend institutional loyalties or friendships: as a scholar of international relations, I also cannot ignore the fact that the role of the UN bureaucracy has been consistently neglected by the IR, UN, and Rwanda literatures—and not only for a lack of primary sources. The assumption that 'power' in IR lies with states has led to a conscious disregard of the UN Secretariat as an object of academic study. In this view, IOs and their bureaucracies only play a role insofar as they reflect, mirror-like, the pre-existing dynamics of its members, rather than being capable of becoming—under certain circumstances and within given limits—self-directed actors. While this statist view has an illustrious history—there is, in fact, evidence in this book supporting it—it only has explanatory value as an arrival rather than as a departure point. Yet in Rwanda the opposite has happened, a circumstance that affects our appreciation of a number of key historical events.

As for Rwanda being 'exceptional', more research is clearly needed to ascertain whether and to what extent the patterns of bureaucratic interaction described in the following pages were reproduced elsewhere. There is, however, suggestive evidence that the events of 1994—so exceptional in terms of casualties—may not have been unique. Since this is a study of the UN bureaucracy that proceeds from the inside out, some of the pathologies displayed by the UN Secretariat of 1994 are likely to have been reproduced in other peace operations—an exciting ground for future enquiry. Further-more, the three factors identified in this book as having contributed to the Secretariat's dysfunctions in Rwanda—namely, the bureaucratic competition between DPA and DPKO, the uses of those departments by different IR actors, and the conceptual confusion surrounding the ideas of peacekeeping and peacebuilding—came to a head in mid-1993, a critical time for the UN when trouble erupted not only in Kigali but also in Mogadishu, Sarajevo, Port-au-Prince, and elsewhere. That a new 'intelligence' system was set up precisely at the time of the Rwanda mission—a system which caused consid-erable friction not only between SG and the UN membership, but also between DPA and DPKO—is also noteworthy.

Twenty years after the Rwandan genocide, I remain a strong supporter of the UN's work in general and of DPA's preventive diplomacy in particular.

---

[29] Marrack Goulding, Letter to G.M., 14 September 2000, p.2 (MIG-PA).

I also fully endorse Herbert Nicholas's view that the UN organization has become necessary before it has become effective.[30] Precisely because I believe that it does matter, however, I am also convinced that it deserves far more scrutiny than it has so far received—indifference is a greater threat to the UN than constructive criticism. A functioning UN bureaucracy is essential to a functional UN organization; studying the uses and abuses of the UN Secretariat by both SGs and states—that critical fault line of IR—is one way of ensuring that the UN fulfils its unique and important mission. It is in this spirit, rather than as an attribution of responsibilities, that this book should be taken.

ARCHITECTURE

Reflecting the view of the UN system as a combination of structures (understood as the distribution of administrative functions) and processes (or patterns of interactions among those units),[31] this book is divided into two parts. The first adopts an 'anatomical' approach and dissects the Secretariat of 1994 by considering the contribution of the key UN units involved in Rwanda, while Part II looks at five long-term, cross-Secretariat processes that impacted on UNAMIR. Processes change more quickly than structures, which can only be understood by looking at how they work in practice. Yet both structures and processes affect—and are affected by—human behaviour, which is why the individual agency of UN officials has a prominent role in this volume. By combining structures and processes, and by suggesting that both shape—but are in turn shaped by—individual agency, *Dangerous Diplomacy* aims to carry out an 'anatomy of influence'[32] by going from the specific to the generic and by moving from the narrow confines of the Rwanda mission, to the larger issues raised by UNAMIR for the UN system as a whole. Through a 'microhistory' of the pathologies of the UN Secretariat in Rwanda, therefore, the book suggests the contours of a 'macro-history' of the UN in the early 1990s and beyond.[33]

---

[30] Chas Freeman, ed., *Diplomat's Dictionary* (Washington, DC: US Institute of Peace Press, 2009), p.234.

[31] Raymond Hopkins and Richard Mansbach, *Structure and Process in International Politics* (New York: Harper & Row, 1973), esp. ch.5; Joseph Nye, *Understanding International Conflict* (New York: Pearson, 2005).

[32] Robert Cox and Harold Jacobson, *Anatomy of Influence* (New Haven: Yale University Press, 1977).

[33] Giovanni Levi, 'On Microhistory', in Peter Burke, *New Perspectives on Historical Writing* (Cambridge: Polity Press, 1991), pp.93–4; Carlo Ginzburg, 'Microhistory: Two or Three Things That I Know About It', *Critical Inquiry*, Vol.20, No.1 (1993), p.10.

Part I

Structures

1

Department of Peacekeeping Operations

In May 1987 the then Secretary-General (SG) of the United Nations (UN), Javier Pérez de Cuéllar, and his adviser, Marrack Goulding, landed at Moscow airport. Greeted by a delegation of senior Soviet officials, they were ushered into a limousine that was soon on its way towards central Moscow. There they met Andrei Gromyko, Soviet Foreign Minister for almost thirty years and Moscow's foreign policy 'supremo' for even longer.[1] Although the three men sitting around that Kremlin table were all diplomats, they could have hardly been more different. Pérez de Cuéllar was a seasoned Chilean who had been appointed as SG in the depths of the Cold War partly because he was seen as docile enough to eschew a superpower veto of his appointment.[2] Goulding was an energetic and outspoken Briton who had run into trouble with the UK Foreign Office for criticizing the pomp and expenses of Her Majesty's diplomatic service.[3] And Gromyko was the most intriguing of the three: secretive and dry in equal measure, he was known for his intellect and bluntness—'If you can face him for one hour and survive, then you can begin to call yourself a diplomat',[4] Kissinger once said of him. In Moscow, what was supposed to be a routine visit turned into a day that the two UN officials would not forget. 'We nearly fell off our chairs',[5] Goulding wrote in his diary.

'The Soviet Union wants to strengthen the political role of the Secretary-General of the United Nations':[6] it was these words that caused the usually composed Goulding to spill his coffee on the Kremlin's floor—and all over his journal. They signalled a Copernican shift in the decades-long Soviet position

---

[1] Michel Tatu, *Power in the Kremlin* (New York: Viking, 1967); Andrei Gromyko, *Memoirs* (New York: Hutchinson, 1989).

[2] Javier Pérez de Cuéllar, *Pilgrimage for Peace* (London: St Martin's Press, 1997); Kent Kille, *From Manager to Visionary* (Basingstoke: Palgrave Macmillan, 2006), ch.2; Romuald Sciora, ed., *À la Maison de Verre* (Paris: Saint-Simon, 2006), pp.97–116.

[3] 'Obituary: Sir Marrack Goulding', *The Telegraph*, 14 July 2010.

[4] Chas Freeman, ed., *Diplomat's Dictionary* (Washington, DC: US Institute of Peace, 2009), p.108.

[5] Marrack Goulding, 'Peacemonger: Book Proposal', 15 June 1998, p.7 (MIG-PA).

[6] Goulding, 'Peacemonger: Book Proposal', p.7.

according to which the SG had no 'political'[7] role to play in international affairs independently of UN member states.[8] 'Coming from the diehard Gromyko, it was an amazing herald of change',[9] Goulding scribbled in his coffee-soaked diary. Proof that Gromyko meant his words came in the following months, when the three men negotiated a long-sought agreement on the withdrawal of Soviet troops from Afghanistan as well as a blueprint ending the eight-year-old war between Iran and Iraq.[10] This was only the start, for a spate of other agreements followed on issues as diverse as the self-determination of Western Sahara, the withdrawal of Cuban troops from Angola, the independence of Namibia, and the conclusion of civil wars in Mozambique, Cambodia, Nicaragua, and El Salvador.[11] The end of the Cold War was making it possible for East and West to resolve conflicts in places where they no longer had direct geopolitical interests. Even more important, it was removing the need for the superpowers to fuel proxy wars in the Third World, long *the* source of global instability.[12] This was a significant development in international affairs—'a 180 degree turn in Soviet policy',[13] as Goulding defined it years later—and one that paved the way for a 'New World Order', as the novel environment came to be known. After years of frustrating immobility the UN was expected to play an active role in world affairs, so the SG and Goulding left Moscow mesmerized. As the highest-ranking officials at the UN, however, they also knew that the organization had been suffering from long-term neglect and superpower rivalry. Was it up to the challenges offered by Gromyko, the two men wondered on their flight back to New York?

From a bureaucratic point of view, the answer was negative. In the mid-to-late 1980s several classified reports—including one by Brian Urquhart, Goulding's predecessor and long-time UN insider—had warned that reform was sorely needed to 'cut through long-accumulated layers of vested interests and organizational traditions'.[14] Urquhart was being conservative, for the decline of the USSR and the end of cross-veto battles required nothing short of a 'cultural revolution' in how the Secretariat worked—a difficult task for any organization, let alone one as resistant to change as the UN of the Cold War.

---

[7] As Part II will suggest, 'political' is a contested term in relation to the SG and the Secretariat.

[8] Boris Ponomaryov et al., *History of Soviet Foreign Policy* (London: ILP Press, 2001).

[9] Goulding, 'Peacemonger: Book Proposal', p.7.

[10] Ilya Gaiduk, *Divided Together* (Stanford: Stanford University Press, 2012); Romain Yakemtchouk, *La Politique Étrangère de la Russie* (Paris: L'Harmattan, 2008).

[11] MIG-PA and Marrack Goulding, *Peacemonger* (London: John Murray, 2002).

[12] Bertrand Ramcharan, *Preventive Diplomacy at the UN* (Bloomington, IN: Indiana University Press, 2008); U Thant, *View from the UN* (New York: Doubleday, 1978).

[13] Marrack Goulding, 'The Evolving Role of the United Nations in International Peace and Security', *Irish Studies in International Affairs*, Vol.3, No.4 (1992), p.1.

[14] Brian Urquhart and Erskine Childers, Confidential: Reorganization of the United Nations Secretariat. A Suggested Outline of Needed Reforms, UN Report, New York, February 1991, p.36 (MIG-PA).

The challenges were thus considerable but so were the potential rewards, for what Gromyko had offered in Moscow was the chance the UN had been waiting for since the erection of the Iron Curtain. 'The opportunities that exist now . . . do not often arise', Urquhart concluded. 'They must not be missed.'[15]

One such opportunity emerged in late 1991, when a self-described champion of global cooperation was chosen to succeed Pérez de Cuéllar as SG. A seasoned diplomat and former professor of international law, Boutros Boutros-Ghali of Egypt promised to strengthen the UN's profile in global affairs and managed to overcome a US veto partly by promising radical reform on First Avenue.[16] So when the new SG moved into his 38th floor suite in January 1992, a sense of optimism reigned at UN Headquarters, where the first area to be affected was peacekeeping. Although UN peacekeepers were deployed as early as 1948, the cross-veto battles of the Cold War rendered peacekeeping largely ineffective, a situation that Boutros-Ghali was determined to change. His first move in this direction was the abolition of Goulding's Office for Special Political Affairs (OSPA)—which had until then combined peacekeeping and peacebuilding—and the creation of two new departments, one dedicated to peacekeeping (DPKO) and the other to peacebuilding (DPA).[17] As Goulding put it, 'Special Political Affairs was a euphemism for "peacemaking and peacekeeping", both of which were United Nations activities that were deemed by the Soviet Union to be illegitimate because there was no specific reference to them in the Charter of the United Nations. The Secretariat also included an office of "Special Political Questions". This', Goulding continued, 'was a euphemism for "Decolonization", a term which would not have been accepted by two other Permanent Members of the Security Council, namely France and the United Kingdom. Such were the complexities caused by the Cold War.'[18]

While the problems associated with the creation of DPA and DPKO lie at the heart of this book, it is important to note that in the early 1990s peacekeeping was by far the fastest growing area where member states expected the SG to make a difference.[19] For several reasons, this included both the 'winners' and the 'losers' of the Cold War: US foreign policy relied heavily on UN peacekeeping to address the challenges of the New World Order, whereas Russia saw peace operations as a cost-effective tool to contain mounting US hegemony. As a result, DPKO quickly established itself as the repository of post-Cold War enthusiasm and as the UN unit embodying the new global

[15] Urquhart and Childers, p.36.

[16] Stephen Burgess, *The UN Under Boutros Boutros-Ghali, 1992–1997* (London: Scarecrow, 2001).

[17] Thant Myint-U and Amy Scott, *The UN Secretariat* (New York: International Peace Institute, 2007).

[18] Marrack Goulding, 'The Rise and Fall of UN Peacekeeping after the End of the Cold War', 8 January 2007, p.1 (MIG-PA).

[19] Paul Kennedy, *The Parliament of Man* (London: Penguin, 2007), ch.3.

'credo'. Importantly, this was also the start of a close and in some respects inevitable relationship between DPKO and UN members, one that survives to this day. Boutros-Ghali's restructuring of the Secretariat in early 1992 mirrored the shift from a divided and neglected organization to one that was becoming engaged in some of the world's most troublesome spots. As the SG stated, 'A new chapter in the history of the UN has begun'.[20]

It is in this context of rapid peacekeeping expansion that the Secretariat began to consider the possibility of establishing a peacekeeping operation to Rwanda.[21] The small African country had a long and bloody history of ethnic strife between the Hutu majority and the Tutsi minority, but by mid-1993 the two parties had reached a compromise and had agreed to set up transitional institutions.[22] So when they jointly requested the SG to oversee the implementation of their peace process, the SC invited Boutros-Ghali to consider a mission and Canadian General Roméo Dallaire was summoned to New York to look into it. The UN Assistance Mission for Rwanda (UNAMIR) was meant to help the Rwandan parties with the implementation of the peace agreements signed at Arusha, Tanzania, in the summer of 1993, and it was on the basis of Dallaire's assessment that the SG was to formally recommend the mission to the SC.[23]

This chapter assesses the role of DPKO in planning and overseeing the Rwanda operation. Although commentators have tended to neglect the earliest stages of UNAMIR and have concentrated their analyses on the deployment of the mission in late 1993, the preparatory period contributed to seal UNAMIR's fate *before* the operation reached Kigali. Four decisions taken by the peace-keeping department led to this outcome and are reviewed in this chapter: the establishment of a reconnaissance mission in mid-1993; the decision on the size of UNAMIR; the cable sent by DPKO to Dallaire in which the Canadian General was asked not to undertake any operation despite disturbing intelligence and mounting tensions in Kigali; and the department's interpretation of the mandate and rules of engagement of UNAMIR.

RECONNAISSANCE MISSION

'Knowledge is of two kinds', the English writer Samuel Johnson wrote. 'We know a subject ourselves, or we know where we can find information on it'.[24]

---

[20] Boutros Boutros-Ghali, 'Empowering the United Nations', *Foreign Affairs*, Vol.71, No.5 (Winter 1992), p.89.
[21] United Nations, *The United Nations and Rwanda* (New York: Department of Public Information, 1996), pp.3–110.
[22] Linda Melvern, *A People Betrayed* (London: Zed Books, 2009), ch.5.
[23] Paolo Mastrolilli, *Lo Specchio del Mondo* (Rome: Laterza, 2005), ch.4.
[24] James Boswell, *The Life of Samuel Johnson* (London: Penguin, 2008), p.34.

By Johnson's standards, Dallaire was largely in the dark on Rwanda. Not only did he know surprisingly little about the African country, he ran into problems as soon as he tried to get information from DPKO.

The briefings he received from New York were clearly inadequate. After a few hastily arranged meetings, the Canadian General was reportedly handed a two-page note with some aggregate data on Rwanda's geography, demography, and economy, together with the names of the country's parties and leaders.[25] There was no sign of the morphological information Dallaire needed to assess the logistical aspects of the mission—instead, a tourist map had to do.[26] 'None in New York seemed to know much about the [strategic aspects of the] mission area or the mission itself', Brent Beardsley, Dallaire's assistant and UNAMIR's Deputy Commander, recalled, '[so] we went in quite blind'.[27] The country's famously complicated ethnic and historical background, in particular, was overlooked: 'I managed to piece together a rough history from newspaper accounts and a few scholarly articles', Dallaire explained, but a little data is often more dangerous than no data at all, and by the General's own admission these sources 'reduced a highly complex social and political situation to a simple inter-tribal conflict'.[28] The absence of information on Rwandan politics was especially troubling, and the clearest indication of Dallaire's lack of information related to the Arusha Peace Agreements. Although these documents took months to negotiate, spanned 170 pages, were written in complicated language, and contained numerous gaps and contradictions, only a clean copy of them was given to Dallaire—a military man with no diplomatic background[29] whose first reaction to being told about the possibility of leading a UN mission in Rwanda was: 'That's somewhere in Africa, isn't it?'[30] He and his aide tried to compensate with a stack of outdated encyclopedias and *Time* magazines. At DPKO, they had neither a desk nor an office, had to camp in a conference room, and were told to borrow laptops.[31]

The official UN explanation for this situation is that resources were scarce in mid-1993, and this was certainly the case. Despite the pomp associated with the 'New World Order', states proved reluctant to bestow the UN with funds proportionate to the tasks they claimed it should perform.[32] In fact, most capitals owed New York large sums in late payments and the most influential of those capitals—and biggest contributor to the UN budget—was under the

---

[25] Roméo Dallaire, *Shake Hands with the Devil* (London: Arrow Books, 2003), p.47.
[26] Brent Beardsley, *PBS Frontline Interview*, 15 November 2003. All PBS Frontline interviews are available at http://www.pbs.org/wgbh/pages/frontline/shows/ghosts/interviews/#3 (accessed 12 November 2016).
[27] Beardsley, *PBS Frontline Interview*, 15 November 2003.
[28] Dallaire, *Shake Hands*, p.47.   [29] Dallaire, *Shake Hands*, p.47.
[30] Dallaire, *Shake Hands*, p.42.
[31] Beardsley, *PBS Frontline Interview*, 15 November 2003; Dallaire, *Shake Hands*, p.42.
[32] Edward Luck, *Mixed Messages* (Washington, DC: Brookings Institution Press, 1999).

spell of a UN-averse Republican Congress that refused to pay US arrears.[33] It is thus understandable that in 1993 the organization was in financial difficulty and that intelligence suffered (Chapter 6 will return to this). 'We began to devote less than adequate time to the research on, and analysis of, the conflicts to which further peacekeepers were to be deployed',[34] Goulding wrote in the mid-1990s in a confidential post-mortem review of peacekeeping. By the time UNAMIR was being considered, Boutros-Ghali had axed jobs, slashed pro-grammes, abolished departments, and replaced the tactful management of his predecessor with an abrupt approach that alienated a good part of his staff.[35] Seen from New York, the new SG had also committed the ultimate sin by placing all Under-Secretaries-General and Assistant Secretaries-General—the UN's highest ranking officials—on one-year contracts, 'a sort of sword of Damocles hanging over the Dionysiuses of the Secretariat'.[36] Even John Bolton, the former US Assistant Secretary of State for International Organ-ization and hardly a UN fan, was taken aback, noting that '[i]n 1992 Boutros-Ghali was very responsive to the United States and its demands for UN reform',[37] and that his restructuring was a 'significant accomplishment'.[38] That there was little UN funding for a mission to a small and strategically insignificant country in faraway Africa is no surprise.[39]

It is nevertheless equally clear that DPKO had far more information on Rwanda than it ever offered Dallaire. In April 1993, the department had despatched a so-called 'technical' mission to Kigali (led by Canadian General Maurice Baril) with the specific aim of gathering data from the field.[40] Also, some of the department's officials had monitored the Arusha peace negoti-ations,[41] and by mid-1993 an extensive UN Report—to which the following chapters will return—compiled by the Special Rapporteur on Extrajudicial, Summary, or Arbitrary Executions had already painted a thoroughly alarm-ing picture of Rwanda's ethnic situation. According to the rapporteur, the country was engulfed in ethnic violence of such a magnitude that acts of

---

[33] Anthony McDermott, *United Nations Financing Problems and the New Generation of Peacekeeping and Peace Enforcement* (Providence, RI: Watson Institute Press, 1994).
[34] Goulding, 'The Rise and Fall', p.7.
[35] Thant Myint-U and Scott, p.90.
[36] Thant Myint-U and Scott, p.84.
[37] My interview with John Bolton, 24 June 2011, Washington, DC (and by email on 28 April 2016).
[38] John Bolton, 'UN Secretariat Restructuring and Unitary UN' (Speech, Geneva Group Consultative Level Meeting, 19–20 March 1992), p.1.
[39] Patrick de Saint-Exupéry, *L'Inavouable: La France au Rwanda* (Paris: Les Arènes, 2004); Didier Tauzin, *Rwanda: Je Demande Justice pour la France et ses Soldats* (Paris: Éditions Jacob-Duvernet, 2011).
[40] United Nations, *The Blue Helmets* (New York: Department of Public Information, 1996), p.341.
[41] Jacques Castonguay, *Les Casques Bleus au Rwanda* (Paris: L'Harmattan, 1998), p.30.

genocide could not be ruled out in the future and had in fact already happened in the past.[42] None of these pieces of information was passed on to Dallaire.

The fact that such data was not shared with General Dallaire is especially problematic since the Rwanda operation was supposed to be established on the basis of his assessment, itself the result of Dallaire's reconnaissance mission to the country. Hastily arranged in August 1993, however, that mission ran into trouble even before leaving New York. Considering the important work that the UN delegation was expected to carry out—looking at the feasibility of an operation and assessing whether Rwanda's politicians were truly committed to peace—the reconnaissance trip was supposed to be headed by a senior political officer from DPA, but because of a last-minute problem the Canadian General was asked to take the lead. 'There was no-one that was an expert on Rwanda', Beardsley stated. 'They were all green on it … so we had to take a lot of stuff on face value. What they told us, we had to accept.'[43] Dallaire agrees: 'Nobody had anything useful to bring to the table and most appeared to be totally out of the loop',[44] he wrote of DPKO staff. The apparent absence of what UN officials problematically refer to as 'political' expertise on Rwanda is especially striking: only two of the eighteen officers forming Dallaire's mission were 'political' experts, while the rest were peacekeeping or humanitarian officers with little negotiating experience. 'A military person thinks in a military way', Major Ezaz Afzal, from UNAMIR's Bangladeshi contingent, stated. 'You cannot suddenly change your whole mindset. You cannot suddenly start thinking like a politician.'[45] A multi-disciplinary mission expected to perform assessments of a strategic, humanitarian, and administrative nature upon which both the SG and the SC would rely was thus headed someone who had no experience of peacekeeping, did not know the UN, and had never been to Africa. 'My eyes were being opened to realities far from my usual military sphere',[46] Dallaire wrote. Goulding sensed danger: '*Ora pro nobis*',[47] he wrote. 'Pray for us.'

The importance of Dallaire's tasks during the reconnaissance mission was reflected in the high-level talks he held in Rwanda. On the government side he met the Prime Minister, the Prime Minister-designate, and President Habyarimana, while on the Tutsi side he saw the RPF leader, Paul Kagame. The trip lasted twelve days and seemed to go smoothly—perhaps too smoothly, since Dallaire's contact person was someone whom Habyarimana distrusted and kept in the dark. Habyarimana himself was hardly a fan of the Arusha Peace

---

[42] United Nations, *Report on Extrajudicial, Summary, or Arbitrary Executions*, August 1993, (E/CN.4/1994/7/Add.1), §79.

[43] Beardsley, *PBS Frontline Interview*, 15 November 2003.

[44] Dallaire, *Shake Hands*, p.55.

[45] My interview with Ezaz Afzal, 20 April 2016, Chittagong, Bangladesh (and via email on 29 April 2016).

[46] Dallaire, *Shake Hands*, p.61.   [47] Goulding, 'Peacemonger: Book Proposal', p.10.

Accords: Alain Juppé, the then French Foreign Minister, stated before a French Parliamentary Commission of Inquiry that 'President Habyarimana did not exactly show great enthusiasm to the idea of renouncing a good portion of his powers [but had] eventually accepted the process established by the Arusha Accords, particularly under French pressure'.[48] Although most of Dallaire's interlocutors expressed enthusiasm for a UN operation, they were all moderates and gave the Canadian General a rosy picture: 'It wasn't a government side and a RPF side', Beardsley recalled long after the events. 'Within the government side there were two distinct factions. There were moderates who were extremely committed to Arusha, and then there was this group of extremists that appeared opposed to it.'[49] Neither did Dallaire and Beardsley realize that paramilitary forces hostile to Arusha were already trying to sabotage the peace process, or that resistance to the Arusha Agreements was mounting within Habyarimana's own camp. For the Canadian General the picture was straightforward: it was on Habyarimana and Kagame that peace depended. 'I was certain that Rwanda was a place that could benefit from a classic chapter-six peacekeeping mission',[50] he wrote. How flawed this assessment was became clear in October 1993, when UNAMIR deployed. By that time, everything had changed.

MISSION SIZE

Two decisions awaited Secretariat officials upon their return to New York. Was a UN operation to Rwanda feasible and, if so, how many troops did it need?

Standard procedures for establishing peacekeeping operations rest on the reconnaissance head and his team, who make recommendations to DPKO, which in turn informs the SG, who brings the proposal to the SC, which makes the final call.[51] Because peacekeeping is a highly specialized business, the decision-making process in New York relies heavily on the initial assessment by—and on the 'technical' expertise of—the military officials in charge of reconnaissance. As Goulding noted, 'All... strategic decisions are taken by either the Security Council or the General Assembly. But of course those bodies are almost invariably acting on the basis of recommendations which have been received from the Secretary-General and his staff. So in practice the

---

[48] Assemblée Nationale, Mission d'Information Parlementaire sur le Rwanda, Audition de M. Édouard Balladur, 2 April 1998, available at http://www.assemblee-nationale.fr/dossiers/rwanda/auditi01.asp (accessed 30 December 2015) (hereinafter, MIPR).

[49] Beardsley, *PBS Frontline Interview*, 15 November 2003.

[50] Dallaire, *Shake Hands*, p.71.

[51] United Nations, *The United Nations and Rwanda, 1993–96*, ch.2.

permanent officials of the United Nations are to a large extent the decision-makers because almost invariably their recommendations are accepted by the Security Council and the General Assembly.'[52] Dallaire was clearly aware of this: 'It was incredible', he stated in an interview, 'just the adrenaline and the fact that you were going to provide the guidance for very senior people [at the UN] to decide whether or not [the Rwandans] would be helped in their path towards peace.'[53] His excitement was nevertheless tempered by a dilemma: he had been warned about the UN financial crisis and had been told that the organization could ill-afford a large and expensive mission—yet he also knew that an inadequately manned operation would be risky both for those in the field and for the reputation of the UN.

Given Dallaire's determination to help Rwandans, his first decision was straightforward. The reconnaissance mission had given him reasons to be optimistic about the tasks ahead, something that Beardsley confirmed by describing UNAMIR in strikingly reassuring terms: 'Very stable situation, two parties, a civil war. There had been a truce, there was a peace agreement, and we were going to implement the peace agreement.'[54] The two military officials were also under the impression that after the recent troubles in Croatia, Bosnia, and Somalia, the Secretariat was counting on a success story to replicate the positive outcomes achieved by the UN in Central America. As a result, the decision to recommend UNAMIR came easily: 'Our report was that this was a winner mission where the UN can redeem itself, that there is a peace agreement with some holes but that everyone is behind it',[55] Beardsley said. Dallaire agreed: 'We knew the UN badly wanted a win and we told them that this was it',[56] adding that '[a] mission was both possible and essential.'[57] UNAMIR was also meant to be the highest point of Dallaire's military career; by his own admission, he was never going to say no.[58]

The decision on troop numbers proved harder to reach. Early estimates had suggested 8,000 but after his reconnaissance mission Dallaire was persuaded that 5,500 would do.[59] In the end, however, he recommended a force of 2,500, less than half the size he thought was necessary on the basis of an already optimistic assessment of Rwanda.

The issue is important since it has been suggested that a stronger mission would have slowed down, or even stopped, the genocide.[60] Beardsley believes

[52] Marrack Goulding, 'The Command and Control of United Nations Peace-Keeping Operations' (Speech, Irish Military College, 8 November 1991) (MIG-PA).
[53] Roméo Dallaire, *PBS Frontline Interview*, 1 April 2004.
[54] Beardsley, *PBS Frontline Interview*, 15 November 2003.
[55] Beardsley, *PBS Frontline Interview*, 15 November 2003.
[56] Michael Barnett, *Eyewitness to a Genocide* (Ithaca: Cornell University Press, 2003), p.65.
[57] Barnett, *Eyewitness*, p.77.   [58] Dallaire, *Shake Hands*, p.45.
[59] Dallaire, *Shake Hands*, p.45.
[60] James Traub, *The Best Intentions* (London: Bloomsbury, 2007), p.53.

so: 'The 450 UN forces that remained on the ground saved the lives of 25,000 people, while General Dallaire stated quite frequently that if 5,500 troops could have come in, we could have arrested it. Do the mathematics, we could have saved over half a million.'[61] Officials on the ground seem to share Beardsley's view: Major Ezaz Afzal, from the Bangladeshi contingent, noted that '[t]he Hutu military forces had poor morale, were corrupt, and lacked professionalism—they could easily have been dealt with',[62] while the head of the UN Humanitarian Assistance Team in Kigali concurs: 'Here is one guy with no gun sitting on a wooden chair all day and all night, not sleeping, and he's able with no gun to convince people that they're not allowed in here to kill people', Gregory Alex stated. 'Yet the whole UN system, with guns or whatever, couldn't do anything. There were some powerful, brave things that were being done by U.N. soldiers, completely devoid of any support from New York.'[63] In January 1997, the Carnegie Commission probed Dallaire's statement that 5,000 troops could have saved thousands of lives and reached a similar conclusion: 'In retrospect', the report noted, 'a capable force of 5,000 troops inserted during April 7–21 could have significantly squelched the violence, prevented its spread from the capital to the countryside, and removed the RPF's pretext for renewing its fight with the Rwandan Government Forces.'[64] This seems to contradict the assertion by Iqbal Riza—Annan's deputy at DPKO—according to whom '...to deal with [the genocide] after it exploded, it would have needed a very large, powerful, well equipped force for enforcement operations with the mandate and political support and will of the international community'.[65] Madeleine Albright also suggested that by the time the situation in Rwanda was clear, it was too late to stop the genocide.[66] Since, as Chapter 5 will show, the SC justified its decision to downsize UNAMIR on the basis that the mission was undermanned, the issue of troop levels deserves careful scrutiny.

One of the reasons why Dallaire settled for 2,500 peacekeepers lies with the phenomenon of the 'anticipatory veto', a tendency by Secretariat officials to recommend to the SC only what the latter is likely to endorse.[67] The informal interactions between UN civil servants and SC members, especially the five permanent members (P-5), mean that the former often try to predict what the

[61] Beardsley, *PBS Frontline Interview*, 15 November 2003.

[62] Interview with Afzal, 20 April 2016.

[63] Gregory Alex, *PBS Frontline Interview*, 18 October 2003.

[64] Scott Feil, 'Could 5,000 Peacekeepers Have Saved 500,000 Rwandans? Early Intervention Reconsidered', Georgetown University's E. A. Walsh School of Foreign Service, Special Issue, Vol.III, No.2 (1997), p.2.

[65] Iqbal Riza, *PBS Frontline Interview*, March 2003.

[66] Madeleine Albright, *PBS Frontline Interview*, 25 February 2004.

[67] Howard Adelman and Astri Suhrke, 'Rwanda' in David Malone, ed., *The UN Security Council* (Boulder: Lynne Rienner, 2004), p.492.

latter is likely to endorse, and prepare recommendations accordingly. DPKO's direct involvement with troop-contributing countries makes its relationship with the P-5 especially complex—another case where Inis Claude's 'two UNs' division can be problematic. In Rwanda, Dallaire reportedly came under pressure from DPKO not to recommend a force exceeding 2,500, regardless of the situation on the ground. Anything more should not even be asked for: 'They told us what the plan should be', Beardsley stated: 'If you are going to recommend a peacekeeping force, then it mustn't exceed 2,500. We estimated that we needed about 5,000–5,500. In fact, one of the earlier missions had gone and said 8,000 would have been the minimum number of soldiers.'[68] Dallaire agrees: 'I knew from my talks with Baril [the DPKO's military adviser] that this recommendation for 5,500 would never leave DPKO.'[69]

Kofi Annan—then head of UN peacekeeping—has openly recognized as much: 'Those of us at Headquarters who knew the situation in the Council and the possibility of whether he will get it or not, sometimes were the ones who had to tell [Dallaire]: "You are not going to get this".'[70] Yet by doing so, Annan noted, DPKO was not questioning Dallaire's judgement but 'indicating what he was likely to get, what was possible and what was not'.[71] 'We knew what the atmosphere was',[72] Riza stated. In his diaries, Goulding too notes the special link between DPKO officials and those countries involved in peacekeeping—especially the largest ones—noting that '...my real power [at DPKO] came from this relationship with the troop contributors',[73] and regretting this loss when the SG moved him from DPKO to DPA. In the case of UNAMIR, this attitude of DPKO—coupled with the intelligence vacuum in which Dallaire and Beardsley found themselves—led the two military officials to settle for 2,500: 'This [smaller size] required the mission to take more risks', Dallaire defensively wrote, 'but it was more likely to be approved and eventually deployed.'[74] A strategic decision supposedly based on the expertise of the head of reconnaissance and on the needs of the field was thus taken by DPKO officials on the ground of what they *thought* the SC wanted.

An argument can be made that DPKO's predictions were likely to be accurate and that, in the wake of growing troubles in Somalia and the former Yugoslavia—the 'first failure of the New World Order',[75] as Goulding describes it—the Council was unwilling to approve a stronger mission, so there was little point in even asking for it. As one source puts it, 'Given close and

---

[68] Beardsley, *PBS Frontline Interview*, 15 November 2003.
[69] Dallaire, *Shake Hands*, p.75.
[70] Kofi Annan, *PBS Frontline Interview*, 17 February 2004.
[71] Annan, *PBS Frontline Interview*, 17 February 2004.
[72] Riza, *PBS Frontline Interview*, March 2003.
[73] Marrack Irvine Goulding, Personal Diary, Vol.B (MIG-PD-B), 14-Jan-1993 (hereinafter, MIG-PD).
[74] Dallaire, *Shake Hands*, pp.75–6.   [75] MIG-PD-B, 20-Oct-1992.

informal relations between the Secretariat and the Security Council, an un-spoken rule in the Secretariat was to discern what the Council was likely to accept, then to prepare policy options within this range.'[76] It should also be noted that DPKO is hardly the only part of the Secretariat to use the 'antici-patory veto': in his memoirs, Boutros-Ghali wrote that as SG he was often pressured by the P-5 to suggest to the Council certain actions rather than others: 'Hannay [the UK Ambassador] pressed me hard to recommend a "light option" of 7,600 troops', the former SG wrote with reference to the UN Mission in the Former Yugoslavia. 'Reluctantly, I agreed to do so....'[77] Goulding too describes several such occurrences, noting that numerous SG reports and suggested courses of action were only approved by the SG 'after receiving the go-ahead from the [Permanent] Five'.[78] As a bitter Boutros-Ghali put it years later, 'Americans do not want you to say yes; they want you to say yes, sir'.[79]

There are a number of problems associated with the practice of the 'antici-patory veto', the most important of which was expressed with unusual candour by former SG Pérez de Cuéllar in a confidential letter to the P-5 'coordinator' in 1991. The Permanent Members had advised Goulding, then head of OSPA, that the SG should release his report on Angola (S/22627) only after clearing it with them. 'After carefully considering this request', Pérez de Cuéllar wrote, 'I have come to the conclusion that it would be wrong in principle for me to accept it.'[80] With unexpected boldness, the SG went on to explain why:

> I am convinced that if I were to accept a request to submit my recommendations in draft to the Permanent Members, or indeed to all members of the Council, I would seriously impair the prerogative of the Secretary-General to present to the Security-Council his own recommendations about how a mandate which the Council may decide to entrust to him could best be implemented. The fact that, on occasions in the past, the Secretary-General may have been specifically instructed by decision of the Security-Council to consult certain Member States, or may on his own initiative and for specific reasons have decided to discuss ideas in a draft report with some or all members of the Council, does not invalidate the fundamental principle described above.[81]

This confidential letter was sent in 1991, during the last year of Pérez de Cuéllar's tenure as SG when this extraordinarily tactful diplomat—described

[76] Adelman and Suhrke, 'Rwanda', p.492. See also Citizens for Global Solutions, 'The Responsibility Not to Veto: A Way Forward' (Washington, DC: CGS Publishing, 2010), p.4.

[77] Boutros Boutros-Ghali, *UNvanquished* (London: I.B. Tauris, 1999), p.86.

[78] MIG-PD-B, 20-Sep-1991.

[79] Roberto Savio, 'Boutros Boutros-Ghali: A Turning Point in the History of the United Nations', *Human Wrongs Watch*, 16 February 2016.

[80] Javier Pérez de Cuéllar, Letter to the Permanent Representative of the Union of Soviet Socialist Republics to the United Nations, Yuli Vorontsov, 21 May 1991 (MIG-PA).

[81] Pérez de Cuéllar, Letter, 21 May 1991.

by a UN specialist as 'the type of person who would not make a splash if he fell out of a boat'[82]—could afford to be a little bolder. It does nevertheless raise an important question about the relationship between member states (the P-5 in particular) and Secretariat officials, namely, how close should it be?

Those who feel strongly about an independent international civil service typically disagree with national diplomats,[83] but there is little doubt that the practice of the 'anticipatory veto' creates problems in terms of accountability and the attribution of responsibilities in times of crisis. In the case of Rwanda, the use of such a practice by DPKO has also been criticized as leading to 'a potentially dysfunctional decision-making process that in Rwanda contributed to the disaster'.[84] While the DPKO's assumption about the Council's hostility to a stronger UNAMIR was perfectly plausible, it was still an assumption—and as Chapter 5 will show, not an entirely accurate one either (France and other countries were at the time advocating for a stronger UN presence in Rwanda). Even assuming that the assessment by DPKO was correct, it is the UN Secretariat that is supposed to inform the SC of what a head of mission requires, rather than the other way around.[85] Similarly, UN officials are expected to provide the Council with impartial advice—based on sound empirical evidence—about the viability of a peacekeeping mission regardless of the presumed opposition of some (or even all) of the Council's members. Clearly, an adviser who only recommends a course of action that the advisee would take anyway is of limited use, something that Annan acknowledges: 'Even in the absence of political will on the Council, those of us in the Secretariat...have a role because we need to be able to press governments as much as we can'.[86] Whether DPKO did so in the case of Rwanda is disputed— it was certainly not vocal in recommending that the Council authorize more troops, as the transcripts of the Council discussions suggest.[87] Despite attending the informal consultations, for instance, Annan's deputy pleaded neither for more soldiers nor for reinforcements once the situation deteriorated. Even at the height of the genocide, in their daily appearances on the Council on 11, 12, 13, 14, and 15 April,[88] DPKO officials did not seem to ask for more means. If they wanted a stronger UNAMIR, there is no trace of it in the minutes.

---

[82] Simon Chesterman, 'The Secretary-General We Deserve?', *Global Governance*, Vol.21, No.4 (2015), p.508.

[83] For the former, see James Jonah, 'Differing State Perspectives on the United Nations in the Post-Cold War World', *ACUNS Report*, No.4 (1993). For the latter, see John Bolton, *Surrender is Not an Option* (New York: Threshold, 2007).

[84] Adelman and Suhrke, 'Rwanda', p.492.

[85] Brian Urquhart, *Hammarskjold* (New York: Harper, 1972).

[86] Dallaire, *PBS Frontline Interview*, 1 April 2004.

[87] The minutes of the Council's informal meetings on Rwanda are available for public consultation at the Linda Melvern Rwanda Genocide Archive in the Hugh Owen Library, Aberystwyth University, Aberystwyth, UK (hereinafter, LMRGA).

[88] See the Minutes of the 13, 14, 15, and 16 April 1994 (LMRGA).

Accurate or not, the assessment by DPKO of the Council's presumed wishes settled the issue of troop numbers. Such an assessment also suggests that what mattered most in 1993 was not the actual but the perceived 'power' of the SC and of its most influential member. 'There is a seeming reflex, in any given situation where the UN is to take a position, to ask first how... Washington will react rather than what is the right position to take', Álvaro de Soto, a long-time Under-Secretary-General and seasoned UN insider, wrote in 2007 in a confidential report. 'I confess that I am not entirely exempt from that reflex, and I regret it.'[89] As the French philosopher Jacques Derrida wrote, 'power' does not only manifest itself through direct condemnations or restrictions of the behaviour of subordinates, but it also teaches subordinates to anticipate its effects.[90] Seen in this light, 'power' works best when it operates behind the scenes—when the 'disempowered' foresee it and censor themselves accordingly.[91] 'I never got around to proposing that this [information] be presented to the Council precisely because of the reflex of self-censorship which I warned against in this report',[92] de Soto concluded. DPKO's decision to predict the stance of the SC is another example of this—and, arguably, of 'power without responsibility'.[93] Rather than considering Dallaire's requirements and referring them to the body which was supposed to take the final decision—the Council—DPKO settled the issue of troop numbers itself. Assumptions about the SC's stance—not the actual needs of Rwanda—thus informed the DPKO's position on troop numbers and Dallaire's decision about them.

Although the UNAMIR leadership should not have recommended numbers which it believed were inadequate, one should note the link between the DPKO's 'anticipatory veto' and Dallaire's intelligence vacuum, for a better picture of Rwanda may have led Dallaire to insist on a larger contingent. 'Am I right?', Dallaire pondered before recommending UNAMIR. 'Am I being ethical? Is this morally correct to take all these risks and to have the mission created and me commanding it? Or should I pull the plug on it?'[94] He decided to abide by DPKO's request, a call to which Chapter 3 will return. Like mushrooms in the rain, doubts feed on ignorance.

[89] Àlvaro de Soto, 'Confidential: End of Mission Report', May 2007, p.49, available at   http://image.guardian.co.uk/sys-files/Guardian/documents/2007/06/12/DeSotoReport.pdf (accessed 10 June 2015).

[90] Jacques Derrida, *Who Is Afraid of Philosophy?* (Stanford: Stanford University Press, 2002), p.79.

[91] Jacques Derrida, *La Voix et le Phénomène* (Paris: Presses Universitaires de France, 1967).

[92] De Soto, p.51.

[93] Though DPKO officials would argue that it was a case of 'responsibility without power' and that the SC is an expert when it comes to privatizing gains and socializing losses.

[94] Dallaire, *PBS Frontline Interview*, 1 April 2004.

'GENOCIDE CABLE'

Few UN decisions attracted more criticism than the reply of DPKO to the so-called 'genocide cable' sent by Dallaire in January 1994.[95] Such a response has been portrayed as a moral failure of the UN Secretariat, the triumph of bureaucratic cynicism in the face of human suffering.[96] If ever a document damaged the reputation of the UN organization, this was it.

The facts are known. On 11 January 1994, three months before the genocide, Dallaire sent a cable to DPKO reporting that '[a] very, very important government politician'[97]—later identified as the Prime Minister-designate—had put him in touch with a member of Habyarimana's Presidential Guard, who also claimed to be the chief trainer of an extremist government militia called *Interahamwe* ('those who fight together'). Code-named Jean-Pierre, this officer had given Dallaire three pieces of information. First, his militia was training men across Rwanda with an emphasis on slaughtering techniques and had been ordered to register all Tutsis in Kigali 'for their extermination'[98]—'Example he gave was that in 20 minutes his personnel could kill up to 1,000 Tutsi.'[99] Second, the militia was planning to kill several Belgian peacekeepers (who formed the bulk of UNAMIR) in order to force Belgium's and the UN's withdrawal from Rwanda. Third, several weapons caches existed in Kigali and Jean-Pierre was willing to show them to Dallaire in exchange for a Western passport.[100] But time was tight—once the arms were distributed, 'there would be no way to stop the slaughter'.[101]

Alarming though this was, Dallaire's cable was not seeking permission to seize weapons; the Force Commander had already decided to do so and was merely asking DPKO to protect his informant.[102] The Canadian General had good reasons to worry about the security situation: by early 1994 it had visibly deteriorated and UNAMIR was witnessing a significant proliferation of weapons.[103] Seizing these caches, Dallaire reasoned, was essential in both strategic and psychological terms to break the cycle of violence in which Rwanda was engulfed. 'We had a chance to seize the initiative',[104] he wrote, and he was

---

[95] Code Cable from Booh Booh to Annan, 11 January 1994. Unless otherwise stated, all Rwanda-related cables in this chapter were accessed through the Rwanda Documents Project (http://www.rwandadocumentsproject.net/, accessed 15 December 2015) (hereinafter, RDP).

[96] Barnett, *Eyewitness*, chs 3 and 4; Melvern, *A People Betrayed*, chs 9 and 10.

[97] Code Cable from Booh Booh to Annan, 11 January 1994.

[98] Code Cable from Booh Booh to Annan, 11 January 1994.

[99] Code Cable from Booh Booh to Annan, 11 January 1994.

[100] Amandou Deme, *Rwanda 1994 and the Failure of the United Nations Mission* (Bloomington: XLibris, 2010).

[101] Dallaire, *Shake Hands*, p.144; Lambertus Ntisoni, *J'ai Traversé des Fleuves de Sang* (Paris: L'Harmattan, 2007).

[102] Dallaire, *Shake Hands*, p.144.   [103] See Chapter 3 for details.

[104] Dallaire, *Shake Hands*, p.144.

willing to take it. 'It was a direct order', Major Ezaz Afzal, from the Bangladeshi contingent, stated. 'It was one of the rules for holding the forthcoming elections that no weapon could get inside Kigali.'[105] The obstacles envisaged by Dallaire were military rather than legal, for he believed that the arms caches were a violation of the Kigali Weapons Secure Area agreement, a contravention of the Arusha Accords, and a direct threat to UNAMIR. 'I knew that such a raid carried a high degree of risk and might include casualties', Dallaire wrote, 'but I also knew it was well within my mandate and capabilities'.[106] This was a volatile situation calling for prompt and decisive action.

Although the DPKO leadership immediately grasped the gravity of the matter, it did not react in the way Dallaire had expected. 'Do not take any action, I repeat, do not take any action',[107] Kofi Annan (under whose name the cable was sent) wrote. Officials in DPKO viewed the operation as 'clearly beyond the mandate entrusted to UNAMIR by Resolution 872/1993'[108] and ordered Dallaire not to carry it out. In the interests of transparency, the Force Commander was also instructed to share his intelligence with President Habyarimana and the US, French, and Belgian ambassadors. While this cable will be considered at length in Chapters 2, 3, and 4, the language used by DPKO left no doubt as to New York's top priority: 'The overriding consideration is the need to avoid entering into a course of action that might lead to the use of force and unanticipated repercussions.'[109] Dallaire was especially surprised by Annan's insistence that the UNAMIR leadership should share their tip with the very government which was suspected of preparing—and that would later carry out—the massacres. 'I was absolutely beside myself with frustration',[110] Dallaire recalled. 'We lost this fantastic opportunity', his aide stated, 'an absolutely incredible opportunity to . . . take this train of genocide and knock it off its rails . . . and prevent what Jean-Pierre told us they wanted to do, which was exterminate Tutsis.'[111] Tragically, in the following weeks all of the informant's predictions materialized.

Why did DPKO officials react this way? The DPKO leadership seemed most concerned about a negative reaction by the SC to a Somalia-type debacle and was apprehensive that some Western capitals—especially Washington— would object to Dallaire's raid. Similarly to what had happened with troop numbers, DPKO anticipated that the SC would disapprove of a military confrontation on hostile soil. 'Quite frankly we had no other option', Annan stated, 'because we knew this mood in the Council. You [were] not going to get them to say: "We are going to send in a brigade . . . [or] reinforcements to Gen

---

[105] Interview with Afzal, 20 April 2016.   [106] Dallaire, *Shake Hands*, p.144.
[107] Code Cable from Annan/DPKO to UNAMIR/Kigali, 12 January 1994 (RDP).
[108] Code Cable from Annan to UNAMIR, 12 January 1994.
[109] Code Cable from Annan to UNAMIR, 12 January 1994.
[110] Dallaire, *Shake Hands*, p.144.
[111] Beardsley, *PBS Frontline Interview*, 15 November 2003.

Dallaire and his men to stop this".'[112] It is partly this assumption that informed the attitude of DPKO towards Dallaire's cable, something that also emerges from Riza's rationalization of the January 1994 events: the Canadian's requests 'were not forwarded to the SC because the Council was expected to turn them down anyway',[113] Riza said. 'I very much doubt... whether the political will had been there on the basis of one cable to say, let us increase the force.... That simply was not going to happen.'[114] Without informing the SC, therefore, DPKO once again assumed that a muscular strategy was bound to fail: 'We did not feel it appropriate to directly address the Security Council [as] we had to consider what the traffic could bear',[115] Riza insisted. Concerned about his department's stance, a DPKO official tried to circulate Dallaire's cable, without success.

It has been suggested that the UN's 'bureaucratic culture' of the time led DPKO officials to conceal Dallaire's cable from the Council out of 'indifference' for the plight of Rwandans.[116] While Part II will return to this position, it is not an entirely convincing one—for several reasons. First, DPKO was barely a year old when UNAMIR was set up and could hardly have developed a strong bureaucratic culture of its own. The following pages will show that relations between DPKO and the SG's office were severely strained at the time of the Rwandan genocide. In 1994, DPKO was also engaged in a sustained turf war with DPA about the scope of peace operations, was distrusted by the SG, and was arguably the least representative part of the UN bureaucracy. By February 1994, a month after Dallaire's cable, Goulding was reporting that Boutros-Ghali had lost faith in both Annan and in the entire peacekeeping department.[117] As for the 'bureaucratic culture' of the UN Secretariat at large, its constituent parts held different views about peacekeeping and about whether, how, and when it ought to be employed; in the Secretariat of the early 1990s there was not a single 'bureaucratic culture' but many, as shown by the fact that DPKO leaders were far more risk-prone in Bosnia and Haiti. '[T]he dependence of DPKO on the US is not healthy, certainly not for the UN', Chinmaya Gharekhan, Boutros-Ghali's Special Representative to the SC, wrote. 'There was a perception in the "House" that DPKO was too beholden to the US, to the extent of losing its objectivity.'[118] Though dismissive of this,

[112] Stanley Meisler, *Kofi Annan* (London: John Wiley, 2007), p.97.
[113] Bjørn Willum, 'Legitimizing Inaction Towards Genocide in Rwanda', *International Peacekeeping*, Vol.6, No.3 (Autumn 1999), p.9.
[114] Riza, *PBS Frontline Interview*, March 2003.
[115] Riza, *PBS Frontline Interview*, March 2003.
[116] Michael Barnett, 'The UN Security Council, Indifference, and Genocide in Rwanda', *Cultural Anthropology*, Vol.12, No.4 (1997), p.562; Michael Barnett and Martha Finnemore, 'The Politics, Power, and Pathologies of International Organizations', *International Organization*, Vol.53, No.4 (1999), p.718.
[117] Marrack Irvine Goulding, Travelling Diary, Vol.IX, 15-Apr-1994 (hereinafter, MIG-TD).
[118] Chinmaya Gharekhan, *The Horseshoe Table* (New Delhi: Pearson Longman, 2006), p.246.

Annan conceded that '[o]ver Rwanda, a key breakdown had taken place in the three-way relationship between the field, the office of the secretary-general, and DPKO.'[119]

Different explanations can—and will—be offered for the breakdown mentioned by Annan, but there is no doubt that the peacekeeping department had strategic objections of its own to Dallaire's plan, fretting that seizing weapons in Kigali might incur casualties due to UNAMIR's poor human resources: 'We were concerned', Annan stated, 'given the limited number of men Dallaire had at his disposal, that if he initiated an engagement and some were killed, we would lose the troops.'[120] Like most diplomats in New York and Washington, DPKO officials had been traumatized by the failure of the Somalia operation; Riza's immediate reaction to Dallaire's cable was: 'Not Somalia again. We were cautious in interpreting our mandate and in giving guidance because we did not want a repetition of Somalia.'[121] Given the amount of criticism the UN was receiving at the time, DPKO officials were reportedly wary of carrying out a dangerous operation with a poorly equipped force in a troublesome spot that could have turned into another Mogadishu. Whatever factor was at play in 1994, it hardly seemed to be caused by indifference: 'Iqbal Riza [at DPKO] is overwhelmed by the Rwanda crisis and seems close to a nervous breakdown',[122] Goulding wrote in his diary. 'Indifference' assumes a uniformed body of opinion in agreement about what to do (which includes doing nothing). The divided Secretariat of 1994 lacked that characteristic.

When it comes to explaining the DPKO's reaction to the start of the Rwandan crisis, however, the department's argument only goes so far. Since UNAMIR's troop numbers had been 'capped' by DPKO, citing the mission's poor human resources as one of the reasons for DPKO's 'cautious' cable is hardly convincing and leads to the conclusion that the department was reacting conservatively to a precarious situation which it had itself contributed to creating. The one signpost that can be reached at this early stage of our analysis is that a part of the UN bureaucracy was making consequential decisions on behalf of—but without consulting—the organ which had mandated the mission in the first instance: the SC. Although Annan has since admitted that '[i]t was probably not a good call',[123] he and his former colleagues remain unapologetic: 'Would it have made any sense', Shashi Tharoor—a former aide to Annan—said, 'for Kofi to do the responsible thing, go to the Security Council, say "We have these warnings, we take them seriously, we seek your mandate to intervene?" It would have blown the whole thing sky-high.'[124] Yet some believe this is precisely what was needed to make the media and the public aware of Rwanda's plight. By this

[119] Kofi Annan, *Interventions* (London: Allen Lane, 2012), p.109.
[120] Traub, *The Best Intentions*, p.53.
[121] Riza, *PBS Frontline Interview*, March 2003.   [122] MIG-TD-IX, 15-Apr-1994.
[123] Traub, *The Best Intentions*, p.53.   [124] Traub, *The Best Intentions*, p.53.

time, however, DPKO had internalized the 'Mogadishu Syndrome' so deeply that it was difficult to say whether it was anticipating the Council's presumed timidity—and Washington's opposition to any action—or helping rationalize it. It is true that the power of suasion of UN officials towards P-5 ambassadors is limited: 'They cannot answer back, they are not allowed to', David Hannay, the former UK Permanent Representative to the UN, stated. 'They might be totally correct, but they cannot win.'[125] The situation is nonetheless different in relation to the E-10 and those capitals which are open to the specific course of action advocated by UN officials. In any event, decisions were taken in the run up to the Rwandan genocide by a part of the Secretariat that had life-or-death effects in the field—for UNAMIR, for the Rwandan people, and for the UN organization—*before* the genocide started. To the extent that anybody was in the driving seat in New York during the crucial months before the genocide, it was the UN bureaucracy.

MISSION MANDATE AND RULES OF ENGAGEMENT

The 'genocide cable' was part of a larger problem between DPKO and Dallaire, namely, a serious misunderstanding about UNAMIR's mandate. Resolution 872 allowed the Canadian General to 'contribute to the security of the city of Kigali, *inter alia*, within a weapons-secure area established by the parties in and around the city'.[126] For DPKO, however, UNAMIR could only *help* the parties recover weapons, rather than doing so autonomously: 'We have to go by the mandate we are given by the Security Council', Riza stated. 'It is not up to the SG or the Secretariat to decide whether they are going to run off in other directions.'[127]

Riza had a point, but since nobody at DPKO seemingly told Dallaire about this, not a strong one. Because the caches mentioned in the 'genocide cable' were within the weapons-secure area indicated by Resolution 872, Dallaire thought that seizing them was firmly within his powers: 'They just don't understand', he told his deputy upon receiving Annan's reply. 'Something's off the rails here, we are off course. We are fully authorized to do this; that's what we are here to do.'[128] Indeed, the recovery of weapons was so important to Dallaire that he had specifically asked DPKO to insert that function into the SG's recommendations to the Council, not least because the Arusha parties

[125] My Interview with David Hannay, 26 April 2010, London, UK (and via mail on 12 May 2016).
[126] Res 872 (S/RES/872), 5 October 1993, §3(a).
[127] Riza, *PBS Frontline Interview*, March 2003.
[128] Beardsley, *PBS Frontline Interview*, 15 November 2003.

had so requested.[129] This, however, was never done and Boutros-Ghali's report only advised that the mission '*assist* in ensuring the security of the city of Kigali',[130] a more timid formula of which Dallaire was unaware. Equally troubling is the fact that the Force Commander had already confiscated illegal weapons in the past and had dutifully reported such activities to DPKO: 'UNAMIR ensured the Kigali Weapons Secure Area so far and is ready for appropriate action in case of violation', Dallaire had cabled New York in early January 1994, adding that the 'Force Commander implemented the first offensive operations planning against armed political militias and suspicious areas'.[131] Various seizures had also been undertaken by UNAMIR at the Kigali airport, where incoming aircraft had been searched and forty tons of ammunition from an *East African Cargo* plane had been confiscated.[132] Since DPKO was informed of these operations but never objected to them, Dallaire's misunderstanding was reinforced: 'We just saw it well within our mandate. The Arusha Peace Agreement had called for the mutual international force— us—to recover illegal weapons; it had authorized us to do that. The mandate that we had told us to contribute to the security of the city of Kigali. In our rules of engagement, we had anticipated the recovery of illegal weapons.'[133] The US Ambassador to Rwanda agrees: 'My own feeling at that time', David Rawson stated, 'which I think I expressed to General Dallaire, was that under terms of the agreement in which Kigali was supposed to be a weapons-free zone, this agreement had been violated, and he certainly had it within his mandate to do this [seize weapons].'[134] Be that as it may, the leadership of a UN mission held a mistaken view of its mandate, and its supervisors in New York did little to correct it.

The confusion surrounding UNAMIR's rules of engagement (ROE) ran even deeper. Since the consent of the parties is crucial to any operation conducted under Chapter VI of the UN Charter, DPKO officials believed that Dallaire could not use force to protect civilians—a problematic scenario in a situation of conflict and civil war, let alone genocide.[135] Confusingly, however, UNAMIR's formal ROE *allowed* Dallaire to protect civilians against gross human rights violations—a contradiction originating in yet another misunderstanding between New York and Kigali. When Dallaire's military attaché approached DPKO in late 1993 to seek instructions on UNAMIR's ROE, New York advised him to produce his own draft and suggested that a previous operation in Cambodia could provide a template.[136] So in November

---

[129] S/725951, 15 June 1993, §B(6).
[130] S/26488, 24 September 1993, §21 (emphasis added).
[131] Barnett, *Eyewitness*, p.84.   [132] Melvern, *A People Betrayed*, p.95.
[133] Beardsley, *PBS Frontline Interview*, 15 November 2003.
[134] David Rawson, *PBS Frontline Interview*, 5 October 2003.
[135] Rawson, *PBS Frontline Interview*, 5 October 2003.
[136] S/1999/1257, 15 December 1999.

1993 Beardsley sent DPKO a document containing UNAMIR's draft ROE, including the following passage: 'There may also be ethnically or politically motivated criminal acts committed during this mandate which will morally and legally require UNAMIR to use all available means to halt them. Examples are executions, attacks on displaced persons or refugees.'[137] Such acts would, the ROE noted, make it necessary for UNAMIR to 'take the necessary action to prevent any crime against humanity'.[138] Because DPKO never objected to this message, Dallaire and Beardsley interpreted it as yet another case of 'silent approval' by New York. Tragically, it was as a result of this misunderstanding that UNAMIR was able to afford some protection to civilians during the genocide—particularly in the *Hôtel de Milles Collines*, a place made famous by the film *Hotel Rwanda*. Had UNAMIR followed DPKO's strict interpretation, even this limited engagement would have been impossible.[139]

DPKO IN RWANDA

Although the DPKO, the position of its leadership, and the department's place within Boutros-Ghali's Secretariat need further scrutiny and will be returned to, three preliminary observations can be made about the role of the peacekeeping department in Rwanda.

First, what officials refer to as 'political analysis' was seriously inadequate in the run-up to the crisis of 1994, for UNAMIR was thrown into the Rwandan maelstrom with less than sufficient knowledge about the minefield that the African country had become. As we will see in Chapter 3, DPKO was hardly the only part of the UN bureaucracy responsible for this, while the UNAMIR leadership too made a number of questionable calls. Nevertheless, the peacekeeping department played a pivotal role in setting up and managing UNAMIR, and thus bears some responsibility for the mission's problems ahead of the genocide. By virtue of its composition—including military personnel from the largest nations—DPKO has 'expert authority', or specialized knowledge that is not widely available and which provides bureaucracies with influence. 'As guardians of this knowledge', two authors observed, 'professionals perceive themselves to be acting in the name of the public good.'[140] This has been referred to as 'epistemic communities', or 'a network of professionals with recognized expertise and competence in a particular domain and an authoritative claim to

---

[137] UN Assistance Mission for Rwanda (UNAMIR), *Rules of Engagement*, undated (on file with the author).

[138] Michael Barnett and Martha Finnemore, *Rules for the World* (Ithaca: Cornell University Press, 2004), p.202, Endnote 64.

[139] *Informal Meetings of the Security Council on Rwanda*, Part I (LMRGA).

[140] Barnett and Finnemore, *Rules for the World*, p.24.

policy-relevant knowledge within that domain or issue-area'.[141] Although, on the eve of UNAMIR, the UN was in a serious financial crisis, DPKO had substantial control over—as well as the ability to create—information, a situation that considerably increased that department's influence over Dallaire. Mark (now Lord) Malloch Brown, a former Deputy SG under Annan, recognizes this 'power' of the UN bureaucracy to frame an issue: 'As a key UN-decision maker during those years, I would say that there is a huge discretion available to the Secretariat to shape the opinion and the response, though it is a discretion within resource constraints and realities.'[142]

Second, the peacekeeping department appeared nonchalant in 'mind-reading' the position of the Council in general and of its most powerful member in particular. As a result, choices were made by a part of the UN bureaucracy not because they were in the best interests of UNAMIR or the Rwandan people, but because DPKO was anticipating a negative reaction to them by the SC. Yet the DPKO's leadership clearly had strategic objections of its own to UNAMIR, and its failure to share them with the rest of the Secretariat suggests that the department was not only anticipating the Council's presumed position, but also agreeing with it. Because of this sensitivity of DPKO to the alleged wishes of the SC, the department ended up taking decisions that unwillingly contributed to mar UNAMIR from the start, a circumstance that undermines the widespread view according to which the Secretariat was unable to influence the events.

Last but not least, the Secretariat was hardly a coherent—let alone monolithic—entity in 1994. Serious miscommunication meant that DPKO and UNAMIR had different readings of the mission's mandate and of its rules of engagement—the two most important components of any peace operation—with extremely damaging effects in the field. Chapter 5 will show why none of this exonerates the UN membership from its responsibility for the events of 1994—indeed, some of the problems mentioned in this chapter resulted from the situation of financial starvation in which the Secretariat was consciously kept in the early 1990s. But it is equally clear that, far from being inconsequential, the decisions taken by DPKO did matter and contributed to the tragic outcome of 1994. Albeit for different reasons, a similar point can be made about DPA.

---

[141] Peter Haas, 'Introduction: Epistemic Communities and International Policy Coordination', *International Organization*, Vol.46 (1992), p.3.

[142] My interview with Mark Malloch Brown, 28 September 2011, London, UK (and by email on 16 June 2016).

2

Department of Political Affairs

It was an unusual place for a Western diplomat. In April 1994, as Rwanda was plunging into chaos, the head of DPA was sitting at Stalin's desk, dialling the phone that the Soviet dictator had used for decades.[1] Important events were taking place at the time—including a bloody conflict in Yugoslavia—and Rwanda was not high on DPA's list of priorities. Partly as a result of this, DPA is the only UN department that has escaped the scrutiny of journalists and academics alike. One of the most highly regarded accounts of the genocide, for instance, dismisses it in a couple of sentences;[2] a number of other well respected analyses barely mention it;[3] and the most rigorous academic study of the UN in Rwanda ignores it altogether.[4] UN insiders have been equally neglectful: the memoirs by Roméo Dallaire give DPA a marginal if unflattering role,[5] as does the book by the Special Representative of the Secretary-General (SRSG).[6] Boutros-Ghali, too, is silent about the input of his 'political'[7] department, an indication that the spotlight has been on DPKO as the UN unit in charge of the Rwanda mission, with DPA supposedly playing a marginal role.

Intriguingly, DPA is also routinely ignored by the UN literature at large. One of the most authoritative treatments of the UN mentions it twice in a thousand pages;[8] another acclaimed (and voluminous) analysis never refers to it;[9] and the index of the best-selling guide to the UN omits it altogether.[10]

---

[1] 'I have had a mystery pain in my jaw ever since'. MIG-TD-X, 5-Apr-1994.

[2] Linda Melvern, *A People Betrayed* (London: Zed Books, 2009).

[3] African Rights, *Rwanda* (London: African Rights, 1995); Linda Melvern, *Conspiracy to Murder* (London: Verso, 2006); Michael Barnett and Martha Finnemore, *Rules for the World* (Ithaca: Cornell University Press, 2004).

[4] Michael Barnett, *Eyewitness to a Genocide* (Ithaca: Cornell University Press, 2003).

[5] Roméo Dallaire, *Shake Hands with the Devil* (London: Arrow Books, 2003).

[6] Jacques-Roger Booh Booh, *Le Patron de Dallaire Parle* (Paris: Éditions Duboiris, 2005).

[7] Boutros Boutros-Ghali, *Mes Années à la Maison de Verre* (Paris: Fayard, 1999).

[8] Thomas Weiss and Sam Daws, eds, *The Oxford Handbook of the United Nations* (Oxford: Oxford University Press, 2008).

[9] Vaughan Lowe et al., *The United Nations Security Council and War* (Oxford: Oxford University Press, 2010).

[10] Linda Fasulo, *An Insider's Guide to the UN* (New Haven: Yale University Press, 2004).

Outside of—and sometimes even *in*—New York, many are unaware of DPA's precise functions. Since the UN organization is often perceived as a sum of its member states, the SG is rarely associated with a strong leadership role in global affairs—and if *he* has not got it, the argument goes, his 'political' department is not really worth engaging with.[11]

There are, of course, excellent historical reasons to be sceptical about the SG's relevance in world politics. From the establishment of the UN until the end of the Cold War, fierce cross-veto battles on the Security Council (SC) often paralysed the organization.[12] The leeway of the SG was then especially limited and the structure of the Secretariat mirrored this: the numerous 'political' departments that mushroomed at Headquarters during the Cold War—such as the Office for Political and General Assembly Affairs, the Department of Political and Security Council Affairs, and the Department for Special Political Questions—were openly controlled by the superpowers and hindered, rather than helped, the SG's work. Indeed, that was their purpose: Àlvaro de Soto, an adviser to both Pérez de Cuéllar and Boutros-Ghali, describes the constraints on the SG's ability to use either the personnel or the material that came out of the existing Secretariat body then called the Department of Political and Security Council Affairs. 'For Cold War reasons', de Soto explains, 'anyone or anything that came out of PSCA, tightly run by the seconded Soviet Diplomat heading it, was viewed with suspicion, and was unusable in the Secretary-General's good offices.'[13] This, however, did not make the SG irrelevant: although peacekeeping is nowhere to be found in the UN Charter, Hammarskjöld carved out a role for himself and Pérez de Cuéllar followed suit by concentrating most of what UN officials refer to as 'political' activities in his Executive Office. But Cold War-era SGs had to be careful: 'It was an extraordinary situation', de Soto elaborates. 'We had to scrounge, beg, borrow, and steal, [we] operated almost clandestinely, and [we] used personnel without admitting it.'[14] The superpowers would have never agreed to this use of the Secretariat, but Pérez de Cuéllar had no intention of telling them.

It was only in 1992, when Boutros-Ghali became SG, that the opportunities afforded by the end of the Cold War could be openly exploited.[15] As Part II will explain, by creating two new departments—one for peacekeeping (DPKO) and the other for peacebuilding (DPA)—the Egyptian had ambitious plans for the organization.[16] One year earlier, the first-ever SC meeting of Heads of State and Government had given him an unprecedented chance to shape the 'New

---

[11] There is a sizeable—notably 'realist'—literature on this. An interesting exception is Thomas Weiss, *What's Wrong with the United Nations and How to Fix It* (Cambridge: Polity, 2009), ch.3.

[12] Paul Kennedy, *The Parliament of Man* (London: Penguin, 2007), ch.2.

[13] My interview with Álvaro de Soto, 20 July 2011, New York, USA (and via email on 4 June 2016).

[14] Interview with de Soto, 20 July 2011.

[15] Leon Gordenker, *The UN Secretary-General and Secretariat* (Abingdon: Routledge, 2010), ch.2.

[16] He describes them in *UNvanquished* (London: I.B. Tauris, 1999), ch.1.

World Order'.[17] Freed from the Cold War constraints that had paralysed his predecessors, Boutros-Ghali was determined to seize this opportunity, and the most important jewel in his crown was to be DPA. It was the department that he cherished and nurtured the most, the vessel through which he intended to ride the uncharted waters of the post-Cold War world. Importantly for our purposes, Boutros-Ghali's administrative 'revolution' came into effect shortly before the Secretariat considered the possibility of setting up a Rwanda operation.

JONAH'S DPA (I): FRICTION WITH DPKO AND MONITORING OF THE PEACE TALKS

Boutros-Ghali's reorganization of the Secretariat coincided with the publication of *An Agenda for Peace*, his ambitious attempt to shift the emphasis of the UN from peacekeeping (i.e. military intervention aimed at solving conflicts) to peacebuilding (i.e. diplomatic efforts to prevent conflicts from arising).[18] As the UN unit responsible for preventive diplomacy, peace-making, and post-conflict peacebuilding, DPA was to have a critical role in this new eco-system, with James Jonah—a long-serving Sierra Leonean diplomat—initially in charge of it.

Every case of bureaucratic re-organization has its losers and Boutros-Ghali's was no exception.[19] While DPA and preventive diplomacy occupied centre-stage in the SG's grand design as cheaper and more promising ways of tackling global instability, DPKO and peacekeeping were increasingly seen from the 38th floor as too expensive and complex for the Secretariat to manage.[20] This went against an important trend since the end of the Cold War, when the disappearance of cross-veto confrontation and the shift from inter-state to intra-state conflicts had turned peacekeeping into the premier tool of member states to promote international peace and security.[21] As mentioned in Chapter 1, DPKO had benefited from this renewed UN activism and had scored a number of successes in the field, while attracting the keen interest of some Western capitals.[22] Since peacekeeping requires the kind of expensive technical and semi-military capacity that powerful countries have but that the Secretariat sorely lacks, DPKO was picked by Western nations as *the* UN department worth investing in, with the result that resources were less

---

[17] Boutros-Ghali, *UNvanquished*, ch.1.
[18] Boutros Boutros-Ghali, *An Agenda for Peace* (New York: Department of Public Information, 1992).
[19] Jack Knott and Gary Miller, *Reforming Bureaucracy* (New Jersey: Prentice Hall, 1987).
[20] Weiss, *What's Wrong*, ch.3.
[21] Javier Pérez de Cuéllar, *Pilgrimage for Peace* (London: St Martin's Press, 1997), ch.1.
[22] Edward Luck, *Mixed Messages* (Washington, DC: Brookings Institution Press, 1999).

reluctantly provided to it than to the rest of the UN bureaucracy.[23] For the only remaining superpower, in particular, the collapse of the USSR provided a good opportunity to re-shape the world organization, and since Washington was by far the largest contributor to the UN budget, US interest in—and influence over—UN peacekeeping steadily increased after the end of the Cold War. As a result, the Secretariat's workload skyrocketed: in his archive, Goulding considered Namibia, Kuwait, Angola, El Salvador, Cambodia, and Mozambique to be UN success stories, but also noted that 'these successes not only amazed; they also intoxicated. Why waste time analyzing political options and military risk when the UN, it seemed, could not put a foot wrong?'[24]

Boutros-Ghali's plan to strengthen DPA at the expense of DPKO threatened the status quo and put him on a collision course with Washington, a move that contributed to his downfall.[25] Though US–UN friction was hardly new, by early 1993 the SG had come to perceive DPKO as a department that was not entirely a part of the UN Secretariat, but rather as US-controlled and largely untrustworthy.[26] The fact that the head of DPKO was Kofi Annan—whom Boutros-Ghali saw as too close to the Americans and, later on, as intent on replacing him at the helm of the UN—contributed to widen the gulf between the SG and one of his key departments.

This is the complex environment that James Jonah faced when he took charge of DPA in early 1992. An African with a deep interest in—and knowledge of—his continent, Jonah went on to serve as Boutros-Ghali's adviser. He also became the 'Africa man' of the most Africa-oriented SGs to lead the UN, somebody who appeared to share Boutros-Ghali's desire to strengthen DPA whilst keeping DPKO at bay.[27] As Part II will suggest, Jonah's mission was made easier by a 1993 directive in which Boutros-Ghali cemented the superiority of his 'political' department by formally requesting that no document produced by DPKO was to reach the SG without Jonah's signature.[28] This meant that DPA usually knew what DPKO was up to, but not necessarily the other way around. That Boutros-Ghali's edict came into effect as the UN was considering a mission to Rwanda virtually guaranteed DPA's involvement there.

Indeed, DPA's involvement was considerable. In the spring of 1993, ahead of his decision to recommend UNAMIR, the SG despatched to Kigali a team led by one of DPA's most senior officers, Macaire Pédanou, who visited the region from 2 to 17 May 1993 and who compiled a report on the local

---

[23] Marrack Goulding, *Peacemonger* (London: John Murray, 2002), ch.2.

[24] Marrack Goulding, 'Peacemonger: Book Proposal', 15 June 1998 (MIG-PA).

[25] Boutros-Ghali, *UNvanquished*, ch.3.

[26] MIG-TD-X, 26-Sep-1994.

[27] James Jonah, *What Price the Survival of the United Nations?* (Ibadan: Evans Brothers, 2006).

[28] My interview with James Jonah, New York, USA, 20 July 2011.

situation, a document that Jonah found 'very useful'[29] and that 'helped [him] to have a better handle on the complexity of the problems in the negotiating process'.[30] Indeed, Pédanou's assessments were deemed to be so informative by Jonah and Boutros-Ghali that the DPA officer was also asked to monitor the talks between the Rwandan government and the rebels of the Rwandan Patriotic Front (RPF) in Arusha, Tanzania. As an observer, Pédanou sent DPA several detailed reports on the ebb and flow of the negotiations; such talks were significant since they resulted in the Arusha Peace Agreements which the UN operation was expected to implement—and the SG was relying on DPA to keep him abreast of events. From the outset and on behalf of the SG, DPA officers encouraged the Rwandan parties to reach an agreement, making it clear that Boutros-Ghali expected them to settle their grievances on the negotiating table rather than on the battlefield (by this time, Boutros-Ghali himself had come under pressure from France to finalize a peace agreement).[31] Yet the Political Affairs department was more than the SG's eyes and ears, for in New York Jonah was himself reportedly advocating for a mission to Rwanda, feeling that the least the UN could do under the circumstances was to have a presence in the African country. According to Jonah, the Americans unambiguously opposed such involvement.[32]

The close ties between DPA and Boutros-Ghali contributed to increased friction with DPKO—at least, this was the perception in the political department and in Boutros-Ghali's Executive Office. According to Jonah, when DPA proposed to the SG that UNAMIR be established, DPKO was sceptical and so were a number of member states, in particular the UK and the USA.[33] France, on the other hand, needed little convincing: its longstanding ties to Rwanda's Hutus meant that Paris strongly supported UNAMIR, a position that—as Part II will explain—nevertheless created a different set of issues. As for Washington, it remained distinctively uninterested in UNAMIR, a circumstance that contributed to exacerbate the rift between the leaderships of the two key Secretariat departments.

Such friction escalated in the following months. Having agreed to consider a Rwanda operation, the perception in DPA was that DPKO felt entitled to take charge of it, and that the peacekeeping department wanted DPA to step aside after the signing of the Arusha Agreements. According to Jonah, the view from DPKO was that it is DPA's task to negotiate, but that once the negotiations are over, DPKO takes charge. The DPA leadership, however, disagreed, seeing the UN presence in Rwanda as a continuum. Issues of a 'political' nature, in

[29] Jonah, *What Price*, p.376.   [30] Jonah, *What Price*, p.376.
[31] Assemblée Nationale, *Mission d'Information Parlamentaire sur le Rwanda*, Audition de M. Edouard Balladur, 2 April 1998, available at http://www.assemblee-nationale.fr/dossiers/rwanda/auditi01.asp (accessed 30 December 2015) (hereinafter, MIPR).
[32] My interview with James Jonah, 20 July 2011, New York, USA. See also Jonah, *What Price*, p.378.
[33] Interview with Jonah, 20 July 2011. See also Jonah, *What Price*, p.378.

particular, were regarded by DPA as a part of *its* mandate; for Jonah, DPKO simply did not have the resources to carry out 'political' analysis.[34] Beyond what was clearly bureaucratic competition, a more substantive difficulty confronted UN officials, one that Part II will consider at length: where do peacekeeping and peacebuilding—and thus the responsibilities of DPKO and DPA—actually begin and end? Jonah in DPA seemed to have no doubts; neither did Annan in DPKO. Yet there was a new mission to plan and since a coordinated approach between DPA and DPKO failed to materialize, the two departments effectively travelled separate ways.

JONAH'S DPA (II): RECONNAISSANCE AND POLITICAL ANALYSIS

While the first stage of DPA's association with UNAMIR included activities such as monitoring the Arusha negotiations and recommending a UN mission to the SG, the second phase was no less significant and concerned the areas of reconnaissance, 'political analysis', intelligence on ethnic killings, and involvement in Dallaire's 'genocide cable'.

Although reconnaissance is critical to any peacekeeping operation, the fact-finding mission of August 1993 was marked by considerable friction between DPA and DPKO, something that resulted in poor information-sharing. For Jonah, this was a DPA-led enterprise whereas Dallaire's and DPKO's roles were thought to be largely 'technical'—rather than 'political'—in nature.[35] When Pédanou's departure was delayed by illness, however, it was decided that the mission would be led by Dallaire instead, a military man with no diplomatic training who went on to perform a wide range of substantive functions. 'My eyes were being opened to realities far from my usual military sphere', Canadian General Dallaire wrote, 'and I was attempting to absorb every nuance of the culture, every distortion of the double-talk of its political leaders.'[36]

Pédanou's illness exposed a serious flaw in the way the UN carried out its assessment on the viability of UNAMIR, for both DPA and DPKO were determined to be in charge of reconnaissance and neither department was willing to leave it to the other. As mentioned, DPA was actively involved in the Arusha peace negotiations and since Jonah was an Africanist, it was felt that the department did not need a large presence during the August trip. Still, DPA felt entitled to be in charge of reconnaissance because the SG's directive

---

[34] Interview with Jonah, 20 July 2011.   [35] Interview with Jonah, 20 July 2011.
[36] Dallaire, *Shake Hands*, p.61.

made the 'political' department hierarchically superior to the peacekeeping one: for Jonah, in particular, it was DPKO that was assisting DPA, not the other way around.[37] This 'primacy' of DPA explains why Pédanou was supposed to lead the mission and was openly recognized by Dallaire: 'DPKO was definitely further down the UN totem pole than DPA', the Canadian wrote, 'a place where many officers flaunted their connections, particularly with the SG.'[38] Yet DPKO had 'political' officers as well and it, too, felt entitled to carry out what it perceived to be 'political' activities: 'Maurice [Baril from DPKO] told me that one of the most difficult problems he and his colleagues faced was DPA's constant interference and maneuvering without consulting DPKO political staff',[39] Dallaire wrote. According to Jonah, when DPKO claimed the right to do the 'political' work, DPA refused given that such issues were within its remit.[40] DPA prevailed.

Unsurprisingly given the institutional friction in New York, personal relations during reconnaissance were also fraught. Dallaire described Jonah's assistant as 'soigné and haughty, a fixer and arranger who thrived in the diplomatic social milieu',[41] while complaining that once Pédanou was finally able to join the delegation, 'he immediately...treated me as his number two'.[42] This confrontation persisted after the mission returned to New York, when officials from both departments 'disappeared to their respective work-places or went on leave'.[43] Tom Quiggin, a Canadian intelligence officer who served in UN peacekeeping missions in the early 1990s, wrote that 'access to [DPA] seemed difficult. They often appeared disinterested or distanced from the real issues on the ground.'[44] As Chapter 6 will show, however, the UN's problem in 1993 was not lack of information—Jonah received extensive briefings from his officials, as did DPKO—but rather the fact that the two departments collected data separately and were reluctant to share it. Given the complexities of Rwanda and the fragility of the Arusha Accords, it was a weakness that would cost the organization dearly: 'The culture of the UN was one of jealously guarded stovepipe fiefdoms where information was power',[45] Dallaire noted. Neither DPA nor DPKO wanted to give up the information they had, least of all to each other.

The handling of intelligence was marred by similar issues. DPKO has been criticized for downplaying reports of ethnic killings prior to the genocide, whereas DPA is thought to have played no role in this. By late 1993, however, Jonah was clearly aware of—and increasingly worried about—the fragile ethnic situation in the Great Lakes region, so much so that when Burundi's

[37] Interview with Jonah, 20 July 2011.   [38] Dallaire, *Shake Hands*, p.51.
[39] Dallaire, *Shake Hands*, p.51.   [40] Interview with Jonah, 20 July 2011.
[41] Dallaire, *Shake Hands*, pp.61–2.   [42] Dallaire, *Shake Hands*, pp.77–8.
[43] Dallaire, *Shake Hands*, p.81.
[44] My interview with Tom Quiggin, 4 May 2016 (by email).
[45] Dallaire, *Shake Hands*, p.52.

Hutu president was killed in a coup by his Tutsi-dominated army in October 1993, Jonah was precipitously sent by the SG to contain the crisis.[46] The head of DPA mediated between the deposed government and the army, set up a UN observer's group, and established a panel of enquiry. Given the similar ethnic composition of Rwanda and Burundi, Jonah was especially worried about a potential spillover of the latter's ethnic conflict into the former: 'Some of the Council members failed to realize the negative impact of developments in Burundi on its neighbor Rwanda', Jonah wrote, '[but] the vitriolic propaganda against the Tutsi leadership [was] inflaming passions [and] I was concerned that it might result in serious consequences.'[47] This was particularly troubling since, by late 1993, DPA was receiving reports that some Rwandan parties were making 'inflammatory pronouncements that increased political and ethnic tension in the country'.[48] Thus, in mid-1993 Jonah and DPA were extremely familiar with the region's problems and were actively trying to contain them on behalf of the SG.

An example of this occurred in December 1993. Four months before the killings began and a few weeks *before* Dallaire sent his 'genocide cable' to DPKO warning of impending massacres, the SG reportedly received an urgent, specific, and top-secret forewarning about large-scale anti-Tutsi killings being planned in Kigali by people close to the Rwandan president.[49] As a result of this piece of information, in December 1993 Jonah was precipitously despatched to Kigali by Boutros-Ghali to warn the Rwandan President that the SG had become aware of 'reported plans for a massacre and to let him know that the United Nations would not tolerate such actions'.[50] According to Jonah, Boutros-Ghali told him that 'people close to President Habyarimana' were planning to use force against the Tutsis, and the SG wanted Jonah to tell Rwanda's Head of State that the UN would not accept that.[51] The warning pushed the SG to despatch one of his highest-ranking officials 'because of the very serious nature of the message':[52] 'I could see that the President was visibly disturbed when he heard the message',[53] Jonah noted. Far from being out of the loop, therefore, DPA was at the forefront of the UN's involvement in Rwanda and was privy to privileged information about the situation at a critical juncture for the country's stability. Did it share it with DPKO? According to Jonah, both Dallaire (the Force Commander) and Booh Booh (Boutros-Ghali's Special Representative in Kigali) were present when the Rwandan President was confronted with the intelligence.[54] Since Dallaire was reporting to DPKO, Jonah assumed that the peacekeeping department

---

[46] Jonah, *What Price*, p.381.   [47] Jonah, *What Price*, p.367.
[48] Jonah, *What Price*, p.380.   [49] Jonah, *What Price*, p.381.
[50] Jonah, *What Price*, p.381.
[51] Interview with Jonah, 20 July 2011; see also *What Price*, p.381.
[52] Jonah, *What Price*, p.381.   [53] Jonah, *What Price*, p.382.
[54] Jonah, *What Price*, p.382.

would be informed by the Canadian General. Yet there is no indication that DPA raised the issue with DPKO directly, nor that the two departments coordinated any specific response to it. Since only a few months later those warnings did materialize, this was a significant development.

DPA was hardly the only UN department guarding its intelligence, for DPKO does not appear to have informed Jonah of Dallaire's 'genocide cable' mentioning plans for similar massacres in January 1994. The former head of DPA, at least, insists that he did not see that cable, nor knew about it, until after the genocide.[55] He also wonders why it was not copied to him by Dallaire—as was customary—but only to DPKO: 'I would have thought that an essentially political matter [such as the one raised in the cable] should have been addressed to me, particularly since I had raised [a similar] issue with the President just a few weeks back on December 7, 1993.'[56] Dallaire knew that Jonah was close to the SG, was involved in the Rwanda operation, and had warned the Rwandan President of the plans for Tutsi massacres. Why, then, did the Force Commander not copy Jonah into his message? At the time of the events, rules for cable traffic worked as follows: those deemed to be of a 'technical' nature were to be sent to DPKO and copied to DPA, whereas those of a 'political' nature were to be sent to DPA and copied to DPKO.[57] What was to count as 'technical' and 'political', however, remained largely unclear. Since we know that Dallaire mistrusted DPA, he might have felt that DPKO represented his best chance for a rapid response. Jonah, however, believes that the cable was concealed from him.[58] Be that as it may, the handling of Dallaire's 'genocide cable' suggests that another critical piece of information had entered the UN chain—this time through DPKO—but was not directly or efficiently shared with the rest of the Secretariat.

GOULDING'S DPA (I): CHANGE OF LEADERSHIP AND CRISIS MANAGEMENT

Until March 1994, DPA was jointly led by James Jonah (who was responsible for Africa) and Marrack Goulding (who dealt with the rest of the world, except Palestine).[59] On 1 March 1994, Jonah retired and Boutros-Ghali entrusted the whole of DPA to Goulding.[60] As a result, a month before the genocide an important change of leadership occurred in New York.

---

[55] Jonah, *What Price*, pp.382–3.   [56] Jonah, *What Price*, p.383.
[57] Interview with Jonah, 20 July 2011. See also Jonah, *What Price*, p.383.
[58] Interview with Jonah, 20 July 2011.   [59] MIG-TD-IX, 4-Feb-1993.
[60] MIG-TD-IX, 4-Feb-1993.

What makes Goulding intriguing is that he was a peacekeeper rather than a 'political' affairs officer at heart. Between 1986 and 1991, before DPKO was created, he had managed UN peacekeeping through the Office for Special Political Affairs (OSPA) at a time when it was both flourishing and successful.[61] As one author noted, 'OSPA was long home to the most important international civil servants below the Secretary-General and therefore a "fabled" UN office, not least due to its famous incumbents Ralph Bunche and Brian Urquhart.'[62] In 1992, following Boutros-Ghali's elevation as SG and his restructuring of the Secretariat, Goulding oversaw the creation of DPKO, which he went on to lead, choosing Annan as his deputy. Yet the SG wanted Goulding to be at the forefront of the UN's preventive diplomacy initiative, so in March 1993 Goulding was abruptly removed from DPKO and found himself co-heading DPA with Jonah. Given the close relationship between DPA and SG, as well as the fact that DPKO was regarded as 'a more technical department',[63] this was supposed to be a promotion, and Goulding went on to become Boutros-Ghali's closest adviser. As somebody who was happier and more at ease in the field than in New York, however, Goulding felt uncomfortable in what he saw as the stuffy environment of DPA. To him, taking over the entire department was a daunting challenge.

This proved to be the case. Almost overnight, Goulding was asked to shift allegiances from DPKO—his 'baby', as he called it—to DPA. More important for our purposes, he was required to leave behind the practical logic of peacekeeping for the murkier arena of peacebuilding. The problem, as he noted early on in his diary, was that he did not really know where one ended and the other began: 'The rest of my life at the UN would be haunted by the question of whether it is possible to separate responsibility for keeping the peace in a particular conflict, from responsibility for mediating a political settlement of it',[64] he wrote. He disagreed with Boutros-Ghali and Jonah that DPA should oversee DPKO, for he recognized that the former was slow and cumbersome in a context where action and prompt decisions were vital. But his allegiance had changed, his colleagues in DPA were looking to him for guidance, and Boutros-Ghali expected him to preach the new gospel: '[When] I raised the "new dispensation" by which DPKO is no longer the overall "backstopping" department but is responsible only for operational and military matters', Goulding wrote in his diary, 'only Kofi supported me', adding that 'it was quite a mean discussion, with Jonah complaining vociferously [about such objections].'[65] Worse was to come, and when the SG asked *him* to produce a

---

[61] Brian Urquhart, *A Life in Peace and War* (New York: Norton, 1987).

[62] Ingvild Bode, *Individual Agency and Policy Change at the UN* (Abingdon: Routledge, 2015), p.153.

[63] Bode, p.153.   [64] Goulding, 'Peacemonger: Book Proposal', p.4.

[65] MIG-PD-B, 20-Mar-1993.

formal division of roles between the two departments, Goulding felt trapped: 'I spent a miserable holiday in Brittany trying to draft a detailed division of labor', he complained. 'It proved impossible.'[66] As Part II will explain, fifteen years later, I faced a similar dilemma at DPA.

Back in New York, events left Goulding little time for these theoretical discussions. By 1994 Secretariat officials were overseeing more than a dozen missions, including those in Bosnia, Haiti, El Salvador, Cambodia, and Angola. Goulding's most pressing problem was thus practical rather than conceptual: money was tight and the British official adhered to DPKO's view that the UN was overstretched and the SC hostile to new operations, something that made him negatively inclined towards them. His journals from his time at the helm of DPA suggest a clear desire for disengagement: he had 'absolutely no enthusiasm'[67] for the Yugoslavia operation; he found Somalia 'deeply worrying'[68] and wondered how the UN could 'escape from its box';[69] he considered the UN successes in El Salvador 'so huge and yet so wholly farcical';[70] and he confessed that 'We have failed in Angola',[71] lamenting the quagmire the UN had found itself in ('How can we disengage is not clear at all', he wrote).[72] He also found DPA depressing, confidentially warning his successor about 'inter-departmental strife',[73] 'vicious fights',[74] 'empire-building',[75] and 'trench warfare'.[76]

As for Rwanda, until February 1994 it was outside of Goulding's remit—not only was Jonah overseeing African matters, he was protective of his role there.[77] As Goulding put it in his handover notes while explaining his areas of competence, 'I fought off Petrovsky's [the DPA's previous co-head] challenges without difficulty (Yugoslavia, Cambodia, Central America) but lost ground to the more experienced Jonah (Liberia, Rwanda, Somalia).'[78] Once Goulding became the sole head of DPA, however, this changed rapidly. From 1 March 1994 the British official began receiving 'all correspondence previously addressed to Mr Jonah',[79] and on 22 March—days before the genocide— Goulding met the Rwandan ambassador and conveyed to him 'the urgency for the prompt and peaceful installation of the transitional institutions [decided at Arusha]'.[80] Beyond customary diplomatic courtesy, however, Goulding was growing visibly impatient about the delays in implementing the Arusha Peace

[66] MIG-PD-B, 20-Mar-1993.   [67] MIG-PD-B, 4-Jun-1992.
[68] MIG-PD-B, 18-Oct-1992.   [69] MIG-PD-B, 7-Sep-1993.
[70] MIG-PD-B, 18-Oct-1992.   [71] MIG-PD-B, 7-Jan-1993.
[72] MIG-PD-B, 21-Nov-1992.
[73] Marrack Goulding, Handover Notes to Sir Kieran Prendergast, 22 February 1997, §4 (MIG-PA).
[74] Goulding, Handover Notes, §19.   [75] Goulding, Handover Notes, §19.
[76] Goulding, Handover Notes, §1.
[77] Goulding, Statement Attributable to the Secretary-General, 1 February 1994 (MIG-PA).
[78] Goulding, Handover Notes, §3.   [79] Code Cable 610, 2-Mar-1994 (MIG-PA).
[80] Code Cable 826, 22-Mar-1994 (MIG-PA).

Accords, and pessimistic about a fruitful resolution of the Rwanda conflict.[81] Yet his diaries leave no doubt that he—like his predecessor—and DPA as a whole were engaged with the Rwanda crisis. When the plane carrying the presidents of Rwanda and Burundi was shot down on 6 April 1994 and the spark of genocide was ignited, Goulding was accompanying Boutros-Ghali on a Russo-European tour. The head of DPA 'decided not to wake the SG'[82] and instead prepared a statement on his behalf expressing concern for the events in Kigali, while the next two days (7–9 April) were spent coordinating the evacuation of foreigners that France, the USA, and Belgium were demanding and in part already carrying out.[83]

The Goulding papers, however, shed more light on the response of the top UN leadership to the start of the massacres. Within hours of the downing of the presidential plane and contrary to what is commonly thought, Boutros-Ghali and Goulding seemed to favour a complete withdrawal of UNAMIR rather than its strengthening, irrespective of the position of the SC.[84] On 10 April 1994, only four days after the start of the killings and despite mounting reports from Kigali detailing vicious massacres on a massive scale, Goulding wrote in his journal that 'the SG told me to tell DPKO that they should withdraw UNAMIR if they and the people on the ground thought this necessary, *without seeking prior authorization from the Council*'.[85] The Goulding diaries also suggest that the Rwanda operation was being seen by UN leaders as a sideshow to Yugoslavia: 'The SG had a full programme of meetings which left little time for Rwanda',[86] Goulding noted on 10 April. Boutros-Ghali's role and what he actually knew about Rwanda remain highly contentious and will be considered in Chapter 4, particularly in view of his abrupt reversal of position later in the crisis. One should also note that by this stage ten Belgian peacekeepers had been killed, so the SG may have concluded that withdrawal, while regrettable, was the only way to ensure the safety of UN officials, for whom he was ultimately responsible. Still, one of the first recorded reactions of the top UN leadership to the start of the massacres clearly favours disengagement: another Goulding diary entry for 15 April 1994—a week after the killings began—confirms that 'the SG would like to get UNAMIR out', but adds that 'the NAM [Non-Aligned Movement] and France won't agree to this'.[87] In his audition before the French Commission of Inquiry into the Rwandan genocide, then Prime Minister Edouard Balladur and Foreign Minister Alain Juppé confirmed that France was at the time putting considerable pressure on the SG to strengthen UNAMIR rather than withdraw it.[88]

---

[81] MIG-PD-B, 20-Mar-1993.   [82] MIG-TD-X, 8-Apr-1994.
[83] MIG-TD-X, 8-Apr-1994.   [84] MIG-TD-X, 10-Apr-1994.
[85] MIG-TD-X, 10-Apr-1994 (emphasis added).   [86] MIG-TD-X, 10-Apr-1994.
[87] MIG-TD-X, 15-Apr-1994.
[88] Audition de M. Balladur et de M. Juppé, 21 April 1998 (MIPR).

In the following days, Goulding appeared increasingly fatalistic about the UN role in Rwanda, writing of 'a horrific conflict [that] is totally beyond the UN's ability to control'.[89] Given that the killings were being carried out with rudimentary weapons such as machetes and that the UN still had 2,500 men on the ground, this is debatable.[90] As the Carlsson Report into the role of the UN in Rwanda highlighted, 'A force numbering 2,500 should have been able to stop or at least limit massacres of the kind which began in Rwanda after the plane crash which killed the Presidents of Rwanda and Burundi'.[91] Ezaz Afzal, from the Bangladeshi contingent, agrees: 'The Hutus could be overthrown just like dust—and it did happen, when 900 Tutsi soldiers [from the RPF] blew off 20,000 Hutus with only small weapons. If the RPF soldiers were able to stop the genocide in a few days with only light firepower, an organized force of peacekeepers with medium fire could have stopped the genocide in the initial days.'[92] In any event, the Goulding diaries refute the view that in the early phases of the genocide, cynical nations stood in the way of an eager UN leadership and opposed its recommendation to strengthen UNAMIR. The Security Council's decision to reduce UNAMIR from 2,500 to 250 while the genocide was in full swing—a decision that is routinely seen as an example of state cynicism and which Chapter 5 reviews in detail—is not surprising. It had, in fact, the backing of the SG.

By mid-May several factors—including an intensification of public criticism— led Boutros-Ghali to reverse his stance and recommend a strengthening of UNAMIR to the Council, which the latter promptly accepted.[93] 'Atrocities continue and estimates of Tutsis killed during the last three weeks now range as high as 200,000',[94] Goulding wrote on 29 April, thus indicating that by the end of the month the top UN leadership was aware of the scale of the tragedy in Rwanda. Although Part II will return to this, what is striking at this stage is Goulding's scepticism about the possibility of any UN involvement: 'There is no hope for a positive response', he wrote of Boutros-Ghali's instructions to send letters to a dozen African leaders. 'But', he fretted, 'his efforts will show where the blame for international inaction really lies.'[95] Goulding's cynicism only increased when it emerged that the SG—who was by then trying to reclaim his leadership—had great difficulty in gathering any troops for UNAMIR: 'Really atrocious things are going on [in Rwanda]

---

[89] MIG-TD-X, 15-Apr-1994.

[90] Scott Feil, 'Could 5,000 Peacekeepers Have Saved 500,000 Rwandans? Early Intervention Reconsidered', E. A. Walsh School of Foreign Service, Georgetown University, Vol.III, No.2 (1997), p.2.

[91] United Nations, *Report of the Independent Inquiry into the Actions of the United Nations during the 1994 Genocide in Rwanda* (S/1999/1257), 15 December 1999, Part III, §1.

[92] My interview with Ezaz Afzal, 20 April 2016, Chittagong, Bangladesh (and via email on 29 April 2016).

[93] Res 918 (S/RES/918), 17 May 1994.

[94] MIG-MD-SG/RWANDA, TF 29APR94, 10.45.   [95] MIG-TD-X, 2-May-1994.

and the major powers are prepared to do nothing',[96] Goulding wrote. 'Suppose such slaughter was taking place in Bosnia-Herzegovina?'[97]

In Goulding's mind, there was no longer a role for the UN in Rwanda because countries were reluctant to send peacekeepers into a maelstrom, and because there was no longer a peace to keep. Writing in August 1994, Goulding also noted that 'We are handicapped by the lack of troops to reinforce UNAMIR and by the usual confusion over coordination of the humanitarian efforts.'[98] Convinced that UN peacekeeping had reached full capacity and that it had to be reduced rather than increased, Goulding was nevertheless extremely concerned about the situation on the ground and the impact of the Rwandan events on the UN's reputation. As Part II suggests, coupled with some personal issues, this partly accounts for his unimaginativeness: 'I was woken at 0530hrs . . . and was asked what to do about the appalling situation in Goma, Zaire, which was being overwhelmed by over a million Hutu refugees from Rwanda', he wrote in July. 'I had no bright ideas.'[99]

GOULDING'S DPA (II): TURF WARS

The head of DPA had bad omens about 1994—'I feel no enthusiasm for [it]', he wrote in his journal, 'but I must think positive.'[100] He was right to worry, for 1994 turned out to be his *annus horribilis*, the second half of it being even worse than the first. With the exception of his involvement in Angola, where he had been a British ambassador, Goulding was a newcomer to Africa. He was also unlucky to be faced with genocide and a million refugees one month after assuming responsibility for Rwanda: 'I was, in the main, a spectator to these events',[101] he defensively wrote in his diary. Although these factors matter, they do not fully explain his subdued reaction and uncharacteristic lack of leadership in the midst of ferocious killing. A more fundamental problem than bad timing and unfamiliarity with Rwanda afflicted him, and it is a problem that came to a head precisely in the toxic environment of early 1994.

Like Jonah, Goulding had been given specific tasks: strengthen DPA, boost preventive diplomacy, and keep DPKO in check. There was clearly an element of empire-building in this—as Chapter 4 explains, the SG had a plan and was wary of state 'interference'—but Boutros-Ghali's goal was a stronger UN, for which he felt he needed a stronger DPA.[102] In the case of Jonah, a veteran civil

[96] MIG-TD-X, 1-May-1994.　　[97] MIG-TD-X, 1-May-1994.
[98] MIG-TD-X, 1-Aug-1994.　　[99] MIG-TD-X, 17-Jul-1994.
[100] MIG-TD-IX, 31-Dec-1993.　　[101] Goulding, 'Peacemonger: Book Proposal', p.12.
[102] Goulding, 'Peacemonger: Book Proposal', p.12.

servant, the SG was preaching to the converted. As a former head of OSPA and DPKO, however, Goulding tended to view field missions from both sides of the peacekeeping/peacebuilding fence—and this partly explains why Boutros-Ghali was intrigued by him. 'The SG felt that the problem during the next year or two was going to be inadequate political analysis', Goulding wrote in early 1993. 'He was thus interested in a redefinition of the relationship between DPKO and DPA, and was thinking of putting me [in charge of it].'[103]

When that switch happened, Goulding faced a conundrum: he genuinely believed in preventive diplomacy and a stronger DPA, but he also wondered about the precise scope of his new department. What *exactly* was DPA responsible for?[104] Anything that involved 'political' negotiations and analysis, he was told by Boutros-Ghali, including those taking place with a peacekeeping mission on the ground.[105] While such a wide mandate delighted Jonah, it gave Goulding significant headaches, for the British official viewed peacekeeping as a 'political' activity and DPKO as a department that needed to have a 'political' role as well: 'The SG's decision, inspired by Jonah ... to make DPA responsible for the "political" aspects of peacekeeping operations is doubtfully workable',[106] he noted in his journal only a few days after joining DPA. However, Goulding's views were hardly popular with his new department and with the UN's top floor, from which instructions came louder and clearer: 'Boutros-Ghali insisted that the drafts [from DPKO] should all be vetted by me before being forwarded to him for approval',[107] Goulding complained. 'I was [also] instructed to insist on my department's responsibility for all "political aspects" of peacekeeping—gamekeeper turned poacher.'[108]

A combination of factors meant that this issue reached a tipping point precisely at the height of the Rwandan crisis. By this time relations between Boutros-Ghali and DPKO were largely compromised, partly as a result of Rwanda and partly due to a clash between the SG and Annan in crises such as Bosnia and Haiti.[109] As Part II will explain, this reinforced Boutros-Ghali's belief that Annan was after the SG's job. Describing a meeting in mid-1994, Goulding noted that 'Kofi, as usual, tended to support the Americans, but the SG and I were firm':[110] 'I have incidentally come to the conclusion—which I discovered to be shared by others—that Kofi fancies himself as SG ... and is therefore bending over backwards to keep in the Americans' good books.'[111] The 'others' to whom Goulding refer include a number of peacekeepers in the field: 'My view, and that of others at the UN in the former Yugoslavia, was that

[103] MIG-PD-B, 10-Jan-1993.   [104] MIG-PD-B, 14-Mar-1993.
[105] MIG-PD-B, 14-Mar-1993.   [106] MIG-PD-B, 14-Mar-1993.
[107] Goulding, *Peacemonger*, p.334.   [108] Goulding, 'Peacemonger: Book Proposal', p.7.
[109] MIG-TD-X, 1-May-1994; MIG-TD-X, 6-Jul-1994; MIG-TD-X, 14-Jul-1994.
[110] MIG-TD-X, 24-Jul-1994.   [111] MIG-TD-X, 24-Jul-1994.

Kofi Annan was running for the SG position and the Americans were going to back him',[112] wrote Tom Quiggin, a Canadian intelligence officer who served in Bosnia in the early 1990s. Goulding also noted that by 1994 DPKO was perceived by the 38th floor as outside of the SG's purview: when Clinton visited UN Headquarters in September 1994, the Briton wrote that 'First Avenue was closed . . . and all six high rise elevators were commandeered so that Clinton could visit DPKO's much-vaunted Situation Centre (in fact an outpost of the Pentagon).'[113] As this comment suggests, Goulding's own relationship with Annan was at times strained, and while he remained sympathetic to DPKO's demands for a 'political' role, he disliked much of DPKO's staff, described Riza as 'a difficult colleague',[114] and complained about Annan's 'slow decision-making, fuzzy compromises [and] lack of intellectual rigor'.[115] The head of DPA was thus stuck between a rock (his desire to keep DPKO involved in peacekeeping) and a hard place (his belief that the department was effectively beyond the SG's control).

The result was an identity crisis and a deterioration of Goulding's own relations with the SG. Throughout 1994, Boutros-Ghali had not been impressed with Goulding's performance, feeling that he could not rely on DPA as he used to (there was, in Boutros-Ghali's view, no question of him relying on DPKO).[116] Among the 'beasts in the jungle'[117] that Boutros-Ghali had required Goulding to fend off—and that Goulding warned his successor to watch out for—were DPKO and UNDP, whose 'people [can] be reluctant to accept political leadership from the SG (ie DPA)'.[118] The SG was also upset with Goulding on a personal level: the latter's extramarital affair with one of Boutros-Ghali's aides had hit the press in the midst of fierce criticism of the UN's role in Rwanda,[119] with the result that in 1994 the organization's two highest ranking officials were making headlines for the wrong reasons.[120] A warning was issued: 'The SG would like me to be more assertive in stopping DPKO encroaching on the political responsibilities of DPA', Goulding wrote, noting that his staff agreed with Boutros-Ghali. 'But I don't relish an interdepartmental war.'[121] By November the situation had degenerated to such an extent that the SG was openly accusing Goulding of offering him little advice and of travelling too much. 'We had a row', the head of DPA scribbled in his journal. '[He said that] my place was in New York, where I should be concerning myself with the major issues of the day (Yugoslavia,

---

[112] Interview with Quiggin, 4 May 2016.   [113] MIG-TD-X, 26-Sep-1994.
[114] MIG-TD-X, 8-May-1994.   [115] Goulding, 'Peacemonger: Book Proposal', p.4.
[116] MIG-TD-X, 13-Sep-1994.   [117] Goulding, Handover Notes, §18.
[118] Goulding, Handover Notes, §18.
[119] 'Tension at UN as Briton Leaves Wife', *The Times*, 21 November 1994.
[120] 'Our Man at UN Dumps Wife for Blonde Secretary', *Daily Mirror*, 22 November 1994.
[121] MIG-TD-X, 13-Sep-1994.

Rwanda, etc)'.[122] Only two days later, another argument ended with the SG 'saying that DPA...gave him a sense of insecurity', and with Goulding 'agreeing with the many who consider [Boutros-Ghali] an erratic and emotional old man'.[123]

DPA IN RWANDA

'A major gale was blowing. The building was swaying [and it was] frightening since I was alone on the 37th floor and the creaking was audible.'[124] Although this is how Goulding describes a Sunday afternoon winter storm at UN Headquarters, it also serves as a good metaphor for his growing professional unease in New York.

One reason for such unease was the confrontation between DPA and DPKO. As we shall see, part of it was clearly a matter of bureaucratic competition, something that should not surprise given the size of the UN Secretariat and the span of its activities. Seen from the SG's office, however, the 110+ military officers who were 'loaned' by member states on a gratis basis and who were stationed at DPKO's 'Operation Centre' meant that this department was seen as an anomaly and its leadership was not to be trusted. 'Since the UN did not pay them', Chinmaya Gharekhan—Boutros-Ghali's Special Representative on the SC—wrote, 'they owed no allegiance to it. They brought with them their own concepts and they saw to it that the UN procured its supplies from their countries. They provided intelligence to their governments.'[125]

In this context, DPA became Boutros-Ghali's key department not only for preventive diplomacy and peacemaking, but also—and crucially—for peace-keeping. Its contribution to UNAMIR was discreet but substantial: it began with the assistance provided on behalf of the SG to the Arusha parties; it continued with its close involvement in the reconnaissance mission; it resulted in extensive gathering of information before, during, and after the genocide; and it resumed after the killings, when UNAMIR was transformed into a post-conflict peacebuilding operation tasked with helping Rwandans overcome the trauma of genocide.

How did the department handle all this? The Africa-dominated leadership of DPA, whose performance will be assessed in Chapter 8, seemed favourably inclined to establish UNAMIR, not least because Boutros-Ghali was critical of

[122] MIG-TD-X, 9-Nov-1994.   [123] MIG-TD-XI, 11-Nov-1994.
[124] MIG-PD-B, 14-Mar-1993.
[125] Chinmaya Gharekhan, *The Horseshoe Table* (New Delhi: Longman, 2006), p.35.

the SC's fascination with the Former Yugoslavia—a 'rich man's war',[126] as he called it—and of its neglect for Africa. Under Jonah, however, DPA also appeared wary of DPKO and reluctant to share information with it, a situation that partly continued when Goulding took charge. Although the British official was concerned about the UN's ability to handle new operations and disagreed with some of his colleagues over the wisdom of establishing them, the change of leadership at DPA in early 1994 did not fundamentally alter the department's priorities. These were set by the SG and evolved little as a result of the fact that the new head of DPA was arguably closer to the positions of DPKO than to those of DPA. While Goulding's performance in Rwanda was hardly stellar and will be returned to, he was nevertheless prescient in raising alarm bells about the UN's lack of intellectual clarity about—and nonchalant approach towards—both peacekeeping and peacebuilding. By 1994, however, Goulding's frustration had visibly turned into cynicism.

The relationship between two of the UN's most important functions (peace-keeping and peacebuilding) and departments (DPKO and DPA) remains one of the UN's most problematic traits and will be returned to in Part II, which will situate it within the historical context of the early 1990s. While this chapter has suggested that the matter has an important conceptual dimension and goes beyond personal friction and turfs, the next chapter will show that it also had practical implications for the Rwanda mission. If diplomats in New York are bureaucratically divided and conceptually confused, UN personnel on the ground are likely to reproduce that division and that confusion. Unfortunately, UNAMIR was riddled with both.

---

[126] Richard Holbrooke, *To End a War* (New York: Modern Library, 1999), p.174.

3

United Nations Assistance Mission for Rwanda

The plight of UNAMIR and of its Force Commander, Roméo Dallaire, has been told many times and has attracted considerable media attention. General Dallaire has written a poignant account[1] and several movies—including a blockbuster[2]—have conveyed UNAMIR's ordeal to the public. Since this was the first (and arguably remains the only) UN mission to witness genocide, such attention is warranted. Academics have also commented extensively on the effects of the crisis upon UNAMIR and its officers. When it comes to explaining the root causes of those events, however, most accounts have focussed on more visible decision-makers such as the DPKO, the SG, and the SC.[3] The internal dynamics of UNAMIR, as well as the relationship between its military (Dallaire) and 'political' (Booh Booh) leadership, have been overlooked. This appears to be the result of two interrelated factors: first, a tendency to see the Secretariat as a coherent whole that works from the top down, rather than a collage of units that often lack coordination and clash with each other; second, an impression that UNAMIR was a marginal decision-maker in Rwanda, the victim of tragic choices made in New York, Washington, and Paris, rather than Kigali.[4] According to this view, the mission had no leeway and did what it could in exceptionally tragic circumstances.

Although there is certainly some truth in these statements, they hide a more complex reality. Being aware of it is especially important since fresh materials have emerged that shed new light on UNAMIR's internal decision-making

---

[1] Roméo Dallaire, *Shake Hands with the Devil* (London: Arrow Books, 2003).

[2] Terry George, dir., *Hotel Rwanda* (Los Angeles: Lions Gate Entertainment, 2005).

[3] Touko Piiparinen, *The Transformation of UN Conflict Management* (Abingdon: Routledge, 2009), ch.1; Michael Barnett and Martha Finnemore, *Rules for the World* (Ithaca: Cornell University Press, 2004), ch.5; Stephen Burgess, *The United Nations Under Boutros-Ghali* (London: Scarecrow, 2001), pp.97–101.

[4] Linda Melvern, *Conspiracy to Murder* (London: Verso, 2006); Jacques Castonguay, *Les Casques Bleus au Rwanda* (Paris: L'Harmattan, 1998); Michael Barnett, *Eyewitness to a Genocide* (Ithaca: Cornell University Press, 2003).

processes. Most of the cables exchanged between New York and Kigali are available, as are a number of first-hand accounts by UNAMIR's officials. Especially significant is the one by the Special Representative of the Secretary-General (SRSG) in Rwanda, Jacques-Roger Booh Booh, who for over a decade had remained silent about his (and Dallaire's) role in 1994.[5] Partly because of a lack of primary materials and the mentioned image of the Secretariat as a monolith, Booh Booh's role has been especially neglected—surprisingly so, since he was the mission's chief. The Head of the UNAMIR's Kigali Sector has also written,[6] while other military officials[7]—including those from the Bangladeshi contingent[8]—have provided their versions of the events. While these materials support the view of a mission in great difficulty due to external factors, they also point to friction *within* UNAMIR as well as *between* Kigali and New York, particularly over what constituted 'political' and 'operational' matters. The present chapter reviews five issues that contributed to such friction: the mission's late deployment; its poor resources and logistical problems; the confusion over UNAMIR's mandate and rules of engagement; the unclear delineation of roles between the mission's military and 'political' leadership; and the nature of the information the UNAMIR leadership possessed about the genocide.

'TIME BOMB': UNAMIR'S LATE DEPLOYMENT

UNAMIR's troubles began well before it reached Rwanda. Although the mission was planned in mid-1993, by the time Dallaire arrived in Kigali in October, the situation had worsened considerably and was forcing Dallaire to play catch up with events that he was largely unable to control. UNAMIR's late arrival also made its mandate, resources, and logistics obsolete, and meant that the transitional institutions set up by the Arusha Peace Agreement—including a functional government—could not be established, thus making it possible for extremists to derail the peace process. 'We are virtually certain that missiles—SAMS and others—threaten our Mystère 50 [jet]; what can be done to avoid being hit'?[9] wrote the French co-pilot of

[5] Jacques-Roger Booh Booh, *Le Patron de Dallaire Parle* (Paris: Éditions Duboiris, 2005).
[6] Luc Marchal, *Rwanda, La Descente aux Enfers* (Brussels: Éditions Labor, 2001).
[7] Amadou Deme, *Rwanda 1994 and the Failure of the United Nations Mission* (Toronto: Xlibris, 2010); Henry Anyidoho, *Guns Over Kigali* (Accra: Woeli, 1997); Lambertus Ntisoni, *J'ai Traversé des Fleuves de Sang* (Paris: L'Harmattan, 2007).
[8] My interview with Ezaz Afzal, 20 April 2016, Chittagong, Bangladesh (and via email on 29 April 2016).
[9] Jean-Pierre Minaberry, Lettre du Pilote du Falcon Présidentiel: Missiles Menaçant la Sécurité des Vols du Falcon, 28 January 1994, *Mission d'Information Parlamentaire sur le Rwanda*, available at http://www.assemblee-nationale.fr/11/dossiers/rwanda.asp (accessed 16 October 2016) (MIPR).

Habyarimana's plane to an acquaintance, a month before dying alongside the President when their aircraft was hit by two such missiles. 'Air France was unable to take off, the air club no longer flies . . . and the Belgian C130 has also been hit.'[10] Were Rwandan politics solely responsible for this precarious situation, or did problems in New York also play a part?

A clash between the unrealistic timetable set by the Arusha Peace Agreement and slow procedures at Headquarters are the main reasons why UNAMIR was deployed later than expected and was quickly overtaken by events. There is no doubt that the Arusha signatories came up with an exceedingly tight schedule: although the agreement was signed on 4 August 1993, the parties required a mission on the ground by 10 September, thus giving the UN little more than a month's notice.[11] In the end, the Security Council approved the operation on 5 October, Dallaire reached Kigali on 22 October, and Booh Booh followed him on 23 November—more than a month behind the Arusha schedule.[12] Since at the time the UN took a minimum of four months to plan, authorize, and deploy even the smallest operation—and considering that by the time Arusha was signed, the SC had not even approved a Rwanda mission—the parties had clearly drawn up an unrealistic plan. All the same, peacekeeping is a complex business requiring careful and time-consuming negotiations with troop-contributing countries, so UNAMIR deployed relatively quickly by UN standards. In normal circumstances, a 37-day delay is unlikely to seal the fate of a peacekeeping operation.

It should also be noted that the Rwandan parties had excellent reasons to be in a hurry, reasons that the UN Secretariat could not have ignored.[13] Since October 1990 their country had been the theatre of a bloody civil war and by the summer of 1993 the two main contenders—the Rwandan Government Forces (RGF) and the Rwandan Patriotic Front (RPF)—were stuck in a precarious military stalemate.[14] As Part II will suggest, early in the conflict the RGF had only survived thanks to the intervention of France and a series of arms deals with Egypt, but in 1991 Mitterrand had reconsidered Paris's involvement in the Great Lakes region and the RPF had made considerable territorial gains.[15] As a skilled military commander, however, Kagame knew how hard it was to defeat an enemy trained by the French, so while by

---

[10] Minaberry, Lettre, p.239.

[11] United Nations, *The Blue Helmets* (New York: Department of Public Information, 1996), p.343.

[12] United Nations, *The United Nations and Rwanda, 1993–96* (New York: Department of Public Information, 1996), p.28.

[13] Présidence de la République, Requête Conjointe du Gouvernement Rwandais et du Front Patriotique Rwandais au Secrétaire-Général des Nations Unies Relative à la Mise en Place d'une Force Internationale Neutre au Rwanda, 11 June 1993 (MIPR).

[14] Gérard Prunier, *The Rwanda Crisis* (London: Hurst, 1998); *Rwanda* (Paris: Dagorno, 1998).

[15] Linda Melvern, *A People Betrayed* (London: Zed Books, 2000), p.24.

mid-1993 both parties were looking favourably to an UN-brokered agreement, they were also aware that a small incident could resume the conflict. Adding to the sense of urgency was the fact that extremists in both camps were vociferously opposed to a power-sharing agreement and were determined to sabotage it.[16] Confirmation of the parties' haste came when these two bitter rivals despatched a joint delegation to New York to plea for a rapid UN deployment. Supporting this delegation, President Habyarimana wrote to the SG 'reiterat[ing his] hope that [the SG] will reserve the advantage of extreme urgency for the request addressed to you jointly by the RGF and the RPF on 11 June 1993 concerning deployment of the neutral international force'.[17] According to Habyarimana's allies in the French government, the Rwandan president had very little desire to share power with the RPF,[18] but being militarily overthrown by it was an even worse option.[19] For both parties, Rwanda was nothing less than a time-bomb.

So it was for Secretariat officials. As mentioned in Chapter 2, Boutros-Ghali had closely monitored the Arusha negotiations via its 'political' department, and the correspondence between him, the Rwandan government, and the RPF shows that he put considerable pressure on them—and on Habyarimana personally—to finalize a deal.[20] The transitional stage of peacekeeping that follows a power-sharing agreement is the trickiest moment of any peace process, a time when factions vie for power and extremists have the best shot at exploiting the institutional vacuum and derailing peace.[21] As the head of the African Union had warned, this was precisely the case of Rwanda, a country where 'a small accident could lead to a reopening of the hostilities'.[22] UN officials knew that, like most peace agreements, Arusha was shaky and depended on the prompt arrival of a UN force, which is why they pressured the parties to sign an agreement.[23] Why, then, would they allow those same parties to set an impossible deadline?

Organizational and communication issues between DPA and DPKO were partly to blame, for Dallaire and DPKO seemed to be taken aback not only

---

[16] Letter from the Rwandan Permanent Representative to the UN, 15 June 1993 (concerning the urgency of stationing a UN-led force in Rwanda). Unless otherwise stated, documents in this chapter are available through the Rwanda Documents Project (http://www.rwandadocumentsproject.net/gsdl/cgi-bin/library, accessed 1 June 2016) (RDP).

[17] Letter from the President of Rwanda to the SG, 3 August 1993.

[18] Télégramme Diplomatique, Dégradation de la Situation au Rwanda, 2 March 1994.

[19] Télégramme Diplomatique, Situation au Rwanda, 7 October 1990.

[20] Letter from the Secretary-General to the Rwandan Ambassador to the UN, 24 February 1993.

[21] Norrie MacQueen, *Peacekeeping and the International System* (Abingdon: Routledge, 2006), ch.10.

[22] United Nations, DPKO, Report of the UN Reconnaissance Mission in Rwanda, Part I, p.14 (undated).

[23] United Nations, UN Reconnaissance Mission, Part I, p.14.

by Arusha's schedule, but also by the fact that the agreement was signed at all. 'On the week-end of August 8, I received an urgent call [informing me that the peace agreement had been finalized]', Dallaire wrote. 'All hell was breaking loose at DPKO as they rushed to cobble together a response, and I was needed back in New York.'[24] While this further highlights the lack of communication—let alone coordination—between DPA (which had monitored the talks on behalf of the SG) and DPKO about an operation that these two departments were supposed to jointly oversee, DPKO rapidly set the wheels in motion. 'We were told right from the beginning "Hurry up, hurry up, hurry up. This will work, but you got to get there fast".'[25] Yet the UN is notoriously difficult to mobilize and the Rwanda mission still needed the Council's approval, which only came in October.[26]

Another reason for the delay had to do with the fact that some capitals had postponed UNAMIR's approval by the SC. Although this certainly presented logistical issues to DPKO and Dallaire, it is not unusual for the planning of peace operations to precede SC approval, a circumstance that partly explains Dallaire's reconnaissance in August 1993. Besides, UN procedures would have probably delayed UNAMIR's deployment anyway: even if the Council had approved the mission on the very day when Arusha was signed, various committees still had to examine its budget and the mission's civilian as well as military personnel still had to be appointed—a process that routinely takes weeks. The time gap between Arusha's schedule and UNAMIR's deployment was partly the result of DPA's inability to influence the unrealistic timetable set up by the parties, and by the SC's delay in approving UNAMIR. The SG and DPKO compounded the issue by allowing the Head of Mission (Booh Booh) to be appointed and reach Kigali in late November, a full month after the Force Commander (Dallaire), thereby sowing the seeds of confrontation between UNAMIR's 'political' and military components. Having the captain board a ship after it has set sail is rarely a good idea.

Far from leading to mere inconvenience, the mission's late deployment proved deadly. The absence of a UN force in the aftermath of the signing of a controversial power-sharing agreement meant that extremists had the opportunity to rally the population against it.[27] As a result, by the time Dallaire arrived in late October 1993, security had deteriorated, political killings had multiplied, militias had become more virulent, and anti-Arusha propaganda had risen.[28] In turn, the transfigured political and security situation meant that the transitional institutions agreed upon at Arusha could not be put in place, with the result that the Rwandan system of governance was at its weakest

[24] Dallaire, *Shake Hands*, p.53.
[25] Brent Beardsley, *PBS Frontline Interview*, 15 November 2003.
[26] Res 872 (S/RES/872), 5 October 1993.   [27] Marchal, *Rwanda*, pp.11–30.
[28] Dallaire, *Shake Hands*, ch.5.

precisely when it was most needed. Bad luck also played a part, for in October 1993 Burundi's (Hutu) President was murdered by his (Tutsi-dominated) army, prompting a series of anti-Tutsi massacres which resulted in a significant flow of refugees into Rwanda.[29] This caused a strategic nightmare for Dallaire: since UNAMIR was being set up in a landlocked country with poor air links and with the closest seaport located thousands of kilometres away, his plans relied heavily on the stability of the Southern flank—an assumption that the Burundi coup shattered overnight.[30] A nation that in August 1993 had seemed on a path to peace was by October seriously threatened by war. Only a well-planned, well-equipped, and highly disciplined mission could have overcome these obstacles. Unfortunately, UNAMIR turned out to be none of those things.

CLAUSEWITZ'S NIGHTMARE: POOR RESOURCES, BAD LOGISTICS, CUMBERSOME BUREAUCRACY

In his book *On War*, Carl Von Clausewitz explains that a lack of proportionality between ends and means is the most common reason for strategic failure.[31] Although the Prussian General was writing in the nineteenth century and was referring to military conflict, his observation also applies to twentieth-century peacekeeping. Indeed, the latter's complexity and the involvement of many stakeholders with different (if not conflicting) interests heighten the risk of a divide between ends and means. Add to this an international organization with limited resources and a large bureaucracy which poses its own challenges to the speed and efficiency required in the field, and the risks increase exponentially. As we shall see in Part II, in early 1994 friction between Boutros-Ghali and the Clinton administration over Somalia, Bosnia, and Haiti further compounded the problem.[32] The SG, Goulding wrote in January 1994, '. . . felt (rightly) that he was again being used cynically as a scapegoat by the Western powers'.[33] At exactly the same time, the Briton explained to the Russian Deputy Foreign Minister the then prevailing realities of peacekeeping in strikingly laconic terms: 'Skeptical and reluctant SecCo [Security Council], no troops, no money, doubtful SG, insistence on return to the established

---

[29] James Jonah, *What Price the Survival of the United Nations?* (Ibadan: Evans Brothers, 2006), ch.6.

[30] Dallaire, *Shake Hands*, ch.8.

[31] Carl von Clausewitz, *On War* (Oxford: Oxford University Press, 2008).

[32] MIG-PD-B, 7-Oct-1993; MIG-PD-B, 21-Mar-1993; MIG-PD-B, 25-Jul-1992; MIG-PD-B, 1-Jan-1992; MIG-PD-B, 26-Dec-1991.

[33] MIG-TD-IX, 12-Jan-1994. See also MIG-PD-B, 7-Oct-1993.

principles and practices of peacekeeping . . . '.[34] Far from being unusual, however, for Goulding this was '[t]he old story'.[35]

Even taking the above into consideration, those in charge of planning, budgeting, and supplying UNAMIR seem to have reversed the logic of Clausewitz's warning, for the mission was marred by alarmingly poor resources and appalling logistics well before trouble started in Rwanda. UNAMIR's leaders could not possibly have ignored the fact that the mission was to be run on the cheap: Dallaire knew that states and Secretariat officials regarded Rwanda as a sideshow to the far more expensive missions in the Former Yugoslavia and Cambodia.[36] Indeed, in setting up UNAMIR, the Council had explicitly ' . . . request[ed] the SG . . . to seek economies and to report regularly on what is achieved in this regard'.[37] Since we know from Chapter 1 that this economy drive was—together with DPKO's use of the 'anticipatory veto'—part of the reason why Dallaire had agreed to request half the troops he thought he really needed, the Force Commander was clearly aware of it. What he ignored was that bureaucratic mismanagement, poor logistics, and a lack of resources would almost starve UNAMIR to death.

The cables between Kigali and New York, together with the daily Situation Reports sent by Dallaire and Booh Booh, show that a mission which was expected to perform critical tasks such as monitoring the cease-fire and assisting with the establishment of an interim government was instead fighting for the most basic supplies. Five days after taking office, the Head of Mission complained that 'HQ must endeavor to . . . expedite the provision of logistics and personnel support',[38] and wrote that UNAMIR 'urgently need . . . an approved budget . . . vehicles and equipment . . . radio and satellite communications, radio operators and technicians [as well as the] medical supply of essential drugs and medicines'.[39] None of this had been provided despite being essential to an already economical mission. Logistics was especially problematic: of the twenty-two armored vehicles requested by Dallaire eight materialized, only five of which were roadworthy.[40] Even those came without spare parts (making them unserviceable) and lacked operating instructions in any language except Russian (which nobody understood).[41] 'I was spending 70%—at least—of my time fighting for batteries and flash lights, just the most simple requirements', Dallaire recalls. 'Even just furniture, chairs and tables.'[42]

Not unlike 'Mayday' messages sent from a stricken aircraft to its control tower, such requests increased exponentially in the following weeks, as did the realization that UNAMIR was in grave danger months *before* the genocide.

---

[34] MIG-TD-IX, 12-Jan-1994.   [35] MIG-TD-IX, 12-Jan-1994.
[36] Dallaire, *Shake Hands*, pp.48–9.   [37] Res 872, §9.
[38] Code Cable, 28-11-1993, p.4.   [39] Code Cable, 28-11-1993, p.4.
[40] Barnett, *Eyewitness*, p.92.   [41] Barnett, *Eyewitness*, p.92.
[42] Roméo Dallaire, *PBS Frontline Interview*, 1 April 2004.

The mission's leadership acknowledged as much thirty days after arriving in Kigali: 'It is becoming extremely difficult to carry out tasks',[43] Booh Booh wrote at the end of November 1993, a warning that he repeated verbatim in every cable thereafter.[44] Two weeks later, the UNAMIR leadership reiterated that 'immediate attention is needed to the state of vehicles and radio sets',[45] without which 'the force reserve has no mobility'.[46] By December the situation had worsened to such an extent that even the most basic items such as eating utensils and paper were missing, a fact that for a while made it impossible to file reports to New York.[47] At one point the mission could rely on just one–two days of drinking water, zero–two days of rations, and two–three days of fuel.[48] 'We are barely at the minimum viable level',[49] the two officials wrote, and by March 1994—a month before the genocide—frustration was replaced by sarcasm: 'Where are the helicopters? The mission will be over before we have seen them.'[50] This turned out to be the case.

UNAMIR also experienced serious human resources problems. The Bangladeshi contingent was supposed to land with an engineering squadron, medical supplies, and a movement-control platoon, but reportedly arrived without water or food, which the UN had to supply.[51] The Ghanaians, too, landed in Kigali without a single vehicle and even the Belgians—the best equipped contingent by far—despatched 400 soldiers despite promising twice as many.[52] 'States in effect inverted the Weinberger doctrine', one author noted: 'It is no longer "Go in with an overwhelming force", but instead is now "Provide minimal force structure and assume a best-case scenario".'[53] A cumbersome bureaucracy also played a part: after spending months begging New York for flashlights, UNAMIR finally received them—without batteries, for Secretariat officials argued that the mission's budget covered the former but not the latter.[54]

It is difficult to overestimate the cumulative effect of these shortcomings. When ten Belgian peacekeepers were captured by militias, they could not be rescued (and were killed, prompting Belgium's withdrawal) partly because the mission 'lacked the heavy ammunition which we had required'.[55] Poor communication was another contributing factor: the Belgians used a radio system that was incompatible with that of UNAMIR, with the result that Dallaire was

[43] Code Cable, 30-11-1993.   [44] Code Cable, 2-12-1993.
[45] Code Cable, 2-12-1993, 6-12-1993, and 8-12-1993.   [46] Code Cable, 18-12-1993.
[47] Code Cable, 18-12-1993.   [48] Carlsson Report, S/1999/1257, §6.
[49] Code Cable, 4-1-1994.   [50] Code Cable, 1-3-1994.
[51] Castonguay, *Les Casques Bleus*, p.63. See also Marchal, p.121; Michael Doyle and Nicholas Sambanis, 'International Peacebuilding: A Theoretical and Quantitative Analysis', *American Political Science Review*, Vol.94, No.4 (2000), pp.778–801.
[52] Jean-Claude Willame, *Les Belges au Rwanda* (Brussels: Éditions GRIP/Complexe, 1997), ch.7.
[53] Barnett, *Eyewitness*, p.168.   [54] Barnett, *Eyewitness*, p.92.
[55] Barnett, *Eyewitness*, p.92.

unable to communicate with his best troops—a Commander's worst night-mare.[56] Like a plane suffering from structural failure, UNAMIR quickly fell apart under the weight of its own logistical problems: 'The mission is desperately short of life and operational sustaining support',[57] Dallaire wrote to New York several months before the genocide. Although the issue of responsibility for inadequate resources involves the SG and the SC, and will thus be considered in Chapters 4 and 5, Resolution 872 pointed out that any economy had to be made 'without ... affecting [the mission's] capacity to carry out its mandate'.[58] Understanding whether this was the case involves assessing the other side of Clausewitz's equation: UNAMIR's goals.

CONFUSED AND CONFUSING: INTERPRETING UNAMIR'S MANDATE

Doubts about UNAMIR's mandate and ROE—and uncertainty over whether these were 'political' or 'technical' matters—created tension not only between New York and Kigali, but also between Dallaire and Booh Booh. While Chapter 1 has underlined the shortcomings of DPKO on this, confusion over the mandate was reinforced by the language of Resolution 872 and by poor coordination between Headquarters and the field. It is thus necessary to consider in detail both the genesis of Resolution 872 and how the UNAMIR leadership interpreted it.

As the first document setting out the tasks that the Rwandan parties wished UNAMIR to perform, the Arusha Agreement of 3 August 1993 is the starting point on which all UN documents on Rwanda were based—and so much so that several of its provisions were incorporated verbatim into Resolution 872. The agreement set out seven tasks for UNAMIR:

1. Guarantee the *overall* security of the country and especially verify the maintenance of law and order by the competent authorities and organs.

2. Ensure the security of distribution of humanitarian aid.

3. Assist in catering for the security of civilians.

4. Assist in the tracking of arms caches and neutralization of armed gangs throughout the country.

5. Undertake mine clearance operations.

6. Assist in the recovery of all weapons distributed to, or illegally acquired by, the civilians.

---

[56] Marchal, p.182.   [57] S/1999/1257, p.40.   [58] Res 872.

7. Monitor the observance by the two parties of modalities for the definite cessation of hostilities provided for in the Peace Agreement.[59]

The Arusha parties clearly expected the UN to make a significant contribution to the security of Rwanda, and this was to be achieved first and foremost by limiting the influx of illegal weapons which were flowing into the country and that were seen as the single biggest threat to peace. In his reconnaissance report of 23 August 1993, Dallaire—who was clearly engaged in matters that went beyond the merely 'technical' or 'operational'—endorsed the conclusions reached by the Arusha parties and recommended seven tasks (among others):

1. Guarantee *national* security . . . and verify the maintenance of law and order . . . ;
2. Provide security for humanitarian aid . . . ;
3. Monitor to ensure the safety of civilians . . . ;
4. Assist in tracking arms and neutralizing armed groups . . . ;
5. Provide for the security of Kigali . . . ;
6. Assist in recovering arms in the hands of civilians . . . ;
7. Monitor the ceasefire. . . .[60]

This convergence between Arusha and Dallaire should not be a surprise, for as mentioned in Chapter 1, his reconnaissance mission had relied heavily on the data provided by the Government of Rwanda and RPF—the Arusha signatories—as well as on the peace agreement itself, a copy of which Dallaire had with him wherever he went. Yet Boutros-Ghali's report to the Council on 24 September 1994 appeared to considerably narrow Dallaire's (and Arusha's) requests as follows:

(a) *Assist* in ensuring the *security of the city of Kigali* [and] in the recovery of arms from civilians;

(b) Monitor the cease-fire agreement, including establishment of an expanded DMZ [De-Militarized Zone] and demobilization procedures;

(c) Continue to monitor the security situation during the final period of the transitional Government's mandate leading up to the elections [including through humanitarian assistance];

(d) Assist with mine clearance. . . .[61]

---

[59] 'Protocol of Agreement between the Government of the Republic of Rwanda and the Rwandese Patriotic Front on the Integration of the Armed Forces of the Two Parties', 3 August 1993, in UN, *The United Nations and Rwanda*, p.193 (emphasis added).

[60] 'Report of the UN Reconnaissance Mission to Rwanda', 23 August 1993, §157 (emphasis added).

[61] 'Report of the Secretary-General on Rwanda' (S/26488), 24 September 1993, §21 (emphases added).

The general provision of ensuring Rwanda's overall security was thus limited to the capital city, and even there the SG thought that UNAMIR should not *guarantee* overall safety (as both the Arusha Agreement and Dallaire had requested) but *assist* the Rwandan parties to achieve it. Furthermore, the reference to 'law and order' disappeared, as did the one relating to the 'safety of civilians'. Given that the Arusha talks were closely monitored by the SG via DPA and that the latter was advising Boutros-Ghali on all matters Rwandan, such a reduced role for UNAMIR is surprising—especially as it came *before* the SC's emphasis on cost-cutting in Resolution 872.[62] Chapter 4 will consider whether this was an autonomous decision by the SG or the result of an 'anticipatory veto' on his part. Against the view of a powerless Secretariat constrained by member states, however, in formally establishing UNAMIR the Council appeared to go slightly beyond Boutros-Ghali's recommendations, though not as far as meeting the Dallaire/Arusha ones. In the end, SC Resolution 872 of 5 October 1993 set out eight tasks for UNAMIR:

1. to *contribute to the security of the city of Kigali*, inter alia, within the weapons-secure area established by the parties in and around the city;
2. to monitor observance of the cease-fire agreement . . . ;
3. to monitor the security situation . . . leading up to the elections;
4. to assist with mine clearance . . . ;
5. to investigate at the request of the parties, or on its own initiative, instances of alleged non-compliance [with Arusha] on the integration of the armed forces of the two parties . . . ;
6. to monitor the process of repatriation of Rwandese refugees . . . ;
7. to assist in the coordination of humanitarian assistance activities . . . ;
8. to investigate and report incidents regarding the activities of the gendarmerie and police.[63]

Intriguingly, at the time none of the Rwandan actors seemed to pay close attention to the language of the Resolution, which was widely regarded as satisfactory. The RPF had no issue with it, while the Interim Prime Minister stated that it 'was very good and in conformity with the [Arusha] Accords—it seemed sufficient to everybody and no-one complained about it'.[64] Both UNAMIR's Head of Mission[65] and its Kigali Sector Chief[66] agreed. Even Dallaire, who had advocated for a more assertive approach, thought that Resolution 872 got the fundamentals right and was broad enough to allow some leeway. 'It was felt the mandate was achievable as a classic peacekeeping

[62] Res 872, §9.   [63] Res 872, 39(a) to 3(h) (emphasis added).
[64] Castonguay, p.44.   [65] Booh Booh, p.30.   [66] Marchal, pp.35–6.

operation', Dallaire's military attaché stated, 'if the necessary force organization and, more importantly, the needed logistics and financial support was provided'.[67] The post-genocide argument that UNAMIR suffered from a narrow mandate was thus not shared by the key stakeholders during the mission's earliest stages.

In the late autumn, however, as the country's security deteriorated, the limits of what UNAMIR could actually do began to emerge. Rwanda was by then becoming increasingly militarized, with caches concealed in government buildings and weapons distributed to the population.[68] More worrying still were the activities at the Kigali airport, from which substantial quantities of weapons and machetes were being smuggled into the country through France and Egypt. Even from as far away as New York such militarization was difficult to miss: in only three years the Rwandan army had grown from 7,000 to 30,000, while two days before the genocide UNAMIR had conservatively estimated the presence in the country of over 85 tons of ammunitions.[69] Unsurprisingly, Rwandan society too was being militarized: in Gitarama, a city of 150,000, the number of machetes before the genocide stood at 50,000 and a grenade could be bought at the Kigali market for as little as 2USD.[70] The issue of weapons had to be tackled, for peace can hardly flourish in a land that is awash with weapons.

Until January 1994, Dallaire and Booh Booh thought their mandate allowed them to *autonomously* seize illegal weapons in Kigali, for Resolution 872 required the mission 'to contribute to the security' of the capital. Since the UNAMIR leadership knew that the Rwandan authorities were involved in weapons smuggling,[71] seizing them was seen as a key contribution to peace.[72] Western diplomats agreed: the Belgian[73] and US[74] ambassadors repeatedly encouraged Dallaire to intervene lest arms be distributed to the militias and, despite its limited resources, from October 1993 to January 1994 UNAMIR did launch multiple recovery operations. 'Several weapons and ammunitions have been confiscated',[75] the Force Commander wrote to New York in early January 1994. As mentioned in Chapter 1, DPKO's silence on such activities was taken by Dallaire and Booh Booh as confirmation that they were doing their job.

This explains Dallaire's astonishment when, on 11 January 1994, having informed New York of his intention to seize an important cache of weapons, he was notified that the verb 'contribute' in Resolution 872 meant that he could only *assist* the Rwandan parties in seizing weapons, rather than acting

[67] Beardsley, *PBS Frontline Interview*, 15 November 2003.
[68] Castonguay, p.68.   [69] Castonguay, p.68.   [70] Castonguay, p.68.
[71] Booh Booh, p.69.   [72] Dallaire, *Shake Hands*, p.149.
[73] Dallaire, *Shake Hands*, p.149.
[74] Rawson, *PBS Frontline Interview*, 5 October 2003.   [75] Code Cable, 7-1-1994.

independently of them.[76] The fact that this came as a surprise to everybody in Kigali shows the extent of the disconnect between Headquarters and the field; it also suggests that for over three months the leadership of a UN mission had carried out actions which DPKO officials regarded as illegal. Even more worrying is the fact that the peacekeeping department knew about those actions but did not object to them, and that Dallaire continued to confiscate arms even *after* the 11 January cable. On 21 January, for instance, 'UNAMIR seized at Kigali International Airport an important amount of weapons onboard a C-130 for the Rwandese army controlled by the Head of State';[77] on 22 January, Dallaire confiscated a 'totally unexpected shipment of military materials';[78] and on 15 February, he 'recovered a few weapons at our road blocks and on our patrols [and] we have established lock-ups for these weapons and ammunition'.[79] Major Ezaz Afzal, from the Bangladeshi contingent, confirmed that 'disarming civilian personnel'[80] and 'checking vehicles for weapons as part of disarming the civilian population'[81] was part of the peacekeepers' roles and was done without the presence of the Rwandan authorities and on a regular basis.

Confusion over UNAMIR's ROE ran even deeper, for the DPKO leadership thought that the principle of consent meant that UNAMIR could only protect Rwandan civilians without using force.[82] This approach nevertheless contradicted UNAMIR's *formal* ROE, which did allow the mission to protect civilians from ethnically motivated crimes.[83] According to Goulding, this disconnect between New York and the field over ROE and over what counted as 'political' and military functions was not unusual. 'It turned out that they have much relaxed ROE . . . and regularly shoot to kill (and do kill) snipers who fire at them or civilians', Goulding wrote about the UN mission in the Former Yugoslavia, noting that '[t]his interesting fact [is] not reported by UNPROFOR [United Nations Protection Force]', and pointing out that ROE were routinely seen as a 'technical' rather than a 'political' matter.[84] What was peculiar in Rwanda was the gulf between the formal ROE—which were seen in New York as an 'operational' issue and, as such, were considered to be the purview of DPKO rather than DPA—and the *interpretation* of those ROE, particularly once the genocide began. Then, a difficult situation spanned out of control and chaos ensued, as Goulding noted in his diary.[85]

---

[76] Code Cable, 19-1-1994.   [77] Code Cable, 27-2-1994.
[78] Code Cable, 22-1-1994.   [79] Code Cable, 15-2-1994.
[80] Interview with Afzal, 20 April 2016.   [81] Interview with Afzal, 20 April 2016.
[82] UNAMIR, *Rules of Engagement*, undated (on file with the author). See also S/1999/1257, p.35.
[83] 'There may also be ethnically or politically motivated criminal acts committed during this mandate which will morally and legally require UNAMIR to use all available means to halt them. Examples are executions, attacks on displaced persons or refugees.' UNAMIR, *Rules of Engagement*, §17.
[84] MIG-TD-IX, 20-Dec-1993.   [85] MIG-TD-X, 15-Apr-1994.

TROUBLES WITHIN: DALLAIRE, BOOH BOOH, AND THE FIGHT FOR UNAMIR'S LEADERSHIP

If communications between New York and UNAMIR were problematic, so was Dallaire's relationship with Booh Booh. It is not unusual for peace missions to experience internal conflict. The high-pressure environment that characterizes most of them, coupled with the daily limitations and frustrations of dealing with a large and unresponsive bureaucracy located thousands of kilometres away, can strain even the best relationship.[86] Rwanda was also a worst-case scenario: poor resources, bad logistics, misunderstandings over mandate, and massacres on a genocidal scale are hardly conducive to interpersonal harmony. Post-mortem recriminations in the form of bitter memoirs—together with the need to 'clear one's name' during one of the worst humanitarian crises of the twentieth century—contribute to amplifying disagreements. Success, it seems, has multiple parents, whereas failure is an orphan.

Even allowing for all this, relations between UNAMIR's Force Commander and his Head of Mission were exceptionally fraught. The two men could not have been more different: Dallaire was a soldier at the pinnacle of his career, whereas Booh Booh was a retired diplomat who had accepted the Rwanda post at the insistence of Boutros-Ghali.[87] Although having a military and a 'political' officer from different backgrounds is standard procedure in peacekeeping, there was (and still is) no love lost between these two men. In his memoirs, Dallaire is scathing about Booh Booh's 'palatial'[88] residence; his frequent requests 'to be ferried around the country in grand diplomatic style';[89] and his love for 'oriental carpets and expensive easy chairs'.[90] 'He was rarely in his office before ten, took a full two-hour lunch and left the office before five',[91] Dallaire complained. The very title of Booh Booh's memoirs (*Dallaire's Boss Speaks Out: Revelations on the Excesses of a UN General in Rwanda*)[92] suggests that the Head of Mission did not appreciate this criticism. After dismissing as 'indecent'[93] Dallaire's claims, he accuses him of being a liar,[94] a racist,[95] a womanizer,[96] a hypocrite,[97] and a megalomaniac.[98] He also charges the Force Commander with being pro-Tutsi, blames him for 'UNAMIR's failure',[99] and

---

[86] Houshang Ameri, *Politics of Staffing the United Nations Secretariat* (New York: Peter Lang, 1996).

[87] Dallaire, *Shake Hands*, pp.114–15; Boutros Boutros-Ghali, *Entre le Nil et Jérusalem* (Paris: Éditions du Rocher, 2011), p.327.

[88] Dallaire, *Shake Hands*, p.175.   [89] Dallaire, *Shake Hands*, p.175.

[90] Dallaire, *Shake Hands*, p.175.   [91] Dallaire, *Shake Hands*, p.118.

[92] Booh Booh, Back Cover.   [93] Booh Booh, Back Cover.

[94] Booh Booh, p.95.   [95] Booh Booh, pp.15 and 139.

[96] Booh Booh, p.10.   [97] Booh Booh, p.134.   [98] Booh Booh, pp.195 and 199.

[99] Booh Booh, Back Cover.

accuses him of placing microphones in Booh Booh's residence.[100] Dallaire 'came to Africa to get promoted at the expense of the dead and wanted to return to Canada as a General McArthur',[101] Booh Booh writes, adding that '[i]t must have been painful for him to work under my authority, given his actions, multiple intrigues and lack of ethics'.[102] Beyond what was clearly personal antipathy, three systemic reasons contributed to mar this relationship.

The first was Booh Booh's tardy arrival in Kigali. That a Head of Mission would take office more than a month after his Force Commander and other colleagues strikes one as a peculiar interpretation of the logic of effective leadership.[103] This is all the more so since by the time Booh Booh arrived, UNAMIR had already been planned (badly), budgeted (poorly), and deployed (belatedly). As Head of Mission, SRSG, and highest ranking UN official in Rwanda, the Cameroonian was expected to take control of an operation that was already in trouble due to its own late deployment, lack of resources, and precarious security situation. Despite UNAMIR's budgetary restrictions, Booh Booh's late appointment is hard to explain other than by mismanagement. If New York had the resources to appoint Dallaire within days of UNAMIR's approval, it could also have appointed the Head of Mission. The fact that it did not do so until the operation was deployed made Booh Booh's already difficult job harder.[104]

Since it is precisely in times of trouble that good leadership is both needed and expected, such a delay is nevertheless unlikely to have caused irreparable damage to UNAMIR. A second, more important reason for the tension between these two men lies with the blurred nature of their roles. In theory the difference was clear: as Force Commander, Dallaire was in charge of the 'technical' side of UNAMIR (understood, loosely and ambiguously, as activities of a military, operational, and logistical nature), whereas as Head of Mission Booh Booh was responsible for its 'political' aspects (such as diplomatic negotiations). Also in theory, this made sense to the extent that Dallaire was an accomplished soldier whereas Booh Booh was a former foreign minister with considerable negotiating experience in Africa. In practice, however, this separation never worked—for at least two reasons. First, Dallaire had conducted negotiations well before Booh Booh's arrival: it was he who had led the reconnaissance mission to Rwanda, who had come up with the structure (even the name) of UNAMIR, who had suggested a draft mandate for it, who had handpicked some of its staff, and who had served as Interim Head of Mission.[105] This intimate involvement put Booh Booh at a distinct disadvantage, not least because Dallaire had reportedly wished to combine the roles of

[100] Booh Booh, Back Cover.   [101] Booh Booh, p.94.   [102] Booh Booh, p.134.
[103] Peter Northouse, *Leadership* (London: Sage, 2009), ch.5.
[104] Booh Booh, p.59 (footnote 12).   [105] Dallaire, *Shake Hands*, chs 2, 3, and 4.

Force Commander and Head of Mission.[106] Second, even after Booh Booh's arrival, Dallaire never performed what UN officials described then—and continue to describe today—as 'operational' functions: he was constantly shuttling between the Rwandan parties, was trying to push them to establish the interim institutions designed at Arusha, was conducting key negotiations, and was in all but name in charge of the operation—hardly 'technical' roles. 'I attended all political meetings', he wrote. '[Booh Booh] wasn't moving.... He had not taken charge of the mission.'[107] The Cameroonian diplomat disagrees: 'It was me who was directing UNAMIR's components and who was in constant contact with the SG, the African Heads of State, the Rwandese political leaders and the Western ambassadors in Kigali',[108] he wrote. '[Dallaire] wanted to do a job for which he had no competence whatsoever: diplomacy and even politics.'[109]

The overlapping roles of Dallaire and Booh Booh point to a systemic problem that goes back to the difficulty of distinguishing between the 'technical' and the 'political' aspects of peacekeeping. Part II will consider in detail the fights, in New York, between the supposedly 'operational' (DPKO) and 'political' (DPA) arms of the UN Secretariat precisely at the time when UNAMIR was deployed. The fact that such a problematic distinction was mirrored in Rwanda should thus not be a surprise: was a cease-fire agreement, for instance, a 'technical' or a 'political' matter? How about a mission's mandate or its ROE? Vocal disagreements existed in both New York and Kigali over what constituted a 'political' issue that needed to be addressed through diplomatic negotiations, on the one hand; and what could be regarded as an operational or logistical arrangement, on the other.[110] 'It seems to me that General Dallaire was trying to carry out political tasks whereas the issue was really military', Major Ezaz Afzal, from the Bangladeshi contingent, stated. 'It is a nightmare when a soldier becomes a politician.'[111] Goulding had raised the problem of the separation between 'political' and 'operational' functions as early as in the 1980s, when trying to formalize the relationship between his Office for Special Political Affairs (OSPA) and the Field Operations Department (FOD)—theoretically, the 'political' and 'administrative' arms of UN peacekeeping. 'FOD must consult OSPA, in advance, about any administrative decisions which have political and military implications',[112] Goulding had written back then. The problem, as he quickly discovered, was that in peacekeeping few administrative decisions are devoid of any 'political' implications. In Kigali, the nebulous separation between the

---

[106] Booh Booh, p.29.   [107] Dallaire, *PBS Frontline Interview*, 1 April 2004.
[108] Booh Booh, p.13.   [109] Booh Booh, p.13.
[110] See MIG-PD-B, 19-Dec-1991.   [111] Interview with Afzal, 20 April 2016.
[112] Marrack Goulding, 'The Relationship between OSPA and FOD', undated (MIG-PA).

two fuelled the tension as well as the confusion of roles between Dallaire and Booh Booh. The result in Rwanda was similar to what Goulding had experienced in New York since the late 1980s: 'There was constant skirmishing in New York between my peacekeeping department and the new Department of Political Affairs', Goulding had written as early as in 1992 about his time at the helm of DPKO.[113]

WHO KNEW WHAT? UNAMIR'S INTELLIGENCE AND 'POLITICAL' ANALYSIS

An example of the overlapping roles of Dallaire and Booh Booh was the issue of 'political' analysis. Since UNAMIR was the eyes and ears of the Secretariat in Rwanda, questions arise about the intelligence the mission had and the way it interpreted it. What did its leaders know about the killings? Did they ring alarm bells in New York? And were they united in their reading of the events of 1994? The issue of intelligence involves the UN system as a whole and will thus be considered in Part II. Still, UNAMIR was the only Secretariat unit to directly witness genocide and was thus ideally placed to recognize its impending signs. Genocides do not happen overnight: they are complex enterprises requiring sophisticated planning at the highest echelons of government, which is why only states usually have the means to carry them out.[114] UNAMIR had been in Kigali since October 1993, the genocide started in April 1994 and lasted three months. How could Dallaire and Booh Booh miss the gathering clouds?

As it turns out, the UNAMIR leadership did see the clouds but not the accompanying storm—for two reasons, the first of which relates to intelligence and the second to 'political' analysis. Dallaire was responsible for intelligence of a supposedly 'technical' nature through his 2,500 men, whose task it was to monitor the situation so that he could file reports to Booh Booh and DPKO. Because of this, the attention has been on Dallaire's reports, which have been scrutinized in forensic detail to understand whether he predicted the impending catastrophe.[115]

What Dallaire's cables confirm is an escalation of anti-Tutsi violence before the genocide. In November 1993, he reported that a group of Tutsi children had been brutally murdered while collecting water from a river.[116] This, he noted, was no ordinary crime, for the children had been raped, choked to

---

[113] Marrack Goulding, *Peacemonger* (London: John Murray, 2002), p.13.

[114] Jacques Semelin, *Purify and Destroy* (New York: Columbia University Press, 2007), chs IV and V.

[115] Barnett, *Eyewitness*, esp. ch.3.   [116] Dallaire, *Shake Hands*, ch.8.

death, and decapitated by well-organized, well-informed, and highly motivated perpetrators.[117] 'Examples of [other] atrocities', Dallaire wrote in another
cable, 'include hands cut off, eyes pulled out, skulls crushed in and pregnant
women cut open'.[118] The Force Commander also warned that 'we have no
reason to believe that such occurrences could not and will not be repeated
again in any part of this country where arms are prolific and political and
ethnic tensions are prevalent'.[119] Ten days after the start of the killings,
Dallaire was even more explicit, reporting that 'the ethnic cleansing continues
and may in fact be accelerating'.[120] Dallaire thus had solid reasons to believe
that more ethnic massacres would occur and he did pass this warning on to
Booh Booh and DPKO. As he wrote years later, however, 'I couldn't even
fathom the term genocide'.[121] Neither could Booh Booh or, for that matter,
Kagame and the RPF.[122] 'We were sure the massacres were being carried out,
and the Tutsi were being targeted, and it had happened before', Kagame stated.
'What we were not sure of was ... the full magnitude and scope of the
problem. We didn't fully understand it at the start.'[123]

Even bearing in mind the difficulty of promptly recognizing the hallmarks
of genocide, the Head of Mission's interpretation of Dallaire's intelligence
remains surprising. Because of his expertise and rank, 'political' analysis was
supposed to be Booh Booh's area of competence as well as his primary
responsibility in Kigali. Yet the cables show it as being consistently mistaken.
In his memoirs, Booh Booh dismisses Arusha as a 'stillborn peace process that
was deliberately rejected by the Rwandan political parties, both on the government and on the rebels side',[124] and argues that this was one of the reasons
for UNAMIR's failure. While this is entirely plausible, as SRSG the Head of
Mission had offered New York strikingly different advice. In November 1993,
shortly after landing in Kigali, he had written of 'genuine readiness' from
all Rwandan leaders 'to support the early implementation of the Arusha
Accords';[125] in December he had commented on the process having 'new
impetus' thanks to the 'friendly and brotherly atmosphere'[126] in the ongoing
discussions; in January he had praised the 'frank and cordial manners'[127] of
both sides; and in February he had noted 'encouraging reactions'[128] and 'true
signs of cooperation'.[129] Indeed, as late as in March 1994—less than a month
before the genocide—Booh Booh had insisted that 'there exists from both sides
the will to continue the dialogue'.[130] Since his memoirs make no *mea culpa* for
overestimating the Arusha peace process, one can only assume that he was

---

[117] Melvern, *A People Betrayed*, p.75.   [118] Melvern, *A People Betrayed*, p.75.
[119] Code Cable, 6-1-1994.   [120] Code Cable, 17-4-1994.
[121] Dallaire, *PBS Frontline Interview*, 1 April 2004.   [122] Booh Booh, p.87.
[123] Paul Kagame, *PBS Frontline Interview*, 30 January 2004.
[124] Booh Booh, p.16.   [125] Code Cable, 28-11-1993.   [126] Code Cable, 12-12-1993.
[127] Code Cable, 28-1-1994.   [128] Code Cable, 2-2-1994.
[129] Code Cable, 9-2-1994.   [130] Code Cable, 4-3-1994.

sceptical about it from the outset—yet his overoptimistic cables to New York offer little sign of this scepticism. On the contrary, they go some way towards explaining the upbeat tone of the SG's reports to the Council.[131]

Booh Booh's 'political' reading also led him to offer New York inaccurate views about who was responsible for the killings. Throughout his time in Rwanda, the Head of Mission was adamant that violence was the result of a confrontation between two equal parties and—after April 1994—of civil war.[132] Both the violence and the war, he argued, could only be stopped with a cease-fire resurrecting the Arusha peace process—seemingly the opposite of what he argues in his book. 'The best assistance we can provide', he wrote two days after the start of the genocide, 'is negotiating a ceasefire and then returning to our mandate tasks for the political process to continue'.[133] He repeated this message in almost every cable to New York from April (when the killings began) to July (when he left Rwanda) because, as he put it, the two sides simply had 'to reconcile their differences'.[134] Yet Rwanda was more than civil war: it was crimes against humanity on a massive scale that were taking place in broad daylight, were carried out with rudimentary weapons such as machetes and kitchen knives, and were resulting in ten thousand violent deaths a day—a higher rate than the Nazis ever managed with gas chambers. Partly because of his background as a diplomat and as the representative of a body that needed to be seen as impartial, the head of UNAMIR was also convinced—against available evidence and Dallaire's view—that both sides were equally responsible for the violence: 'The RPF, like the Rwandan Army, has incontestably committed crimes against humanity and deserves to be treated as such',[135] he noted years later. It is important to note that Booh Booh was not alone in blaming the RPF for crimes against humanity: 'A five-week survey for UNHCR in Rwanda [has] come to the well-documented conclusion that the RPF are systematically killing Hutus', Goulding wrote in his diary in September 1994, adding that '[t]his is potentially *very* damaging for the UN which has been encouraging Hutu refugees to return to their homes'.[136] Habyarimana's pilot had raised similar issues in a letter sent before the start of the genocide, in which he noted that 'the UN ... sees nothing [despite the fact that] entire families on both sides are massacred ... '.[137] The problem with Booh Booh's analysis, therefore, is not so much that it was 'pro-Hutu' but that it offered little assistance to the SG: if the two sides wanted to settle their grievances on the battlefield, the Special Representative concluded, there was little the UN could do: 'We can bring a thirsty horse to the

---

[131] See Chapter 4.   [132] Booh Booh, p.184.   [133] Code Cable, 8-4-1994.
[134] Code Cable, 5-1-1994.
[135] Booh Booh, p.184. For a supportive view of Booh Booh's position, see Ntisoni, p.123. For how the BBC too required its correspondent to be 'even-handed', see Mark Doyle, *PBS Frontline Interview*, 12 December 2003.
[136] MIG-TD-X, 16-Sep-1994 (original emphasis).   [137] Minaberry, Lettre, p.239.

river, but we cannot force him to drink.'[138] For him, UN impartiality required absolute neutrality—an interesting comment in light of the accusations of bias directed at Booh Booh by the RPF.[139]

Rwanda had been on the UN radar since 1992 and the Secretariat had considerable expertise on it through the SG, DPKO, and DPA, so Booh Booh's assessments were hardly the only information upon which New York relied (especially since they often clashed with Dallaire's cables). What is striking about Booh Booh's 'political' analysis, however, is that it remains as question-able today as it was in 1994: 'I did not even manage to conclude a ceasefire, despite this being so necessary to reinvigorate the peace process',[140] he writes in a book published ten years after the events. Given that one of the govern-ment's *raisons d'être* was ethnic extermination and that the RPF had no intention of reaching a truce until this stopped, Booh Booh's insistence on a cease-fire was both an impossibility and an irrelevance. 'People were dying because of the massacres, not the war',[141] a survivor noted. 'Some of the areas most affected by large-scale massacres . . . have seen no battles whatsoever.'[142] Although the SRSG was hardly the only diplomat in Kigali who was pushing for a cease-fire—the US ambassador did the same and later regretted it[143]— Booh Booh's claim that both sides should be treated equally was over-shadowed by accusations of partiality towards the Hutus. In any event, the SRSG lost the trust of many in Rwanda—by late April the RPF refused to deal with him on the ground that he was 'pro-Habyarimana'—and, it now emerges, also in New York: 'Boutros-Ghali, Kofi [Annan] and I agreed that Booh Booh was not *à la hauteur* of [or up to] the job', Goulding wrote in his diary in mid-May 1994, adding that the Cameroonian appeared '[c]onfused, fearful [and] lacking in diplomatic clout'.[144] He was replaced soon afterwards.

UNAMIR IN RWANDA

'The UN is a law unto itself operationally and seems to run on the principle that anything logical and militarily sound of plan should be ignored and the opposite principles applied. The consequence is complete and utter chaos— particularly on the logistics and operational side—to the extent that for the first eight days when the HQ was deployed, the UN was unable to get a water bowl to us and we were having to wash in bottled water.'[145] Though this note was written in 1991 by a peacekeeper serving in Kuwait after the First Gulf

---

[138] Minaberry, Lettre, p.202.   [139] Part II returns to this.
[140] Booh Booh, pp.184 and 189.
[141] 'UN Seeks Rwanda Ceasefire', *Reuters*, 8 July 1994.
[142] 'UN Seeks Rwanda Ceasefire', *Reuters*, 8 July 1994.
[143] Rawson, *PBS Frontline Interview*, 5 October 2003.   [144] MIG-TD-X, 13-May-1994.
[145] Typewritten note in the Goulding Archive, 16-May-1991 (MIG-PA).

War, his Rwanda colleagues would have recognized the sorry picture it paints. They may even have concurred that the 'major enemies are the heat, the dust, and UN procedures, not our opponents'.[146] Peacekeeping in the 1990s clearly posed serious challenges and UNAMIR was hardly the only mission facing them.[147] In March 2016, a former Assistant Secretary-General resigned after thirty years with the UN because of similar dysfunctions. 'If you locked a team of evil geniuses in a laboratory', Anthony Banbury wrote, 'you could not design a bureaucracy so maddeningly complex, requiring so much effort but in the end incapable of delivering the intended result.'[148] '[T]he UN bureaucracy', he concluded, 'is getting in the way of its peacekeeping efforts.'[149]

Though none of this would come as a surprise to UN peacekeepers, the Rwanda operation remains uniquely flawed, with several factors contributing to its failure. Its delayed arrival meant that Dallaire had to play catch up with a transfigured situation which he had neither the tools nor the mandate to control. UNAMIR was also hampered by severe logistical problems that stretched it beyond its limits and that turned out to be very costly in terms of human lives. Equally serious was the fact of having an ambiguous mandate that was interpreted conservatively by DPKO and liberally by the UNAMIR leadership. As this chapter has suggested and as Part II will explain, however, this disconnect was part of a larger breakdown in communications between New York and Kigali, the reasons for which lie within UN Headquarters rather than in Rwanda. In particular, the exceptionally difficult relationship between the 'military' and the 'political' leadership and tasks of UNAMIR—including the ill-defined and overlapping jobs of Dallaire and Booh Booh—partly reflect the confusion in New York between the so-called 'operational' and 'political' aspects of peacekeeping. On top of the mission's already considerable problems, such lingering confusion made it even harder for UNAMIR's leaders to advise New York and to coordinate their own responses to the crisis.

On reflection, Clausewitz's paradigm should thus be rephrased, for worse than a divide between ends and means is the fact of having unclear ends. That is the point when a difficult mission becomes impossible, and that is what arguably happened to UNAMIR. Unable to sustain itself in the best of scenarios, the mission could hardly be expected to prevail against some of the worst atrocities of the twentieth century. Why, then, was it allowed to deploy in the first instance, and why was it not strengthened or withdrawn? The answers to these questions lie thousands of kilometres away from Rwanda and require us to climb to the top of the UN hierarchy, first into the SG's office and then into the Security Council's chamber.

---

[146] MIG-PA, 16-May-1991.
[147] Alex Bellamy et al., *Understanding Peacekeeping* (Cambridge: Polity Press, 2010), esp. ch.4.
[148] Anthony Banbury, 'I Love the UN, But it is Failing', *The New York Times*, 18 March 2016.
[149] Banbury, 'I Love the UN, But it is Failing'.

4

Secretary-General's Office

In his *Inferno*, Dante afflicts the inhabitants of Hell with a sadistic form of punishment called *contrappasso* (from the Latin *contra* and *patior*, 'suffering the opposite'): sorcerers have their heads twisted and walk backwards (an allusion to the twisted nature of magic); the hateful are condemned to an afterlife with the hated; and the greedy are damned to an eternity of starvation.[1] For Dante, the highest form of punishment contrasts with the sin committed, a technique that Seneca and Aquinas had already used, but that the Italian poet popularized.

Although it is questionable whether Boutros Boutros-Ghali committed the many sins that his many critics blame him for during his time in New York (1992–96), he appears to have already been punished through *contrappasso* and a term of office replete with paradoxes and contradictions. While he was one of the most scholarly chiefs to lead the Secretariat, he was also the first—and remains the only—SG to be denied a second term. Although he was independent and strong-willed, he was accused by many—including himself—of failing to stand up to the Security Council (SC). An intellectual powerhouse, he nevertheless suffered the ignominy of losing his job to the person whom he saw as his nemesis, civil servant Kofi Annan. Despite his claims to be an ardent believer in equality, he left the UN with a reputation for autocracy and with the unflattering nickname of 'Pharaoh'. Last but not least, while he advocated an ethical approach to global affairs, he was involved in a potential conflict of interest that casts doubt about his ability to treat the Rwandan parties fairly.

For the highly unregimented and famously short-tempered Boutros-Ghali, it is the accusations of subservience that are most hurtful: 'I do need to calm down', he wrote in his diaries, 'but will I be able to?'[2] Even Dante's truculence, however, could not have envisaged a more gruesome punishment for this lively, cultured, and most contradictory of SGs than having his term associated with genocide. How did the first African SG—and the staunchest advocate of humanitarian intervention on his continent—end up being accused of

---

[1] *Enciclopedia Dantesca* (Milan: Treccani, 2005), Vol.7 ('*Contrappasso*').
[2] Boutros Boutros-Ghali, *En Attendant la Prochaine Lune* (Paris: Fayard, 2004), p.39.

passivity during one of the bloodiest humanitarian crises of the twentieth century, one that happened, of all places, in Africa? To answer this question, it is necessary to return to the peculiar international environment of the early 1990s and to consider how, and for what purposes, Boutros-Ghali used what he saw as the 'political' functions of his office. While Part II will review in detail the various ways in which Boutros-Ghali *as a leader* used 'his' bureaucracy to implement his peacekeeping agenda, this chapter will highlight the paradoxes associated with his role in Rwanda, paradoxes that reflect the contradictions of his term in office. That the SG is both a principal organ of the UN as well as an individual agent makes it all the more important to ascertain what Boutros-Ghali's goals were and how he used his office to achieve them.

ENTHUSIASM: BOUTROS-GHALI, THE UN, AND THE 'NEW WORLD ORDER'

When Boutros Boutros-Ghali of Egypt took office as the sixth SG of the UN in January 1992, the collapse of the Soviet Union had just brought the Cold War to an end and was offering new opportunities to the SC, a body which had long been paralysed by superpower vetoes.[3] In this respect, the Gulf War of 1991 did more than liberate Kuwait from Iraqi troops; it signalled the start of a multilateralist dawn and promised to bring out the best that UN diplomacy had to offer.[4] It is these opportunities that Boutros-Ghali wished to seize when he started campaigning for the top UN job. A former professor of international law at Cairo University and a committed multilateralist, he had no interest in the Secretariat of the Cold War but relished the opportunity to make an impact in the early 1990s—'Now there was a real role to play and a chance to put into effect ideas I had been working on for years',[5] he wrote. Those ideas included international law, human rights, and economic development.[6] A francophone Arab of Christian Coptic faith from Africa, he gathered the support of most countries except the USA—but when the preferred American candidate failed to muster enough support, Washington abstained and the Egyptian was elected (a move that the US government would come to regret).[7]

---

[3] David Malone, ed., *The UN Security Council* (Boulder: Lynne Rienner, 2004); Edward Luck, *The UN Security Council* (Abingdon: Routledge, 2006).

[4] David Hannay, *New World Disorder* (London: I.B. Tauris, 2008).

[5] Boutros Boutros-Ghali, *UNvanquished* (London: I.B. Tauris, 1999); Boutros Boutros-Ghali, *Mes Années à la Maison de Verre* (Paris: Fayard, 1999), p.18.

[6] Kent Kille, ed., *The UN Secretary-General and Moral Authority* (Washington, DC: Georgetown University Press, 2007), pp.270–4.

[7] MIG-PD-B, 27-Dec-1991 and 2-Jan-1992; Romuald Sciora, ed., *À la Maison de Verre* (Paris: Saint-Simon, 2006), p.39.

As with his predecessors, the job of the new SG consisted in adapting the UN Charter to a new era—but unlike his colleagues, Boutros-Ghali came to office at a time of unparalleled optimism for the organization.[8] The ending of the Iran–Iraq war, the eviction of Saddam's troops from Kuwait, and the Namibia, Afghanistan, and Nicaragua operations were all regarded as UN successes, an optimism that percolated to *An Agenda for Peace*. A month after Boutros-Ghali's appointment, the Council convened for the first time at the level of Heads of State and Government and—under the presidency of John Major and with the active participation of George H. W. Bush and Boris Yeltsin—asked Boutros-Ghali to outline 'recommendations on ways of strengthening and making more efficient the capacity of the UN for preventive diplomacy, peace-making and peacekeeping'.[9] As mentioned in Chapter 1, after the Cold War these were unprecedented requests. 'Our new Secretary-General is a lucky man', Major stated. 'He is the first in many years to inherit a UN that is confident in its own ability to solve problems while still being conscious of the magnitude of its task.'[10] *An Agenda for Peace* provided the intellectual framework through which Boutros-Ghali wished to push the UN towards new paths, and a unique opportunity for 'the most combative of Secretaries-General'.[11] 'I wanted [the 1992 summit] to result in a more effective role for the UN chief',[12] he stated.

'Ambitious' is an apt adjective to describe the *Agenda*, which formalized concepts such as peacebuilding, early-warning, and preventive diplomacy. Early in his tenure, Boutros-Ghali favoured a muscular approach to peacekeeping—'international intervention must extend beyond military and humanitarian tasks', he wrote, 'and must include the promotion of national reconciliation and the re-establishment of effective government'.[13] Among his boldest proposals (which the Council never approved) were plans for rapid-deployment peace-enforcement units under the SG's command (opposed by the North); an early-warning system (rejected by the South); and devolution of the Council's peacekeeping authority to the General Assembly (disliked by virtually everybody).[14] Any SG was going to face opposition to such ambitious plans, but the convergence of the US and Russian 'planets' along the UN 'orbit' was promising. As David Hannay, the UK Permanent Representative in New York, observed at the time, 'Here is an organization undergoing a renaissance [and] every speech . . . proclaims the fact. . . . But', he

---

[8] Ian Clark, 'Another "Double Movement": The Great Transformation after the Cold War?', *Review of International Studies* (2001), pp.27 and 237–55.

[9] Boutros-Ghali, *UNvanquished*, p.25.   [10] Boutros-Ghali, *UNvanquished*, p.25.

[11] Thant Myint-U and Amy Scott, *The UN Secretariat* (New York: International Peace Academy, 2007), p.96.

[12] Boutros-Ghali, *UNvanquished*, p.23.

[13] Boutros Boutros-Ghali, *An Agenda for Peace* (New York: Department of Public Information, 1992), p.9.

[14] Boutros-Ghali, *An Agenda for Peace*, p.39.

warned, 'there is a tendency to underestimate the fragility of the renaissance [and] to forget that this heady wine is being poured into some pretty cracked old bottles.'[15] Goulding too saw problems coming, especially 'in terms of the command of peace enforcement operations, Article 2(7) [the clause on the domestic jurisdiction of member states], the capacity of the Secretariat, and finance'.[16] But the new credo left little time for such concerns in the SC or in the Secretariat. 'I was intoxicated like anyone else',[17] the British official admitted.

It took the new SG only a few months to discover the fragility of those 'old bottles'. The 1992 summit had offered more power of initiative to Boutros-Ghali than to most of his predecessors, but while they had the luxury of choosing their battles carefully, post-Cold War optimism and the shift from inter-state to intra-state conflict meant that the new SG was expected to take a stand on almost every international event—a circumstance that contributed to constrain rather than cement his influence. Against the advice of some of his aides, including Goulding, Boutros-Ghali pushed the SC into a high-risk role in Somalia (a state where the UN tried—and failed—to impose peace);[18] he oversaw—albeit reluctantly and, as we shall see, under significant pressure from Western powers—an imposing mission in Yugoslavia;[19] he promoted peace efforts in Afghanistan; and he launched new operations in Mozambique, Namibia, El Salvador, Cambodia,[20] and Haiti, all of which happened almost simultaneously.[21] In the early 1990s the UN was very active, which is precisely what the 1992 summit had asked for. The problem is that such a ballooning list of activities—there were more UN missions in the four years between 1990 and 1994 than in the previous forty—could only be carried out with more resources. Such resources were not provided, and since Boutros-Ghali claimed that these difficulties affected both UNAMIR and his decisions on Rwanda, they ought to be considered at the outset.

DISAPPOINTMENT: PEACEKEEPING BOOM AND FINANCIAL CRISIS

The newly appointed SG found one dossier towering over all the others: the fiscal one. Despite the pomp associated with the 1992 summit, UN finances

---

[15] Hannay, *New World Disorder*, pp.10–11.   [16] MIG-PD-B, 15-Aug-1991.

[17] Marrack Goulding, 'Peacemonger: Book Proposal', 15 June 1998 (MIG-PA).

[18] United Nations, *The United Nations and Somalia* (New York: Department of Public Information, 1996).

[19] Samantha Power, *Chasing the Flame* (London: Penguin, 2007), chs 8 and 9.

[20] Power, ch.7. See also James Mayall, *The New Interventionism* (Cambridge: Cambridge University Press, 1996).

[21] Boutros-Ghali, *UNvanquished*, pp.97, 162, 221, 346, 358, and 405.

were in a state of considerable disarray. Administrative mismanagement, increased peacekeeping, and member states' reluctance to pay their dues were some of the reasons behind the crisis, with US arrears a cause of particular concern as they amounted to 20 per cent of the overall UN budget.[22] US–UN frictions go back to the foundation of the organization, but during the Clinton presidency (which, to Boutros-Ghali's dismay, virtually overlapped with the SG's term in office)[23] they had especially serious implications. Bill Clinton and Madeleine Albright claimed to be committed multilateralists and pledged support for the UN, but the President soon lost control of Congress and the Republican majority tied US payments to UN reform.[24] Partly as a result of this, under both Boutros-Ghali and Annan the organization almost faced bankruptcy.[25] Both SGs implemented major reforms, with Boutros-Ghali axing hundreds of jobs and cutting expenses as well as other benefits.[26] John Bolton, the US Assistant Secretary of State for International Organization (1989–93) and later the controversial US ambassador to the UN (2005–06), noted that one important reason why the USA did not veto Boutros-Ghali's appointment in late 1991 was that the Egyptian had promised Washington drastic administrative changes: 'I knew him before he was elected in 1992 and I talked to him several times about what our priorities were in picking the SG in 1991', Bolton stated. 'We wanted somebody who was going to come in and do the management. He said he would and . . . he did do a lot of reform, getting off to a good start and being hugely criticized for being a tool of the US.'[27] 'I assured [Bolton] of my interest for US positions', Boutros-Ghali wrote in his diaries with a sentence that sounds both ironic and prescient given his later fallout with Washington, 'and I told him that without US support, the UN would be paralyzed.'[28]

Financial stringency nevertheless persisted and UN activities were affected, especially the most expensive of them all, namely, peacekeeping. 'The US arrears compelled me to focus almost entirely on financial expedients', Boutros-Ghali wrote, 'such as shifting funds out of peacekeeping accounts to cover regular budget expenses. The United Nations was living hand to mouth.'[29] Precisely at a time when appeals by states to initiate new operations were multiplying, therefore, the organization stood on the verge of insolvency.

---

[22] Boutros-Ghali, *Mes Années*, ch.2.

[23] My interview with John Bolton, 24 June 2011, Washington DC (and by email on 28 April 2016).

[24] James Vreeland and Axel Dreher, *The Political Economy of the UN Security Council* (Cambridge: Cambridge University Press, 2014), esp. ch.1.

[25] Marrack Goulding, Talking Points for the Secretary-General at the ACC Meeting, 12 October 1995 (MIG-PA); Edward Luck, *Mixed Messages* (Washington, DC: Brookings Institution Press, 1999).

[26] 'Vested Interests at the UN a Test for Ghali', *The Independent*, 3 January 1992.

[27] Interview with Bolton, 24 June 2011.

[28] Boutros Boutros-Ghali, *Entre le Nil et Jérusalem* (Paris: Éditions du Rocher, 2011), p.454.

[29] Boutros-Ghali, *UNvanquished*, p.20. See also pp.16–17.

'By mid-1992 I had to take the unprecedented step of notifying member states that the United Nations might not have enough money to operate beyond the end of summer',[30] Boutros-Ghali wrote. Even then UN finances did not improve—indeed, the running of costly operations in Somalia and the Former Yugoslavia, coupled with Republican congressional control, further worsened the UN's balance sheets.[31] Writing about the UN's core task of preventing conflict, Goulding noted: 'That is what the UN was set up to do. The question now was whether the United States would let it do it.'[32] It is in this context of financial crisis that the Rwandan parties asked the SC to approve a UN operation in the African country[33] and that the Council established, in June 1993, first the Observer Mission (UNOMUR)[34] and then, in October 1993, the Assistance Mission for Rwanda (UNAMIR).[35] As Dallaire stated, this was an operation to be run 'on the cheap'[36]—still, it was not customary for financial parsimony to percolate to UN resolutions. Yet this is precisely what happened with Resolution 872, a document in which the fifteen diplomats sitting around the horseshoe table made it clear that UNAMIR had to be as cost-effective as possible.[37]

Perhaps because—as mentioned in Chapter 1—the assessment on UNAMIR's troop levels had already been subject to an 'anticipatory veto' by both Dallaire and DPKO, Boutros-Ghali seemed mindful that further cuts would undermine the mission's effectiveness. 'I will continue to seek economies through the phased deployment and withdrawal of UNAMIR personnel', the SG wrote to the Council in December 1993; 'I am however convinced that . . . a reduction in the projected resource levels would negatively affect the performance and credibility of UNAMIR in the discharge of its mandate. It could also jeopardize the peace process in Rwanda.'[38] Despite this stance, the New York diplomats were determined to contain expenses further and, when the Council reconvened in January 1994, it 'reiterate[d] its request to the SG to continue to monitor the size and cost of the Mission to seek economies'.[39] An identical demand was inserted in the resolution of early April 1994 extending UNAMIR,[40] and it was only after the genocide began that the quest for savings disappeared from SC resolutions.[41]

---

[30] Boutros-Ghali, *UNvanquished*, p.20.   [31] Luck, *The UN Security Council*, ch.1.
[32] Goulding, 'Peacemonger: Book Proposal', p.15.
[33] Permanent Mission of Rwanda to the UN, Letter to the President of the Security Council Requesting Deployment of UN Military Observers to the Rwanda-Uganda Border, 22 February 1993 (S/25355).
[34] Res 846 (S/RES/846), 5 June 1993.
[35] Res 872 (S/RES/872), 5 October 1993.
[36] Roméo Dallaire, *PBS Frontline Interview*, 1 April 2004.   [37] Res 872, §9.
[38] UN Secretary-General, *First Report on UNAMIR*, 30 December 1993 (S/26927), §30.
[39] Res 893 (S/RES/893), 6 January 1994.   [40] Res 909 (S/RES/909), 5 April 1994.
[41] Res 912 (S/RES/912), 21 April 1994.

Partly as a result of recurring problems with the UN operation in Somalia, the first paradox of Boutros-Ghali's term thus consisted in having been given an unprecedented mandate but little financial means to carry it out. Early in his term of office, Boutros-Ghali found out that war is expensive but always affordable, whereas peace has to be self-supporting. Goulding had similar complaints: describing the limits of the SG's action in world politics, the British official noted that 'MS [member states] monitor closely what the Secretary-General does [and] the vast majority of them do not want a powerful Secretary-General.'[42] Boutros-Ghali found the financial stringency of member states especially irritating in light of what he saw as the gratuitous generosity by Western powers in Yugoslavia. 'Why don't they make as much fuss about Rwanda . . . as they do about one dissident in China?',[43] he wrote in 1999 in his memoirs. During a press conference in 1995, he also complained that member states were willing to pay $5 million *a day* for the UN mission in the Former Yugoslavia, but only $25 million *a year* for the one in Liberia.[44] In a talking point to the SG, Goulding wrote that '[t]his distortion discriminates especially against Africa and the republics of the former Soviet Union', and noted that 'If, as it appears to be the case, there is a low ceiling on what Member States are ready to pay for such services, we will have to avoid any more expensive operations like Somalia or Yugoslavia.'[45] Predictably, the paper was not well received by the P-5.

Since these statements were made *after* the Rwandan genocide, it is legitimate to ask whether Boutros-Ghali raised the issue of UNAMIR's finances and logistics just as forcefully during the crisis. The answer is largely negative: the SG did propose (and obtain) further personnel for UNAMIR on an ad hoc basis,[46] but he did not officially plead for more resources. In 1993 and early 1994, the SG was also silent about supplies which had already been approved by the SC but which—as the previous chapter has shown—had failed to materialize. It has been suggested that this indicates the SG's lack of interest in the African country. I argue (later in this chapter) that Boutros-Ghali had considerable interests in Rwanda, and that his reluctance to push the Council to approve more resources for UNAMIR amounted to post-Somalia fatigue and to an assumption that the SC would have declined his requests anyway. 'Perhaps I had not been insistent enough with the Council', Boutros-Ghali acknowledged in his memoirs. 'In private talks with ambassadors I was repeatedly told that my effort was hopeless.'[47] Still, if he believed that

---

[42] Marrack Goulding, 'Power Politics at the United Nations', Remarks to the O'Neill/Roberts Seminar, All Souls' College, Oxford, 5 December 1997, p.3.
[43] Boutros-Ghali, *UNvanquished*, p.141.
[44] Goulding, Talking Points, 12 October 1995.
[45] Goulding, Talking Points, 12 October 1995.
[46] Res 893.   [47] Boutros-Ghali, *UNvanquished*, p.141.

UNAMIR's budget—one that he had himself submitted to the Council—was unrealistically low, he ought to have proposed a different one. Concern that a more muscular position on Rwanda would antagonize veto-yielding members at a time when the SG had controversially announced his decision to run for a second term may have also played a role.[48] While Boutros-Ghali's brusqueness is well known, the SG saw himself as a politician rather than a diplomat and was a shrewd tactician. 'The Secretary-General asked me why I thought the US was so hostile to him', Chinmaya Gharekhan, his Special Representative on the SC and a member of the Executive Office of the Secretary General (EOSG), wrote in his memoirs. 'I said it was partially because he had the audacity to give them his views as he saw them. He agreed, "They want stooges". But the fact was that he had done several things that the US wanted from him...;[49] even he admitted he had accommodated the Americans on most issues.'[50] As Part II will suggest, the fact that Boutros-Ghali was carving out a role for himself in peace operations did not make him 'anti-American'.[51]

Whatever his conduct in private, the SG failed to push the issue of UNAMIR's resources publicly—the daily press briefings by his spokesman, for example, are silent about this.[52] As for his appearances before the Council, the minutes of the informal consultations suggest that in April and May 1994—the peak of the Rwandan crisis—Boutros-Ghali briefed ambassadors only once, preferring to leave the task to his Special Representative[53] while prohibiting most of his senior officials (including USGs) from attending SC sessions altogether, a circumstance that drastically reduced direct communication between two principal UN organs precisely when the opposite was needed.[54] 'He found the meetings a bit of a bore', Gharekhan wrote. 'He did not form a high opinion of most of the ambassador members of the Council... [and] it was a big relief [for him] not to have to put up with the mediocrity, as he saw it, of the ambassadors.'[55] On 13 April 1994 Álvaro de Soto, Boutros-Ghali's Special Adviser, did brief the Council, noting that 'UNAMIR's tasks *as presently conceived* cannot be carried out without Belgium'[56] and that 'UNAMIR is no longer viable'.[57] But de Soto did not explicitly ask for more resources, and neither did Gharekhan during his regular appearances in the informal briefings.[58] While financial constraints were certainly an obstacle to

---

[48] Chinmaya Gharekhan, *The Horseshoe Table* (New Delhi: Longman, 2006), p.247.
[49] Gharekhan, p.289.   [50] Gharekhan, p.303.
[51] My interview with David Hannay, London, UK, 26 April 2011 (and by email on 12 May 2016).
[52] United Nations, Press Briefing of the Office of Spokesman for Secretary-General, 12 April 1994, p.2.
[53] Minutes of the Security Council's Informal Meetings on Rwanda, 6 April 1994 to 22 May 1994, Linda Melvern Rwanda Genocide Archive (LMRGA), Aberystwyth University, UK (hereinafter, Minutes).
[54] Gharekhan, p.25.   [55] Gharekhan, pp.24–5.
[56] Minutes, Part I, p.121. (original emphasis).   [57] Minutes, Part I, p.121.
[58] On April 18, 19, 21, and 22, as well as on May 3 and 12 (LMRGA).

Boutros-Ghali's peacekeeping strategy and contributed to increasing the tension between the SG and some member states, the UN chief did not seem to use all the opportunities available to him to make a case for more resources, nor did he bring to the attention of the SC the sorry state of UNAMIR before the killings started. A similar observation can be made about his (and the EOSG's) planning and analytical decisions.

FAILURE TO SEE? BOUTROS-GHALI'S INVOLVEMENT IN RWANDA AS SECRETARY-GENERAL

Lack of accurate assessments and overestimation of the solidity of the Arusha Accords have been recurrent themes of this book. The latter has so far suggested that DPKO entrusted a military official with the task of setting up a complex and multidimensional peacekeeping operation, failed to provide Dallaire with appropriate intelligence on Rwanda, and contributed to the friction and confusion between UNAMIR's 'military' and 'political' components. Earlier chapters have also noted the limitations of the assessments carried out by DPA and UNAMIR, the fact that Dallaire recommended troop numbers with which he was uncomfortable, and Booh Booh's questionable reporting. While overall accountability for these shortcomings rests *de jure* with the UN's Chief Administrative Officer, it is important to ascertain whether the SG's responsibility was nominal (i.e. whether Boutros-Ghali, while indirectly accountable, had limited involvement in an issue that never reached his level)[59] or whether he was fully engaged in Rwanda and could have done more to shift the balance.

There is suggestive evidence to support the latter view, especially when it comes to what UN officials call 'political analysis'. The Arusha Peace Agreements are a case in point: unlike Dallaire and Booh Booh, the SG was ideally placed to assess the viability of those accords because in early 1993 he had despatched a good-will mission to oversee the peace talks in Tanzania headed by DPA's Pédanou,[60] as well as a technical mission headed by DPKO's Baril.[61] This was in addition to Dallaire's reconnaissance trip of August 1993. Indeed, Boutros-Ghali was so involved in Arusha that the peace agreement had been signed 'in the presence of the Representative of the Secretary-General of the

---

[59] Boutros Boutros-Ghali, *Twenty-Twenty Interview*, Transcript of Tape 76, p.3 (undated).
[60] United Nations Secretariat, Interim-Report of the Secretary-General on Rwanda, 20 May 1993 (S/1993/25810), §4.
[61] UN Secretariat, Interim-Report of the Secretary-General on Rwanda, §3.

United Nations'[62] and head of the UN's Geneva Office Vladimir Petrovsky, another DPA official. Boutros-Ghali was also best positioned to contain the DPA–DPKO rivalry and instruct the two departments to cooperate. Whatever the shortcomings of Arusha, therefore, the SG could hardly plead ignorance about the genesis and contents of that peace agreement, particularly since he had personally intervened to pressure Habyarimana into signing it.[63] In his memoirs, Booh Booh defines the former SG as somebody who 'followed so closely the Rwanda and Great Lakes operations',[64] and as I point out in the section 'Neutral and Impartial?' below, Boutros-Ghali knew Habyarimana extremely well, having done business for years with the Rwandan government until his elevation to SG in 1992. Previously confidential diplomatic correspondence also shows that President Mitterrand of France—a close ally of Habyarimana as well as a personal friend of Boutros-Ghali—was increasingly concerned about Rwanda's ethnic cauldron and was exerting significant pressure on the SG to establish UNAMIR.[65]

Boutros-Ghali's correspondence, meetings, and conversations confirm his involvement in and commitment to Rwanda and the Arusha Agreement. Yet they also suggest that the SG placed considerable faith in the signatories despite their less-than-exemplary behaviour and the turbulence of the talks they were engaged in. While this is not unusual in peace negotiations, the SG's surprise at the failure of Rwandan politicians to abide by the Arusha timetable in the autumn of 1993 bordered on naiveté—in line with his (as well as DPA's and France's) desire to despatch a mission, but at odds with Rwanda's increasingly precarious situation. In an April 1993 letter, Boutros-Ghali had himself informed the Council of 'disturbing reports that the Arusha discussions are at an impasse. As a result', he wrote, 'there are fears that fighting may resume'.[66] Since war did indeed restart a little later, tougher questions should have been asked about the parties' commitment to peace and, at a minimum, a contingency plan should have been drawn up in case the situation deteriorated. This was another oversight by the SG, the assumption in New York having been that Arusha was solid and that the UN simply needed to 'show the flag' in Rwanda. The country's famously complicated ethnic composition, coupled with the SC's stinginess on Rwanda, should have pushed the SG to demand an

[62] Letter Addressed to the United Nations Secretary-General Transmitting the Peace Agreement Signed at Arusha, 23 December 1993 (A/48/824-S/26915).
[63] United Nations, Letter from the SG to the President of Rwanda, 27 January 1994.
[64] Jacques-Roger Booh Booh, *Le Patron de Dallaire Parle* (Paris: Éditions Duboiris, 2005), p.20.
[65] Télégrammes Diplomatiques, 7 October 1990; 15 October 1990; 19 December 1990; 15 October 1992; 12 January 1994; 2 March 1994; 22 April 1994. In Assemblée Nationale, *Mission d'Information Parlamentaire sur le Rwanda*, available at http://www.assemblee-nationale.fr/11/dossiers/rwanda.asp (accessed 24 February 2017) (MIPR).
[66] Boutros Boutros-Ghali, Letter to the President of the Security Council, 8 April 1993, in Charles Hill, ed., *The Papers of United Nations Secretary-General Boutros Boutros-Ghali*, Vol.1 (New Haven: Yale University Press, 2003), p.557.

exit strategy in the event that the parties disappointed or the mission ran into trouble. Instead, a best-case scenario was applied to actors that were systematically displaying worst-case behaviour.

Part II will show the disjuncture existing at the time between the SG and DPKO (which is responsible for contingency planning), a situation that hampered communications in New York. Such a divide, however, cannot fully explain Boutros-Ghali's performance in Rwanda. Indeed, the SG's proclivity to dismiss DPKO as a 'technical' department meant that he could and did rely on several other sources of information and advice, including DPA, EOSG, and France. Mitterrand, in particular, knew that Habyarimana was opposed to Arusha: 'President [Habyarimana] has attacked vigorously what he perceives as a peace agreement signed against his interests by the Foreign Minister, Mr Boniface Ngulinzira, and the RPF', a French diplomatic cable noted in 1992. 'Whenever political concessions have been asked of him in the past, Habyarimana has mentioned his country's public opinion (read his partisans) which he says will not accept the current arrangements.'[67] According to French sources, DPKO was aware of Habyarimana's opposition to Arusha: 'One of my aides has today contacted Mr Annabi [from DPKO] who has expressed the same fears [about Arusha]', another French telegram reads. 'The Secretariat acknowledges that the Rwandan President has systematically sabotaged all initiatives which tried to bring about a consensus.'[68] More worrying signs were coming from Kigali: in August 1993, while Arusha was being finalized and UNAMIR planned, a disturbing UN report had warned that Rwanda's anti-Tutsi violence had been 'institutionalized' by the authorities: 'It has been shown time and time again that government officials were involved directly [in these anti-Tutsi attacks] by encouraging, directing or participating in the violence',[69] the UN Special Rapporteur on Extrajudicial, Summary, or Arbitrary Executions wrote. The latter had no doubts about the authors of anti-Tutsi massacres: 'Youth organizations of some political parties have been converted into militias', and these 'have been guilty of incitement to ethnic violence against the Tutsi, of massacres of civilian population and of political assassinations.'[70] Waly Bacre Ndiaye, the special rapporteur, also warned about a 'catastrophic situation' and noted that Rwanda was 'nothing short of a time bomb with potentially tragic consequences'.[71] That such an alarming report—produced by his own organization—was not used by the SG

---

[67] Télégramme Diplomatique, Mission du Général Quesnot au Rwanda, 15 October 1992 (MIPR).

[68] Télégramme Diplomatique, Dégradation de la Situation au Rwanda, 2 March 1994 (MIPR).

[69] United Nations, Report by the Rapporteur on Extrajudicial, Summary, or Arbitrary Executions in Rwanda, 11 August 1993 (E/CN.4/1994/7/Add.1), §28.

[70] United Nations, Report, 11 August 1993, §40.

[71] United Nations, Report, 11 August 1993, §24.

to demand more resources and a contingency plan is a shortcoming ultimately lying with the UN chief, who nevertheless seemed oblivious to the report's very existence.

FAILURE TO ACT? BOUTROS-GHALI REACTS TO THE GENOCIDE

The SG's direct involvement in Rwanda was not confined to the initial stages of the UN operation but continued—indeed, intensified—once UNAMIR got into trouble. In this post-deployment phase, Boutros-Ghali again placed considerable trust in the ability of the Rwandan parties to fulfil the promises made in Arusha. By this time, however, he had little choice since the UN had committed to the operation and had been invited to the country by the Rwandan government, with the result that by this stage the SG needed to rely on the ability of local politicians to deliver peace. To his credit, Boutros-Ghali went beyond the role of privileged spectator: in late 1993, when the situation on the ground deteriorated and the Rwandan parties proved unable to establish the transitional institutions agreed at Arusha, the SG instructed his Special Representative to put pressure on them and solve the stalemate.[72] He also pleaded with President Habyarimana personally on several occasions, by letter and by phone, urging him to fulfil his side of the Arusha deal.[73] This was in keeping with the SG's desire to strengthen the UN presence in Africa while disengaging from expensive operations in the Former Yugoslavia. 'African issues continue to take an immense amount of time, partly because the SG is so minutely interested in them',[74] Goulding—who was by this time the sole head of DPA—wrote in his diary in March 1994, a month before the genocide.

Boutros-Ghali's involvement in Rwanda and his knowledge of the country become clearer if one recalls from Chapter 2 that in December 1993 Jonah was despatched to Kigali to warn Habyarimana that the SG had been made aware of plans involving large-scale anti-Tutsi massacres. According to Jonah, there was a very active Egyptian Embassy in Rwanda and it is possible that Boutros-Ghali learned this from them.[75] In his diaries, Goulding too appears to conflate Boutros-Ghali's intelligence system with the Egyptian Diplomatic Service.[76]

---

[72] United Nations, Draft Letter from SG to President of Rwanda, 25 January 1994 (on file with the author).

[73] Draft Letter, 25 January 1994.

[74] MIG-TD-IX, 12-Mar-1994. See also MIG-TD-IX, 7-Mar-1994.

[75] My interview with James Jonah, 20 July 2011, New York, USA.

[76] MIG-TD-IX, 20-Dec-1993 and MIG-TD-XII, 24-Jan-1996.

Although the issue of intelligence will be considered at length in Chapter 7, the December 1993 episode is significant in relation to the SG for a number of reasons. First, it confirms that Boutros-Ghali had independent information about Rwanda and that he was closely involved with the country's affairs. Indeed, he seemed to know more about Rwanda than his own Africa adviser (Jonah), and to some extent even more than UNAMIR officials on the ground. Second, the advance warning of December 1993 reached Boutros-Ghali a month *before* Dallaire's cable to DPKO of January 1994 alerting of arms caches being hidden with the purpose of committing anti-Tutsi massacres. Thus, Boutros-Ghali's claim that DPKO never brought the cable to his attention and the fact that he only saw it after the genocide—a claim that Jonah confirms[77]—should be weighed against the fact that the SG had learned of similar plans in late 1993. The incident also suggests that the SG saw his intelligence as serious, specific, and reliable enough to justify the extraordinary step of warning a sitting Head of State about the existence of damning evidence against him. Boutros-Ghali must have been absolutely convinced of its authenticity.

This makes the SG's reaction to the onset of the massacres puzzling. From its privileged position as an elected member of the SC, the Rwandan government predictably denied any involvement in the killings and attributed them to 'certain military personnel . . . who had reacted spontaneously in attacking certain persons'.[78] This, however, was a far cry from the truth and by mid-April thousands of bodies were floating down Rwanda's rivers into Lake Kivu. The authorities were also adamant about 'the need to establish an immediate cease-fire with a view of putting an end to the hostilities and create a climate conducive to full implementation of the Arusha peace agreement'.[79] Since the Rwandan Patriotic Front was heading for Kigali to unseat the government, the Hutu ambassador's stance was unsurprising. More perplexing is the fact that the SG appears to have bought into it: on 20 April, more than two weeks after the start of the massacres, Boutros-Ghali incorrectly informed the SC that 'unruly members of the Presidential Guard'[80] were to blame for the violence, noting that 'the most urgent task was . . . the effort to secure a cease-fire through contacts with representatives of the armed forces and the RPF'[81]—precisely the position of the *génocidaires*. This was repeated on 29 April when the SG again blamed 'uncontrolled military personnel' and an 'armed group of civilians taking advantage of the complete breakdown of

---

[77] Interview with Jonah, 20 July 2011.

[78] Letter from the Government of Rwanda to the President of the Security Council, 13 April 1994 (S/1994/470), §3.

[79] Letter from the Government of Rwanda, 13 April 1994, §3.

[80] United Nations, Special Report of the SG on UNAMIR with a Summary of the Developing Crisis, 20 April 1994 (S/1994/470), §3.

[81] United Nations, Special Report of the SG on UNAMIR, 20 April 1994, §3.

law and order in Kigali'.[82] In mid-May—more than a month after the genocide began—the SG was still insisting, like Booh Booh, that 'it is clearly necessary that a cease-fire be agreed and be put into effect at the earliest possible date'.[83]

Given the horrific scenes broadcast from Rwanda and Boutros-Ghali's insider's knowledge of Habyarimana's anti-Tutsi plans, the SG's position is highly problematic, especially in light of evidence from the Goulding papers suggesting that the SG was aware of the scale and nature of the killings early on (by the end of April, the Secretariat had estimated the number of Tutsi killed during the first three weeks at 200,000).[84] Clearly, this is not something that could have been done by 'unruly' army officers. Yet two weeks later, the SG was still bowing to the UN's neutrality principle and appeared to blame the Rwandan parties equally: 'Both sides have adopted rigid positions', the SG wrote to the Council, echoing Booh Booh's reports but certainly not Dallaire's cables, 'with the RPF presenting preconditions [the end of massacres] that Rwandan Government Forces reject'.[85] Since the RGF was bent on exterminating the RPF and the entire Tutsi population, a cease-fire between them was both unfeasible and immaterial.

An important qualification needs to be made here, for even those on the ground were slow to recognize genocide. Dallaire acknowledged that his January 1994 cable was warning of anti-Tutsi *massacres*.[86] Likewise, the intelligence tip that Jonah had received from the SG in December 1993 referred to some form of use of force against the Tutsis but did not explicitly mention 'genocide' (although according to Jonah, when confronted with the warning, Habyarimana had 'vehemently denied that any massacres *or genocide* were being contemplated...').[87] For a while, even Kagame failed to recognize that genocide was taking place.[88] The optimistic tone of Booh Booh's assessments may have also played a role in delaying Boutros-Ghali's realization of the gravity of the situation, a circumstance that was worsened by the disconnect existing at the time between DPKO and the SG's office—and thus between UNAMIR's 'military' officials and the top UN leadership. It would be unfair, then, to blame the SG for failing to foresee something that took most people by surprise, especially since Boutros-Ghali was actually the first world leader to speak publicly of 'genocide' (on 25 May)[89] at a time when Washington was prohibiting its diplomats from even uttering the word, lest it

---

[82] United Nations, Letter from the SG to the President of the SC, 29 April 1994 (S/1994/518).
[83] United Nations, Report of the Secretary-General on Rwanda, 13 May 1994 (S/1994/565), §27.
[84] MIG-MD-SG/RWANDA, TF 29APR94, 10.45.
[85] United Nations, Report, 13 May 1994, §6.
[86] Dallaire, *PBS Frontline Interview*, 1 April 2004.
[87] James Jonah, *What Price the Survival of the United Nations?* (Ibadan: Evans Brothers, 2006), p.382 (emphasis added).
[88] Paul Kagame, *PBS Frontline Interview*, 30 January 2004.
[89] Gharekhan, p.247.

triggered Genocide Convention obligations.[90] Still, from someone as active in Africa and as involved in Rwanda as Boutros-Ghali, one would have expected a more steadfast condemnation of those whom he knew were behind the massacres. Commenting on the difficulty of the SG's job, Goulding likened Boutros-Ghali to Dag Hammarskjöld:

> Two Secretaries-General—DH and BBG—have seen that the compliance de-manded by the majority gives Secretaries-General an unattractive set of options. Either the Secretary-General takes no initiatives unless specifically mandated to do so; or he tries to ensure that, taken overall, his initiatives are equally offensive to all power groups; or he blatantly takes sides. Hammarskjold and Boutros-Ghali hoped that they would escape from this box by asserting and strengthening the independence of the Secretary-General and the Secretariat, as envisaged in the Charter. This is and remains an extraordinarily difficult task.[91]

Goulding's quote highlights another Boutros-Ghali paradox: some states clearly had opportunistic reasons to remain quiet in 1994, but why was the first African SG—a keen interventionist perfectly ready to criticize Western capitals, as he saw it, for wasting money in the Former Yugoslavia—so guarded on Rwanda? Part of the reason lies with the composition of the SG's office and with the kind of advice offered to Boutros-Ghali on Rwanda.

RESTRICTED ADVICE? THE SECRETARY-GENERAL'S EXECUTIVE OFFICE

The fragmented nature of Boutros-Ghali's Secretariat meant that in late 1993 and early 1994 the SG was relying on a small inner circle of officials—described by Goulding as 'the Pharaoh's Court'—which included five people: Ismat Kittani, Álvaro de Soto, Chinmaya Gharekhan, Jean-Claude Aimé, and Gould-ing himself. 'I worry about the growing power of the "Special Advisers" on the 38th floor', Goulding wrote—not entirely disinterestedly—on 30 January 1994 with reference to the EOSG, 'all of them Third Worlders, as are Boutros Boutros-Ghali and Aimé [the SG's Chief of Staff]'.[92] According to the head of DPA, this was '[n]ot good for the Organization's image with the principal donors/contributors',[93] and in his handover notes, Goulding warned his successor that he should be firm to stand his ground against the special advisers on the top floor: 'You will need to guard against any tendency to

---

[90] Boutros-Ghali, *Mes Années*, ch.4.
[91] Goulding, 'Power Politics at the United Nations', p.4.
[92] MIG-TD-IX, 30-Jan-1994.   [93] MIG-TD-IX, 30-Jan-1994.

regard African matters as a *chasse gardée* from which you are excluded',[94] Goulding confidentially wrote to his successor upon leaving DPA. At a time of budgetary battles and bureaucratic friction, Goulding was especially concerned about Boutros-Ghali's isolation from—and difficult relationship with—both the USA and DPKO.

The role of Boutros-Ghali's advisers is all the more important since the SG was travelling in Europe during the crisis and was thus further insulated from other sources of information at Headquarters—particularly the 'operational' side and DPKO—while being overexposed to Gharekhan and Goulding, who were travelling with him. This situation had a number of implications for the Rwanda events. Until a meeting with the German Foreign Minister early in the second week of April 1994, the SG's involvement in the Great Lakes region and his commitment to maintaining the UN in Rwanda appeared relatively established, with Boutros-Ghali even forecasting a long-term UN presence in the region: 'The Secretary-General took credit for keeping the situation in Burundi calm', Gharekhan wrote in recounting Boutros-Ghali's meeting with the German official. 'He added [that] Rwanda had no government, like in Somalia, and [that] UNAMIR might have to stay in the country for a year or two.'[95] Hours *after* the start of the massacres, therefore, Boutros-Ghali had not yet made up his mind, but seemed inclined to keep UNAMIR put. This is confirmed by a Goulding diary entry dated 9 April 1994 where a meeting between the French Ambassador to the UN and the SG is discussed:

> The French Ambassador said that France was very worried about the security of its nationals in Rwanda and was considering possible actions to ensure their evacuation. The SG said don't do it; it would oblige him to withdraw UNAMIR and would be 'a gift' to those in Russia who want to take unilateral action in the New Abroad. The Ambassador spoke of divided councils in Paris . . . and said that the SG would be informed immediately if any concrete decision was taken. He duly was [informed] by telephone at 0100 hrs and this morning's BBC reported that the French troops had already landed and secured the airport at Kigali. The Belgians subsequently told him that their troops would be going in at midnight tonight. The Americans seem to be mounting some operation of their own out of Bujumbura but have said not a word to the SG or UNNY.[96]

What happened, then, between this meeting on 9 April and Goulding's remark, on 10 April and mentioned in Chapter 2,[97] that the SG wanted to pull UNAMIR out of Rwanda?

According to Gharekhan, events on the ground, the SC's presumed wishes, and the nature of the advice offered to Boutros-Ghali by his advisers—including Gharekhan himself—explain the SG's stance. On 14 April 1994,

[94] Marrack Goulding, Handover Notes for Sir Kieran Prendergast, 22 February 1997, §62 (MIG-PA) (emphasis in the original).
[95] Gharekhan, p.241.　　[96] MIG-TD-X, 9-Apr-1994.　　[97] MIG-TD-X, 10-Apr-1994.

Gharekhan forwarded from Europe to the SC the SG's recommendations on Rwanda. 'We suggested two alternatives', Boutros-Ghali's Special Representative to the Council wrote. 'The Secretary-General had to be prudent. What he would really have liked to propose was an increase in UNAMIR's strength by about 3,000 troops and keep UNAMIR in Rwanda for at least another year. Since the Council would not agree to such a large increase (or even a smaller one), the Secretary-General would prefer to pull UNAMIR out altogether. But these options would be unpopular, so some provisional solutions were sent to New York.'[98] By this time, Boutros-Ghali was also coming under pressure from the Belgian government (which had lost ten peacekeepers in gruesome circumstances) to withdraw UNAMIR. The SG put great weight on Belgium's recommendation, for he believed that as a former colonial power Brussels understood Rwanda better than the UN did.[99] Yet Dallaire and his colleagues wanted to stay, with the result that the SG was getting contradictory advice.

As the massacres multiplied, Boutros-Ghali's office put three alternatives to the Council—increase UNAMIR, reduce it, or withdraw it altogether—without nevertheless recommending any one of them. The SG reportedly 'did not favor' Option 3, but neither was he clear which between Option 1 and Option 2 he recommended. In Gharekhan's view, Boutros-Ghali would have wanted the UN to have a more muscular presence in Rwanda, but his advisers—including Gharekhan himself—reportedly managed to dissuade him from recommending Option 1:

> The Secretary-General rejected the withdrawal option though several in the Council favored it, especially the US and UK. The Secretary-General's own strong preference was for the first option and he wanted to recommend it to the Council. But we, his advisers, told him that there was not the slightest chance of the Council embracing it. The Secretary-General knew that as well as anyone else, in fact better. But he felt that as an African he had to recommend it. I told him that he would be accused of trying to win kudos with the Africans; he should certainly propose the alternative but not recommend it. He agreed, most reluctantly.[100]

In his memoirs, Gharekhan regrets offering this piece of advice to Boutros-Ghali: 'I soon developed doubts whether we, the Secretary-General's advisers, had been right in persuading the Secretary General to change his mind', adding—in a fascinating afterthought—that '...the UN as an organization ought perhaps to have taken a moral, principled stand.'[101]

By the late April, with the Rwandan tragedy on TV screens, the SG reversed his stance and recommended a strengthening of UNAMIR. 'The main event of the day was the SG's decision to write to the Council recommending that it reconsider the use of force to restore law and order, and end the massacres in

[98] Gharekhan, pp.242–3.   [99] MIG-TD-X, 9-Apr-1994.
[100] Gharekhan, p.244.   [101] Gharekhan, p.244.

Rwanda',[102] Goulding wrote in his diary. 'He knows the Council won't accept this recommendation; but he feels obliged to draw attention publicly to the double standards applied in B.H. [Bosnia Herzegovina] and in Africa.'[103] According to Gharekhan, this time Boutros-Ghali asserted himself and went against the counsel of his aides: 'The SG had discussed the matter with his advisers. [Like the SC] he too felt the need "to do something". He regretted he had not thrown his weight behind the first alternative in his report of a week earlier, and did not fail to remind us that we had persuaded him not to do so.'[104]

Several factors make Gharekhan's and Goulding's comments intriguing. First, they are unlikely to be self-serving, for neither aide comes out especially well from this version of the events. Gharekhan concedes to having given in to the presumed wishes of the SC, admittedly a more convenient explanation than confessing to having looked the other way during a genocide but still a short cry from the tendency of political memoirs to 'clear one's name' and distance their authors from problematic decisions, while taking credit for the 'good' ones. Gharekhan's role within the so-called 'Pharaoh's Court' makes this noteworthy: 'I was the eyes, ears and voice of the Secretary-General on the Security Council',[105] Gharekhan wrote. As for Goulding, Chapter 8 will show that he never concealed his opposition to peacekeeping where conditions were unfavourable and was never apologetic about it. This is different from Gharekhan: although admiring of Boutros-Ghali, Gharekhan criticizes his former boss on a number of issues, but on Rwanda he actually praises the former SG's instincts:

> The advisers of the Secretary-General ought to have advised him not to put forward that option in the first place, but they had not dissuaded him for practical political reasons. We in the Secretariat should have let the Secretary-General follow his instinct and recommend the more robust option. The Secretariat officials are not immune from political considerations.[106]

In this account, the EOSG contributed to recommending an important policy decision, namely, UNAMIR's drastic reduction from 2,500 to 270 men. Although Gharekhan's comments are consistent with Boutros-Ghali's activism in Africa before, during, and after the genocide, it is worth bearing in mind that such activism was not fully shared by Boutros-Ghali's advisers: 'On Burundi, the SG and all of us remained very worried about a Rwanda-type collapse', Goulding wrote in his diary after the genocide. 'He . . . had the idea of getting some Western troops into Bujumbura, under humanitarian guise, to establish a "humanitarian base" at the airport. But where will the troops come from?', a sceptical Goulding asked. 'And how can the 95% Tutsi army

---

[102] MIG-TD-X, 1-May-1994.   [103] MIG-TD-X, 1-May-1994.
[104] Gharekhan, pp.244–5.   [105] Gharekhan, p.239.   [106] Gharekhan, p.257.

be persuaded to accept this?'[107] In another entry Goulding noted—again disapprovingly—that Boutros-Ghali 'also fretted about not being able to do anything to forestall another disaster in Burundi [and] startled the Council on Friday by asking that France, the US and other Western powers should keep troops in Zaire as a standby intervention force for Burundi'.[108] While these comments bear witness to Boutros-Ghali's interest for Africa, they make his Rwanda vacillations even more surprising. Several pieces of the Boutros-Ghali 'puzzle'—pieces that complicate the task of assessing his leadership—are clearly missing from the above account and will be considered in detail in Part II. They include the most controversial of them all, namely, Boutros-Ghali's association with the Hutus prior to becoming SG.

NEUTRAL AND IMPARTIAL? BOUTROS-GHALI AND THE HUTU GOVERNMENT

A series of little known documents shows that from October 1990 until his elevation to the top floor of the UN Secretariat in January 1992, Boutros-Ghali had been instrumental, as Egyptian Minister of State for Foreign Affairs, in facilitating a series of arms deals between the Mubarak and Habyarimana governments, with the specific purpose of helping Habyarimana's Hutus defeat Kagame's Tutsi-dominated RPF.[109] Although the ethical implications of these events and of Boutros-Ghali's links to the Hutu (via Habyarimana) and to the French (via Mitterrand) will be explored in Part II, it is important to note that Boutros-Ghali did not inherit the Rwanda arms dossier from his predecessors in the Egyptian government but initiated it, actively pleading with President Mubarak to reverse his long-term policy of not supplying weapons to Kigali for the specific purpose of helping the Hutus defeat the Tutsis.[110]

Importantly, Boutros-Ghali succeeded. In December 1990, in the midst of the civil war between Habyarimana's Hutus and Kagame's Tutsi rebels, a letter from the Rwanda Ambassador in Cairo to his Foreign Minister confirms Boutros-Ghali's involvement in the conflict and credits him with nothing less than saving Habyarimana from a certain RPF defeat. Referring to 'Egypt's supply of military materials which have been of great assistance during the difficult moments we have just experienced', the ambassador wrote to his boss

---

[107] MIG-TD-X, 14-Aug-1994.   [108] MIG-TD-X, 24-Aug-1994.

[109] Unless otherwise stated, the documents in this section are available for public consultation at the Linda Melvern Rwanda Genocide Archive in the Hugh Owen Library, Aberystwyth University, UK (LMRGA). All translations are mine.

[110] Howard Adelman and Astri Suhrke, 'Rwanda', in Malone, p.489.

that 'the personal intervention of Foreign Minister Boutros Boutros-Ghali has been crucial [*"déterminante"*] in concluding such a contract, since he was closely following the situation on our borders. I would suggest that you write a personal letter of thanks which I could deliver to him personally'.[111] This followed another document—marked 'SECRET'—which the same ambassador sent to Boutros-Ghali with a request for further supplies: 'I have the honour of forwarding you the list of materials which the Rwandan Ministry of Defence has given... your Embassy in Kigali. The Rwandan Government would like you to use your influence with your Government in order to obtain this assistance as rapidly as possible, given the situation in the North-East following the 1st October aggression [by the RPF] of which Rwanda is a victim.'[112]

Boutros-Ghali made extensive use of his influence, for the above request led to several business trips by him to Kigali and to a long series of arms deals with Habyarimana. 'In a spirit of mutual support and assistance', one of the contracts reads, '[t]he Arab Republic of Egypt... pledges to deliver to the Rwandese Republic... the military materials with the price and details specified in Annex A of the present contract... for a total sum of 6,000,000 US$.'[113] As for the nature of the armaments supplied, another document—on Egyptian Defence Ministry's letterhead—mentions '4,000 bombs 120mm, 500,000 Rounds 7.62×51 (Tracer), 1,000,000 Rounds 7.62×51 (Normal), 500,000 Rounds 7.62×39 and 2,000 Rocket PG7' for a value of 6,722,400 US$.[114] A further letter refers to 'about 300 tons to be transported, that is to say, 8 [Cairo-Kigali] round-trips',[115] which another two documents confirm having been shipped by Egyptian airline ZAS[116] and for which authorization to overfly Sudan was obtained.[117] A cargo flight also left Cairo for Kigali on 28 October 1990 with 35,570 kilos of weapons (including bombs of various types),[118] the delivery of which is confirmed by a receipt for US$2,941,800 signed by the Egyptian Ministry of Defence and paid for by the Habyarimana government.[119]

While this is not an insignificant amount of weapons for a small country like Rwanda, Part II will show that it was only the first of a long list of military

---

[111] Rwanda Embassy in Cairo, Confidentiel: Lettre au Ministre des Affaires Etrangères et de la Coopération Internationale, 19 December 1990, §2.

[112] Rwanda Embassy in Cairo, Lettre à M. Boutros Boutros-Ghali, 15 October 1990, §2.

[113] Ministère de la Défense du Rwanda, Contrat n.1/92 Entre le Gouvernement de la République Rwandaise et le Gouvernement de la République Arabe d'Egypte sur la Fourniture par l'Egypte d'un Crédit d'Assistance Militaire, Art.1 and 2.

[114] Egyptian Ministry of Defence, Offer Letter by Col Sami Said (undated).

[115] Rwanda Embassy in Cairo, Letter to Rwanda Ministry of Foreign Affairs, 27 October 1990.

[116] Rwanda Embassy in Cairo, Fax 085/(C)4 I to Rwanda Foreign Ministry, 26 October 1990, §1. See also Rwanda Embassy in Cairo, Fax 082/(C)4 I to ZAS Airlines (undated).

[117] See Rwanda Embassy in Cairo, Letter to Rwanda Ministry of Defence, 28 October 1990, §1.

[118] See Rwanda Embassy in Cairo, 'Chargement sur le Vol Spécial du 28 Octobre 1990', 28 October 1990.

[119] See Rwanda Embassy in Cairo, 'Reçu', 31 October 1990.

deals between Egypt and Rwanda spanning the years 1990, 1991, 1992, and 1993[120]—indeed, the transactions became so frequent that at one time a Rwanda Embassy document suggested that 'the purchase will be done at the usual conditions'[121] and for the usual reasons, namely, to assist Habyarimana's Hutu government in defeating Kagame's Tutsi-dominated RPF. Chillingly, several delivery sheets show that weapons and technical training were supplied as a result of contracts facilitated by Boutros-Ghali up to July 1994, that is to say, the end of a genocide that caused almost a million violent deaths.[122]

BOUTROS-GHALI IN RWANDA

'There are still plenty of mysteries, plenty of questions that have not been answered, plenty of questions that have never even been asked, despite all the inquiries, auditions and reports',[123] Boutros-Ghali wrote in relation to the Rwandan genocide. The former SG is right, and some of those questions refer to his own involvement in the tragic events of 1994.

It is important to note that there is no evidence that Boutros-Ghali directly facilitated the supply of weapons to Habyarimana *after* his accession to the UN Secretariat. Furthermore, he was no apologist, condemned the genocide, and tried—although belatedly—to convince world leaders to intervene in Rwanda. Given his track record and active engagement in Africa, this is unsurprising. In the critical hours following the start of the killings, however, the SG reacted tardily and hesitantly, with a number of factors affecting his decisions.

The first relates to the paradox of an SG with a reputation for toughness who ends up being blamed for passivity. Of all the UN units, the SG was in the best position to assess the Rwanda situation, estimate the needs, viability, and costs of UNAMIR, and oversee Arusha's implementation. Indeed, this was his job. It is true that the decision to launch a peacekeeping mission rests with the Council and that the latter often pressures SGs to recommend certain courses of action, as the Brahimi Report noted.[124] It is also true that Boutros-Ghali was constrained by an exceptionally stingy membership and that the financial crisis negatively impacted on his peacekeeping strategy. Still, the SG had

---

[120] See Egyptian Ministry of Defence, 'Offer', December 1991.

[121] Rwanda Embassy in Cairo, Fax 119/(C)4M to Rwanda Foreign Ministry, 28 August 1991, §2.

[122] Egyptian Ministry of Defence, Delivery Sheet 13 July 1992 (for 456,320 US$); Delivery Sheet 11 July 1992 (for 555,000 US$). See also Rwanda Embassy in Cairo, Fax 35/(C)2F, 13 July 1994.

[123] Boutros-Ghali, *En Attendant*, p.38.

[124] Lakhdar Brahim et al., Report of the Panel on UN Peace Operations, 21 August 2000 (A-55-305–S/2000/809).

general oversight as well as some power of initiative; his failure to raise UNAMIR's logistical issues with the SC and his argument that he was 'not in close touch with the Rwanda situation'[125] since he was in Europe do not go very far, as he repeatedly refused to return to New York to handle the crisis.

The second factor affecting the SG's decisions was the fragmented nature of Boutros-Ghali's Secretariat. The SG's misgivings about DPKO meant that communications in New York were poor, a situation that was compounded by Boutros-Ghali's absence during the crisis. 'He made a long, rambling, unprepared speech', Goulding wrote of Boutros-Ghali's last day as SG, 'mainly about where he had gone wrong (not enough attention paid to the US, too much insistence on the independence of the UN), but also about his claims to virtue (no decisions without consultation with Department Heads concerned!!)'.[126] Goulding's sarcastic use of punctuation is especially justified in relation to Annan, whom Boutros-Ghali hardly consulted. Because his advisers in the EOSG (and Goulding in DPA) were aware of the SG–DPKO friction, of what they saw as the Council's hostility to UNAMIR, and of the risks associated with a UN presence in Rwanda, the advice they offered the SG was strikingly homogeneous. For a leader, lack of dissent among advisers is rarely conducive to well-informed decisions, particularly since at the time of the crisis DPKO and its leadership were not actively involved in the SG's decisions. As Part II will suggest, the fact that Boutros-Ghali was antagonizing a number of Western capitals over other peace operations did not help; neither did his contempt for ambassadors and his decision to appoint a representative to the Council while prohibiting his aides from appearing before the very organ responsible for international peace and security.

A third contributor to Boutros-Ghali's decision-making involves intelligence and the quality of the information he received. Booh Booh's mistaken reporting and the revered principle of UN impartiality may have pushed the SG, even after the onset of the massacres, to treat the Hutu government as a reliable interlocutor when several signals suggested otherwise. The fact that the SG had his own intelligence network, coupled with multiple indications from the Goulding archive and from his aides that Boutros-Ghali was heavily involved in—and deeply knowledgeable about—Rwanda means that the UN's intelligence failure was also his failure.

These three factors—leadership, bureaucracy, and intelligence—involve the UN as a whole and will be considered at length in Part II. So will the fourth and arguably most controversial contributor to the SG's decisions of 1994, namely, Boutros-Ghali's association with the Hutus before becoming SG.[127] On the face of it, such a link undermines Boutros-Ghali's (and the UN's) moral authority: that genocide happened before the eyes of the international

---

[125] Boutros-Ghali, *UNvanquished*, p.130.   [126] MIG-PD-D, 19-Dec-1996.
[127] See Chapter 9.

organization which is supposed to prevent it is tragic enough; that the organization's chief had been instrumental in sustaining—indeed, in keeping in power—the very government responsible for that genocide is extraordinary. It is true that SGs are prone to conflicts of interests since the UN has a global span and most SGs come from high-level political careers in their own countries. Yet as Egyptian Minister of State, Boutros-Ghali had unequivocally supported one side of Rwanda's ethnic divide (Habyarimana's Hutus) against the other (Kagame's Tutsis), a clear obstacle to impartiality. That as SG he went on to impose an arms embargo against weapons which he had himself contributed to supplying is disturbing and deserves further analysis.

'It is those with whom one is in touch that one helps, whether they are democratic or not, whether they commit atrocities or not', Boutros-Ghali told a French audience in an attempt to justify Paris's support for the *génocidaires*. 'And since in 1994 it was the Hutus who were in power, it is they whom governments—French, Belgian and others—were supporting . . . for states always support those who are in power.'[128] Whether that should also be true of the UN and its SG, given their obligations to prevent genocide under the Geneva conventions, is debatable. Since Boutros-Ghali argues that an ethical approach—one that he claims to have preferred—was made impossible by the fact that '[n]o government had any intention of stepping in to stop the Rwandan holocaust',[129] the final chapter of Part I will review the remaining— and arguably most powerful—UN body involved in the Rwanda decisions, the SC.

[128] Sciora, p.189.   [129] Boutros-Ghali, *UNvanquished*, p.140.

5

Security Council

The decision taken by the Security Council on 21 April 1994 to reduce the size of UNAMIR from 2,500 to 270 in the midst of genocide has been extensively commented upon by journalists and scholars alike.[1] Almost universally criticized as one of the most ill-advised moves ever made by the UN, it has also been portrayed as the triumph of cynicism over human dignity, an example of how the greed of self-interested states prevails over international solidarity. While a number of national diplomats would dispute this assessment, even they would concede that few UN decisions match the drama of Resolution 912. 'There was no interest in getting involved', Kofi Annan wrote in his memoirs.[2] His predecessor as SG, Boutros Boutros-Ghali, agreed: '[M]embers pursue their own national agenda without worrying about wider considerations of morality or even legality.'[3]

Since Resolution 912 effectively left the African country to its own destiny and made it easier for the *génocidaires* to exterminate almost a million people, the decision-making process leading to that document deserves strict scrutiny. Yet there is another, more specific reason why the SC's interactions matter: not only do they offer important clues about the power relations among member states back in 1994, they also shed light on those states' interactions with the UN bureaucracy. The Secretariat is a discreet but important presence on the Council: it feeds it with information, provides guidance to it, and executes its decisions.[4] To be sure, it does not appear on vote counts and its influence on the SC is contested, but its very presence among the world's powerful warrants consideration. The fact that this is rarely done comes down

---

[1] Linda Melvern, *Conspiracy to Murder* (London: Verso, 2006); Linda Melvern, *A People Betrayed* (London: Zed Books, 2007); Roméo Dallaire, *Shake Hands with the Devil* (London: Arrow Books, 2003); Roméo Dallaire, *PBS Frontline Interview*, 1 April 2004; Michael Barnett, 'The UN Security Council, Indifference and Genocide in Rwanda', *Cultural Anthropology*, Vol.12, No.4 (1997), pp.551–78.

[2] Kofi Annan, *Interventions* (London: Allen Lane, 2012), p.58.

[3] Chinmaya Gharekhan, *The Horseshoe Table* (New Delhi: Longman, 2006), p.x.

[4] Connie Peck, 'Special Representatives of the Secretary-General', in David Malone, ed., *The UN Security Council* (Boulder: Lynne Rienner, 2004), p.325.

to a practical reason—informal Council–Secretariat interactions are very seldom recorded—but also to the ingrained view according to which states are the only 'inhabitants' of the SC 'planet'. However, since the Council needs the Secretariat in order to function, they cannot be. Not for nothing has the UN bureaucracy been referred to as the Council's 'Sixth Permanent Member'.[5]

This chapter looks at the Council's decision-making process on Rwanda and considers its most visible conundrum: why did states unanimously decide to reduce UNAMIR in late April 1994, only to reverse their position in early May? As one of the ambassadors wondered ten years after the events, 'Why did we vote in favor of this resolution?'[6] The following pages address this question by considering an important but neglected source—the Council's informal (or secret) consultations of April and May 1994—and by assessing it alongside the recollections of UN officials (including the SG's Special Representative to the Council), the Goulding Archive, and other records.[7] In doing so, the chapter questions a number of assumptions about the crisis of 1994: that the SC was united in its opposition to UNAMIR; that states merely pursued their national interests; and that the Secretariat had little influence over the Council's decisions. The above sources also convey the complexity of the situation facing UN officials in mid-1994, adding colour and texture to the Rwanda 'mosaic'. 'Only by examining the informal debates and discussions can an observer begin to understand the difficulties faced by the Security Council in attempting to discharge its responsibilities',[8] a high-ranking UN diplomat wrote, while expressing regret that reports of such discussions do not usually exist. 'In the informals', another official noted, 'no records, either summary or verbatim, are kept [and] delegates have the great advantage of deniability.'[9] For Rwanda, this is no longer the case.

FRUSTRATION: THE COUNCIL AND RWANDA
BEFORE THE GENOCIDE

The Council's much-criticized decisions in the darkest hours of the genocide can only be understood in light of its attitude towards the Rwandan parties

[5] Howard Adelman and Astri Suhrke, 'Rwanda', in Malone, p.485.

[6] Ibrahim Gambari, *PBS Frontline Interview*, 15 January 2004.

[7] The minutes of the Council's informal meetings on Rwanda, upon which this chapter is based, are available for public consultation at the Linda Melvern Rwanda Genocide Archive (LMRGA) in the Hugh Owen Library, Aberystwyth University, UK (hereinafter, Minutes). The nature of these documents—which were scribbled during the SC's secret sessions—explains the occasional fragmentation, the absence of ellipses, and my explanations in brackets.

[8] James Jonah, 'Differing State Perspectives on the United Nations in the Post-Cold War World', J. W. Holmes Memorial Lecture, *ACUNS Reports*, No.4 (1993), p.13.

[9] Gharekhan, p.23.

ahead of the killings. Although the Arusha Peace Agreement had committed Kigali's politicians to form a transitional government by January 1994, in April there was still no sign of it, negotiations had stalled, and the country's security had deteriorated. Seen from New York, Rwandan politicians looked untrustworthy and by early April a consensus had emerged among ambassadors that pressure should be put on them to implement their engagements. While official documents and transcripts of formal meetings around the horseshoe table do contain polite invitations to the parties to honour their commitments, it is during the secret meetings behind the closed doors of the Consultations Room that the Council's impatience with UNAMIR emerges most clearly.

This frustration came to a head on 4 April 1994, two days before the start of the genocide, when the Council was discussing the SG's proposal to extend UNAMIR for six months. On this occasion, Nigerian Ambassador Ibrahim Gambari expressed concern for the delay in the implementation of Rwanda's transitional institutions; agreed with Boutros-Ghali's suggestion that UNAMIR should be extended for no more than six months; and noted that 'possibly the timetable had been too ambitious'.[10] The Council's president, Colin Keating of New Zealand, went further and stated that it was crucial to put 'pressure on the parties to reach an agreement':[11] a shorter, three-month extension was preferable since a longer one would 'encourage the parties to delay' the implementation of transitional institutions, which Keating defined as a 'major obstacle to peace'.[12] For him, the UN had been 'boxed in' by Arusha.[13]

This position was shared by US Ambassador Madeleine Albright. After pointing out that the United States 'genuinely want Rwanda to be stable', she stated that Washington 'does not support a six-month extension' and warned that 'if there are no concrete steps [the UN should] reduce the size of the operation or close [it] down altogether [as we should] only help if the parties will help themselves'.[14] In this, the USA was far from isolated: the Spanish ambassador agreed and so did the UK's David Hannay, who emphasized that while the 'Rwanda situation calls for continued engagement by the UN, which is doing a valuable job [there], progress is patently insufficient'.[15] London, Hannay concluded, 'favour[s] a short mandate putting the onus on the parties to come to an agreement'.[16] Russia, too, concurred and so did Brazil and China.[17] In April 1994, Rwanda's representative to the UN was sitting on the Council as an elected member and he was asked to explain his government's delay in implementing the peace accords, but sidelined the question by stating

---

[10] Minutes, 4 April 1994, p.18.   [11] Minutes, 4 April 1994, p.18.
[12] Minutes, 4 April 1994, p.18.
[13] Colin Keating, 'An Insider's Account', in Malone, p.501.
[14] Minutes, 4 April 1994, p.18.   [15] Minutes, 4 April 1994, p.19.
[16] Minutes, 4 April 1994, p.19.   [17] Minutes, 4 April 1994, p.19.

that Kigali was 'grateful to troop-contributing countries for UNAMIR [which] facilitates the negotiations, while the extension of the UN mandate will contribute to peace'.[18] Unimpressed by the ambassador's reluctance to elaborate further, Albright expressed a 'strong preference for [an additional] two-months [since] a lengthy extension would send the wrong signal to the parties',[19] and even Nigeria agreed on four months. By passing Resolution 909, therefore, the Council effectively put Kigali on notice.[20]

Two preliminary observations can be made about the Council's position ahead of the genocide. The first confirms the sceptical stance of the USA towards UNAMIR—perhaps unsurprisingly, as only a few months had passed since the crisis of the United Nations Operation in Somalia (UNOSOM), in which eighteen US soldiers had died.[21] Because of this traumatizing experience and the UN-averse stance of a Republican-controlled Congress, President Clinton had publicly announced a reduction in peacekeeping:[22] 'It is not US policy to seek to expand either the number of UN peace operations or US involvement in such operations', he had written in early 1994. 'Instead this [new] policy, which builds upon work begun by previous administrations and is informed by the concern of the Congress and our experience in recent peace operations, aims to ensure that our use of peacekeeping is selective and more efficient.'[23] The USA had never shown much interest in UNAMIR and had only agreed to its establishment in exchange for France's support for a UN mission to Liberia.[24] Consequently, Albright's position in the informals was consistent with her country's lack of strategic interest in UNAMIR and with its post-Somalia selectiveness towards peacekeeping operations. 'If the US is to say "yes" to peacekeeping operations, the UN must learn to say "no"',[25] Clinton had told the General Assembly in September 1993. In his diaries, Goulding mentions a difficult meeting, in February 1994, between Boutros-Ghali and Albright to discuss precisely this new US policy on peacekeeping. 'Our visitors asked the SG to support the new Presidential directive, shortly to be presented to Congress, without being free to reveal what it said', Goulding wrote, noting that 'The SG rightly declined to sign a blank cheque.'[26] Curiously, Washington's position on peacekeeping contrasted sharply with that of Russia: during a visit to the Kremlin two days before the start of the Rwandan genocide, Moscow's Defence Minister had assured Goulding

[18] Minutes, 5 April 1994, p.40.   [19] Minutes, 5 April 1994, 5pm, p.37.
[20] Minutes, 4 April 1994, p.41.
[21] United States Senate, *U.S. Participation in Somalia Peacekeeping* (Washington, DC: US Senate, 2012).
[22] David Ambrosetti and Mélanie Cathelin, 'Les Enjeux du Leadership au Conseil de Sécurité', *Revue Internationale et Stratégique*, No.68 (Winter 2007–08), pp.69–77.
[23] United States Department of State, *The Clinton Administration's Policy on Reforming Multilateral Peace Operations* (Washington, DC: State Department, 1994), p.6.
[24] George Moose, *PBS Frontline Interview*, 21 November 2003.
[25] Gharekhan, pp.245–6.   [26] MIG-TD-IX, 6-Feb-1994.

and Boutros-Ghali that Russia's policy had changed: 'We are ready to send our soldiers anywhere in the world with the UN',[27] Grachev had said.

The informal consultations further suggest that Washington was hardly the only capital tired of the Rwandan parties. Indeed, doubts were being voiced by most ambassadors about UNAMIR's feasibility and a consensus was emerging that Kigali was being unresponsive. This frustration was fully shared by the SG and Secretariat: having repeatedly called on President Habyarimana and his fellow politicians to implement the peace agreement, Boutros-Ghali was privately irritated by their inaction and made it clear to his staff.[28] As a result, the suggestion that UN members routinely try (and fail) to control the USA in the same way as the Roman Senate tried (and failed) to control the Roman Emperor does not seem to apply to Rwanda.[29] Indeed, the Council's unanimous decision to extend UNAMIR for only four months expressed both a desire to put peace operations under a stricter scrutiny, as well as a sense of frustration at the unreliability of the Rwandan parties. Somalia had changed the peacekeeping game and the SC as a whole—not just the USA—was determined to 'learn' from it. There was 'political pressure, particularly from the United States, for the United Nations to be able to demonstrate that it could "shut down" a peacekeeping operation', Keating wrote, noting that 'It almost did not matter which operation; the momentum was for symbolic closure.'[30] On the eve of the genocide, both the Council and the Secretariat were asking hard questions about UNAMIR. An overnight explosion over Kigali would only amplify those doubts.

DISAGREEMENT: THE COUNCIL REACTS TO THE START OF THE MASSACRES

'This is the last thing we needed.'[31] So spoke a frustrated Colin Keating upon hearing that the plane carrying the presidents of Rwanda and Burundi had crashed at the Kigali airport (President Mobutu of the Democratic Republic of the Congo was also supposed to be onboard, but had changed plans at the last minute).[32] It was 4.30 pm on

---

[27] MIG-TD-X, 5-Apr-1994.

[28] Boutros Boutros-Ghali, *Mes Années à la Maison de Verre* (Paris: Fayard, 1999), pp.194–5; Gharekhan, p.252.

[29] Thomas Weiss and Sam Daws, eds, *The Oxford Handbook on the United Nations* (Oxford: Oxford University Press, 2008), p.9.

[30] Keating, p.504.   [31] Minutes, 6 April 1994, 4.30pm, p.45.

[32] Assemblée Nationale, *Mission d'Information Parlementaire sur le Rwanda*, Audition de M. François Léotard, Ministre de la Défense, 21 April 1998, available at http://www.assemblee-nationale.fr/dossiers/rwanda/auditi01.asp (accessed 30 December 2015) (MIPR).

Wednesday 6 April 1994 and Keating was chairing another meeting of the SC when this event turned Rwanda into a full-fledged emergency. Although the fifteen ambassadors had little information on the cause of the accident, they knew that its effects would be devastating for Rwanda's rickety peace process, especially since reports of violence in Kigali were already surfacing. 'It was quite clear that a tragedy was about to happen',[33] Gambari recalled years later. Keating agreed: 'I sensed that an awful tragedy was at hand.'[34] What is intriguing about this initial phase after the plane crash is that the Council's unity in putting pressure on the Rwandans was abruptly replaced by disagreement about what to do—and that such a division was supplanted by a unanimous resolution reducing UNAMIR. How did the Security Council come to this?

During these early stages of the crisis the Council was not in favour of UNAMIR's withdrawal, as the records of the informals show. Speaking after Keating, French ambassador Jean-Bernard Mérimée confirmed that the news from Kigali were 'indeed serious'[35] but fretted to add that 'people in Rwanda count on the continued action of the SC and the international community to face this tragedy at [this] most critical time'.[36] Paris's immediate reaction, therefore, was that UNAMIR should not only be maintained but reinforced—a confirmation of the Goulding diary entry mentioned in the previous chapter. 'Planned dinner with Stoltenberg delayed because the French Ambassador is coming to see the SG at 1930 hrs to talk about military intervention in Rwanda',[37] Goulding—who was travelling with the SG at the time—wrote in his diary.[38] After the Spanish and Argentinean representatives expressed their concern, the Council moved on to discuss Iraq so that ambassadors could consult their capitals about the Rwandan crisis.[39] Two days later, on 8 April 1994, Keating reported back: the situation in Rwanda was 'extremely precarious' with 'large numbers killed, mostly Rwandese'.[40] However, the French ambassador noted that 'UNAMIR seemed to play a positive role and that the Force Commander and Special Representative [were] trying to establish some initial authority'[41]—though by this time Paris, against Boutros-Ghali's advice and without even informing its ambassador in New York, was already evacuating French nationals. For his part, Gambari noted that Rwanda's plight was disturbingly similar to that of the Congo in the 1960s and cautioned about a 'very dangerous period ahead':[42] 'If [we] don't do something quickly, the UN might be involved in something bigger.'[43]

---

[33] Gambari, *PBS Frontline Interview*, 15 January 2004.   [34] Keating, p.505.
[35] Minutes, 6 April 1994, 4.30pm, p.45.   [36] Minutes, 6 April 1994, 4.30pm, pp.45–6.
[37] MIG-TD-X, 8-Apr-1994.   [38] See also MIG-TD-X, 9-Apr-1994.
[39] Minutes, 6 April 1994, 4.30pm, pp.45–55.   [40] Minutes, 8 April 1994, p.61.
[41] Minutes, 8 April 1994, p.61.   [42] Minutes, 8 April 1994, p.61.
[43] Minutes, 8 April 1994, p.62.

As hours turned into days, divisions within the Council widened. Nigeria 'urge[s] UNAMIR to continue its efforts to set up some interim authority', Gambari stated, adding that the 'African group prefers a multilateral solution to this problem'.[44] His Pakistani colleague conveyed his country's commitment to Rwanda, voiced 'concern [at] the SG's letter relating to the evacuation of UNAMIR', and emphasized that 'action can [be] taken straightaway to amend the mandate and rules of engagement',[45] thus leaning towards a strengthening of the mission. By this time, however, ambassadors were mostly worried about the evacuation of their nationals, with Mérimée being one of them. Paris's decision to evacuate 'French nationals and others [was a] humanitarian operation [that had] nothing to do with UNAMIR', he noted. 'My government felt [it was] its duty to act swiftly [and] didn't take this decision lightly',[46] but UNAMIR itself should stay. Noting that SC members seemed more worried about evacuating foreigners than about protecting 'the innocent citizens of Rwanda', Gambari raised the possibility of 'beefing up UNAMIR',[47] something that led the UK's Hannay to note that a 'UN decision [is] needed whether UNAMIR can perform [a] useful function in the present situation.'[48] Although Russia, China, and Spain were undecided, one point on which all ambassadors agreed was the need to keep journalists at bay: '[We] prefer that fewer details [be given] to the press', the French representative said; 'merely [say] that the SC met [to discuss] evacuation and exchange views ... otherwise [it's like we are] trying to hide something'.[49] Along similar lines, London expressed a 'preference for not being too specific in suggesting when/ how [we will] come back to this issue',[50] while the Brazilian ambassador recommended 'not even taking notes'[51] of the meetings. Media pressure was clearly being felt by the fifteen diplomats.

In the early hours of the crisis, Washington did not come across as uncompromisingly opposed to UNAMIR—indeed, Albright's first reaction was to ask the SG for more input: '[We] don't have anywhere near sufficient information',[52] she observed on 8 April, noting that it was important to hear the 'advice of the SG and FC as to their recommendations on the fate of UNAMIR',[53] and hinting that the US position would depend on such advice.[54] As time passed, however, Albright appeared to be increasingly opposed to the idea—put forward by Gambari and others—of strengthening UNAMIR: 'The

[44] Minutes, 8 April 1994, p.64. See also Ibrahim Gambari, 'Rwanda: An African Perspective', in Malone, p.513.

[45] Minutes, 8 April 1994, p.66.   [46] Minutes, 9 April 1994, p.72.

[47] Minutes, 9 April 1994, p.73.   [48] Minutes, 9 April 1994, p.73.

[49] Minutes, 9 April 1994, pp.77–8.   [50] Minutes, 9 April 1994, p.79.

[51] Minutes, 9 April 1994, p.80.   [52] Minutes, 9 April 1994, p.65.

[53] Minutes, 9 April 1994, p.72.

[54] Madeleine Albright, *Madam Secretary* (London: Pan Books, 2004), pp.147–55.

mandate is already wide enough',[55] she brusquely replied to those calling for a broadening of the mission's legal framework, before noting that the evacuation of foreigners (which Washington had already carried out) was necessary. Yet the clearest indication of the US position came five days after the start of the killings, when Albright expressed 'doubts about the viability of UNAMIR in Rwanda', pointed out that the mission 'can't do its mandate', and suggested that a 'withdraw[al] might be necessary'.[56] There is a 'strong feeling in Washington that UNAMIR is not appropriate now and never will be', she said, so the USA 'can't agree with Gambari'.[57] Echoing Clinton's 1993 speech before the General Assembly, the USA was saying 'no' to the UN.

Yet Albright's stance was not widely shared. Keating strongly opposed a UN departure from Rwanda,[58] Gambari reiterated the need for a new mandate,[59] France noted that 'if UNAMIR withdraws, [the situation is] likely to get even worse and spread to Burundi',[60] Brazil made it clear that 'UNAMIR should not be withdrawn',[61] and even the UK resisted outright departure. Being opposed to a withdrawal, however, was not the same as being ready to offer troops, with the result that a week after the Kigali air crash the Council remained thoroughly undecided on what to do. As a result, diplomats turned to the SG for advice.

GUIDANCE: THE COUNCIL–SECRETARIAT INTERACTIONS

On 11 April 1994 Iqbal Riza, Annan's deputy at DPKO, was asked to brief the ambassadors about Rwanda and reported that artillery had hit a hospital and killed several people.[62] His appearance in the Consultations Room, however, matters for another reason: after the Brazilian representative praised UNAMIR, which in his view 'played an extensive role in protecting civilians',[63] Riza noted that 'the protection of civilians is not in [the UN's] mandate although UNAMIR is doing this—the first priority is to protect UN personnel, then help evacuate [foreigners], then help the concentration of refugees'.[64] For Riza, sheltering Rwandans was thus low on the UN's 'to do' list, an intriguing observation in light of the fact that, as Chapter 3 has shown, Dallaire thought that his rules of engagement *required* him to protect civilians (thousands of whom were already

---

[55] Minutes, 9 April 1994, p.66.   [56] Minutes, 12 April 1994, p.101.
[57] Minutes, 12 April 1994, p.110.   [58] Minutes, 13 April 1994, p.117.
[59] Minutes, 13 April 1994, p.118.   [60] Minutes, 13 April 1994, p.118.
[61] Minutes, 13 April 1994, p.119.   [62] Minutes, 13 April 1994, p.87.
[63] Minutes, 13 April 1994, p.87.   [64] Minutes, 13 April 1994, p.87.

dying).[65] Equally notable is the fact that at this stage and according to the minutes, the DPKO official did not seem to offer any assessment or recommend any course of action in the face of increasing bloodshed.

In the following days, Keating repeatedly queried Riza about the underlying causes of the violence. 'The media unfairly treated this as a tribal conflict', Keating noted on 12 April, but 'it is a political conflict [and surely] the imminent objective [must be] to stop the killing'[66]—what was the SG's view on this? 'The situation is chaotic', Riza is reported to have replied, and Rwanda was experiencing 'ethnic random killings'[67]—a far cry from the systematic campaign mentioned in Dallaire's cables to DPKO. This prompted Gambari to stress that, whatever the situation, 'tens of thousands of people are dying— what is the UN doing? What is the UN responsibility for the civilian population?'[68] UNAMIR had 'already taken measures to protect thousands in stadiums and schools',[69] Gambari concluded, and should continue to do so. The French ambassador agreed: it is 'not good for UNAMIR to leave' as this 'would add to the chaos [given that] UNAMIR [is] also a stabilizing factor'.[70] London and Washington were far more cautious: Hannay noted the total lack of security in Kigali and the 'urgency to reach a conclusion about UNAMIR',[71] whereas Albright pointed out that the mission was unable to fulfil its mandate.[72] A sense of stalemate thus reigned, with the result that several ambassadors made a direct appeal to Boutros-Ghali. '[Russia] urgently request[s] the SG to convey news so that [we] can take a decision tomorrow',[73] Moscow's representative stated, while the Czech ambassador noted that his country would 'reserve its position until it hears from the SG'.[74] Keating was blunter still: is the 'SG going to recommend [UNAMIR's] termination?'[75]

With Boutros-Ghali in Europe, the answer arrived by letter on 13 April. 'In light of [the] decision by the Government of Belgium [to withdraw its troops from UNAMIR following the death of ten Belgian peacekeepers], it is my assessment that it will be extremely difficult for UNAMIR to carry out its tasks effectively. I have [thus] asked my Special Representative and the Force Commander to prepare plans for the withdrawal of UNAMIR, should this prove necessary.'[76] Although Boutros-Ghali maintained that this letter was trying to 'provoke' the SC into action, the Goulding diaries paint a different picture, that of a hesitant SG who in the early stages of the Rwandan tragedy was leaning

---

[65] See Chapter 3 for details.   [66] Minutes, 12 April 1994, p.97.
[67] Minutes, 12 April 1994, p.98.   [68] Minutes, 12 April 1994, p.99.
[69] Minutes, 12 April 1994, p.99.   [70] Minutes, 12 April 1994, p.100.
[71] Minutes, 12 April 1994, p.101.   [72] Minutes, 12 April 1994, p.101.
[73] Minutes, 12 April 1994, p.102.   [74] Minutes, 12 April 1994, p.103.
[75] Minutes, 12 April 1994, p.110.
[76] Letter from the Secretary-General to the President of the Security Council, 13 April 1994, in United Nations, *The United Nations and Rwanda* (New York: Department of Public Information, 1996), p.259.

towards withdrawal. In any event, what emerges from the minutes is that ambassadors were unhappy with Boutros-Ghali's letter: 'I don't agree with the SG that because Belgium is withdrawing, UNAMIR must be withdrawn—[there is] no automatic connection',[77] France noted. Brazil, Djibouti, Spain, and even China concurred,[78] while the USA and the UK also complained—not because the SG wanted to withdraw, but because he had rebuked a fellow member state. Brussels 'had reasons for withdrawal',[79] Albright complained, while Hannay was 'disappointed'[80] that the SG's letter provided 'no altogether satisfactory response. It is not justified to place responsibility on Belgium for UNAMIR's inability to carry out its mandate', the British diplomat noted, 'and it is even more bizarre to believe that if Belgium changed [its] mind all would be well—the conditions are not there for UNAMIR to succeed. There is a practical element', Hannay concluded: 'What can the UN do? It needs to protect civilians and UNAMIR with [its] present technical means cannot achieve this.'[81] De Soto clarified that it was 'not the SG's intention to blame Belgium for the present state of affairs. What the SG meant was that UN-AMIR's tasks *as presently conceived* cannot be carried out without Belgium—UNAMIR is no longer viable',[82] so 'the SG is not submitting options as to how UNAMIR (as presently conceived) can carry out its duties'.[83] Hesitant UN officials thus appeared to lean towards withdrawal—at this stage, there was certainly no mention of UNAMIR's strengthening.

Leaving aside for a moment the merits of the SG's argument, why did Boutros-Ghali decide not to return to New York and brief the Council in person? The fact that a week after the eruption of an exceptionally virulent humanitarian crisis the top UN official had still not directly consulted the fifteen ambassadors is unusual for an SG—though not necessarily for Boutros-Ghali. A seasoned diplomat with decades of international experience and an encyclopedic phonebook, the SG was so used to dealing with presidents, prime ministers, and foreign ministers that he refused to attend the Council's informals. Chinmaya Gharekhan, his Representative to the Council, has written scathingly about the 'secret confabulations'[84] of the fifteen ambassadors, has noted that 'they are not governed by any rule',[85] and has conceded that Boutros-Ghali looked down on the Council: 'The Secretary-General always maintained that unless we in the Secretariat gave them ideas, the [SC] members would simply not know what to do. He was right.'[86] In his papers, Goulding confirms that 1994 was a difficult year for the relationship

---

[77] Minutes, 18 April 1994, p.118.   [78] Minutes, 18 April 1994, pp.119–22.
[79] Minutes, 18 April 1994, pp.119–22.   [80] Minutes, 18 April 1994, pp.119–22.
[81] Minutes, 18 April 1994, pp.119–22.
[82] Minutes, 18 April 1994, p.121 (emphasis added).   [83] Minutes, 18 April 1994, p.121.
[84] Gharekhan, p.4.   [85] Gharekhan, p.15.   [86] Gharekhan, p.253.

between SG and SC, especially the P-5,[87] noting that Boutros-Ghali's absences from the SC '. . . made it more difficult for him to "get the feel" of the Council and perhaps prevented him from seeing early enough how determined the United States was to deny him a second term'.[88] By mid-1994 the SG's relationship with the USA was so strained that Albright told senior UN officials that 'her government was "fed up" with the Secretary General'.[89] David Hannay acknowledged that tension existed: 'Pérez de Cuéllar used to sit in the . . . informals for hours, often not speaking at all, just listening. Boutros hated that and after a bit he stopped doing it. So . . . of course there was a good deal of antagonism.'[90] But the British diplomat added that such friction was 'far more strongly felt by the smaller member states than by the P-5. We could always see Boutros whenever we wanted, of course. We had no trouble. They couldn't.'[91]

At the time of the Rwandan genocide, the President of the SC was quarrelling with Boutros-Ghali precisely about the lack of direct access to the SG: 'Throughout 1993–1994', Keating wrote, 'I and some others on the Council had been in a sustained dispute with the Secretary-General about his policy of seeking to manage operations without any transparency or accountability to the Council and his personal inclination to selectively deal with only a few permanent members for discussion of difficult issues.'[92] The repeated requests for information by the E-10 to UN officials during the Rwandan crisis should thus be seen in this light.[93] It is true that Boutros-Ghali had a far heavier workload than Pérez de Cuéllar—during the latter's ten-year term the SC had adopted an average of 22.6 resolutions per annum, whereas during Boutros-Ghali's five-year stint that had trebled to 73.4. In his diaries, Goulding also wonders 'how much briefing to give to a Council whose appetite for information has become insatiable, in the apparent belief that endless informal consultations (six or seven hours a day is not abnormal) are a substitute for decisions and action'.[94] Nevertheless, for an SG who saw himself as a champion of the 'democratization' of international relations,[95] particularly in the developing world, Keating's observations are damaging. So are the frequent derogatory comments made by the SG about smaller states: 'He told me that I could not go to Myanmar [since] it was a third-rate country and

[87] MIG-TD-IX, 30-Jan-1994.
[88] Marrack Goulding, 'The UN Secretary-General', in Malone, p.276.
[89] Gharekhan, p.282.   [90] My interview with David Hannay, London, UK, 26 April 2011 (and by email on 12 May 2016).
[91] Interview with Hannay, 26 April 2010. See also David Hannay, *New World Disorder* (London: I.B. Tauris, 2008), pp.164–72.
[92] Keating, p.503.   [93] Gambari, 'Rwanda: An African Perspective', p.512.
[94] Marrack Goulding, Handover Notes for Sir Kieran Prendergast, 22 February 1997, §74 (MIG-PA).
[95] Boutros Boutros-Ghali, *An Agenda for Democratization* (New York: Department of Public Information, 1996); Boutros Boutros-Ghali, *Démocratiser la Mondialisation* (Paris: Éditions du Rocher, 2002).

unworthy of my attention',[96] Goulding wrote in his diary. In the midst of the Rwanda slaughter, after lunching with the ambassadors of the Nordic countries, Goulding came to the conclusion that they too 'feel very neglected by the SG'.[97] To Boutros-Ghali, some member states seemed to be more equal than others.

CONSENSUS: THE COUNCIL DRASTICALLY REDUCES UNAMIR

With reports of massacres multiplying and no idea about what to do, by 13 April the UK was calling for the SG to come up with clear 'options about what is realistic'.[98] These were delivered in a report on 20 April and it is on its basis that the controversial decision to reduce UNAMIR was unanimously taken the following day. Yet what happened behind the closed doors of the Consultations Room in between the commissioning and the delivery of this report? Did national positions become clearer? And what role did the SG and the Secretariat play?

Three important developments took place during that crucial April week: a rare appearance by Boutros-Ghali in the informal meetings; a shift in the French and Nigerian positions; and Belgium's lobbying for UNAMIR's departure. 'The abrupt withdrawal of UNAMIR is neither feasible, nor wise, nor possible',[99] the SG said during the 14 April consultations, while noting that a 'fundamental change in the situation [is] preventing UNAMIR from carrying out its mandate'.[100] As a result, Boutros-Ghali verbally offered three options to the SC:

1. Keep a reduced mission in place (UNAMIR without Belgium) [and] inform [the parties] that they have three weeks to reach an agreement and return to the Arusha peace process;

2. Total withdrawal [if it is] not sustainable to maintain UNAMIR;

3. A combination of the two.
   Option 1 is the SG's preference and could slide into Option 2.[101]

Rather than bringing clarity, however, this statement left the door open to a range of possibilities—except for UNAMIR's strengthening, which as Gharekhan has admitted at this stage Boutros-Ghali did not even mention (let alone

[96] MIG-TD-XI, 9-Nov-1994.   [97] MIG-TD-X, 15 June 1994.
[98] Minutes, 13 April 1994, 4.30pm, p.124.   [99] Minutes, 14 April 1994, p.127.
[100] Minutes, 14 April 1994, p.127.   [101] Minutes, 14 April 1994, p.128.

recommend) as an option.[102] If anything, the SG's advice appears to have convinced France and Nigeria to accept a *reduction* of UNAMIR—albeit a largely inevitable one following Belgium's departure. '[I] prefer the first option', Mérimée stated, 'but it would have to be in safety and serving some useful purpose'—'[France is] prepared to accept the first option but is ready to reconsider if there is no progress.'[103] Speaking for the Non-Aligned Movement, Gambari 'like[d] the first option because UNAMIR cannot do what is doing'[104]—although ten years later the Nigerian diplomat would criticize his own decision as 'disastrous'.[105] Whatever the intention of the SG, his appearance in the Consultations Room contributed to cool—rather than embolden— the Council's most 'interventionist' members, especially since few countries were prepared (e.g. the USA) or able (e.g. Nigeria) to send peacekeepers to Rwanda.

Belgium's lobbying for withdrawal was another significant development. Brussels had been traumatized by the murder of ten of its highly skilled—and UNAMIR's best trained—peacekeepers: 'For any UN personnel to remain . . . would be risky and [there would be] grave consequences for their safety',[106] Belgium's Foreign Minister wrote in a letter to the Council which was strongly resented by the Non-Aligned Movement. '[I] note the special relationship between Belgium and Rwanda both historically and at present', Gambari stated, 'but with all due respect—however weighty their advice is—a former colonial country cannot dictate to the SC how to respond to [this] tragedy.'[107] Despite Nigeria's protestations, the murder of Belgium's peacekeepers further deterred those who might have been able to provide troops, especially since the circumstances of those deaths in Kigali looked eerily similar to those in which eighteen US rangers had been killed in Mogadishu in October 1993. As if this were not enough, the third week of April was proving to be problematic on another critical UN front: 'In BH [Bosnia-Herzegovina] the use of airpower against Bosnian Serbs . . . has led to the sort of reaction which many of us had always predicted, putting at risk the whole UNPROFOR operation',[108] Goulding wrote in his diary on 15 April, pointing out that DPKO officials were at the time facing immense pressure.[109] Back in the Consultations Room, meanwhile, Albright noted that 'hopefully conditions will change and a different approach [will become necessary, but if the USA were] called to make a decision *today*, there is no role which can be played by UNAMIR'.[110] Despite this stance, Boutros-Ghali's informal recommendation drew the approval of a majority of the Council (Nigeria, France, Rwanda, Oman, Djibouti, China, Brazil, Pakistan,

---

[102] Gharekhan, p.257.   [103] Minutes, 14 April 1994, p.128.
[104] Minutes, 14 April 1994, p.133.   [105] Gambari, 'Rwanda: An African Perspective', p.512.
[106] Minutes, 15 April 1994, AM Session, p.134.
[107] Minutes, 15 April 1994, AM Session, p.136.   [108] MIG-TD-X, 15-Apr-1994.
[109] MIG-TD-X, 15-Apr-1994.   [110] MIG-TD-X, 15-Apr-1994 (emphasis added).

and Spain). After the SG's intervention and the murder of the Belgian peace-keepers, however, strengthening UNAMIR was clearly off the table.

Two other factors led ambassadors to be increasingly sceptical about UNAMIR's chances of success, the first being a further deterioration of security. 'It is irresponsible for anyone to urge anyone else to stay',[111] Albright stated, before noting that '[we] will make further action in Africa harder if [there is] a slaughter [of UN troops].'[112] Conveying the mood in DPKO and among troop-contributing countries, Riza agreed that 'Belgium's assessment [must be taken] very seriously, I don't think it can be ignored',[113] and even Keating noted that while there was no question of 'abandoning Rwanda, [the Council] has very short [leeway]'.[114] Equally important in steering the fifteen ambassadors towards a reduction of UNAMIR was the picture painted by the SG's Representative to the Council: on 18 April Gharekhan offered the bleakest portrait of Rwanda yet, reporting that 'massacres continued in Kigali [and that] the humanitarian situation deteriorates and is becoming very serious'.[115] He reiterated these points the following day, when he also expressed doubts about the mission's viability: 'Under these circumstances', he stated, 'it is almost impossible for UNAMIR to carry out its mandate.'[116]

Given this situation, the SG's report to the Council of 21 April 1994 came as no surprise and sealed the deal in terms of reducing UNAMIR. After noting that 'tens of thousands of deaths'[117] might have occurred, Boutros-Ghali blamed—wrongly—'unruly members of the Presidential Guard'[118] and pointed out that 'the most urgent [task] is the effort to secure a cease-fire'[119] between the Rwandan parties, a position that—as noted in Chapter 4—reflected what Booh Booh had been recommending to DPA and the EOSG, rather than what Dallaire had been reporting to DPKO.[120] The SG then offered, in writing, three options to the Council which differed from those he had informally and verbally suggested a week earlier. The first option consisted in the 'immediate and massive reinforcement of UNAMIR and a change in mandate so that it would be equipped and authorized to coerce the opposing forces into a ceasefire, and to attempt to restore law and order and to put an end to the killings'.[121] This, Boutros-Ghali noted, 'would require several thousand add-itional troops and UNAMIR might have to be given enforcement powers under Chapter VII of the UN Charter'[122]—the dreaded Somalia approach. The second alternative would reduce UNAMIR to 'a small group headed by the Force Commander...to act as intermediary between the parties in an

---

[111] MIG-TD-X, 15-Apr-1994, p.142.   [112] MIG-TD-X, 15-Apr-1994, p.142.
[113] Minutes, 15 April 1994, PM Session, p.145.
[114] Minutes, 15 April 1994, PM Session, p.146.   [115] Minutes, 18 April 1994, p.151.
[116] Minutes, 19 April 1994, 4.30pm, p.12.   [117] S/1994/470, 20 April 1994, §3.
[118] S/1994/470, 20 April 1994, §5.   [119] S/1994/470, 20 April 1994, §7.
[120] See Part II for details.   [121] S/1994/470, 20 April 1994, §13.
[122] S/1994/470, 20 April 1994, §13.

attempt to bring them to an agreement on a ceasefire'.[123] A total of 270 peacekeepers would remain in Rwanda while 'the remainder of UNAMIR personnel would be withdrawn but UNAMIR, as a mission, would continue to exist'.[124] The third option—withdrawal—'was not favored by the SG',[125] and while Boutros-Ghali expressed no preference between Option 1 or Option 2, most ambassadors—particularly from the E-10[126]—thought that the SG was recommending Option 2. A diplomatic cable from the French ambassador in New York reached the same conclusion: 'The SG's report has been released today. Unlike his first intervention, Mr Boutros-Ghali presented three options but discarded the first (Chapter VII and several thousand troops) and the third (total withdrawal of UNAMIR). He thus recommended, without ambiguity, the second option which consists in keeping in Kigali a small group of approximately 270 people, under the current Force Commander.'[127]

How did the Council react to the SG's report? After complaining that there was 'no political will or resources for Alternative 1'[128] and that 'Africa was being treated with a different yardstick',[129] Gambari conceded that he 'may be able to live with Option 2':[130] Nigeria 'cannot contemplate total withdrawal and the immediate death sentence of 14,000 under UNAMIR protection',[131] he added. Hannay, who described himself as 'mildly disappointed' with the SG's report, noted that London would 'prefer [to hear] a clear choice on the basis of the Force Commander and Special Representative [since] we are not as good a forum as the FC, SRSG and SG'.[132] In response to Gambari, Hannay also pointed out that Option 1 was 'not on the cards [and] impractical not because [there are] no troops but [because], to think back to Somalia, what would we ask them to do? Wage war against the RPF or RGF, take over the country completely and deal with two heavily armed groups? [Option 1] is impractical not because of a lack of resources', the British diplomat concluded, 'but because it is not feasible.'[133] The USA concurred: on 15 April, Secretary of State Warren Christopher had written to Madeleine Albright that 'there is insufficient justification to retain a UN peacekeeping presence in Rwanda and the international community must give highest priority to full, orderly withdrawal of all UNAMIR personnel as soon as possible'.[134] Her initial instructions were thus to terminate UNAMIR, but she managed to have

[123] S/1994/470, 20 April 1994, §15.   [124] S/1994/470, 20 April 1994, §16.
[125] S/1994/470, 20 April 1994, §19.   [126] S/1994/470, 20 April 1994, §19.
[127] Télégramme Diplomatique, Réduction des Effectifs de MINUAR, 22 April 1994, 'Annexes', p.305 (MIPR).
[128] Minutes, 21 April 1994, 4pm, p.24.   [129] Minutes, 21 April 1994, 4pm, p.24.
[130] Minutes, 21 April 1994, 4pm, p.24.   [131] Minutes, 21 April 1994, 4pm, p.24.
[132] Minutes, 21 April 1994, 4pm, p.25.   [133] Minutes, 21 April 1994, 4pm, p.25.
[134] Code Cable from SECSTATE WASHDC to USUN, 15 April 1994, §4, available at http://nsarchive.gwu.edu/ageofgenocide/VOLUME%202%20COMPLETE.pdf (accessed 15 November 2016).

them changed and eventually supported Option 2 rather than Option 3.[135] So did China and Djibouti, which defined it as the 'most reasonable [option]'.[136] 'It is not our preferred one', Brazil acknowledged, 'but [we] bow to certain realities [in that the UN should be] resuming traditional peacekeeping with the consent of the parties.'[137] The latter comment is particularly significant if one bears in mind the parallel travails the UN was undergoing in the Former Yugoslavia, where Western ambassadors were actively pushing the SG to be far more aggressive. As a result of this, by early 1994 Boutros-Ghali was clashing not only with the North Atlantic Treaty Organization (NATO) leadership but also with most Western capitals, including Paris: 'The SG, with Madame and party, arrived from Paris at 2215 hrs', Goulding wrote in his diary in January 1994. 'He was very tired . . . very agitated by a difficult meeting he had had *à trois* with Balladur (PM) and Juppé (FM) immediately before leaving Paris',[138] and ' . . . distressed by the terrible press he is receiving in France'.[139] Boutros-Ghali's relations with Washington were worse still: 'Madeleine Albright pushed for air strikes', Goulding wrote, 'especially for Tuzla and Srebrenica, in total disregard for the political and military realities.'[140] For the SG, such activism in Bosnia contrasted sharply with Washington's stance on UNAMIR,[141] resulting in a serious crisis between the UN and NATO in May 1994.[142]

   Back in New York, meanwhile, the Council felt increasingly pressured by the media. The Argentinean ambassador pointed to 'reports in the press and public opinion that there is indifference by the UN about what is happening there. [We must] make it clear that we are not indifferent but [that we just] can't do anything about it.'[143] His Spanish colleague concurred, noting that the SG's 'report clearly indicates the course to take: [we must] translate Option 2 into a Resolution'.[144] At the end of the discussion, Gambari conceded that while '[it] undermines the credibility of the UN to reduce [UNAMIR] to the minimum, [the UN] needs to carry on the intermediating efforts [and to retain] a political presence'.[145] He and his colleagues then left the Consultations Room, took their seats around the horseshoe table, and unanimously voted Resolution 912 reducing UNAMIR from 2,500 to 270.

REGRET: THE COUNCIL STRENGTHENS UNAMIR

The best indication that several ambassadors were uncomfortable with Resolution 912 lies with its ninth paragraph: 'The Council states its readiness to

---

[135] Code Cable from SECSTATE WASHDC to USUN, 15 April 1994, §26.
[136] Minutes, 21 April 1994, 4pm, p.26.   [137] Minutes, 21 April 1994, 4pm, p.26.
[138] MIG-TD-IX, 12-Jan-1994.   [139] MIG-TD-IX, 24-Jan-1994.
[140] MIG-TD-IX, 23-Jan-1994.   [141] MIG-TD-X, 1-May-1994.
[142] MIG-TD-X, 1-May-1994.   [143] Minutes, 21 April 1994, 4pm, p.42.
[144] Minutes, 21 April 1994, 4pm, p.27.   [145] Minutes, 21 April 1994, p.30.

consider promptly any recommendations which the Secretary-General may make concerning the force level and mandate of the Mission in the light of developments'.[146] Such developments—including the acknowledgement that Rwanda was engulfed in genocide—led the SC to make a U-turn only three weeks later, on 17 May, when ambassadors strengthened UNAMIR from 270 to 5,500. Once again, it is important to understand what happened in between these two resolutions—and, once more, the best indications come from the Consultations Room.

While the extent to which Council members were aware of the Rwandan events remains disputed, after the passage of Resolution 912 ambassadors felt increasingly under pressure to act. 'The members had been suffering from a guilt complex', Gharekhan wrote. 'They wanted "to do something" to demonstrate to others, and to themselves, that they were concerned.'[147] By late April, Keating was worried enough to note that the 'slaughter of innocent civilians increases' and went so far as to say that Rwanda was 'a shameful situation offending all norms of civilized behavior'.[148] The Czech ambassador shared this outrage, pointing out that '80% of [our] preoccupation [has been] on getting UNAMIR out and 20% on [the] ceasefire—[we] did not focus on the slaughter [despite] much information from the NGOs'.[149] Even the USA was 'increasingly stunned', Albright acknowledged, and the pictures coming out of Rwanda are 'hard to believe at the end of the 20th century'.[150] The Russian ambassador agreed—'100,000 are dying [and yet we are] taking very timid steps'[151]—while Hannay spoke of an 'appalling situation' but was quick to point out that 'non-Africans can't be in the lead of this—we have spent the last weeks removing non-Africans from Rwanda—but Africa legitimate[ly] looks at the UN for a joint approach to helping'.[152] By the end of April, with reports of massacres multiplying, the Council thus found itself in a quandary: ambassadors did not know what to do, yet doing nothing was no longer an option. As the Argentinean representative put it, '[We have] a serious moral problem'.[153]

By then such a problem was also being openly recognized by the SG.[154] On 29 April, Boutros-Ghali informed the Council of ongoing 'massacres' and noted that 'as many as 200,000 people may have died during the last three weeks'.[155] For this reason, he wrote, 'I urge the SC to re-examine the decisions which it took in Resolution 912 and to consider again what action, including forceful action, it could take . . . to end the massacres.'[156] This was the first official and unambiguous attempt by the SG to urge intervention from the fifteen ambassadors, the moment when Boutros-Ghali abandoned his

[146] Res 912 (S/RES/912), 21 April 1994, §9.   [147] Gharekhan, p.244.
[148] Minutes, Late April 1994, p.81.   [149] Minutes, Late April 1994, p.81.
[150] Minutes, Late April 1994, p.82.   [151] Minutes, Late April 1994, p.83.
[152] Minutes, Late April 1994, p.84.   [153] Minutes, Late April 1994, p.87.
[154] Gharekhan, p.244.   [155] Res 518 (S/1994/518), 29 April 1994, §4.
[156] Res 518, §9.

ambivalence and started puncturing the SC in the process. 'In making this recommendation', the SG noted, 'I am of course aware that such action would require a commitment of human and material resources on a scale which Member States have so far proved reluctant to contemplate. But I am convinced that the scale of human suffering in Rwanda and its implications for the stability of neighboring countries leave the Council with no alternative but to examine this possibility.'[157] For this reason, Goulding wrote, Boutros-Ghali sent letters 'to a dozen African leaders asking if they would contribute troops to a regional effort to restore law and order in Rwanda'.[158] The SG's missive led Keating to hint, in a statement on the Council's behalf, that genocide may have been committed in Rwanda, though he stopped short of using the word directly: 'The Security Council recalls that the killing of members of an ethnic group with the intention of destroying such a group in whole or in part constitutes a crime punishable under international law.'[159] Though belatedly, the *génocidaires* were warned.

Back in the Consultations Room, meanwhile, ambassadors were still agonizing over possible action. The USA 'continue to be deeply distressed and agree with the SG's letter . . . looking at possible action in Rwanda',[160] Albright stated, before suggesting that the African Union should get involved. The UK concurred but pointed out that 'a lot of care [is] needed about [the words] "intervention" or "use of force" or the SG's "forceful means". [We should exercise] caution because [we] won't get many [troop-contributing countries] involved', Hannay noted, adding that 'maybe we should talk about SC action as "support" rather than intervention?'[161] Reflecting Russia's shift in its peacekeeping policy, Moscow disagreed and argued in favour of a Chapter VII operation 'to provide emergency humanitarian assistance to Rwandese refugees in neighboring countries',[162] while New Zealand noted that '[we] must contemplate "forceful action" to reinstate order—the SG today has been more helpful', Keating stated, 'but we need a further proposal.'[163] As for Nigeria, Gambari reiterated that it was 'shameful for the SC to miss an opportunity for action',[164] while France concurred with the SG's letter but also noted that any operation was 'not to pursue political goals, [a] ceasefire or [a] peacekeeping role, [but] humanitarian objectives only'.[165] This led the USA to express 'serious doubts about a large peacekeeping operation with [a] mandate to pacify the population': Washington, Albright said, had 'several problems with it, including the fact that neither the UN nor the OAU [Organization of African Unity] demonstrates the capability to do this with success; that it is

---

[157] S/1994/518, 29 April 1994, §9.   [158] MIG-TD-X, 2-May-1994.
[159] S/PRST/1994/21, 30 April 1994, §3.   [160] Minutes, 3 May 1994, p.108.
[161] Minutes, 3 May 1994, p.109.   [162] Minutes, 3 May 1994, p.109.
[163] Minutes, 3 May 1994, p.109.   [164] Minutes, 3 May 1994, p.109.
[165] Minutes, 11 May 1994, p.130.

unclear whether the [Rwandan] parties would use force to oppose [it]; that it is unlikely that there will be sufficient pledges to maintain large operations; and that there will be logistical problems.'[166] Any mission should thus be based *outside* of Rwanda, a position that Albright's colleagues dismissed outright. Although the Council remained divided, ambassadors were at least converging on the need for a humanitarian operation.

On 13 May 1994, Boutros-Ghali wrote to the Council recommending intervention because 'nearly 2 million persons have been displaced'.[167] In his view, a new, 5,500-strong humanitarian operation called UNAMIR II was necessary: 'The world community has witnessed with horror and disbelief the slaughter and suffering of innocent civilians in Rwanda [and] the international community cannot ignore the atrocious effects of this conflict on innocent civilians', he wrote. 'I therefore recommend to the SC that it approve the phased expansion of UNAMIR to enable the mission immediately to help alleviate the humanitarian crisis in Rwanda.'[168] Four days later, the fifteen ambassadors approved UNAMIR II, the aim of which was to 'contribute to the security and protection of displaced persons, refugees and civilians at risk in Rwanda'.[169] However, full-scale enforcement under Chapter VII was only provided for arms embargoes—the subject of heated debates during the previous day's consultations. 'Make sure [that UNAMIR II does not have] full scale enforcement', the Spanish ambassador had urged, while Hannay had pointed out that 'here [we must] try to focus on what will be welcomed by all parties'[170] lest Rwanda become another Somalia, where there was an 'inability to secure the harbor [and where] we got stuck for months'.[171] The Czech ambassador agreed: 'It is clear from the SG that UNAMIR falls within Chapter 6—[it would be] unrealistic to get [it] under Chapter 7',[172] while Albright noted that the resolution should 'authorize UNAMIR to use force as necessary to protect persons', but added that the USA 'does not agree to Chapter 7-type language'.[173] More than a month after the start of the massacres, states were still dreading a Somalia-style failure. The end result was the cautious language of Resolution 918.

LEADERSHIP, CONSENSUS, LEGITIMACY

'I wish sometimes that we had the documentation for the closed sessions of the Council on critical issues like [Rwanda] that have become really

---

[166] Minutes, 11 May 1994, p.131.   [167] S/1994/565, 13 May 1994.
[168] S/1994/565, 13 May 1994, §31.   [169] Res 918 (S/RES/918), 17 May 1994, §3a.
[170] Minutes, 12 May 1994, p.144.   [171] Minutes, 12 May 1994, p.145.
[172] Minutes, 12 May 1994, p.146.   [173] Minutes, 13 May 1994, 10.30 am, p.151.

of tremendous interest and have consequences for international peace and security',[174] Gambari stated. Jonah agrees: 'None knows what future scholars will find when they try to closely examine how the Security Council dealt with such sensitive issues as [Yugoslavia or Rwanda, for] no meaningful official records of the Security Council proceedings will exist on these and other important issues.'[175]

This documentation is now available and several conclusions can be drawn from it, the first being the Council's distinctive lack of leadership during the crisis. Rather than supporting the widespread perception of diplomats cynically united in their determination to leave Rwanda and UNAMIR to their destiny, the informal consultations suggest considerable uncertainty and procrastination in New York. Both the decision to reduce *and* to expand UNAMIR were reached after the Council had repeatedly sought the advice of the SG. Indeed, at almost every stage of the process ambassadors appeared in need of guidance, something that Boutros-Ghali was initially unwilling to provide. His reluctance to participate in the informal meetings made interactions between Secretariat and SC—two of the UN's principal organs—unnecessarily strained. Obviously this does not mean that the SG would have succeeded in pushing states to strengthen UNAMIR—had they wanted to, they would have intervened regardless of his views. But the fact that his formal advice was both sought *and* heeded at virtually every step of the process gave the SG more influence than is generally assumed.[176]

A second point concerns 'national interests'. While much is made in the international relations literature of the Council as the highest expression of *realpolitik*, the informals only partly support this view. Ambassadors clearly defended what they perceived to be their countries' priorities (non-involvement in the case of the USA, engagement in the case of France) and their positions were certainly affected by domestic political considerations (a hostile Congress in Washington, an interventionist president in Paris). Nevertheless, the stance of all states—including, indeed especially, the most powerful ones—evolved considerably during the Council's informal discussions. Despite the existence of stringent post-Somalia restrictions on new peacekeeping operations, Washington found itself increasingly isolated and its position appeared so out of touch with the rest of the Council that Albright insisted on having it changed.[177] As a result the USA, as the world's superpower at the time, ended up agreeing on precisely the kind of sizeable peacekeeping operation in a faraway place devoid of any strategic American significance

[174] Gambari, *PBS Frontline Interview*, 15 January 2004.

[175] Jonah, 'Differing State Perspectives', p.12.

[176] David Ambrosetti, *Normes et Rivalités Diplomatiques à l'ONU* (Brussels: Peter Lang, 2009).

[177] Albright, p.150.

that Clinton had warned against only a few months earlier.[178] Consensus and legitimacy, it seems, were more important to Washington than its ability to wield a veto.[179] Furthermore, the old adage, according to which when a representative of the King sits on the board his or her vote constitutes a majority, does not accurately describe Albright's role on the Council. France's position, too, changed considerably during the debates: notwithstanding its failed bid to retain a full-strength UNAMIR in Rwanda—and despite witnessing its francophone Hutu allies overthrown by its anglophone Tutsi arch-enemies—Paris had little 'currency' on the Council, never threatened a veto, and, like the USA, ended up voting in a way that was hardly in its 'national interest'. As for smaller countries like New Zealand and Nigeria, despite being vocal during the debates, they voted for a resolution which they largely disliked. As it has been noted, under certain circumstances institutions can be instruments of political control,[180] especially high profile ones such as the UN Security Council. Back in 1994, the latter's decisions expressed something more than the narrow interests of its members, not least because of the process of socialization of national diplomats into the Council's unique environment.[181]

What else did the informals reflect? Media pressure was one factor, for not only were ambassadors acutely aware that the eyes of the world were upon them, they often expressed concern about the impact of their decisions (and *in*-decision) on the reputation of the UN and the Council. There is an irony here, for ambassadors retreat to the Consultations Room precisely in order to shelter themselves from the media. Yet the latter seemed to follow them everywhere—figuratively if not physically—and it did appear to matter in several ways. To begin with, media pressure reportedly contributed to mollify the previously rigid stances of some capitals (there are indications, for instance, that Albright used both the media and the Council's opposition to a complete withdrawal in order to have her instructions changed).[182] Second, such pressure could conceivably have been used by the SG and Secretariat to push ambassadors to react more swiftly during the darkest hours of the killings, especially given that much of the SG's influence lies with his or her 'bully pulpit' prerogative.[183] As Part II will suggest, a major debate in

---

[178] The White House, Presidential Decision Directive No.25 Establishing U.S. Policy on Reforming Multilateral Peace Operations, available at https://fas.org/irp/offdocs/pdd/pdd-25.pdf (accessed 2 July 2015).

[179] Rosemary Foot, Stephen MacFarlane, and Michael Mastanduno, *US Hegemony and International Organizations* (Oxford: Oxford University Press, 2003), esp. p.51. See also Yves Buchet de Neuilly, 'Devenir Diplomate Multilatéral', in David Ambrosetti et al., eds, *Crises et Organisations Internationales* (Paris: L'Harmattan, 2009), p.79.

[180] Foot et al., p.51.

[181] Ambrosetti, *Normes et Rivalités Diplomatiques à l'ONU*, esp. ch.IV.

[182] Albright, pp.150-1.

[183] Leon Gordenker, *The UN Secretary-General and Secretariat* (Abingdon: Routledge, 2010); Simon Chesterman, ed., *Secretary or General?* (Cambridge: Cambridge University Press, 2007).

normative theory and the theory of humanitarian intervention revolves around the discussion of whether decisions for action and inaction should be based on assessments of what is 'possible', 'realistically achievable', and 'likely to be successful'.[184] The Rwanda tragedy suggests that assessments of this kind can be: (a) inaccurate; (b) founded on problematic assumptions about what states and the SC 'want' (e.g. the 'anticipatory veto'); and (c) intertwined with self-interest. The Council's informal discussions on Rwanda show how problematic it is to base one's moral arguments solely—or even mostly—on assessments of what is 'possible'. The 'possible' should be taken into account, but it is a notoriously tricky and subjective yardstick which should neither circumscribe nor overshadow other considerations (such as the 'just').[185]

The secret consultations are also instructive in relation to the issue of 'indifference'.[186] The informal meetings do not support the view of Council members cynically ignoring the fate of Rwandans; indeed, ambassadors seemed to be concerned about the situation and repeatedly asked the SG and Secretariat to be briefed about it. While a plausible argument can be made that states knew far more about Rwanda than the SG and Secretariat officials, this was only partly the case. It is true that the largest nations had embassies in Kigali and were knowledgeable about the situation there. Yet the complete breakdown of law and order following the presidential air crash meant that most of those diplomats were evacuated as soon as the massacres began, while the few who remained had limited contact with the outside world.[187] More importantly and unlike the P-5, the Council's elected members did not have diplomats in either Kigali or on the upper floors of the UN Secretariat (such as in DPA or DPKO). They clearly resented their lack of direct access to the SG, another factor that makes Boutros-Ghali's reluctance to attend the informals problematic. 'In the absence of good information from the Secretariat', Keating wrote, 'I began having personal meetings [with NGOs. Gharekhan's] oral reports significantly muddied the waters. The media, the NGOs, and the force commander had a much clearer view of the situation'.[188] The fact that the Council's President felt the need to ring an outside Rwanda expert—rather than Secretariat officials—on a Sunday morning to be briefed about what was actually going on in Rwanda confirms

[184] Richard Price, ed., *Moral Limit and Possibility in World Politics* (Cambridge: Cambridge University Press, 2008); Judith Gardam, *Necessity, Proportionality and the Use of Force by States* (Cambridge: Cambridge University Press, 2011); Stefano Recchia and Jennifer Welsh, *Just and Unjust Military Intervention* (Cambridge: Cambridge University Press, 2013).

[185] Don Scheid, *The Ethics of Humanitarian Intervention* (Cambridge: Cambridge University Press, 2014).

[186] Barnett, pp.551–78.

[187] David Ambrosetti, *La France au Rwanda* (Paris: Karthala, 2001).

[188] Keating, p.506.

the neglect felt by the E-10.[189] It also suggests that the SG and Secretariat could have done more to brief the Council as a whole, rather than a part of it. 'It is true that the Secretariat followed existing conventions in reporting to the Council and that its sources of information were very limited', Keating wrote. 'But there were a large number of people in academia, in NGOs, in private life, and in the UN agencies who knew much more about Rwanda. Had the Council been exposed to a slice of this wisdom, it might have proceeded quite differently at a later time when confronted with the crisis.'[190]

In light of the above, an argument can also be made that, given the circumstances of 1994, the decision to reduce UNAMIR was not, *at the time when it was made*, illogical. Faced with unreliable parties, a weak mandate, an undermanned and under-resourced mission, a deteriorating security situation, the deaths of several peacekeepers, and the shadow of Somalia, the choice to temporarily reduce UNAMIR after putting the Rwandan politicians on notice may even have been sensible. Throughout the activist period of the 1990s, the Council only authorized military action when there was a prior offer by a state or group of states to lead that action; whether there were nations willing to provide troops was thus the key determinant on whether the SC acted.[191] In the absence of such an offer, arguably, no muscular Council action was possible, and Somalia had made that offer much harder to come by. On the other hand, and critically, the decision to reduce UNAMIR became morally problematic—as well as legally questionable—as soon as it emerged that *genocide* was taking place. Understanding this complex balance between political, moral, and legal considerations requires us to widen our perspective and to look into a number of cross-Secretariat processes which not only affected the UN organization in the early 1990s, but that arguably still influence it to this day.

[189] Alison Des Forges, *PBS Frontline Interview*, 1 October 2003.   [190] Keating, p.501.
[191] Malone, Parts 2 and 4. See also Vaughan Lowe et al., eds, *The United Nations Security Council and War* (Oxford: Oxford University Press, 2008).

Part II

Processes

The preceding analysis of the five structures involved in the Rwandan geno-cide leaves a number of questions unanswered, both in relation to UNAMIR and to the way the SG and Secretariat conceptualized and conducted peace operations in the early 1990s. What did Boutros-Ghali mean exactly by 'political' and 'technical' activities? What role did individuals (as opposed to bureaucratic structures) play during the Rwanda events? What does the experience of UNAMIR tell us about the Secretariat's institutional history? What are the precise functions of DPA and DPKO in peace operations? And what are supposed to be the borders—both at the practical and conceptual level—between peacekeeping and peacebuilding? UNAMIR was hardly the first mission to struggle with such issues, but it does have a special place within UN institutional history because of its human costs but also because it was one of the first peacekeeping operations to bear the brunt of Boutros-Ghali's restructuring and of his conceptualization of peace missions, both of which still largely stand.

The five structures mentioned in Part I differed from each other and were supposedly responsible for distinct parts of the Rwanda mission. However, they were also linked by several processes, or patterns of interaction.[1] After having carried out a post-mortem of the different components of the UN Secretariat in Rwanda in Part I, Part II will thus broaden the perspective and concentrate on the 'body' as a whole. Some of the interest and difficulty of international organization lies with the fact that national and international administrations differ—in how they relate to the organs that dictate their policy, for instance, but also in the ability of their executive heads to influence those policies.[2] In highlighting five cross-Secretariat processes that affected the UN bureaucracy of 1994, Part II will move away from the narrow confines of the Rwanda mission and will consider a number of larger issues that affected the UN in the 1990s. From a 'micro-history' of the UN Secretariat in Rwanda,

[1] Joseph Nye, *Understanding International Conflict* (New York: Pearson, 2005), p.37.
[2] Stephen Goodspeed, *The Nature and Function of International Organization* (New York: Oxford University Press, 1967), p.380.

therefore, the book aims to suggest the contours of a 'macro-history' of the Secretariat as a whole—a way of proceeding which is faithful to the historical fact that structures (such as DPKO and DPA) developed in New York *before* processes (such as peacekeeping and peacebuilding) could be tested in the field.

The first such process is bureaucracy. The dysfunctions of DPA and DPKO in Rwanda should be seen within the context of broader attempts by Boutros-Ghali to disenfranchise the UN bureaucracy from member states. Chapter 6 will thus return to the issue of bureaucratic competition in New York by considering the attempts made by Boutros-Ghali in 1992–94 to limit the influence of states over the Secretariat. UN intelligence was the most visible product of this effort and will be reviewed in Chapter 7. While intelligence has always been a sensitive issue in New York, this was especially the case in 1993–94. Then, reflecting the truism that information is power, UN intelligence became the arena for a rivalry between an assertive SG and guarded UN members, a state of affairs that both DPA and DPKO used to expand their functions. Chapter 8 will assess how UN officials handled the Rwanda crisis in light of the challenges of the early 1990s, while Chapter 9 will consider the 'moral authority' of Boutros-Ghali, arguably one of two sources of the SG's 'influence' (the other being oversight over the UN bureaucracy). Lastly, Chapter 10 will highlight the contested concepts of peacebuilding and peacekeeping.

6

Bureaucracy

Although bureaucracy is essential to the modern state, its role within it is contested.[1] Even more controversial is its relevance within international organizations (IOs) in general and the UN in particular. While the impact of bureaucracy at the state level has attracted the attention of scholars since the nineteenth century, international bureaucracies have only recently become objects of academic study.[2] This reflects the relatively recent rise of IOs but also a growing awareness that, far from merely executing the wishes of governments, IOs can under certain conditions be 'self-directed actors'.[3] Writing in the early twentieth century, Max Weber focussed on *verband* or organization, a concept of wide significance that included states, parties, churches, and firms. For Weber, *verband* was an ordering of social relations, and he saw a hierarchical chief and an administrative staff as the key traits of such an organization.[4] Also essential for him was the existence of an *ordnung*, a set of rules governing the behaviour within the organization, including the legal authority of the chief over its staff. For Weber, the combination of these three factors—a chief, an administrative staff, and a set of rules—formed a bureaucracy, a feature of the modern world that was then on the rise. 'The development of modern organizational forms in all spheres (state, church, army, party, the economy, interest groups, voluntary associations, charitable bodies, or whatever) is simply identical to the development and continuous increase of bureaucratic administration',[5] Weber wrote.

---

[1] B. Guy Peters, *The Politics of Bureaucracy* (Abingdon: Routledge, 2009); Charles Goodsell, *The New Case for Bureaucracy* (Thousand Oaks, CA: CQ Press, 2014); Kenneth Meier, *Politics and the Bureaucracy* (Belmont, CA: Wadsworth Publishing, 2006).

[2] Michael Barnett and Martha Finnemore, 'The Politics, Power, and Pathologies of International Organizations', *International Organization*, Vol.53, No.4 (1999), pp.699–732; David Beetham, *Bureaucracy* (Minneapolis: Minnesota University Press, 1966).

[3] Martin Albrow, *Bureaucracy* (London: Macmillan, 1970).

[4] Max Weber, *The Theory of Social and Economic Organization* (Oxford: Oxford University Press, 1947).

[5] Weber, p.337.

Most theories of bureaucratic organization, including Weber's, identify as an 'ideal' form of bureaucracy one that involves the following seven features:

(a) *impersonality*, or the fact that staff members only fulfil the duties of their offices;

(b) *hierarchy*, or a chain of command for offices and clear reporting lines between them;

(c) *role separation*, or a situation where the offices' functions are clearly delineated;

(d) *contracts* on the basis of which officials are appointed;

(e) *professional qualifications*, and a competitive entry into the system;

(f) *salary* and career structures;

(g) a *disciplinary system*.

For Weber, these were the requirements which a bureaucracy needed in order to exercise authority over—and attract the obedience of—individuals. What distinguishes 'power' (*Macht*) from 'authority', in Weber's view, was the fact that obedience to an organization depends on a belief in its legitimacy, whereas 'power' can be enforced despite people's resistance to it. Although some of Weber's ideas can easily be applied to the UN bureaucracy and the international civil service, others are more difficult to square with it. In the context of Rwanda, two Weberian ideas that pose some challenges are the existence in the Secretariat of a hierarchy of offices, and the delineation of well-defined spheres of competences.

This chapter questions the effectiveness of these two features in the UN Secretariat of 1994 by taking a closer look at the origins of the bureaucratic confrontation between DPA and DPKO in the early 1990s. This was a critical period for the UN Secretariat, a time when both Pérez de Cuéllar and Boutros-Ghali took advantage of the opportunities arising from the collapse of the USSR, the end of the Cold War, and the demise of a bi-polar system. These two officials shared a vision—strengthening the role of the SG—but used different bureaucratic tools to achieve it, for while Pérez de Cuéllar kept peacekeeping and peacebuilding firmly under the purview of his Executive Office, Boutros-Ghali created two new entities, DPA and DPKO. Importantly for the events leading up to 1994, as UNAMIR was being considered, Boutros-Ghali also redefined the roles of these two departments, so that DPA became his 'political' office and was charged with substantive decision-making responsibility ('the big picture'), whereas DPKO was largely meant to be downgraded to 'operational' tasks. Although this distinction was partly based on Boutros-Ghali's desire to increase the SG's influence over the Secretariat, it turned out to be problematic and it further increased friction between two key UN departments in a way that still affects the Secretariat today.[6] Fresh documents from the Goulding Archive also suggest that while the DPA–DPKO competition manifested itself in bureaucratic fashion from as early as 1992, it was the result of a larger phenomenon, namely, the SG's attempt to disenfranchise itself from member states through what Boutros-Ghali saw as a powerful 'political' office to be opposed to the 'operational'—and, in his view, US-dominated—DPKO.

PÉREZ DE CUÉLLAR: CARVING OUT A 'POLITICAL' ROLE FOR THE SG

One of the ironies surrounding the birth of the UN after the Second World War is that its Secretariat was meant to have a humble role. In 1945, upon the recommendation of the Preparatory Commission for the United Nations, the General Assembly (GA) required the SG to 'take immediate steps to establish an administrative organization which will permit the effective discharge of his administrative and general responsibilities under the Charter and the efficient performance of those functions and services required to meet the needs of the several organs of the United Nations'.[7] The Assembly also decided that the new Secretariat was to have a slim structure, with only six departments and two services in addition to the Executive Office of the Secretary-General.[8] Of these six departments, only two were meant to possess what UN insiders and documents routinely refer to as a 'political' role (loosely and inconsistently understood as the ability to develop substantive policy): the Department of Security Council Affairs and the Department of Trusteeship and Information from Non-Self-Governing Territories. With this kind of administrative set up, the SG of the UN—then a largely 'imperial' institution under the control of the Western victors of the Second World War[9]—was hardly going to overshadow the world's capitals. As one author wrote with a degree of hesitation that is symptomatic of the task ahead, '...in the interest of the organization, as well as that of the efficiency and integrity of the staff, *ideally* politics should have no role to play in the administrative affairs of the Secretariat'.[10]

---

[6] As we shall see, confusion also surrounds the meaning of the term 'political' in 'DPA'.
[7] Res 13(I), 14 February 1945.   [8] Res 13(I).
[9] Mark Mazower, *No Enchanted Palace* (Princeton: Princeton University Press, 2009).
[10] Houshang Ameri, *Politics of Staffing in the United Nations Secretariat* (London: Peter Lang, 1996), abstract (emphasis added).

Yet the onset of the Cold War and the confrontation between capitalism and socialism went on to produce one of the most bloated and polarized bureaucracies in the world, a place where the Great Powers—particularly those at the extreme ends of the ideological spectrum—expected the SG to appoint their nationals to key positions, while jealously protecting 'their' senior UN posts as *chasses guardées*.[11] Goulding himself had been pushed into the Secretariat by a Great Power: 'The British Government had pressed [SG] Waldheim and then Pérez de Cuéllar to accept a nominee of theirs to succeed Brian Urquhart, who was retiring after 41 years with the UN', Goulding wrote in his papers. 'The Secretariat would have preferred another insider. I was the nominee, reluctantly accepted and liable to rejection as an alien implant in the UN body.'[12] In addition to 'imposed' appointments, another sign of Cold War times was the proliferation—against the wishes of the inaugural GA in 1945— of so-called 'political' offices in the Secretariat, a place that filled up with officials reporting to their capitals rather than to the SG, as international civil servants are supposed to do.[13] In a further twist of irony and despite the visibly partisan state of the Secretariat, the USSR expected the SG *not* to acquire policy-making functions and to remain neutral at all times. By the end of the Cold War the UN bureaucracy was dominated by states and included as many as eight departments supposedly dealing with 'political' affairs, to which temporary offices were added on an ad hoc basis.[14] A Secretariat that was meant to be slim, agile, and at the service of the SG thus became increasingly controlled by member states as well as bitterly divided along the East–West confrontation. Unsurprisingly, its adversarial bureaucracy was also strikingly inefficient and unable to sustain the SG in his functions. In the same way as cross-veto battles were blocking the SC, a system of bureaucratic stonewalling was paralysing the Secretariat.

It was partly to remedy this situation that Pérez de Cuéllar—who was elected SG in 1984 at the height of the Cold War when the Council was largely ineffective—decided to strengthen the role of his Executive Office within the

---

[11] Thant Myint-U and Amy Scott, *The UN Secretariat* (New York: International Peace Academy, 2007); James Jonah, 'Independence and Integrity of the International Civil Service', *International Law and Politics*, Vol.14 (1982): p.841; Roger Coate et al., *United Nations Politics* (Abingdon: Routledge, 2010).

[12] Marrack Goulding, 'Peacemonger: Book Proposal', 15 June 1998 (MIG-PA).

[13] James Jonah, 'Differing State Perspectives on the United Nations in the Post-Cold War World', J. W. Holmes Memorial Lecture, *ACUNS Reports*, No.4 (1993).

[14] These included the Executive Office of the Secretary-General; the Office for Special Political Affairs; the Office for Political and General Assembly Affairs and Secretariat Services, including the Division of Palestinian Rights; the Office for Research and Collection of Information; the Office for Ocean Affairs and the Law of the Sea; the Department of Political and Security Council Affairs, including the Centre against Apartheid; the Department for Special Political Questions, Regional Cooperation, Decolonization and Trusteeship; and the Department for Disarmament Affairs.

Secretariat. As Part I has explained, by the end of the 1980s an increasingly weak Soviet Union was no longer opposed to a proactive role for the SG and in fact welcomed it. In 1987, Pérez de Cuéllar and Goulding had returned from their Moscow meeting with Gromyko determined to carve out a more assertive role for the SG, and to address the bureaucratic issues that were blighting the Secretariat. At first, Pérez de Cuéllar relied on the Office for Special Political Affairs led by Urquhart and then by Goulding, which combined peace and security missions,[15] while using a Field Operations Department for supposedly 'technical' matters.[16] With Moscow weaker by the day and the prospect of a revitalized UN gaining momentum, however, in 1988 the Peruvian diplomat tightened his grip over peace operations by assuming direct responsibility through his EOSG of the key regions of the Middle East, Cyprus, and Afghanistan.[17] This was a significant strategic move by an SG who had recognized the importance of UN operations and the need for him to oversee them, but who was also wary of the influence of states on the Secretariat and who resisted calls to use departments outside the purview of his EOSG. 'Pérez de Cuéllar ... reduce[d] OSPA's functions, limiting us to the management and planning of peacekeeping operations and nothing else',[18] Goulding complained. Despite having been 'imposed' on the SG by Thatcher, the Briton was side-lined: 'I revelled in the attention I received', Goulding wrote of his early years, 'But it nearly caused my downfall. A baron had become too powerful.'[19] When the SG tried to transfer him to Geneva, the UK government reacted and—by Goulding's admission—'Mrs Thatcher wielded her handbag. I remained in New York, but I was stripped of responsibility for peacemaking ... and half my senior staff were removed from me and transferred into the Secretary-General's office.'[20] Even the *New York Times* noticed this fall from grace: 'The main loser in the [1988] reorganization [was] the Under-Secretary-General for Special Political Affairs ... who was in charge of United Nations efforts to promote settlement in the three regions.'[21] Pérez de Cuéllar was determined to fend off not only the ingrained temptation of the UN bureaucracy to grow, but also the well-oiled tendency of states to infiltrate it. His solution was to concentrate as many functions as possible into the EOSG.

The peculiar circumstances of the early 1990s and the growth of peace missions after the Cold War made this centralizing approach untenable in the

[15] Marrack Goulding, *Peacemonger* (London: John Murray, 2002).
[16] Marrack Goulding, 'The Relationship between OSPA and FOD', undated (MIG-PA).
[17] 'Change on the First Avenue', *The New York Times*, 22 November 1988.
[18] Goulding, *Peacemonger*, p.29.
[19] Goulding, 'Peacemonger: Book Proposal'.
[20] Goulding, 'Peacemonger: Book Proposal'.
[21] Goulding, 'Peacemonger: Book Proposal'.

long run. In early 1991 Brian Urquhart wrote in a confidential report that 'a reorganization of the Secretariat . . . is essential to its effectiveness',[22] and noted that 'the appointment of a new SG in the closing months of 1991 provides an appropriate occasion for making major changes'.[23] In particular, Urquhart directly criticized the influence of member states upon the New York bureaucracy as well as the 'long-accumulated layers of vested interests and organizational traditions',[24] while also noting that the 'present set-up makes it virtually impossible for the Secretary-General to obtain the best assessments and syntheses in matters covered by more than one office'.[25] Yet Urquhart also rebuked Pérez de Cuéllar's centralizing tendencies and heavy reliance on the EOSG, which in Urquhart's view 'has assumed a number of functions in the political and security field. It cannot also cope with the task of detailed substantive direction, coordination, and follow-up of the complex work of so many units which the present structure imposes upon it. The result', the report noted, 'is a significant gap between the 38th floor and the rest of the house.'[26] According to Urquhart, a veteran international civil servant, the EOSG had too much on its plate and the SG needed to create a separate administrative architecture dealing specifically with UN peace operations. For Urquhart, the most important step forward was to recognize—without inhibitions—that the SG's functions *are* eminently 'political', and that he or she needs an efficient bureaucratic structure—free of state influence—to fulfil them. This is precisely what the new SG-elect set out to accomplish.

BOUTROS-GHALI: BUREAUCRATIC REVOLUTION IN NEW YORK

'One of the primary managerial shortcomings encountered by the Team is the lack of clear and unambiguous definition and assignment of responsibility for specific functions', a report on UN peace operations noted in late 1991. 'On more than one occasion, the Team found that more than one official claimed to have responsibility for the same function(s) and, generally, there was lack of clear understanding of the scope of functions for which others were responsible.'[27] This was the sorry state of the UN Secretariat inherited by the new SG in January 1992. As mentioned in Part I, Boutros-Ghali undertook a sweeping

---

[22] Brian Urquhart and Erskine Childers, Reorganization of the United Nations Secretariat: A Suggested Outline of Needed Reform, UN Report, New York, February 1991, p.1 (MIG-PA).

[23] Urquhart and Childers, 'Reorganization', p.1.

[24] Urquhart and Childers, 'Reorganization', p.36.

[25] Urquhart and Childers, 'Reorganization', p.1.

[26] Urquhart and Childers, 'Reorganization', p.5.

[27] C. Wallroth et al., Report to the Secretary-General on the Review of the Planning and Management of Peacekeeping Operations and Other Special Missions, 6 September 1991, p.7 (MIG-PA).

programme of reform by slashing budgets, eliminating departments, and cutting senior posts, none of which endeared him to First Avenue mandarins more familiar with continuity than with the abrupt and acrimonious reorganizations that became the hallmark of Boutros-Ghali's term.[28] Nevertheless, the new SG was in a curious position: he had overcome a US veto to his election on a platform of bureaucratic reform,[29] yet like Pérez de Cuéllar, he was aware of the influence of states over the UN bureaucracy—all this while being committed to a stronger profile for the SG.[30] As his first months in office showed, he did cherish what he routinely referred to as a 'political' role for the SG and was determined to create a bureaucratic structure that reflected it.[31] Coupled with his support for an independent international civil service, this meant that Boutros-Ghali's elevation worried not only bureaucrats in New York, but also those politicians in the world's capitals who were eager to 'place' their nationals in key UN posts, particularly in DPA and DPKO.[32]

(i) March 1992: Birth of DPA and DPKO

As it turned out, both constituencies had reasons to worry, for in early 1992 Boutros-Ghali's restructuring hit the Secretariat harder than a New York storm. Determined to heed Urquhart's advice and make the most of a unique historical juncture, the new SG chose change over continuity and implemented a bureaucratic revolution that played out in two episodes, both of which are relevant not only for the Rwanda story, but also for understanding a fundamental weakness of the current UN architecture. The first phase began in March 1992 when, three months into his mandate, Boutros-Ghali abolished in one stroke all six 'political' offices of the Cold War era. Yet the new SG went further and walked where none of his predecessors had gone: he broke the unity of UN peace operations by creating two entities supposedly autonomous of the EOSG, one of which (the Department of Political Affairs, DPA) was put in charge of peacebuilding while the other (the Department of Peacekeeping Operations, DPKO) was to be responsible for peacekeeping.[33] As mentioned, both functions had in the past been managed by the SG via his Executive Office rather than through Secretariat departments. No longer, and the harsh

---

[28] 'Boutros Cracks Down on National Perks', *UN Staff Report*, February 1993; 'Apartheid Alleged in UN Postings', *The Daily Times*, 2 July 1993.

[29] My interview with John Bolton, 24 June 2011, Washington, DC (and by email on 28 April 2016). See also Romuald Sciora, *À la Maison de Verre* (Paris: Saint-Simon, 2006), pp.117–36.

[30] Boutros Boutros-Ghali, *Mes Années à la Maison de Verre* (Paris: Fayard, 1999), chs 2 and 3.

[31] Boutros Boutros-Ghali, *UNvanquished* (London: I.B. Tauris, 1999).

[32] Marrack Goulding, Letter to N.B., 28 May 2001 (MIG-PA).

[33] James Jonah, *What Price the Survival of the United Nations?* (Ibadan: Evans Brothers, 2006), ch.3.

reaction to the move—including from Boutros-Ghali's own entourage—suggests that the 'Secular Pope'[34] had committed apostasy.

The creation of DPA and DPKO, along with the separation of peacebuilding and peacekeeping, marked a critical moment for the evolution of the UN security architecture. The assumption behind this move was straightforward: the end of the Cold War had multiplied those situations where peace missions were needed, an exponential growth in the organization's activities that was bound to continue in the years to come.[35] The changing character of war—from inter-state to intra-state conflict—was only one of a number of global shifts that had accompanied the collapse of the Soviet Union and the disintegration of the system of 'tutelage' of the Cold War, especially in Africa. Add to this the unprecedented mandate given by states to Boutros-Ghali in January 1992 during the first Security Council meeting at presidential level, and it is easy to see why—as Urquhart had urged—the UN bureaucracy needed to be adapted to the new circumstances, but also why the EOSG no longer seemed an adequate tool to handle the 'New World Order'. It should also be noted that the separation between peacekeeping and peacebuilding suited Boutros-Ghali's long-term plans, particularly with reference to his programme of reform whereby the Egyptian drew connections between human rights, democracy, and peace, arguing for a stronger UN role in all of these areas.[36] In the SG's eyes, the rationale for an efficient bureaucracy was twofold: first, the UN needed to sustain the peace processes reached by the parties to a conflict; second, it had to build upon that peace in order to establish the foundations for democratic states respectful of human rights.[37] For Boutros-Ghali, the creation of DPKO and DPA, respectively, met this dual need.

(ii) March 1992–March 1993: Bureaucratic Confusion

As the months following Boutros-Ghali's restructuring showed, however, the birth of DPA and DPKO further increased the bureaucratic confusion and lack of coordination lamented by so many UN reports, including the one quoted at the beginning of this section. A fundamental problem concerned the nature of those departments: what did their mandates involve? How was their work to be coordinated? How did they relate to the EOSG? And what did the distinction on which they were based—between 'political' and 'operational' matters—entail exactly?

---

[34] Thus Hammarskjöld famously defined the SG.
[35] Boutros-Ghali, *Mes Années*; Jonah, *What Price*, chs 2–5.
[36] Boutros-Ghali, *UNvanquished*, chs 1 and 3; Stephen Burgess, *The United Nations under Boutros-Ghali, 1992–1997* (London: Scarecrow, 2001).
[37] Boutros-Ghali, *UNvanquished*, chs 1 and 3.

Fresh documents paint a picture of considerable administrative uncertainty in 1992 and 1993. Several months after the establishment of the new architecture, the top UN leadership seemed at a loss not only to make it work, but also to identify the exact roles of the new departments. Given the undetermined and all-encompassing reference to 'political' affairs in DPA's title, in particular, it was not readily apparent what this department was supposed to accomplish. In his diaries, Goulding—who had by this time become the unenthusiastic head of DPA—dismissed the political department as a 'large and amorphous department. It had been hastily composed by sweeping together more than 300 officials from six "political" offices which Boutros-Ghali had decided to abolish or transform in his restructuring of the Secretariat. [Yet] there had been no time to assess how well those officials' skills would match the tasks of preventive diplomacy and peacemaking which he intended to be the new department's primary responsibility.'[38] As for DPKO, Annan was put in charge of it—a move that Boutros-Ghali would later regret—in the hope that the Ghanaian would smooth relations with peacekeeping donors and troop-contributing countries, especially the USA.[39]

By creating these two new departments, however, Boutros-Ghali opened a Pandora's box that not only negatively impacted on UNAMIR, but that arguably continues to affect the Secretariat today. Annan defined the DPKO of the early 1990s as 'a department whose authority was unclear',[40] while, on the eve of the Rwanda operation and upon assuming the helm of DPA, Goulding described his department as 'squalid and totally demoralized'.[41] The British official also explained how—in an effort to find out who worked for DPA and what they did—he had made a curious discovery: 'On the 30th floor I found a small unit with three professionals whose working language is Russian and two thirds of whose staff have evident drink problems!'[42] Yet Moscow wanted these officials to be—and to remain—there as a source of information. 'I feel depressed about my prospects in DPA', Goulding concluded. 'I'm not at all sure I will be able to turn it into an effective instrument of peacemaking and preventive diplomacy and I miss the realities of peacekeeping.'[43] Goulding's distress was compounded by the fact that while DPA was visibly unprepared, Boutros-Ghali had ambitious plans for the department: 'Spent much of the day drafting a paper on a possible redistribution of responsibilities between DPKO and DPA',[44] Goulding wrote in early 1993, a year after the 'birth' of the two departments and when UNAMIR was being considered.

[38] Goulding, *Peacemonger*, p.333.
[39] Stanley Meisler, *Kofi Annan* (London: John Wiley, 2007), p.65.
[40] Kofi Annan, *Interventions* (London: Allen Lane, 2012), p.38.
[41] MIG-PD-B, 21-Mar-1993.   [42] MIG-PD-B, 21-Mar-1993.
[43] MIG-PD-B, 24-Mar-1993.   [44] MIG-PD-B, 10-Jan-1993.

[The SG] said that he had decided that an effort had to be made to strengthen the Organization's peace-making capability [and] had decided to appoint me to [DPA]. This was some shock. I spoke, confusingly I fear, about the relationship between peacekeeping and peacemaking, suggesting that perhaps the peace-makers should take over when pkos [peacekeeping operations] ran into trouble, with DPKO being more of a technical department.[45]

Although this was a suggestion that Goulding would later regret, by early 1993 the Briton was increasingly concerned about the future of intra-Secretariat relations, especially vis-à-vis Annan's department. 'I suspect that I am going to end up doing quite a lot of the political side of peacekeeping', Goulding noted in another entry, 'with Kofi and Iqbal running the actual operations. But I must try to bring this about without damaging relations with them'.[46]

(iii) March 1993: Reorganization of Functions

While the creation of DPA and DPKO marked a departure from Pérez de Cuéllar's centralized Secretariat, Boutros-Ghali agreed with his predecessor about the need for a bureaucratic structure that supported what he saw as the 'political' role of the SG. This became apparent in March 1993, when the second phase of Boutros-Ghali's restructuring materialized. In addition to peacemaking, peacebuilding, and preventive diplomacy, the SG ruled that DPA was to be responsible for the 'political' aspects of *all* peacekeeping missions—including 'political' analysis, mandate interpretation, and diplo-matic negotiations. Conversely, as the peacekeeping department, DPKO was to be merely 'operational'—it would deal with the logistical aspects of field missions but it would leave policy direction to DPA and the EOSG. What this meant in practice was that DPA acquired a higher status in the Secretariat than DPKO: not only was it the closest department to the SG, it performed key functions on his behalf (such as peacebuilding, peacemaking, and preventive diplomacy) *and* it was to be involved with the policy direction of peacekeeping missions. The difference between DPA and DPKO is often painted—including in New York—as one of a Foreign Ministry/Defence Ministry type. Yet Boutros-Ghali was clear that he wished to turn DPA into an extension of— to retain the national analogy—a President's Office rather than a Foreign Ministry.[47] Given his emphasis on the 'operational' functions of DPKO, how-ever, the Ministry of Defence comparison suits the peacekeeping department fairly well: 'I . . . raised the "new dispensation" by which DPKO is no longer the overall "back-stopping" department but is responsible only for operational and

---

[45] MIG-TD-IX, 4-Feb-1993. See also MIG-PD-B, 10-Jan-1993.
[46] MIG-TD-IX, 13-Feb-1993.   [47] MIG-TD-IX, 13-Feb-1993.

military matters, with DPA handling political aspects', Goulding—who was becoming increasingly sceptical about the new arrangements—wrote, highlighting the tension that this caused in 1993. 'Only Kofi supported me in questioning the practicability of this arrangement. It was quite a mean discussion, with Jonah complaining vociferously about being cut out of Angola by me.'[48]

TROUBLE AT THE TOP: 'POLITICAL' DPA VERSUS 'OPERATIONAL' DPKO?

Boutros-Ghali's decision to put DPA in charge of the 'political' aspects of peacekeeping matters on several levels—for the relationship between DPA and DPKO; for the relationship between Boutros-Ghali and member states; and for events in Rwanda. The travailed way and peculiar timing of this decision—which was conceptualized as UNAMIR was being considered and which entered into force as Dallaire's mission was being deployed—deserve close scrutiny, not least because Boutros-Ghali's architecture still stands at the time of writing.

(i) Boutros-Ghali's Memo: 'Political' versus 'Operational'

On 3 October 1993 Boutros-Ghali sent a confidential memo to his closest aides, the purpose of which was to 'avoid duplication of efforts and inefficient use of resources'[49] within the UN bureaucracy. In this document, the SG tried to separate the functions of DPA and DPKO, with the aim of bringing clarity to the UN architecture. 'The Department of Political Affairs is the *political* arm of the Secretary-General in matters relating to the maintenance of international peace and security and the control and resolution of conflicts within states', Boutros-Ghali wrote. 'As such, it advises the Secretary-General on policy in these areas and is responsible for *political* research and analysis. It also has executive responsibilities in the fields of preventive diplomacy and peacemaking, including negotiations and other diplomatic activities. All these functions and responsibilities *as they relate to field operations* are to be prepared and carried out by DPA under the direction of the Secretary-General.'[50]

---

[48] MIG-PD-B, 22-Mar-1993.
[49] Boutros Boutros-Ghali, Memorandum: The Establishment and Conduct of United Nations Field Operations, 2 October 1993, §2 (MIG-PA). Although the memo is dated 2 October, it was signed and issued on 3 October.
[50] Boutros-Ghali, Memorandum, §4 (emphases added).

Two points should be noted. First, the fact that this clarification was made almost two years after the creation of DPA and DPKO suggests that, for a significant amount of time, confusion reigned in New York over the core functions of the UN's key departments. Second, one should note the wide range of tasks attributed to DPA as well as the inclusion of substantive policy functions within its remit, as my italics indicate. Compare this with the far narrower mandate given by the same document to DPKO: 'The Department of Peacekeeping Operations is the *operational* arm of the Secretary-General for all United Nations field operations, in particular for the *day-to-day* management of peacekeeping forces and observers.'[51] The memo also clarified the reporting responsibilities of the two departments, noting that 'DPKO is responsible for preparing the first draft of reports of the Secretary-General to the Security Council or the General Assembly on field operations. The draft is passed to DPA for its input and onward submission to the Secretary-General for approval'.[52] This effectively gave DPA a power of veto over any draft produced by DPKO, a fact that the peacekeeping department resented, Jonah welcomed, and Goulding begrudged: 'Boutros-Ghali insisted that the drafts should all be vetted by me before being forwarded to him for approval', the British official wrote in his diaries, '[a situation that] caused understandable resentment in DPKO'.[53]

(ii) Aimé's Draft and DPKO's Opposition

Boutros-Ghali's memo matters not only for what it said but also for what it did *not* (and arguably could not) say. The Goulding Archive contains three drafts of this document and comparing them offers fascinating insights into Boutros-Ghali's term of office, the bureaucratic confusion surrounding his Secretariat, and the constraints from states that the SG faced—as had all of his predecessors. On 1 October 1993 a longer (eight pages against three) and heavily annotated draft was sent to Goulding by the SG's Chief of Staff, Jean-Claude Aimé, which is remarkable for its hesitation to define the role of DPKO. 'The Department of Peacekeeping Operations is the chief executive office for all United Nations operations in the field',[54] the draft notes. Yet somebody (presumably Goulding) bracketed the term 'chief executive office' and replaced it with 'executing agency', adding on the margin that 'executive office has rather humble administrative connotations'.[55] Aimé's document then goes on to review the competencies of the two departments in the 'Establishment

---

[51] Boutros-Ghali, *Memorandum*, §5 (emphases added).
[52] Boutros-Ghali, *Memorandum*, §6.   [53] Goulding, *Peacemonger*, p.334.
[54] Boutros-Ghali, *Memorandum*, 2 October 1993, §5 (MIG-PA).
[55] Boutros-Ghali, *Memorandum*, 2 October 1993, §5.

and Planning of Field Operations', and is peppered with expressions like 'only after consultation with DPA';[56] 'DPKO consults DPA';[57] and 'DPKO keeps DPA informed'.[58] The draft also notes that when a new field operation is being considered, 'DPKO starts contingency planning... but only after consultation with DPA',[59] a circumstance that partly explains the active role of the political department early in the Rwanda operation. It is nevertheless on what the document refers to as the 'political' aspects of peacekeeping that Aimé's draft is most fascinating: 'DPA is responsible for identifying how the *political* objectives of a new operation can best be achieved [whereas] DPKO's responsibility is to assess the proposal's *operational* feasibility, especially from the military (where appropriate) and logistic point of view.'[60] The memo also points out that 'DPKO clears with DPA the language describing the new operation's *political* context and objectives'.[61]

Fresh evidence suggests that this document caused quite a stir when it was shown to the DPKO leadership in early August 1993. 'Tense meeting at 1700hrs to discuss "Aimé's paper" on DPA–DPKO relationships', Goulding wrote in his diary in August 1993, precisely when—in the same building— General Dallaire was being briefed by DPKO officials about its forthcoming Rwanda mission. 'James Jonah was strident and Kofi Annan wounded and defensive. JCA [Jean-Claude Aimé] tried unsuccessfully to railroad it through, using crude threats about the SG's office taking everything over unless we USGs [Under-Secretaries-General] responded better to his wish for a powerful Political Department.'[62] Such a charged atmosphere in New York conveys the hesitation that accompanied the gestation of Boutros-Ghali's memo, a hesitation that was partly due to the difficulty of separating the functions of DPA from those of DPKO,[63] and partly to the perceived pressures coming from influential member states, especially the USA.[64] 'The SG's decision, inspired by Jonah and Aimé, to make DPA responsible for the "political" aspects of peace keeping operations is doubtfully workable',[65] Goulding worried. As mentioned in Part I, Washington staffed a large part of DPKO, contributed most of its peacekeeping budget, and staunchly opposed Boutros-Ghali's redefinition of roles, as well as the 'operational' functions of DPKO.[66] It should also be recalled that this confrontation was taking place within the difficult context of mid-1993, when conflict in the Former

---

[56] Boutros-Ghali, Memorandum, 2 October 1993, §7.
[57] Boutros-Ghali, Memorandum, 2 October 1993, §12(a).
[58] Boutros-Ghali, Memorandum, 2 October 1993, §12(b), §12(d), and §12(f).
[59] Boutros-Ghali, Memorandum, 2 October 1993, §7.
[60] Boutros-Ghali, Memorandum, 2 October 1993, §8 (emphasis added).
[61] Boutros-Ghali, Memorandum, 2 October 1993, §12(e) (emphasis added).
[62] MIG-PD-B, 3-Aug-1993.   [63] MIG-PD-B, 14-Mar-1993.
[64] MIG-PD-B, 1-Oct-1993.   [65] MIG-PD-B, 14-Mar-1993.
[66] MIG-PD-B, 14-Mar-1993.

Yugoslavia and troubles in Somalia were already straining the relationship between Boutros-Ghali and the Clinton administration. As Chapter 7 will suggest, it was a confrontation that significantly reduced direct and open communications between DPKO and the SG—not only in Rwanda but across several other peacekeeping operations. In February 1994, for instance, the slow delivery by DPKO of a cable from the head of NATO to the SG over Bosnia reportedly caused a 'tremendous tantrum'[67] from Boutros-Ghali, who openly criticized Annan for siding with the USA. 'I was the drafter and the person the SG consulted the most', Goulding wrote of a top-level meeting. 'Poor Kofi was rather pushed to one side and clearly resented this. His problem is that he can't draft and the SG distrusts his subservience to the Americans.'[68]

(iii) Goulding's Draft: DPKO Subordinated to DPA

An even earlier draft of the SG's memo—originally written by Goulding in July 1993 on Boutros-Ghali's instructions—is even more straightforward about the ancillary role which DPKO was expected to play from mid-1993 onwards. 'The field operations managed by DPKO are means to the achievement of political ends defined by DPA',[69] the document noted in a passage that was omitted in the final version, but that left little doubt as to which department was to have priority in New York. 'To that extent, the activities for which DPKO is responsible are secondary or subordinate to those for which DPA...is responsible.'[70] Why did these sentences disappear from the document eventually issued by Boutros-Ghali? Indeed, why were Goulding's and Aimé's drafts bolder and more explicit in setting out the DPA–DPKO framework than the one finally approved by the SG? This is important since we know from his diaries that Goulding had serious misgivings about his own draft. 'At Jean-Claude's request', he wrote, 'I have tried my hand at a redefinition of responsibilities of DPA and DPKO and faxed it to him from France. He is putting it to the SG, with the recommendation that he promulgate it *tel quel* [as it stands]. Fur will certainly fly over this—and my own position could become painful. I am not at all sure that my scheme will be workable without...the cooperation of DPKO (which is unlikely to be forthcoming)....'[71] In another document, a frustrated Goulding noted the sheer difficulty of coming up with a division of labour between DPA and DPKO, adding that 'There is no universally applicable solution. The problem

---

[67] MIG-TD-IX, 12-Feb-1994.   [68] MIG-TD-IX, 12-Feb-1994.
[69] Marrack Goulding, *Note to Mr Aimé: The Establishment and Conduct of United Nations Field Operations*, 19 July 1993, §4(a) (MIG-PA).
[70] Goulding, *Note to Mr Aimé*, §4(b).
[71] MIG-TD-X, 31-Jul-1993.

depends so much on personalities.'[72] As for why the section on the subordination of DPKO was omitted from the final version, Goulding pointed out that Boutros-Ghali came under sustained pressure from Washington to issue a different document: 'Jean-Claude Aimé sends me a copy of the final draft of the SG's directive on the division of labour between DPA and DPKO', Goulding wrote on 1 October 1993—precisely while UNAMIR was being deployed. 'This is an immensely watered down, and less detailed, revision of the draft I prepared in Brittany in July. Kofi has successfully lobbied the Americans to block that draft with the result, I fear, that difficulties between the two departments will continue.'[73] The extent of DPA–DPKO friction during the following months makes Goulding's prediction prescient.

NEW YORK TO KIGALI: EFFECTS OF BOUTROS-GHALI'S MEMO ON UNAMIR

Boutros-Ghali's reorganization of the Secretariat and redistribution of functions between DPA and DPKO was conceived in early to mid-1993, at a time when the Rwandan parties were concluding a peace agreement (August 1993) but well before the approval and deployment of UNAMIR (October 1993), as well as significantly before the preparation (October 1993–April 1994) and perpetration (April–July 1994) of the genocide. It is thus unsurprising that several aspects of the Rwanda operation were affected by the bureaucratic changes at Headquarters. More intriguing is the fact that Boutros-Ghali's memo was inconsistently applied due to conflicting interpretations about what DPA's 'political' competences actually involved. Three areas—diplomatic negotiations, 'political' analysis, and intelligence—were affected by the SG's division of responsibilities, whereas three others—mandate interpretation, rules of engagement, and the chain of command—were not because the SG's directive was effectively disregarded.

(i) Implementing the SG's Memo in Rwanda

Diplomatic negotiations and the signing of the Arusha Peace Agreement are phases when Boutros-Ghali's desire for a stronger DPA was fulfilled. As mentioned in Part I, the department was largely in charge of relations between the SG and the Rwandan parties, as well as of facilitating the peace agreement

[72] Goulding, 'Peacemonger: Book Proposal'.
[73] MIG-PD-B, 1-Oct-1993.

of August 1993. A DPA official had also been despatched to Arusha to represent the SG with the task of monitoring the negotiations and putting pressure on Habyarimana and Kagame to sign the peace agreement. This is consistent with Boutros-Ghali's view of DPA as an extension of his EOSG in matters related to the 'control and resolution of conflict within states'.[74] As his October 1993 memo noted, DPA 'has executive responsibilities in... negotiations and other diplomatic activities'.[75] There are several signs of the trust and responsibilities bestowed by Boutros-Ghali on DPA from mid-1993 onwards. When he formalized the areas of geographical competence for his aides in the EOSG (Gharekhan, de Soto, and Kittani) and made Kittani responsible for 'Africa South of the Equator (except Lesotho) plus Nigeria',[76] the SG put DPA—not Kittani—in charge of the Rwandan negotiations. Also, after receiving notice of the impending ethnic massacre and likely involvement of the Rwandan President, Boutros-Ghali sent a DPA official (Jonah) rather than his EOSG aide (Kittani) to warn Habyarimana. It is true that, with typical administrative bluntness, the document also pointed out that 'The Secretary-General can, at any time, modify the division of roles without informing the parties in question'.[77] Yet it is difficult to see Pérez de Cuéllar using a part of the UN Secretariat to carry out such mission; from mid-1993, it was clearly DPA—not the EOSG—which was in charge of the diplomatic aspects of UNAMIR.

'Political' analysis is the second area where the new delineation of responsibilities at Headquarters impacted on UNAMIR. Again, Boutros-Ghali's memo left little doubt about it, noting that DPA 'is responsible for political research and analysis'.[78] As mentioned in Part I, in the case of Rwanda, this process began by assessing whether UNAMIR was worth deploying, and it was DPA that advised the SG on this. Yet the issue of what the SG referred to as 'political' analysis is most important in relation to the reconnaissance trip of August 1993, for although the latter was supposed to be led by DPA's Pédanou, Dallaire and DPKO ended up taking charge of it, thus potentially disrupting Boutros-Ghali's rationale. As the Canadian General pointed out, however, when Pédanou did join the delegation, he made it clear that, by virtue of Boutros-Ghali's dispensation about the division of roles between DPA and DPKO, it was the DPA official who was in charge of the so-called 'political' aspects of that reconnaissance operation.[79] This is something that Jonah confirmed[80] but that DPKO reportedly resented, since for them reconnaissance

[74] Boutros-Ghali, Memorandum, §4. [75] Boutros-Ghali, Memorandum, §4.
[76] Jean-Claude Aimé, Sécret: Répartition des Compétences au Cabinet du Secrétaire Général, 11-Jan-1994 (MIG-PA).
[77] 'Now we know', a handwritten note addressed to Goulding and attached to this document reads. Aimé, Sécret.
[78] Boutros-Ghali, Memorandum, §4.
[79] Roméo Dallaire, *Shake Hands with the Devil* (London: Arrow Books, 2003), p.132.
[80] My interview with James Jonah, 20 July 2011, New York, USA.

missions had both 'operational' and 'political' aspects. 'The political side remained the purview of the DPA',[81] Dallaire wrote. The result was that, as Part I has hinted and as Chapter 7 will show in detail, both departments gathered intelligence and carried out what they saw as 'political' assessments, but neither of them efficiently shared those assessments with each other upon returning to New York.[82] As the next chapters will show, neither were DPA or DPKO clear about the meaning of 'political'. 'The fights within the Secretariat had such a big impact on the success or failure of an operation',[83] Goulding noted.

Back in 1994, similar frictions afflicted the handling of intelligence after UNAMIR was deployed, the third area to be affected by Boutros-Ghali's directive. The SG's memo stated that 'DPKO will act as the main channel of communication between United Nations Headquarters and the field',[84] and 'will submit weekly reports to the Secretary-General on the current status of field operations, with the observations on situations of particular importance'.[85] Yet the memo also tasked DPA with gathering data from DPKO, processing it, and turning it into intelligence for the SG and SC.[86] This is why from October 1993 DPA effectively functioned as a reporting filter between DPKO and the SG, with most DPKO reports vetted by DPA before going to the SG. As we shall see in Chapter 7, however, there was to be little coordination between the suppliers of information in the field (UNAMIR and DPKO) and the producer of intelligence in New York (DPA), a situation that seriously constrained the analytical capacity of the Secretariat. 'Boutros-Ghali maintained strict, private control over his personal communications with representatives and leaders of member states, as well as Special Representatives of the Secretary-General (SRSGs), who ran the political side of operations on the ground', Annan wrote in his memoirs. 'This meant that, at any stage, we in DPKO could never be sure who knew what, or what had been agreed to in the day-to-day running and direction of operations'.[87] The same cannot be said for DPA.

(ii) Disregarding the SG's Memo in Rwanda

Partly because of doubts over what counted as 'political' and 'operational' activities, Boutros-Ghali's memo was inconsistently applied in Rwanda—it was in fact often disregarded, an example being UNAMIR's mandate. As the

---

[81] Dallaire, *Shake Hands*, p.55.   [82] Dallaire, *Shake Hands*, p.132.
[83] Goulding, 'Peacemonger: Book Proposal'.
[84] Boutros-Ghali, Memorandum, §5.   [85] Boutros-Ghali, Memorandum, §5.
[86] 'On strictly political matters...[DPA] will be, when required, in contact with the field'. Boutros-Ghali, Memorandum, §5.
[87] Annan, *Interventions*, p.38.

depository of policy direction for all peacekeeping operations, DPA was supposed to clarify doubts about UNAMIR's mandate as approved by the SC, a mandate that had been informed by the Arusha Accords and by the SG's recommendation to establish the mission. Since DPA had overseen all of these passages (Arusha, the SG's recommendation, and the SC mandate), the department was arguably in the best position to interpret UNAMIR's mandate. Presumably, this is also what the SG meant when he wrote in his memo that DPA 'is the political arm of the Secretary-General in matters relating to the maintenance of international peace and security and the control and resolution of conflict within states'.[88] Dallaire's multiple requests for clarification on UNAMIR's mandate, however, were addressed to—and replied to by—DPKO rather than DPA.[89] This included the question of whether Dallaire was allowed to seize weapons without the knowledge of the Rwandan parties, seemingly a substantive—or 'political'—rather than an 'operational' issue which, according to the SG's memo, should presumably have been handled by DPA rather than DPKO. Uncertainty over the borders between 'political' and 'operational' roles, however, and faulty reporting lines in New York, meant that the interpretation of mandates was seen by DPKO as part of its remit, with the result that—to Jonah's dismay[90]—no DPA input was reportedly requested or received. As for Goulding, as head of DPKO he had 'defended the principle that if a peace-keeping operation was deployed the "political" work belonged to DPKO, not DPA',[91] so he was hardly in a position to complain about a situation which he had himself contributed to creating.

The handling of UNAMIR's rules of engagement is another area that failed to conform to Boutros-Ghali's dispensation. Although UNAMIR's ROE became a matter of life-or-death as soon as the genocide started, DPKO maintained—controversially—that such rules did not allow UN peacekeepers to open fire to protect civilians, but only to protect themselves. As Part I has shown, 'Fire only if fired upon' was the message (confusingly) conveyed by DPKO to Dallaire, one that he nevertheless disobeyed while saving hundreds of people. In light of Paragraph 17 of UNAMIR's ROE—according to which peacekeepers *could* use force to stop 'ethnically or politically motivated criminal acts' and *should* 'take the necessary action to prevent any crime against humanity'[92]—DPKO's interpretation is questionable. Nevertheless, this was another issue that according to Boutros-Ghali's memo should have been brought to the attention of DPA. The fact that this was not done shows the

[88] Boutros-Ghali, Memorandum, §4.
[89] Dallaire, *Shake Hands*; Roméo Dallaire, *PBS Frontline Interview*, 1 April 2004.
[90] Interview with Jonah, 20 July 2011.
[91] Marrack Goulding, Handover Notes for Sir Kieran Prendergast, 22 February 1997, §3 (MIG-PA).
[92] Barnett and Finnemore, *Rules for the World*, p.202.

inconsistent application of the SG's memo as well as the confusion surrounding the distinction between 'political' and 'operational' functions in peacekeeping operations. It also suggests that the Secretariat of 1993 was a far cry from the 'coherent, cooperative and smoothly functioning team'[93] that the SG's memo wished to establish.

While the division of roles between a 'political' DPA and an 'operational' DPKO created confusion and competition in New York, it produced chaos in Rwanda—especially with reference to UNAMIR's chain of command. There is no better example of the problems associated with the SG's distinction of mid-1993 than the fraught relationship between UNAMIR's Force Commander and the mission's 'political' head. As Chapter 3 has shown, the division of labour between Dallaire and Booh Booh was dysfunctional and involved a military official with no negotiating experience providing a large part of UNAMIR's 'political' direction, while the mission's nominal head essentially duplicated Dallaire's work. The issue was compounded by the fact that the two officials reported to different units of the UN bureaucracy (Dallaire to DPKO, Booh Booh to DPKO, DPA, and EOSG), with the result that their problematic relationship in Kigali partly mirrored the flawed separation of roles between DPA and DPKO in New York. Once again, there was no 'responsible and collegial consultation and clearance process'[94] between DPA and DPKO, as requested by Boutros-Ghali's memo. UNAMIR was apparently not the only mission where the SG's dispensation caused trouble: '[SRSG] Michel Pelletier telephoned this evening to agonize over how it could be applied in the case of El Salvador',[95] Goulding noted in his diary, pointing to a fundamental problem with Boutros-Ghali's memo which likely affected UN operations worldwide. Albeit for different reasons, Annan was equally frustrated: 'Much of UNOSOM II was run by Boutros-Ghali in his secretive style. Through his personal negotiations with troop contributors, Boutros-Ghali kept most people at the UN, including the leadership of DPKO, out of much of the decision making.'[96] As Goulding readily admitted, Boutros-Ghali's management '... led to much bad blood both within the Secretariat and between it and the troop-contributing countries'.[97]

BUREAUCRATIC POLITICS VERSUS POWER POLITICS

An assessment of the UN bureaucracy ahead of the establishment of UNAMIR suggests that, in Boutros-Ghali's grand design and immediately before setting

---

[93] Boutros-Ghali, Memorandum, §9.   [94] Boutros-Ghali, Memorandum, §9.
[95] MIG-PD-B, 14-Mar-1993.   [96] Annan, *Interventions*, p.44.
[97] Goulding, 'Peacemonger: Book Proposal'.

up the Rwanda mission, DPA was supposed to be the key department in New York. As Chapter 9 will explain, DPA's remits for preventive diplomacy, peacebuilding, and peacemaking were precisely the kind of activities that Boutros-Ghali saw as elevating the UN's influence in global affairs and upon which he wished the organization to focus.[98] Boutros-Ghali was also the first SG to take a leap of faith in the UN bureaucracy (or, rather, in a part of it) by trying to turn it into an effective mechanism for handling a growing number of complex operations. Beginning with the Rwanda mission, this meant that DPA was to assume responsibility for *all* 'political' aspects of *all* peacekeeping operations, a sweeping mandate that kept the department busy before, during, and after Rwanda's genocide.

Boutros-Ghali's preference for DPA aggravated the bureaucratic friction in New York precisely as UNAMIR was being considered. On the one hand, DPA was hardly a model of speed and efficiency in the early 1990s, as Goulding had repeatedly warned. On the other, DPKO never accepted Boutros-Ghali's dispensation, disagreed with the SG's 'political' versus 'operational' division, and was actively involved in Rwanda—through Dallaire—in substantive (or 'political') issues including diplomatic negotiations, the interpretation of the mission's mandate, and UNAMIR's rules of engagement. A dangerous duplication thus ensued which was worsened by the inability (indeed, the unwillingness) of the two departments to share what they knew with each other. Writing in mid-1995, Goulding recalled a difficult meeting with Boutros-Ghali about the DPA–DPKO relationship: 'From the SG's point of view', the British official wrote, 'I could give him much more support, and of a wider nature, from DPA than from DPKO where I would be a victim of the success we had had in recent months in cutting DPKO down to size and asserting the supremacy of the Political Department.'[99] As the next chapter will show, in Rwanda this confrontation meant that important leads were missed; the information flow was disrupted; the intelligence cycle was dysfunctional; and 'political' analysis was flawed, a situation that Boutros-Ghali's memo exacerbated and that led his bureaucratic strategy to fail shortly after it was launched. The first victim of it was UNAMIR.

Yet the situation of friction at Headquarters had deeper roots than the standard bureaucratic competition that is so common to large organizations,[100] for in the middle of the Rwandan tragedy the UN bureaucracy seemed to be at the centre of a power struggle between the SG on the one

[98] Boutros Boutros-Ghali, *An Agenda for Peace* (New York: UN Department of Public Information, 1992); Boutros Boutros-Ghali, *An Agenda for Development* (New York: UN Department of Public Information, 1995); Boutros Boutros-Ghali, *An Agenda for Democratization* (New York: UN Department of Public Information, 1996).

[99] MIG-TD-XII, 14-Aug-1995.

[100] Barnett and Finnemore, *Rules for the World*, chs 1 and 2; Michael Barnett, *Eyewitness to a Genocide* (Ithaca: Cornell University Press, 2003), pp.7–10.

hand and member states—particularly the USA—on the other. At least, this was the perception from the Secretariat's top floor: 'I believe that DPKO at this time was very much involved with the American administration and was acting taking into consideration the demand or the recommendation of the American administration',[101] Boutros-Ghali stated in an interview and confirmed in his memoirs. 'The American administration was very powerful. They have a control on DPKO.'[102] Jonah agrees[103] and so does Goulding (although, as we will see in Chapter 8, with reservations about his boss, whom he described as 'an intellectual powerhouse with a wicked wit, but erratic in judgement and prone to irrational likes and dislikes'.)[104] Given Boutros-Ghali's reluctance to deal directly with the SC and even allow UN officials to appear before the ambassadors, the SG's views of DPKO were partly a self-fulfilling prophecy and a matter of perceptions. Yet in the Secretariat of 1994, as in politics more generally, perceptions matter. So does the fact that the SG saw himself as engaged in a confrontation with some states *and* UN officials over his control of the New York bureaucracy.

The history of the UN Secretariat since the early 1990s is the story of how SGs tried to carve out a role for themselves in the post-Cold War environment. Both Pérez de Cuéllar and Boutros-Ghali understood the UN bureaucracy as a means to an end, namely, the SG's disenfranchisement from member states. The fact that bureaucracies have a tendency to grow and compete with each other—the 'bureaucratic politics' side of things—thus goes in tandem, in New York, with power politics and with the perceived influence of the UN membership over the Secretariat. Although the relationship between bureaucratic and power politics at UN Headquarters remains largely unexplored, it makes the story of the UN Secretariat of 1994 even more intriguing. So does the fact that this conflict involved two key players of international relations—states and the SG, or the so-called 'Two UNs'.

How did this confrontation play out in the early 1990s? As the next chapter suggests, first and foremost through the issue of intelligence. Bureaucracies are often seen as specific forms of social organization,[105] and there is merit in looking at international organizations as bureaucracies.[106] As part of the literature has noted, bureaucracies in general and the UN Secretariat in particular matter not only because of their material and informational resources, but also because they interpret the information *they* have in the

[101] Boutros Boutros-Ghali, *PBS Frontline Interview*, 21 January 2004.
[102] Boutros-Ghali, *PBS Frontline Interview*, 21 January 2004.
[103] Jonah, *What Price*, p.106.
[104] Goulding, 'Peacemonger: Book Proposal', 15 June 1998.
[105] Max Weber, 'Bureaucracy', in Hans Gerth and Charles Wright Mills, eds, *From Max Weber: Essays in Sociology* (Oxford: Oxford University Press, 1978), pp.196–244. See also Weber, *Theory of Social and Economic Organization*.
[106] Barnett and Finnemore, *Rules for the World*, p.3.

way *they* see fit to achieve the aims *they* agree with.[107] In so doing, bureaucracies invest that information with meaning and transform it into knowledge.[108] This is what happened in the early 1990s, when UN intelligence became a battleground between an increasingly assertive SG and its 'political' unit, on the one hand, and a frustrated US administration exerting financial and logistical influence over DPKO, on the other.[109] For these reasons, intelligence is the second process that ought to be considered.

---

[107] Burkart Holzner and John Marx, *Knowledge Application* (Boston: Allyn and Bacon, 1979).

[108] Barnett and Finnemore, *Rules for the World*, p.7.

[109] Joel Oestreich, ed., *International Organizations as Self-Directed Actors* (Abingdon: Routledge, 2012), esp. Part I; Paolo De Stefani, 'Lo Spazio dell'ONU nei Processi di Produzione Normativa Internazionale', in *Pace, Diritti dell'Uomo, Diritti dei Popoli*, Vol.7, No.2 (1993), pp.69–81; and Daniele Archibugi et al., *Cosmopolis: E' Possibile una Democrazia Sovranazionale?* (Rome: ManifestoLibri, 1993).

7

Intelligence

'The UN has no intelligence'.[1] So wrote Boutros-Ghali in 1993, describing what he saw as the chronic lack of information-gathering and analytical capacity in New York. U Thant, one of his predecessors, concurred: 'The limitations [in collecting information] are inherent in the very nature of the United Nations and therefore of any operation conducted by it'.[2] There is no doubt that, historically speaking, the UN has had an awkward relationship with the idea of intelligence: since the organization is based on the principles of neutrality and impartiality, diplomats in New York have traditionally viewed the possibility of the UN covertly acquiring and analysing information with suspicion. Secretariat officials, in particular, worry that doing so would compromise the institution's most cherished asset: its legitimacy. It is not the role of an organization of states founded on ideas of inclusiveness and cooperation to surreptitiously gather information about its members, they argue. Even Dag Hammarskjöld rejected the idea of UN intelligence on the ground that, like the Red Cross, the UN must have 'clean hands'.[3] As for national leaders, they often have self-serving reasons to be hostile to the idea of UN intelligence, including a fear that the SG might become too influential.[4] The matter of what and how the Secretariat 'knows' thus remains highly controversial in New York, where the consensus is that, as an inter-*national* body, the UN should rely on what states are willing to share.

This, however, is problematic. Few organizations can function effectively without collecting and analysing information, especially an organization as structurally complex and as functionally multifarious as the UN, and particularly in the context of peacekeeping operations, where knowledge can make

[1] Simon Chesterman, 'Does the UN Have Intelligence?', *Survival*, Vol.48, No.3 (2006), p.152.
[2] Walter Dorn and David Bell, 'Intelligence and Peacekeeping', *International Peacekeeping*, Vol.2, No.1 (1995), p.11.
[3] Conor O'Brien, *To Katanga and Back* (New York: Grosset and Dunlop, 1962), p.76.
[4] Pavel Larsson, *The United Nations, Intelligence, and Peacekeeping* (Lund: Lund University, 2007).

the difference between life and death.[5] Besides, states are not necessarily the most reliable suppliers of intelligence, especially when it comes to certain operations. 'I had no means of intelligence on Rwanda', Dallaire wrote. 'Not one country was willing to provide the UN or even me personally with accurate and up-to-date information [so] we always seemed to be reacting to, rather than anticipating, what was going to happen.'[6] Compare this with the run-up to the Iraq invasion of 2003, when the US administration was more than eager to offer the UN (questionable) intelligence to the extent that it suited Washington's goals.[7] This paradox of an organization that *needs* intelligence in order to function, but that is not supposed—sometimes not even *allowed*—to gather it independently is the subject of this chapter.

The issue of who knew what in New York is especially important in relation to Rwanda, for there is a link between the institutional pathologies of the Secretariat raised in this book, UN intelligence, and UNAMIR. Precisely on the eve of the Rwanda operation, a new system of data-collection and analysis was established by Boutros-Ghali[8] which was supposed to rely heavily on both DPA and DPKO as the eyes and ears of the SG. Indeed, an argument can be made that Boutros-Ghali originally set up these departments precisely in order to strengthen the intelligence capability of the Secretariat *vis-à-vis* that of member states, on which New York had long depended. As this chapter will show, however, the escalating feud between DPA and DPKO, together with Boutros-Ghali's increasing reliance on his 'political' department, negatively affected the way in which the Secretariat handled the Rwanda intelligence. Boutros-Ghali's memo on the DPA–DPKO interface raised further questions, for is intelligence a 'political' or an 'operational' matter? As this chapter suggests, it is precisely in the domain of intelligence that the institutional pathologies and ambiguous roles of DPA and DPKO were most visible.

And yet, UN documents continue to refer to 'information' but studiously avoid the word 'intelligence' altogether. Far from merely expressing a semantic preference, this vocabulary points to a distinction which is familiar to intelligence analysts, for whom 'information' refers to the gathering of raw data whereas 'intelligence' indicates the process of assessing such data for a given purpose.[9] In line with the controversial nature of intelligence mentioned above, Secretariat officials have in the past readily acknowledged the necessity

[5] Pär Eriksson, 'Intelligence in Peacekeeping Operations', *Intelligence and Counterintelligence*, Vol.10, No.1 (1997), pp.1–18.

[6] Roméo Dallaire, *Shake Hands with the Devil* (London: Arrow Books, 2003), p.90.

[7] Kenneth Pollack, 'Spies, Lies, and Weapons', *The Atlantic Monthly*, January–February 2004. See also 'Full Text of Colin Powell Speech at the UN', *The Guardian*, 5 February 2003.

[8] Chesterman, p.153.

[9] Paul Johnston, 'No Cloak and Dagger Required: Intelligence Support to UN Peacekeeping', *Intelligence and National Security*, Vol.12, No.4 (1997), p.105; André Roux, 'Intelligence and Peacekeeping: Are We Winning?', *Conflict Trends*, No.3 (2008), pp.18–25.

for their organization to handle *information* but have consistently denied that Headquarters needs (or has) *intelligence*.[10] The 1994 edition of the semi-official *Peacekeepers' Handbook*, for instance, notes that '[t]he UN has resolutely refused to countenance intelligence systems as a part of its peacekeeping operations',[11] and brusquely points out that 'intelligence, having covert connections, is a dirty word'.[12] Yet if by 'intelligence' we mean—as I do—the collection *and* analysis of information, then there is no doubt that the UN Secretariat has it and regularly uses it. On the eve of the Rwanda genocide, the Force Commander of the operation in the Former Yugoslavia—while confirming the UN's unease with the term 'intelligence'—conceded as much when he wrote to Headquarters that '[g]reat care is taken in the mission to refer to "information gathering" as opposed to "intelligence gathering". Indeed, we refer to information officers *vice* intelligence officers, and avoid any overt actions that might raise suspicion *if* we are in fact involved in the intelligence function.'[13]

As this chapter suggests, the same was true for UNAMIR. Not only was intelligence produced in both Kigali and New York; in the run-up to 1994, gathering it was a central aim of the UN Secretariat. It is true that several states were reluctant to share what they knew with UN officials and that New York lacked the means for thorough 'political' analysis. It is also true that, as mentioned in Part I, warnings were missed and emerging threats went unheeded. Yet this does not mean that UN Headquarters was unable to rely on its own intelligence—as one analyst put it, for a UN mission '[t]o refuse to "do intelligence" is merely to manage one's information poorly.'[14] The events of 1994, however, were at least partly an intelligence failure to the extent that various Secretariat units (such as the SG, DPKO, and DPA) did not efficiently share what they knew with each other. Furthermore, many of the intelligence challenges faced by the mission in Kigali reflected the difficult separation of roles in New York between DPA and DPKO described in the previous chapters. This emerges most clearly from the way in which the UN Secretariat handled the four critical stages of the so-called 'intelligence sequence' in Rwanda, namely, the planning, collection, analysis, and dissemination of the intelligence that was available in the run-up to the Rwandan genocide. This chapter considers how each of these stages reflected at least in part the institutional pathologies highlighted in this book.

[10] Melanie Ramjoué, 'Improving United Nations Intelligence: Lessons from the Field', Geneva Centre for Security Policy Papers No.19, August 2011.

[11] International Peace Academy, *Peacekeepers Handbook* (New York: Pergamon Press, 1994), p.39.

[12] International Peace Academy, p.39.

[13] Johnston, p.104 (emphasis added); Tom Quiggin, 'Intelligence Support to UN Peacekeeping Missions', *Intelligence and National Security*, Vol.14, No.4 (1998), pp.203–7; Tom Quiggin, 'Intelligence in Support of UN Peacekeeping in Bosnia during the 1990s', 11 February 2013, *Spy Museum*, available at http://www.spymuseum.org (accessed 28 April 2016).

[14] Johnston, p.106.

PLANNING: WHY AND HOW WAS INTELLIGENCE ON RWANDA PRODUCED?

The first stage of any intelligence cycle is strategic, that is to say, is centrally managed and comes down to the following question: why should information be collected and analysed?[15] In the case of UNAMIR, the answer is straightforward: because the Rwandan parties had asked the SG to despatch a mission and he needed to assess its viability.[16] The key task of the UN system in Rwanda consisted in assisting the country's politicians with their reconciliation process and in ensuring that the conditions for a peacekeeping mission existed. This aim was consistent with the first article of the UN Charter, according to which the UN is 'to maintain peace and security and, to that end, to take effective measures for the prevention and removal of threats to peace'.[17] Like other peacekeeping operations, the Rwanda mission stemmed from a request by a state (Rwanda) to the head of the UN (the SG) which was eventually approved by the UN body responsible for international peace and security (the SC). While these phases are significant, this section will focus on the role played by the UN bureaucracy—particularly DPA and DPKO—in gathering the intelligence which was then used by the SG to advise the Council. In particular, I will address the following question: how did Boutros-Ghali reach his decision, one that—given the financial crisis of the early 1990s and Washington's disinclination towards UNAMIR—was in no way a foregone conclusion?

Since the first step for the UN system was to gather as much information on Rwanda as possible, in the months preceding his decision the SG took a number of initiatives which were aimed at collecting data of—to use the Secretariat's problematic terminology—a 'political' (via DPA) and 'technical' (via DPKO) nature. This is why, as mentioned in Part I, in March 1993 Boutros-Ghali sent a DPA mission to the region to negotiate a possible deployment of UN military observers along the Rwanda–Uganda border.[18] Regional tensions between anglophone, Tutsi-dominated Uganda and francophone, Hutu-controlled Rwanda had escalated in the early 1990s into public

---

[15] Bram Champagne, *The UN and Intelligence* (New York: Peace Operations Training Institute, 2006), p.4.

[16] United Nations, Letter from the Permanent Representative of Rwanda to the United Nations Requesting Deployment of United Nations Military Observers to the Rwanda-Uganda Border, S/25355, 3 March 1993. Unless otherwise stated, documents in this chapter have been downloaded from the Rwanda Documents Project (RDP), available at http://www.rwandadocumentsproject. net/ (accessed 2 June 2016).

[17] United Nations, *Charter of the United Nations* (New York: Department of Public Information, 2006), p.5.

[18] James Jonah, *What Price the Survival of the United Nations?* (Ibadan: Evans Brothers, 2006), p.376.

accusations by Kigali that Kampala was smuggling weapons for the benefit of Kagame's Rwandan Patriotic Front (RPF).[19] The first UN task in the region was thus to monitor the border area between the two countries, which is why in April 1993 a 'technical' mission—led by DPKO's Maurice Baril—was despatched by Boutros-Ghali with the aim of reporting on whether the UN should deploy observers to the area.[20] It was on the basis of this expedition that the UN Observer Mission for Uganda–Rwanda (UNOMUR) was established in June 1993 to 'monitor the border [and] to verify that no military assistance reaches Rwanda'.[21]

Before any peacekeeper set foot in Kigali, therefore, the UN system was already collecting, analysing, and assessing data in view of a possible engagement there—in other words, it was already producing intelligence rather than simply gathering information. UNOMUR would have been unable to operate without (and was itself a product of) UN intelligence—not only of raw data but of its processing. According to John Ruggie, peacekeeping missions have an 'umpire' role and 'toward that end, they observe and report'.[22] Not coincidentally, words like 'monitor', 'observe', 'report', and 'fact-find' regularly appear in UN documents and confirm that it is the nature of UN peace operations to observe, gather, *and* assess information—thus producing intelligence.[23] As another author put it, 'Collecting information on military forces and processing it in order to assess what those military forces are doing is, of course, the very essence of "military intelligence".'[24] This is exactly what UNOMUR did in 1993.

The same can be said of the UN Assistance Mission for Rwanda (UNAMIR), which was established by the SC as a result of intelligence collected through UNOMUR.[25] Nevertheless, while the information gathered by—and the intelligence produced on the basis of—UNOMUR was supposedly 'technical' or 'operational' in nature, UNAMIR's mandate was said to also include 'political' functions. Although this expression remained undefined, it pointed to a wider role than UNOMUR, as one would expect from a significantly larger operation (UNOMUR counted 81 unarmed observers while UNAMIR could

[19] United Nations, *The Blue Helmets* (New York: UN Department of Public Information, 1996), p.342.

[20] United Nations, *The Blue Helmets*, p.342.

[21] Res 846 (S/RES/846), 22 June 1993.

[22] John Ruggie, 'The UN: Stuck Between Peacekeeping and Enforcement', in William Lewis et al., eds, *Peacekeeping: The Way Ahead?* (Washington, DC: Institute for National Strategic Studies, 1993), p.3. See also Brian Urquhart, 'Thoughts on the 20th Anniversary of Dag Hammarskjöld's Death', *Foreign Affairs*, Vol.60 (1981), p.6.

[23] Walter Dorn, 'The Cloak and the Blue Helmet: Limitations on Intelligence in UN Peacekeeping', *International Journal of Intelligence and Counterintelligence*, Vol.12, No.4 (1999), pp.414–17.

[24] Johnston, p.105.   [25] United Nations, *The Blue Helmets*, p.243.

rely on 2,500 armed peacekeepers).[26] As mentioned in Part I, UNAMIR's mandate included a lessening of the military conditions of Rwanda and required the mission to 'contribute to the security of Kigali'[27] by 'monitoring a weapons-secure area established by the parties in and around the city',[28] as well as 'observance of the cease-fire agreement'[29] set up by the Arusha Accords. Importantly, UNAMIR was also tasked to 'investigate, at the request of the parties or on its own initiative, instances of alleged non-compliance'[30] of the Arusha Peace Agreements; 'to monitor the process of repatriation of Rwandan refugees';[31] 'to assist in the coordination of humanitarian assistance activities';[32] and 'to investigate and report on incidents regarding the activities of the gendarmerie and police'.[33] Far from being a data-gathering machine, UNAMIR's core aim was thus the production of intelligence for Headquarters, particularly DPKO.

This point should not be underestimated. As the repeated requests for information by the ambassadors of the ten elected members of the Security Council suggest, the intelligence produced by a field mission can be as important as that generated by the upper echelons of the UN, including the SG.[34] In the early phases of the UN engagement in Rwanda and in coming to an assessment on whether to establish the operation, Boutros-Ghali relied heavily on the intelligence provided by UNOMUR and would have been unable to make a decision without it. Furthermore, the deteriorating security situation meant that once UNAMIR was despatched, the need for intelligence in New York grew rather than diminished. There were thus excellent strategic reasons why the UN system wanted to 'know' as much as possible about Rwanda and it is unsurprising that, before the genocide, the entire UN machine was geared towards the production of intelligence. What kind of intelligence was generated, by whom, and for whom it was produced are the next questions that ought to be addressed.

COLLECTION: WHAT KIND OF INTELLIGENCE DID THE UN SYSTEM PRODUCE?

As a mission set up on the basis of Chapter VI of the UN Charter, it has been suggested that UNAMIR lacked the military, 'political', and legal tools to

---

[26] United Nations, *Uganda–Rwanda UNOMUR Background*, available at http://www.un.org/en/peacekeeping/missions/past/unomurbackgr.html (accessed 9 July 2015).

[27] Res 872 (S/RES/872), 5 October 1993, 3(a).   [28] Res 872, 3(a).

[29] Res 872, 3(b).   [30] Res 872, 3(e).   [31] Res 872, 3(f).

[32] Res 872, 3(g).   [33] Res 872, 3(h).

[34] 'Intelligence in Integrated UN Peacekeeping Missions', *International Peacekeeping*, Vol.15, No.4 (2008), pp.517–27.

independently gather intelligence on Rwanda.[35] Since traditional peacekeeping relies on the consent of the parties, this view suggests that any information collected and analysed by a UN mission had to be open, transparent, and shared with member states, especially in places like Rwanda where the UN had a limited presence while several nations could rely on strong diplomatic ties with Kigali.[36] While Part I has shown that UNAMIR faced formidable challenges on several fronts, the mission gathered at least four types of intelligence: 'technical', 'human', 'surveillance', and 'open-source'. A close examination of these types of intelligence suggests that a large portion of UNAMIR's problems stemmed from long-standing issues in New York—including Boutros-Ghali's distinction of 'political' and 'operational' functions—rather than from a lack of information in Kigali.

(i) 'Technical' versus 'Human' Intelligence

The Rwanda operation produced extensive 'technical' intelligence. Known as 'TECHINT', this refers to the collection and analysis of information through technological means and, in the case of Rwanda, preceded the arrival of the Blue Helmets in Kigali. The very aim of the early Reconnaissance Mission despatched by the SG in the summer of 1993 and headed by Dallaire was to 'assess the situation on the ground and gather the relevant information so as to enable the SG and the SC to reach a decision [on whether to establish UNAMIR]'.[37] Despite the customary absence of the word 'intelligence' from UN documents, the mission's final report included detailed recommendations on issues as diverse as command and control, personnel, vehicles, aviation, logistics, and infrastructure—assessments that were carried out through the independent processing of so-called 'technical' information.[38] Substantially the same can be said of UNOMUR, the other side of the UN presence in the region and the main purpose of which was the production of intelligence through situation reports ('SITREPS') which informed the Canadian General—on a daily basis—of what was happening along the Uganda–Rwanda border.[39] Thirdly and finally, once UNAMIR deployed, it too started producing intelligence through technical means, this time for DPKO. The cables between Dallaire and the peacekeeping department show that, from November 1993 until July 1994, thousands of SITREPS gave New York detailed assessments on demining, weapons caches, patrols and escorts, logistical and deployment

---

[35] Jacques-Roger Booh Booh, *Le Patron de Dallaire Parle* (Paris: Éditions Duboiris, 2005).
[36] Boutros Boutros-Ghali, *UNvanquished* (London: I.B. Tauris, 1999), p.129.
[37] Roméo Dallaire, Report of the Reconnaissance Mission to Rwanda, August 1993, ICTR-98-41-T, §2.
[38] Dallaire, *Report*, §4.   [39] Cables from 4-1-1994 to 11-4-1994 (6006/MILOB).

matters,[40] but also more general—or what UN officials would call 'political'—advice on what to do.[41] Dallaire also filtered UNOMUR's reports for DPKO, adding his comments and offering recommendations of what he regarded as both an operational *and* a 'political' nature.

The second form of intelligence upon which the UN system relied in Rwanda was 'human' and involved the gathering of information through people (HUMINT).[42] Since intelligence gathered by technical means is expensive and collecting it can be legally problematic, contacts with the local population offer peacekeepers a more discreet way of knowing what is happening. This was especially the case in Rwanda, where the Force Commander was bilingual and made a point of winning the hearts and minds of the local population.[43] It is thus not accidental that the most significant and controversial piece of intelligence gathered by UNAMIR was 'human' and involved the member of an extremist group linked to President Habyarimana.[44] As explained in Part I, according to this informant, his group was bent on provoking the Belgian contingent into leaving Rwanda; was planning the extermination of the Tutsi population at a rate of 1,000 in 20 minutes; and hid illegal weapons throughout Kigali.[45] Dallaire promptly informed DPKO of all this in his 'genocide cable'—yet while New York's reply has been widely commented upon, two aspects of it have been overlooked. First, what Dallaire sent to New York was *intelligence* rather than information, for his message included assessments of the informant and his reliability.[46] Significantly, the cable also outlined Dallaire's plans and expressed a clear desire for action ('*Peux ce que veux. Allons-y*', he signed off).[47] That DPKO deemed it proper, on the basis of Dallaire's cable, to oppose his plans and notify the Rwandan authorities of the tip it had received from its Force Commander shows that the intelligence process was indeed used by Headquarters to come to a decision—a clear (if controversial) application of the 'intelligence cycle'.[48] Second, the informant episode confirms the presence in New York of the so-called 'fear of intelligence' mentioned at the outset, especially in a department such as DPKO that was staffed by military observers 'loaned' by several states.[49] Equally significant is the fact that the decision to share Dallaire's intelligence with the Rwandan authorities

---

[40] Situation Reports (hereinafter, SITREPS) from No.1993-22-23A to No.1994-04-07D.

[41] Of special importance are the SITREPS from 23 November 1993 to 11 July 1994.

[42] Walter Dorn, 'United Nations Peacekeeping Intelligence', in Linton Johnson, ed., *The Oxford Handbook of National Security Intelligence* (Oxford: Oxford University Press, 2010), p.279.

[43] Dallaire, *Shake Hands*, esp. ch.7.

[44] United Nations, Report of the Independent Inquiry into the Actions of the United Nations during the 1994 Genocide in Rwanda, 15 December 1999, S/1999/1257.

[45] United Nations Report of the Independent Inquiry, p.10.

[46] See his code cables from 25 October 1993 (No.203) to 25 April 1994 (No.213).

[47] 'Where there is a will, there is a way. Let us do it.'   [48] Johnston, p.111.

[49] Thant Myint-U and Amy Scott, *The UN Secretariat* (New York: International Peace Academy, 2007), pp.74–5.

was seen by DPKO as 'operational' rather than 'political', with the result that it was taken by Riza and Annan in DPKO without direct consultation with DPA, the EOSG, or the SG, as Boutros-Ghali's memo seemingly required. Back in 1994, at least some DPKO officials thought that the UN should share what it knew with member states and should refrain from using intelligence against them.[50] Indeed, the existence of covert UN surveillance seemed to worry some of these officials more than any threat of ethnic violence.

(ii) 'Covert' versus 'Open-Source' Intelligence

Yet UNAMIR had already used covert surveillance, not least because this third form of intelligence—involving the monitoring of the behaviour of the Rwandan parties—was explicitly included in the mission's mandate.[51] It is true that, according to the latter, certain activities could only be performed by UNAMIR with the help of local authorities (e.g. '*contribute* to the security of the city of Kigali';[52] '*assist* in the coordination of humanitarian assistance activities';[53] and '*assist* with mine-clearance'[54]). Nevertheless, several other tasks were to be carried out independently by Dallaire (e.g. '*monitor* observance of the ceasefire agreement';[55] '*monitor* the security situation';[56] and '*monitor* the process of repatriation of Rwandese refugees').[57] Also, two of UNAMIR's core tasks could only be performed covertly ('*investigate* at the request of the parties, or on its own initiative, instances of alleged non-compliance';[58] and '*investigate* and report on incidents regarding the activities of the gendarmerie and police').[59] As Chapter 3 has shown, Dallaire had already gathered covert intelligence by seizing illegal arms caches from extremist groups and had duly reported such activities to DPKO.[60] This is why his 'genocide cable' never asked New York for *permission* to seize the weapons mentioned by his informant: the Force Commander assumed that it was his job to do so and was only asking DPKO to protect his source.[61] As a result, not only was UNAMIR covertly gathering intelligence on Rwanda; it was doing so with the knowledge of DPKO, whose officials repeatedly failed to object to it.

---

[50] Iqbal Riza, *PBS Frontline Interview*, March 2003; Kofi Annan, *PBS Frontline Interview*, 17 February 2004.
[51] Res 872, §3(e).   [52] Res 872, §3(a) (emphasis added).
[53] Res 872, §3(g) (emphasis added).   [54] Res 872, §3(d) (emphasis added).
[55] Res 872, §3(b) (emphasis added).   [56] Res 872, §3(c) (emphasis added).
[57] Res 872, §3(f) (emphasis added).   [58] Res 872, §3(e) (emphasis added).
[59] Res 872, §3(h) (emphasis added).
[60] Michael Barnett, *Eyewitness to a Genocide* (Ithaca: Cornell University Press, 2003), p.83.
[61] Barnett, p.83.

As for the fourth and last type of intelligence used by the UN system in Rwanda, it was 'open-source' (OSINT) and included public information, media outlets, and reports by governmental, intergovernmental, and non-governmental organizations.[62] Although Rwanda was hardly making front page news before the genocide, Part I has shown that information did exist about the country's situation, including a series of alarming UN reports that the Secretariat missed. Besides, after the start of the killings the scale of the tragedy quickly gained prominence in the media: 'It was clear who was being targeted', a BBC journalist reported, 'and it was also clear that the militia and the army were working together'.[63] Unlike Nazi Germany, Rwanda's *génocidaires* operated in broad daylight, used rudimentary weapons, and relied on the local media. 'Every day, many times a day, [there was] this radio/television [propaganda] which was encouraging people to kill with machetes and screwdrivers',[64] the head of the Red Cross stated.

(iii) 'Military' versus 'Political' Intelligence

Although Part I has already noted that the division of labour between the Force Commander (Dallaire) and UNAMIR's head (Booh Booh) was unclear and that the former was supposedly responsible for the 'operational' side whereas the Cameroonian was nominally in charge of 'political' matters,[65] the ambiguity surrounding their roles is most visible in relation to the issue of intelligence. Dallaire had been entrusted with reconnaissance and it was upon his recommendations that UNAMIR was set up; he had also been the interim chief of mission until Booh Booh arrived. It is thus unsurprising that Dallaire's role was never purely 'operational' but included substantive activities such as 'political' analysis and the production of intelligence for the benefit of what Boutros-Ghali's memo defined as the 'operational' DPKO. Booh Booh, too, produced intelligence—that was partly his job—but his training and the nature of his ambassadorial role meant that he was largely concerned with assessments of what New York called a 'political' nature for the UN's 'political' departments, namely, DPA and the EOSG. It is true that in 1994 cables deemed to be of a 'technical' nature were sent to DPKO and copied to DPA, while cables seen as involving 'political' matters were sent to DPA and copied to DPKO—a system that was meant to facilitate coordination and keep everybody in the loop. In practice, however, this system failed to work due to the high volume of cables exchanged and the fact that the separation

---

[62] Johnston, p.7.   [63] Mark Doyle, *PBS Frontline Interview*, 12 December 2003.
[64] Philippe Gaillard, *PBS Frontline Interview*, 12 December 2003.
[65] United Nations Report of the Independent Inquiry, pp.7–9.

between 'technical' and 'political' intelligence was subject to different inter-pretations by two departments which were not only reluctant to communicate with each other, but also determined to use that confusion to expand their functions. The ill-defined distinction between 'political' and 'operational' roles in Kigali mirrored at least in part the problematic division in New York mentioned in Chapter 6, with the result that a parallel system of intelli-gence was created in the field which mirrored the pathologies present at Headquarters.

ANALYSIS: WHICH PART OF THE UN SYSTEM ASSESSED THE RWANDA INTELLIGENCE?

In exercising their functions, SGs rely on a wide range of sources, including UN field personnel (for fact-finding), DPA (for what officials refer to as 'political' assessments), DPKO (largely for the 'operational' aspects of peace-keeping), the UN's specialized agencies (for humanitarian purposes), mem-ber states (though selectively and only when they feel the UN 'needs' to know something), NGOs, and the media.[66] Not all of these sources are available to the SG all the time for all peacekeeping missions, and their importance depends on the nature, location, and size of each operation.[67] Yet there are several 'eyes' through which the SG can 'see', although the vision of some of them is decidedly better than others. While the previous section focussed on the intelligence gathered by UNAMIR in the run-up to the genocide, the present section concentrates on how DPA and DPKO analysed that intelligence in New York. Since these two departments were supposed to filter information *and* intelligence coming from the field to the SG, they were important 'lenses' through which Boutros-Ghali was supposed to see the Rwanda 'universe'. Before dealing with their roles in Rwanda, however, the overall intelligence functions of DPA and DPKO need to be mentioned, for the establishment of these two departments in early 1992 can be seen as the latest in a series of attempts by SGs to strengthen the intelligence and analytical capacity of the UN bureaucracy against the wishes of several member states.

---

[66] Linda Melvern, *Conspiracy to Murder* (London: Verso, 2006), esp. chs 3 and 8; Allan Thompson, *Media and the Rwanda Genocide* (London: Pluto Press, 2007); Robert Rotberg and Thomas Weiss, *From Massacres to Genocide* (Washington, DC: Brookings Institution Press, 1996).
[67] Ramjoué, 'Improving United Nations Intelligence'.

(i) UN Intelligence before 1992

While the wariness of national capitals towards the idea of UN intelligence has a long history, it peaked during the years of the Cold War, when the organization was paralysed by cross-veto battles that severely constrained its effectiveness.[68] Even in this difficult context, however, SGs were able to rely on limited forms of covert intelligence.[69] For one thing, the two super powers were eager to offer intelligence to the SG if and when doing so was in their interests—and given the polarized approaches of Moscow and Washington to most issues, the UN chief often had at least one 'willing' source of intelligence.[70] For another, the Cold War stalemate in some respects enhanced the mediating role of the SG and, in the late 1980s, occasionally translated into increasing UN responsibilities in the areas of peace and security.[71] Although opportunities for the top UN official were limited, they were nevertheless growing.

Still, throughout the 1980s intelligence at the UN remained largely confined to espionage by and against the governments represented in New York, while numerous attempts by various SGs to enhance the analytical capacity of the Secretariat were systematically frustrated by member states.[72] When, in 1987, a Political Division (headed by a US citizen) was established within the Department for Special Political Questions (led by a Soviet), the impasse reached its zenith and Pérez de Cuéllar tried to overcome it by creating the Office for the Research and Collection of Information, or ORCI (note the avoidance of the word 'intelligence' in the title).[73] According to Álvaro de Soto, its former head, ORCI 'was supposed to be an office for policy planning, analysis, and also assistance to the SG on political questions. But', de Soto continues, 'for Cold War reasons we could not use in the title or in the terms of reference either the term "political" or the term "analysis", which is why you had this ridiculous title "Research and Collection of Information".'[74] ORCI was one of the earliest attempts by SGs to create an early-warning system in the Secretariat to deal with crises: 'It served as the focal point for the gathering, processing and reporting of international data', James Jonah, another former ORCI official, wrote. 'It was designed to provide early warnings in the Secretariat about looming trouble spots around the globe.'[75] Although ORCI was small and had few officers, it was seen by some states (especially the USA and the USSR) as a threatening sign of a new UN 'intelligence' apparatus,

---

[68] Brian Urquhart, *Peacemaking, Peacekeeping and the Future* (Toronto: GREF Publishing, 1990).

[69] Jonah, *What Price*, esp. chs 3, 4, and 6.

[70] David Hannay, 'Intelligence and International Agencies', in Harold Shukman, ed., *Agents for Change* (London: St Ermin's, 2000).

[71] Jean-Pierre Alem, *L'Espionage* (Paris: Lauvauzalle, 1987).   [72] Alem, p.465.

[73] Chesterman, 'Does the UN Have Intelligence?', p.152.

[74] My interview with Álvaro de Soto, 20 July 2011, New York, USA (and via email on 4 June 2016).

[75] Jonah, *What Price*, p.86.

while several US senators worried that it might provide a cover for Soviet spying in the USA.[76] Most national diplomats were thus relieved when newly-appointed SG Boutros-Ghali abolished ORCI in 1992.

Such relief was, nonetheless, short-lived, for Boutros-Ghali did not disband ORCI in order to weaken the analytical capacity of the Secretariat, but to strengthen it through the creation of DPA and DPKO. Despite reassurances to the contrary, the rationale for the establishment of these two entities was precisely to provide the SG with enhanced intelligence capabilities ('operational'—to use New York's problematic terminology—in the case of DPKO, 'political' in the case of DPA) which were seen as all the more necessary given the growth of peacekeeping after the end of the Cold War.[77] Since it was the SC itself, during its January 1992 summit, that had asked the SG to expand the role of the organization in preventive diplomacy, states were hardly in a position to openly oppose Boutros-Ghali's move.[78] They nevertheless controlled the all-important UN budget, and the distribution of resources left little doubt as to which of these two departments mattered most to the world's capitals. So while in the early 1990s DPKO flourished, DPA suffered—and with it the SG's capacity for 'political' analysis and intelligence: 'What happened in the 1990s was that you had this peacekeeping bonanza, so the peacekeeping budget grew exponentially', a UN official said. 'But the equivalent never happened for the preventive diplomacy budget. And the reason was that DPA was consciously starved of resources, because the member states did not want a powerful political department.'[79] This appeared especially true of the superpower: when, in 1992, the European Community, Australia, Canada, and New Zealand proposed an independent UN intelligence-gathering facility for early warning and preventive diplomacy, the USA vetoed it.[80] 'The proposition touched off a furious response from the US', one observer noted, 'which appears to be resolutely opposed to any moves that would enhance the UN's ability to gather and analyse sensitive information in an independent fashion.'[81] Writing of the UN's ability to enable governments to find common solutions to transnational problems, Goulding noted that 'That is what the UN was set up to do. The question now was whether the United States would let it do it.'[82] In the early 1990s, the scene was thus set for a confrontation between a pro-active SG eager to make

[76] Chesterman, 'Does the UN Have Intelligence?', p.152.

[77] Boutros-Ghali, *UNvanquished*, esp. ch.2.

[78] Boutros-Ghali, *UNvanquished*, esp. ch.2.

[79] My interview with a UN official, New York, USA, 14 July 2011. See also Marrack Goulding, 'Power Politics at the United Nations', Remarks to the O'Neill/Roberts Seminar, All Souls' College, Oxford, 5 December 1997, p.3.

[80] Mark Curtis, *The Great Deception* (London: Pluto, 1998). See also William Durch, ed., *UN Peacekeeping, American Policy and the Uncivil Wars of the 1990s* (Basingstoke: Palgrave Macmillan, 1996).

[81] Curtis, pp.200–1.

[82] Marrack Goulding, 'Peacemonger: Book Proposal', 15 June 1998 (MIG-PA).

his mark on the world stage, and a superpower that, having—in the view of many Americans—won the Cold War and while ready to enhance the role of the UN in theory, was eager to micro-manage it in practice.[83] Importantly for our purposes, all this was happening in mid-1993, when UNAMIR was being planned.

(ii) UN Intelligence after 1992

The different intelligence roles played by DPA and DPKO in Rwanda did not only reflect their supposedly distinct areas of expertise, but also a clash between Boutros-Ghali and the UN membership. Given the UN's notorious problems with logistics and the fact that the use of force is traditionally associated with states rather than international organizations, in the early 1990s military attachés from Western capitals—rather than Secretariat officials—came to dominate DPKO.[84] This became most apparent in April 1993, when a Situation Centre was established within the peacekeeping department with the task of monitoring UN operations and gathering military intelligence for the benefit of the wider UN 'family'—in theory, an 'operational' development that was supposed to assist the SG's 'political' role in peacekeeping. In September 1993, the Centre was also equipped with an Information and Research Unit (again, note the absence of the word 'intelligence' from the title) in order to enhance the analytical capacity of DPKO.[85] Like the Centre, however, the Unit was staffed with military officers 'loaned' to the Secretariat and drawn from national intelligence branches—especially the USA, which footed most of the bill.[86] While the DPKO's intelligence facilities were thus nominally under the control of the SG, they were heavily reliant on national officials, particularly those coming from the country that provided 20 per cent of the UN budget and that boasted the world's largest military output.[87] Writing about the DPKO's Information and Research Unit, a former military adviser noted that it is 'not clear *who* is in charge of this section, *how* it is managed, and *who* is responsible for *what*. In addition, many officials inside the Secretariat looked at the product of this section with great distrust and not without reason.'[88] In his handover notes, Goulding warned his successor that the DPKO's Situation Centre '...maintains a 24-hour watch and its staff get

[83] Marrack Goulding, *Peacemonger* (London: Murray, 2002), ch.18; Jonah, *What Price*, pp.97–108; Boutros Boutros-Ghali, *Mes Années à la Maison de Verre* (Paris: Fayard, 1999), ch.4.

[84] Frank Van Kappen, 'Strategic Intelligence and the United Nations', in *Peacekeeping Intelligence* (London: OSS, 2003), p.6.

[85] Chesterman, 'Does the UN Have Intelligence?', p.154.

[86] Chesterman, 'Does the UN Have Intelligence?', p.154.

[87] Edward Luck, *Mixed Messages* (Washington, DC: Brookings Institution Press, 1999), esp. ch.7.

[88] Van Kappen, p.5.

from their Governments interesting intelligence which is not normally made available to other Departments' or the SG.[89]

This was the complex environment that awaited Dallaire in August 1993 when he was summoned to New York to consider the Rwanda mission.[90] Although he reported to DPKO and provided to it most of UNAMIR's intelligence, Boutros-Ghali's instructions mentioned in Chapter 6 seemed to suggest that responsibility for gathering intelligence of a 'political' nature fell on DPA rather than DPKO.[91] It is, of course, normal for different bureaucratic units to have different areas of expertise—were this not the case, chaos would ensue. What is interesting about 1993, however, is that DPA and DPKO seemed to have not only different intelligence *roles* in Rwanda, but also different *constituencies* (i.e. the SG *vis-à-vis* certain states) with seemingly different strategic interests and approaches to the African country. Boutros-Ghali was a committed interventionist intent on turning DPA into the most important jewel in his crown and into New York's key department, a determination that clashed with Clinton's post-Somalia peacekeeping strategy and emphasis on DPKO. The elevation of DPA over DPKO, therefore, did not purely express a bureaucratic preference but was meant to strengthen the SG's role in intelligence-gathering; as Chapter 6 has shown, it also reflected Boutros-Ghali's determination to control the UN bureaucracy by limiting the influence of member states—especially the USA—over it and by cutting DPKO out of 'political' matters. '[The SG] wants to correct the impression that the UN has become an instrument of American policy', Goulding wrote, '[and] claims to have detected in Bonn and Paris much unease about American dominance.'[92] More than any other department, for Boutros-Ghali DPKO reflected precisely such US dominance.

DISTRIBUTION: HOW WAS THE RWANDA INTELLIGENCE SHARED WITHIN THE UN SYSTEM?

Even the best intelligence is of limited use unless it is shared and acted upon. This is especially the case in a large organization such as the UN, where bureaucracy and power disparities create peculiar challenges to the 'intelligence cycle'.[93] Peacekeeping presents its own problems because information tends to be fragmentary, collection methods are often limited, and intelligence

---

[89] Marrack Goulding, Handover Notes for Kieran Prendergast, 22 February 1997, §16 (MIG-PA).
[90] Dallaire, *Shake Hands*, ch.5.   [91] Jonah, *What Price*, pp.9–10.
[92] MIG-TD-IX, 20-Jan-1993.
[93] Alexandre Dumulon-Perreault et al., Peacekeeping Intelligence, Unpublished Conference Report, 2003.

rarely adheres to the rules of regular warfare.[94] In spite of this, and as we have seen above, the UN system did gather a considerable amount of intelligence on Rwanda. Yet to what extent was it disseminated within it? Seeing how three pieces of intelligence mentioned in Part I were handled by the Secretariat— and asking to what extent they fit within the 'technical' versus 'political' distinction set by Boutros-Ghali's memo—addresses some of these questions.

Rwanda's pitiful human rights record had been an open secret in New York long before the genocide. The vicious civil war between Habyarimana's French-supported forces and Kagame's Uganda-sponsored RPF meant that atrocities were committed by both sides, ethnic tensions were long-standing, and the country was awash with weapons.[95] Indeed, it is because the situation was so precarious that UN officials were keeping Rwanda under close observation.[96] Although various UN reports were produced in the early 1990s, Ndiaye's stands out because of the level of detail, prescience, and its publication date. Despite visiting the country for only a week in mid-1993, the UN Special Rapporteur on Extrajudicial, Summary, or Arbitrary Executions had no doubt about the causes of Rwanda's violence. '[T]he victims of the attacks, Tutsis in the overwhelming majority of cases, have been targeted solely because of their membership of a certain ethnic group, and for no other objective reason',[97] he wrote—with language that is customarily used in international law to define the crime of genocide. As for the perpetrators, Ndiaye noted that '[i]t has been shown time and time again that government officials were involved... directly by encouraging, planning, directing or participating in the violence',[98] and he suggested that unless weapons were confiscated the situation would get out of control since 'one spark is all that is needed to cause the situation to degenerate'.[99] What makes this report significant for intelligence purposes is its publication date, namely, a week *after* the signing of the Arusha Peace Agreement and precisely when UNAMIR was being planned.[100] Alarmingly, nobody in New York seemed to be aware of this report: not DPA (which was monitoring the Arusha negotiations and was responsible for UNAMIR's 'political' issues); not DPKO (which was organizing the logistical aspects of UNAMIR but was also clearly dealing with substantive matters); and not the SG (who was expected to oversee the entire operation). That such a disturbing report

---

[94] Dumulon et al., Peacekeeping Intelligence.

[95] Melvern, ch.3; Dallaire, *Shake Hands*, ch.4.

[96] United Nations, *The Blue Helmets*, ch.16.

[97] United Nations, Report by the Special Rapporteur on Extra-Judicial, Summary, or Arbitrary Executions on his Mission to Rwanda, pp.8–17, April 1993, (E/CN.4/1994/7/Add.1), 11 August 1993, p.79.

[98] United Nations, Report by the Special Rapporteur, §28.

[99] United Nations, Report by the Special Rapporteur, §74.

[100] Dallaire, *Shake Hands*, ch.4.

produced from within the organization remained unfamiliar to the upper echelons of the Secretariat is especially troubling in light of Dallaire's complaints that he was given virtually no information on Rwanda.[101] As one observer noted, 'Ndiaye said later that for all the attention his report received he might as well have thrown it into the sea'.[102]

The second piece of intelligence involves the advance warning, given directly to Boutros-Ghali in December 1993 and mentioned in Part I, of impending anti-Tutsi massacres. Four months before the start of the genocide and one month before Dallaire sent his 'genocide cable', Jonah was told by Boutros-Ghali that people close to the Rwandan president were planning to use force against the Tutsis. The SG confidentially asked Jonah to tell Habyarimana that the UN would not accept this and, according to Jonah, when confronted with such evidence Habyarimana denied any involvement and asked where the SG had obtained this information.[103] This episode matters in relation to the issue of intelligence for what it says about the 'intelligence cycle' within the UN 'family': while the SG shared what he knew with Jonah and DPA—his chief 'political' officer and department—he seemed to keep DPKO in the dark partly because the matter, for the SG, was 'political' rather than 'technical', and partly because he distrusted Annan (given Boutros-Ghali's view that the SC should not 'micro-manage' peacekeeping operations, it is unsurprising that the SG did not inform the SC).[104] By this time, Goulding was writing in his diary that Riza, too, was seen by Boutros-Ghali as unfaithful to the SG and untrustworthy.[105] 'Relations with DPKO were difficult in a number of areas', Goulding wrote in August 1994, days after the Arusha parties had signed the peace agreement, 'most of them due to the prickliness of Iqbal Riza, who cannot accept any role in DPA in relation to peacekeeping'.[106]

This makes the circumstances surrounding Dallaire's 'genocide cable'—the third problematic example of how the UN used its Rwanda intelligence—all the more intriguing. Chapter 3 has mentioned how the Force Commander gathered his intelligence, and that he promptly reported it to DPKO.[107] Yet two points should be noted. First, and once again, there was no attempt in the UN Secretariat to share this piece of information—which corroborated the other two already mentioned—with the rest of the UN 'family', partly as a result of the dysfunctional chain of command (Dallaire reported to DPKO) but also because of the presumed 'technical' nature of Dallaire's information.

---

[101] Dallaire, *Shake Hands*, ch.4.

[102] United States Holocaust Memorial Museum, 'Briefing by Linda Melvern: Question and Answers', available at https://www.ushmm.org/confront-genocide/speakers-and-events/all-speakers-and-events/briefing-by-linda-melvern/briefing-by-linda-melvern-questions-and-answers (accessed 13 May 2016).

[103] My interview with James Jonah, 20 July 2011, New York, USA. See also Jonah, *What Price*, p.382.

[104] MIG-TD-IX, 12-Feb-1994.   [105] MIG-TD-XII, 25-Jul-1995.

[106] MIG-TD-IX, 31-Jul-1994.   [107] Code Cable No.1994-01-11J, 11-1-1994.

The Force Commander sent his cable to DPKO's military adviser, Maurice Baril, who shared it internally only with Annan (head of DPKO) and Riza.[108] Dallaire did not copy his message to DPA or to the SG's office, despite the fact that—going by Boutros-Ghali's memo—such a cable supposedly involved substantive 'political' issues.[109] Importantly, DPKO did not seem to have shared it either: Annan's reply to Dallaire was marked 'UNAMIR ONLY—NO DISTRIBUTION'[110] and it was not copied to DPA, nor shared with the SG, nor notified to the SC.[111] While referring the cable to the SC would have been unusual, directly informing DPA and the SG would have been appropriate. In January 1994, precisely at the time of the 'genocide cable', Goulding was complaining about 'the management and flow of information within the Secretariat'[112] and regretting that 'secretiveness and turf protection still prevail in some quarters'.[113] '[That cable] never reached the level of the Secretary-General, no', Boutros-Ghali stated with reference to Dallaire's document. 'There was a very important decentralization. We received only a report from DPKO based on the different telegrams, and this report was given to the ambassador-general, who read this report to the Security Council.'[114] Far from being exceptional, the 'genocide cable' offers another example of how different parts of the UN system were not proactive in sharing with each other the intelligence they did have. Boutros-Ghali's division between 'technical' and 'political' roles compounded the matter and made it easier for his two key departments to use both information and intelligence as they saw fit.

THE UN, INTELLIGENCE, AND RWANDA

A key question surrounding the role of the UN in Rwanda involves the extent to which Secretariat officials knew what was happening in 1994. This is a sensitive—even emotional—issue in that attempts by successive SGs to strengthen the intelligence and analytical capacity of the organization before *and* after 1994 have been studiously frustrated by member states. Since the world's most powerful capitals had stronger ties with Kigali than the Secretariat and were able to rely on embassies there, UN officials claim that, in Rwanda like elsewhere, the real problem lay with those nations. 'The member

---

[108] Code Cable No.1994-01-11J, 11-1-1994.
[109] Code Cable No.1994-01-11J, 11-1-1994.
[110] Code Cable No.1994-01-11A-1, 11-1-1994.
[111] Code Cable No.1994-01-11A-1, 11-1-1994.
[112] Marrack Goulding, 'Recent Development in Peace-Making', Presentation given at the International Peace Academy, 31 January 1994, p.4 (MIG-PA).
[113] Goulding, 'Recent Development in Peace-Making', p.4.
[114] Boutros-Ghali, *PBS Frontline Interview*, 12 November 2008.

states, to maintain a kind of pressure on the United Nations, will not give you all the information', Boutros-Ghali noted in relation to the crisis of 1994. 'But definitely, when a decision is taken, or when you are trying to oppose a decision, you are in a weaker position than member states, because they know more about the situation than you. We gave information [on Rwanda], but they never gave us any information.'[115]

Two factors should be noted. First, states may have legitimate concerns about sharing what they know with the UN Secretariat. 'I understand the reluctance of the nations to share intelligence with DPKO', one of the department's military advisers wrote. 'Often... the nation that owns the information is afraid [that] its intelligence sources may be compromised, or else that certain technical capabilities may be revealed. The Secretariat is as watertight as a sieve [and] it is nearly impossible to keep anything under wrap.'[116] Second, the fact that states are reluctant to share what they know with the UN does not address the question of how *the Secretariat* manages its own intelligence. As this chapter has suggested, fragmentation rather than ignorance was the critical issue in 1994: DPA was supposed to gather information of a 'political' nature and was responsible for diplomatic negotiations; DPKO was theoretically in charge of the 'operational' aspects of peacekeeping and of collecting data about them; Humanitarian Affairs oversaw the issue of refugees and produced intelligence on that; and so on. Yet this division of labour visibly failed to work. 'No central unit was charged with collecting even "soft" intelligence, including information available in the vast structure of the UN agencies', one author wrote, 'and to translate assessments into policy options and strategic planning.'[117]

While the main reason lay with member states' opposition to an effective intelligence-gathering system, there is another explanation behind the lack of coordination in New York: the various units of the UN Secretariat were unwilling—rather than unable—to do so. This was especially the case for DPA and DPKO: the institutional rivalry between them—exacerbated by Boutros-Ghali's memo and by a clash of personalities between Jonah and Annan—meant that the intelligence gathered by one department was not directly or efficiently passed on to the other, despite the two offices being located next to each other. Although both departments possessed privileged intelligence pointing to advanced plans for a humanitarian crisis—DPA via the SG's warning of December 1993, DPKO through Dallaire's 'genocide cable' of January 1994—neither department appears to have gone out of its way to share what it knew with the other, let alone coordinate its responses. In few cases did the old dictum that information is power have more tragic outcomes than in Rwanda, where intelligence became an

---

[115] Boutros-Ghali, *PBS Frontline Interview*, 12 November 2008.

[116] Van Kappen, p.7.

[117] Astri Suhrke and Bruce Jones, 'Preventive Diplomacy in Rwanda', in Bruce W. Jentleson, ed., *Opportunities Missed, Opportunities Seized: Preventive Diplomacy in the post-Cold War World* (Lanham: Rowan & Littlefield, 2000), p.259.

instrument employed by the SG, by member states, *and* by the UN bureaucracy to achieve different objectives.

Different parts of the UN Secretariat thus knew different things about Rwanda, yet neither an institutional arrangement for coordinating such knowledge (because of states' opposition to it) nor a desire to do so (because of intra-departmental rivalries and the SG's lack of confidence in DPKO) existed in 1994. As Chapter 10 will suggest, far from being a relic of the past, poor—often opportunistic—handling of intelligence is a problem that affects the Secretariat to this day. In November 2012, an internal report on the role of the UN bureaucracy during the Sri Lanka civil war concluded that senior officials in the EOSG 'were receiving almost no information from the [lower echelons of the] Secretariat on the international human rights and humanitarian law situation [in the country, and] began relying on reports from Human Rights Watch (HRW) and other international NGOs to learn about the killing of civilians'.[118] Although in true UN style the word 'intelligence' is nowhere to be found in this 128-page document whereas 'information' appears on every other page, the questions raised by that report and by this chapter—why, how, and by whom intelligence is produced and shared within the UN Secretariat—remains topical.

Back in 1994, it was the SG's job to manage the different parts of the Secretariat and ensure that they overcame their bureaucratic rivalries, as any good administrator would do. Although Boutros-Ghali did attempt to establish a UN-wide intelligence unit, there is no evidence that he tried to smooth relations between his two key departments—quite the reverse, since we know from Chapter 6 that he mistrusted DPKO even more than DPA officials did. '[T]he trench warfare with Annan's DPKO continued', Goulding wrote. 'As Boutros-Ghali's difficulties with the Americans increased and it became clear that Annan was their African candidate to replace him, Boutros-Ghali used me more and more as a counterweight to Annan, thereby adding tension between our two Departments.'[119] Rather than a resource, DPKO was increasingly seen as a liability for Boutros-Ghali's plans and Annan as a threat to the SG's job security; the more the peacekeeping department and its leaders were kept in the dark, the better. Bureaucratic friction was therefore hardly the only reason behind the DPA–DPKO tensions of 1994; although the SG had a solid reputation for handling cumbersome organizations, including the Egyptian civil service,[120] he discovered that bureaucrats enjoying the protection of the Council's veto-wielding members raise a peculiar set of problems. Since individuals, their professional interactions, and their personal inclinations clearly mattered in 1994, it is to them that Chapters 8 and 9 will turn.

---

[118] *Report of the Secretary-General's Internal Review Panel on the United Nations Action in Sri-Lanka*, December 2012 (New York: UN Department of Public Information, 2013), p.82.

[119] Goulding, 'Peacemonger: Book Proposal'.

[120] Kevin Cahill, *Preventive Diplomacy* (Abingdon: Routledge, 2000), p.254.

8

Leadership

In the midst of the military campaign he was waging in Spain on behalf of Her Majesty's government, the Duke of Wellington sent the following note to his boss, the War Minister—a note that Goulding admiringly mentions in his diaries and kept in his archive: 'Sir—were I to reply to all the correspondence that I receive from you, I would be unable to attend to the important matter for which I am here: the war. I thus remind you—for the last time—that so long as I am in charge of this army, I will ensure that nobody under my command is embarrassed by the futilities emanating from your office'.[1] While Wellington's message is widely seen—including by the 'peacekeeper' Goulding—as a sign of strength of purpose and military resolve in the face of the micro-managing tendencies originating in faraway centres of 'political' power, different circumstances and a more authoritarian politician at Westminster may have led to different outcomes (such as the Duke's removal for insubordination). Several factors—including Wellington's personality, his military skills, and the Minister's strategic dependence on him—made it easier for the Duke to resist pressures coming from London.[2] By far the most critical among those factors, however, was war. As the most destructive of human endeavours, war requires discipline—bypassing the chain of command can be deadly—but also the flexibility to adapt to the battlefield.[3] The more tragic the circumstances, the more legitimately are rules bent and leaders made, and few circumstances test leadership as thoroughly as war.[4]

One of those circumstances is genocide.[5] The destructive combination of civil war and ethnic strife on a vast scale—but also the friction between 'military' and 'political' leadership that so incensed the Duke of Wellington—were in full display during the Rwandan genocide, with one significant complication. As an international organization based on consensus and limited enforcement

---

[1] Marrack Goulding, 'Code Restricted', Folder V, Z-262, 2/2 (MIG-PA).
[2] Christopher Hibbert, *Wellington* (New York: HarperCollins, 2010).
[3] Sun Tzu, *The Art of War* (London: CreateSpace, 2013).
[4] James MacGregor Burns, *Leadership* (New York: HarperCollins, 2010).
[5] Jacques Semelin, *Purify and Destroy* (London: Hurst, 2007).

mechanisms, the UN is notoriously inept at handling conflict.[6] Although the chain of command in New York can be confusing at the best of times, in 1994 the division between 'operational' and 'political' roles in peacekeeping—and between the supposedly 'technical' DPKO and the 'political' DPA—contributed to straining relations among UN officials in both New York and Kigali, making it even more difficult to implement strategic decisions.[7] Partly because of this, in the run-up to the Rwanda crisis, individuals mattered as much as their departments and their contributions should be taken into account. While the next chapter will consider Boutros-Ghali's long-standing involvement with Rwanda, the present one looks at how the other top UN officials involved in the events of 1994 managed the challenges posed by the Rwanda crisis: Kofi Annan and Iqbal Riza in DPKO, James Jonah and Marrack Goulding in DPA, Jacques-Roger Booh Booh and Roméo Dallaire in UNAMIR, Madeleine Albright and Ibrahim Gambari in the Security Council. What were their approaches to UNAMIR and peacekeeping? How did they cope with the Rwanda events, with the distinction between 'technical' and 'political' roles emanating from Boutros-Ghali's memo, and with the blurring of functions in both New York and Kigali? And can we speak of leadership at all in relation to them—did these officials have a vision and a sense of purpose, or were they simply bureaucrats handling a complex emergency?

Leadership[8] and international leadership[9] are contested concepts, but writing of them in relation to UN officials is especially problematic. While several studies have looked at how the UN handles crises, the focus has been on the Council rather than the Secretariat.[10] Since states are thought to control the world body, no 'real' leadership is considered possible within the New York bureaucracy—even writing of it with reference to the SG is a recent and disputed endeavour.[11] UN officials, too, tend to see themselves as executors of policy decisions made *by* the SG and SC, rather than as leaders with decision-making discretion and an ability to influence their departments' policies, let alone those *of* the SG and SC.[12] Yet as this chapter suggests, that

---

[6] Spyros Economides and Mats Berdal, eds, *United Nations Interventionism, 1991–2004* (Cambridge: Cambridge University Press, 2007).

[7] Ralph Zacklin, *The UN Secretariat and the Use of Force in a Unipolar World* (Cambridge: Cambridge University Press, 2010).

[8] Burns, esp. pp.1–5; Peter Northouse, *Leadership* (London: Sage, 2012); Michael Foley, *Political Leadership* (Oxford: Oxford University Press, 2013), esp. pp.1–28.

[9] Foley, ch.10; Simon Chesterman, ed., *Secretary or General?* (Cambridge: Cambridge University Press, 2007); Ngaire Woods et al., *Effective Leadership in International Organizations* (Geneva: World Economic Forum, 2014), p.7.

[10] Vaughan Lowe et al., eds, *The United Nations Security Council and War* (Oxford: Oxford University Press, 2010).

[11] Kent Kille, *From Manager to Visionary* (Basingstoke: Palgrave Macmillan, 2006).

[12] Kille, *From Manager to Visionary*, ch.1. See also Ingvild Bode, *Individual Agency and Policy Change at the United Nations* (Abingdon: Routledge, 2015).

perception is not entirely accurate. The fragmented nature of the Secretariat in the early 1990s means that UN officials had a considerable margin of manoeuvre in terms of policy direction, a discretion which they did use to achieve the outcomes *they* saw as optimal, but which they often failed to coordinate with other parts of the Secretariat, *including* the SG and SC.[13] Institutional leadership as seen so far is thus insufficient to explain the role of the Secretariat in 1994 and the contribution of its individual leaders must also be considered, especially given their different approaches to peacekeeping and to the scope and limits of the SG's role in world politics. The turf wars of the early 1990s, the friction between SG and parts of the UN membership, and their disagreements over the very nature of peacekeeping, simultaneously restricted and emboldened UN officials. To them, such factors represented threats as well as opportunities, and they affected their performance both in New York and in Rwanda.

KOFI ANNAN AND IQBAL RIZA

The first question to ask when considering the role of Kofi Annan in what he described as the 'very painful and traumatic experience'[14] of Rwanda is the extent to which he was in charge of UNAMIR. As Under-Secretary-General for Peacekeeping, the Ghanaian was supposedly responsible for managing the 'operational' aspects of peacekeeping missions, including large ones in Somalia, Bosnia, and Cambodia.[15] Although it is not unusual for routine matters to be left to aides—the most important of whom, in Annan's case, was his deputy Iqbal Riza (who would become his Chief of Staff when Annan was promoted to SG)—it was Riza who took some of the most consequential and controversial decisions on UNAMIR. While Annan's proclivity to delegate complicates the task of assessing his performance in 1994, it is nevertheless indicative both of his 'consensual' approach to leadership and of the challenges it poses in times of crisis.

(i) Annan, Riza, and UNAMIR

Reflecting the widespread feeling of 'fatigue' with traditional peacekeeping which was being felt by troop-contributing countries and most SC members following the death of eighteen US rangers and the near collapse of the

---

[13] Keith Grint, *Leadership* (Oxford: Oxford University Press, 2010), p.4.
[14] Kofi Annan, *PBS Frontline Interview*, 17 February 2004.
[15] Michael Doyle, *Keeping the Peace* (Cambridge: Cambridge University Press, 1997).

Somalia operation in October 1993, Annan—like Goulding—was increasingly concerned about the viability of setting up missions in the absence of financial and logistical means to support them. As the next section will suggest, however, unlike Goulding's, Annan's concerns were practical rather than conceptual: 'Handed to us by the SC were over a dozen operations that we now had to manage worldwide with a tiny DPKO staff',[16] Annan wrote in his memoirs. Far from being a sign of 'indifference',[17] at the strategic and logistical level—which was supposed to be the remit of DPKO—such reluctance was understandable. If the world's only superpower was unable to control a few hundred Somali militias despite its state-of-the-art technology and top-notch command-and-control mechanisms, how could an organization like the UN with its limited budget and well-known operational shortcomings—including its complete reliance on voluntary troop contributions—be expected to succeed? 'The debacle in Somalia meant the aversion to taking any risks now ran even harder through the instincts of the troop-contributing nations',[18] Annan pointed out. 'But peacekeeping operations continued to be deployed to complex and rapidly shifting civil war zones elsewhere',[19] including Rwanda. There was also the issue of workload, for Annan's involvement in the Former Yugoslavia and Haiti meant that UNAMIR became a sideshow to those crises. 'The assistant secretary-general was dealing with [Rwanda]', Annan wrote with reference to Riza, 'and I had my hands full at that time also with Yugoslavia.'[20]

Since UNAMIR was predicted to be a cheap success story, the limited support it had plummeted as soon as its troubles started. As previous chapters have shown, it was a mission that France wanted (in order to prevent the RPF from overthrowing the Paris-backed Hutus),[21] that Boutros-Ghali favoured (in order to counterbalance what he saw as the Council's Western-centric approach to peacekeeping), and that Jonah encouraged (in order to implement Boutros-Ghali's agenda). Annan was far more cautious: worried about the logistical challenges of setting up another mission and of finding troops for it, the head of DPKO was also painfully aware that after Somalia the USA—the nation that was paying 27 per cent of the entire UN peacekeeping budget—remained thoroughly unconvinced about UNAMIR. 'As an administrator', one author noted, '[Annan's] sense of what ought to be done was profoundly shaped by his understanding of what could or, rather, couldn't be done'.[22] So the Ghanaian diplomat found himself between a rock (an administration in Washington that was essential to the smooth running of DPKO but which

---

[16] Kofi Annan, *Interventions* (London: Allen Lane, 2012), p.52.
[17] Michael Barnett, *Eyewitness to a Genocide* (Ithaca: Cornell University Press, 2003).
[18] Annan, *Interventions*, p.46.   [19] Annan, *Interventions*, p.46.
[20] Annan, *PBS Frontline Interview*, 17 February 2004.
[21] Andrew Wallis, *Silent Accomplice* (London: I.B. Tauris, 2014).
[22] James Traub, *The Best Intentions* (London: Bloomsbury, 2007), p.48.

disliked UNAMIR) and a hard place (an SG in New York who saw Rwanda as an opportunity to redeem the UN from the reputational disaster of Somalia).

In this environment of fractious leadership, peacekeeping fatigue, and budgetary crisis, it is important to note that Annan's response to Dallaire's 'genocide cable' did not convey the position of the SG or the Secretariat, but that of the peacekeeping department, for neither DPA, nor Boutros-Ghali, nor the SC seem to have been directly consulted about it.[23] Annan correctly notes that '[a]ll cable traffic from force commanders was automatically copied to over a dozen people, both among senior staff in DPKO and the secretary-general's office'.[24] Yet with tens of thousands of troops on the ground, several large-scale operations worldwide, and thousands of messages going back and forth, Dallaire's cable could not reasonably be expected to pop up on the SG's desk. More important still, the department's response was neither coordinated with, nor communicated to, anybody outside of DPKO. While Chapter 9 will show that Boutros-Ghali's own position is highly problematic, Annan was supposedly in charge of day-to-day activities—including early-warnings—something that neither Jonah nor Boutros-Ghali were in a position to monitor. Yet Annan and Riza made little visible effort to solicit the advice of the top echelons of the UN, as bureaucrats usually do when confronted with a thorny issue. For a document that the DPKO chief acknowledged to have 'caused a stir' in his department, this is surprising. 'There are a number of cables that we get of this nature', Riza stated, 'but not of this magnitude. Not with such dire predictions.'[25] Neither can the contents of Annan's response to Dallaire be seen—to use the vocabulary employed at the time by UN officials—as 'technical' in nature. On the contrary, it conveyed a substantive decision which reflected a certain (conservative) interpretation of what UNAMIR's priorities were and how they should be implemented. Thus the need to avoid military confrontation, rather than the necessity to prevent an ethnic massacre, was thought to be the 'paramount consideration' for UNAMIR. There was nothing 'technical' about such an assessment or the decision underpinning it.

From a leadership perspective, it should also be noted that Annan was not actively involved in drafting the DPKO's response to Dallaire, which was sent by Riza under Annan's name. 'I was in charge of the mission and I decided on what instructions were sent', Riza stated, so 'those instructions [to Dallaire] were sent under my signature'.[26] Indeed, Riza has conceded that Annan was only briefed about the cable *after* it was sent to Dallaire: 'We must have briefed [Annan] the following day or maybe a day or two later',[27] Riza noted, a

---

[23] Boutros Boutros-Ghali, *Mes Années à la Maison de Verre* (Paris: Fayard, 1999); James Jonah, *What Price the Survival of the United Nations?* (Ibadan: Evans Brothers, 2006); Chinmaya Gharekhan, *The Horseshoe Table* (London: Longman, 2006).

[24] Annan, *Interventions*, p.54.   [25] Iqbal Riza, *PBS Frontline Interview*, March 2003.

[26] Riza, *PBS Frontline Interview*, March 2003.

[27] Riza, *PBS Frontline Interview*, March 2003.

circumstance that Annan confirms.[28] As mentioned, it is hardly unusual for deputies to take decisions in the absence of their bosses, especially in an under-staffed office like DPKO which back in 1994 was juggling several large operations. One should also note that Annan never objected to Riza's wording and, to his credit, never tried to shift responsibility to his deputy—quite the reverse: 'We believed it to be the best—indeed, the only—option that we could take',[29] Annan insists. Still, the DPKO head was neither on leave nor travelling during the Rwanda crisis, and Dallaire's cable was clearly exceptional—Annan himself described it as 'urgent and deeply disturbing'.[30] The fact that Riza thought it appropriate to respond to Dallaire without asking for Annan's advice (let alone permission) indicates not only Riza's considerable influence within DPKO, but also the comparatively low priority given to UNAMIR by Annan.

The confusion surrounding the mission's mandate and rules of engagement is another example of Annan's penchant to delegate substantive decision-making authority to his deputy—and of DPKO's tendency to make conse-quential choices in 'splendid isolation' from the rest of the Secretariat, while framing them as 'operational' in nature. 'They did not need instructions from New York. They have their weapons, those weapons are loaded and ... while lives are threatened ... they could have opened fire',[31] Riza stated in relation to the uncertainty about UNAMIR's rules of engagement. Yet not only were Riza's views not clearly conveyed to Dallaire, peacekeepers in Rwanda thought that permission from DPKO *was* necessary to open fire to protect civilians. 'I cannot understand that', Riza replied when asked about this. 'I cannot recall ... a cable [from us] going back and saying "Let hell run its course, don't open fire".'[32] Still, if confusion reigns in the field on what peacekeepers can and cannot do, responsibility for it cannot but rest first and foremost with the DPKO leadership. Consequential—and, to use the UN's lexicon, 'political'—decisions such as the interpretation of a mission's mandate and its conduct were thus taken by Riza and Annan independently of the SG and the SC. As Chapter 10 will suggest, this is not entirely surprising to the extent that peacekeeping-related tasks include to this day a wide range of activities such as 'assisting the parties in their negotiations';[33] 'preparing peacekeeping mandates';[34] 'day-to-day management *and* political decisions';[35] as well as 'issuing legal opinions'.[36] None of these roles can reasonably be regarded—even by New York's flimsy vocabulary—as 'technical' in nature.

Different views have been put forward to explain Riza's and Annan's failure to consult the top UN leadership about Dallaire's cable, UNAMIR's mandate,

---

[28] Annan, *PBS Frontline Interview*, 17 February 2004.   [29] Annan, *Interventions*, p.48.
[30] Annan, *Interventions*, p.47.   [31] Riza, *PBS Frontline Interview*, March 2003.
[32] Riza, *PBS Frontline Interview*, March 2003.   [33] Bode, p.154.
[34] Bode, p.154.   [35] Bode, p.154.   [36] Bode, p.154.

and its rules of engagement, as well as to solicit a Secretariat-wide response. Jonah—hardly an Annan fan—believes that this was done deliberately to cut DPA and the SG out of the picture,[37] while Boutros-Ghali argued that Annan and DPKO were under the influence of a UNAMIR-adverse US administration.[38] 'It was accurate that there was very keen US involvement', Annan acknowledges. 'They were big players. They showed keen interest in peacekeeping operations...from a budgetary point of view where...they were paying about 27 percent-plus of the costs, they were also anxious to see what happens....So there was very keen interest. In that sense, he [Boutros-Ghali] was right. But I think the leadership of the UN also had a responsibility. I reported to the secretary-general. I took my orders from him, not from the Americans.'[39] Although Chapter 10 will show that, as SG, Annan did try to tackle some of the issues highlighted by the crisis of 1994, in the early 1990s a serious disagreement emerged at UN Headquarters over Washington's role in peacekeeping and over which task counted as 'technical' or 'political', a disagreement that went beyond Rwanda and that also affected missions in Somalia, Haiti, and Yugoslavia. Since this dispute played a role both in the events of 1994 and in convincing Washington that Boutros-Ghali should be denied a second term and ought be replaced with Annan, it is necessary to temporarily broaden the analysis and to consider Annan's views on peacekeeping and on the role of the USA in it. This will also clarify why Annan found himself closer to Washington precisely at a time when Boutros-Ghali was travelling in the opposite direction.

(ii) Annan, Peacekeeping, and the USA

Personality-wise, Annan and Boutros-Ghali could hardly have been more different, the former being the embodiment of calm and politeness whereas the latter was passionate and combative. Their backgrounds also separated them: Annan was the consummate bureaucrat who had joined the UN as a budget specialist and knew the New York machinery inside out. As mentioned, his was an administrative rather than a 'visionary' approach to peacekeeping; the 'Responsibility to Protect' would only come later, during Annan's tenure as SG. 'He's a bureaucrat by temperament and training', Edward Mortimer, one of Annan's closest aides, stated. 'His way of thinking is: I was doing the job assigned to me, I was not really the main person responsible [in Rwanda]'.[40] Whether Annan's work was effective or not depended on whether he could find logistical support for an operation. As a result, Annan appeared

---

[37] My interview with James Jonah, 20 July 2011, New York, USA.
[38] Boutros-Ghali, *PBS Frontline Interview*, 21 January 2004.
[39] Annan, *PBS Frontline Interview*, 17 February 2004.   [40] Traub, p.114.

to look more favourably on missions which had the strong backing of troop-contributing countries, especially the USA. By contrast, Boutros-Ghali was an academic who had written extensively about peacekeeping, was determined to strengthen the 'political' functions of the SG within it, and despised bureaucracies. What Annan had in administrative skills Boutros-Ghali matched in intellectual power, and had they managed to establish a good relationship, they would have made a formidable duo. Yet this was not to be, and the deterioration of their relationship matters not only for its impact on UNA-MIR, but also because it reflects two very different approaches to peacekeeping and to Washington's role in it.

Although Somalia in 1993 marked the start of the downward spiral in the relationship between Boutros-Ghali and Annan, as well as between the SG and Washington, the two men actually agreed—against Goulding's advice—about the need for the UN to get involved in the Horn of Africa once the USA had departed. Early in his term, Boutros-Ghali was far more amenable to US ideas of peacekeeping than he would later claim, whereas a fundamental difference persisted between Boutros-Ghali and Goulding in their interpretation of the nature and scope of peacekeeping. This difference emerged most visibly in March 1993—two months after the Clinton administration came into power and precisely when the Somalia crisis deepened—when Goulding was moved from DPKO to DPA and Annan was promoted to Under-Secretary-General and put in charge of peacekeeping. Although Boutros-Ghali explained this shift with the need 'to strengthen Africa's presence in the highest echelons of the United Nations',[41] it has been speculated—including within the SG's office—that Washington was frustrated with Goulding's traditionalist interpretation of peacekeeping and that Clinton wanted Annan at DPKO.[42] Yet Boutros-Ghali's decision also reflected a genuine difference between the SG and Goulding: 'You are always telling me, Goulding, that we can't do this and we can't do that because that's not the way we do peacekeeping in the United Nations',[43] Boutros-Ghali complained to Goulding after summoning him to his office to convey the news of his imminent removal from DPKO. Annan, on the other hand, was far more amenable on Somalia: 'Caught in the upbeat UN mood after the Persian Gulf War', one author noted, 'Annan believed it was worth bending the rules to save many African lives'[44]—precisely the opposite of what he was later accused of doing in Rwanda. 'With his innate optimism and almost naïve trust in the goodwill of the Americans, Annan hoped that the Americans could be persuaded to engage in "more aggressive" disarmament [in Somalia].'[45] This was a different approach from Goulding's, who continued to steadfastly oppose an aggressive UN role in the Horn of Africa on the

[41] Stanley Meisler, *Kofi Annan* (London: John Wiley, 2007), p.65.
[42] MIG-TD-IX, 4-Feb-1993.   [43] Meisler, p.64.   [44] Meisler, p.61.
[45] Meisler, p.63.

ground that the UN lacked the means to succeed there. 'UN military officers who dealt with the UN on Somalia found Goulding rigid on the issue, but Kofi Annan, one officer told me, "is more flexible than Goulding about the new role for the peacekeepers".'[46] When the US President opportunistically blamed the death of eighteen US rangers on the UN, Goulding was shocked, writing in his diary of 'the impossibility of having US troops in UN peace-keeping operations'.[47]

Boutros-Ghali was equally outraged. Having brought Goulding into DPA and closer to his office, the SG started to see the benefits of Goulding's conservative views and became increasingly influenced by the Briton. In this respect, Yugoslavia was to be a more formidable testing ground than Rwanda for Boutros-Ghali's relationship with the USA: in Bosnia, Washington wanted the UN to be more involved but Goulding and Boutros-Ghali[48] opposed this because of the SG's focus on the developing world.[49] Goulding's views of Clinton and Albright had by this time further deteriorated: the British official wrote in his diaries of 'dishonesty'[50] from the US government in Bosnia, berated 'the total misinterpretation of the Americans'[51] there, and recalled: 'the advice I have been giving [Boutros-Ghali] for some weeks [is] that his best course of action is to lie low and let the discord among the major powers reveal itself more clearly as the real reason for the ineffective UN performance in B-H [Bosnia Herzegovina]'.[52] Annan, on the other hand, was far more positively inclined towards a UN involvement in Bosnia, and when Boutros-Ghali despatched him to Zagreb in what was widely seen at the time as an attempt by the SG to get a potential competitor away from New York, the head of DPKO impressed Washington for his activism in supporting air strikes. As Richard Holbrooke, Clinton's top official in the Former Yugoslavia, noted, 'More than any other issue, it was [Boutros-Ghali's] performance on Bosnia that made us feel he did not deserve a second term—just as Kofi Annan's strength on the bombing [of Serb positions] in August already made him the private favourite of many American officials.'[53]

Annan's desire for UN involvement in Yugoslavia and Haiti suggests that post-Somalia fatigue alone cannot account for his wariness towards UNAMIR. Likewise, the idea that Annan was negatively inclined towards all new peacekeeping missions because of Somalia and because of the UN's 'bureaucratic culture' is not convincing either. Neither is the suggestion that Annan played an ancillary—or 'technical'—role as head of DPKO. As Hol-brooke said of Annan when the latter took a far harder line on air strikes than the SG had wished him to do,

---

[46] Meisler, p.63.   [47] MIG-PD-B, 12-Oct-1993.

[48] MIG-TD-IX, 2-Mar-1993, p.24.   [49] MIG-TD-IX, 19-Jan-1994.

[50] MIG-TD-XII, 22-Jul-1995.   [51] MIG-TD-XII, 25-Jul-1995.

[52] MIG-TD-XII, 22-Jul-1995.

[53] Edward Luck, *Mixed Messages* (Washington, DC: Brookings Institution Press, 1999), p.189.

Kofi made a historic decision. Without that decision, we might never have gotten
to the table. As long as the Serbs believed we were never going to hit them hard,
they would never have been incentivized to act.[54]

This was hardly the behaviour of a bureaucrat involved in 'technical' matters,
and so much so that Annan's activism was not nearly as appreciated on the
Secretariat's top floor as it was in Washington. 'In my absence', Goulding
wrote in his diary, 'this wholly political subject [of air strikes against the
Bosnian Serbs] had been taken over by DPKO and I would not even have
known about [it] if I hadn't called Kofi this morning to say Hi, I'm back.'[55] As
another observer noted, 'When [Clinton and Albright] pressed the button for
action in Bosnia in the summer of 1995, Annan sprang to life, and at Albright's
request—without consulting Boutros-Ghali as secretary-general—authorized
Nato to start heavy bombing of Serb positions.'[56]

The fact that Annan appeared to look more favourably to US-sponsored
operations (such as Somalia, Yugoslavia, and Haiti) than to those opposed by
Washington (such as Rwanda) has a charitable as well as an uncharitable
explanation. The latter, put forward by his critics, is that Annan was simply
trying to keep in the Americans' good books. Tom Quiggin, the Canadian
intelligence official who served in Bosnia in the 1990s, believes so and is
stridently critical.[57] For those holding such views, Annan's strategy was
successful. James Steinberg, Clinton's deputy national security adviser, stated
that by 1994 Boutros-Ghali was seen in Washington as 'an implacable
obstacle...'[58] to US peacekeeping goals. Steinberg's colleagues at the US
Mission to the UN agreed: 'On former Yugoslavia and a whole host of other
issues, we felt that Kofi Annan was an extremely nuanced, an extremely
serious man with whom we agreed most of the time.'[59] 'People personalized
it, that we hated Boutros-Ghali and we liked Kofi Annan', stated Robert Orr,
an officer at the National Security Council who worked on 'Operation Orient
Express', a secret task-force established by Madeleine Albright to replace
Boutros-Ghali with Annan as SG. 'In fact, it was all about the policy. Kofi
could do it. Very few secretaries-general had worked with the US military.'[60]
Only a considerable show of leadership (from Washington's perspective) or
betrayal (in Boutros-Ghali's view) by Annan could have led Clinton to that
conclusion, a performance that involved issues as substantive as the scope of
UN peacekeeping and the role of the USA in such operations. 'If Bosnia

[54] Traub, p.64.   [55] MIG-PD-B, 3-Aug-1993.
[56] Perry Anderson, 'Our Man', *London Review of Books*, 10 May 2007.
[57] Tom Quiggin, 'Intelligence in Support of UN Peacekeeping in Bosnia during the 1990s',
Spy Museum Podcast, 11 February 2013, at 32:44, available at http://www.spymuseum.org
(accessed 16 May 2016); Tom Quiggin, 'The Rwanda "Genocide Fax": What We Know', *Network
on Intelligence History and Studies Discussion Forum* (15 January 2014, 12:26AM); Tom Quiggin,
email to the author, 4 May 2016.
[58] Traub, p.62.   [59] Traub, p.64.   [60] Traub, p.65.

destroyed Boutros-Ghali's reputation [in US eyes]', one author noted, 'it confirmed Annan's as someone willing to contemplate the use of force, and likelier to heed Washington's preferences'.[61]

A more charitable explanation is that Annan's pragmatic approach to peacekeeping led him to believe that it would be counterproductive to engage the UN in missions which lacked the support of large troop-contributing countries, especially the USA. Although this version squares with Annan's view of peacekeeping mentioned above, what is clear for the purposes of this book is that DPKO and its leadership were involved in a plethora of consequential (and value-ridden) decisions in Rwanda. To be sure, certain functions (e.g. the selection of personnel, the harnessing of resources, and the implementation of administrative decisions) were more practical than others (e.g. meeting with the parties, setting up the mission's mandate, and negotiating cease-fires). DPKO was involved in both, a situation that often frustrated DPA officers and Boutros-Ghali because, for them, DPKO was supposed to *execute* the SG's policies, not craft new ones. This is why, as Chapter 6 has shown, by the summer of 1993 Boutros-Ghali was engaged in a war of nerves with DPKO about the latter's very role and functions. According to Goulding,

> The SG, egged on by Aimé, wants DPA to have primacy in all 'political' matters with DPKO playing a secondary, 'technical' role. This concept is anathema to Kofi, as it would have been to me, and he and his staff have been clever in obstructing its implementation.[62]

For Annan, as for Washington, DPKO *had* to deal with both 'political' and 'operational' matters once peacekeepers deployed—a position that horrified DPA, Boutros-Ghali, and most of the EOSG, but that also contradicted Annan's and Riza's projection of their role in Rwanda as being largely 'operational' in nature (recall Annan's quote at the start of this subsection that he was merely taking orders from Boutros-Ghali). On the contrary, not only were assessments made by the two DPKO officials 'political' according to the SG's memo of October 1993; both of them appeared to disregard the letter as well as the spirit of that document. 'Over Rwanda', Annan stated, 'a key breakdown had taken place in the three-way relationship between the field, the office of the secretary-general, and DPKO.'[63] Years later, he also noted that 'Riza and I had gone through the experience of the Rwandan genocide together in the [DPKO] and its lessons were never far from our minds.'[64] For Annan, that breakdown was the key message of 1994, one that—as Chapter 10 will show—he was determined to heed once he became SG. For Boutros-Ghali, however, the message was very different and came down to the

[61] Mark Mazower, *Governing the World* (London: Penguin, 2012), p.385.
[62] MIG-TD-IX, 31-Jul-1993. [63] Annan, *Interventions*, p.109.
[64] Annan, *Interventions*, p.109.

realization that Annan was not to be trusted. 'The SG threw a justified tantrum when he discovered that Kofi had waltzed off to Zagreb, without telling him, as soon as the NATO ultimatum in Sarajevo had passed without incident',[65] Goulding wrote shortly before the Rwanda genocide. In the following months that relationship worsened further, although the nadir was reached well after the end of the Rwandan massacres:

> A roar rumbled all day between the SG and Kofi who, contrary to what all the rest of us thought had been agreed the previous evening, had sent the British and the French a draft summary of their proposal, without consulting Chinmaya [Boutros-Ghali's representative on the Council] or me. The SG was furious, referring to 'Mr. Annan's unilateral stupidity' and telling me that Kofi had an ulterior motive. When I tried to defend him, BBG [Boutros Boutros-Ghali] accused me of being 'always the boy scout'![66]

Importantly, in the Secretariat of the Boutros-Ghali era, personal dislikes also had significant professional implications: 'The SG', Goulding noted about another such crisis, 'blew his top and ruled that in future any DPKO traveller should be accompanied by someone from DPA!'[67]

JAMES JONAH AND MARRACK GOULDING

Although DPA was involved in UNAMIR from the start, a month before the genocide responsibility for the supposedly 'political' aspects of the mission passed from Jonah to Goulding—a handover between two officials with very different views on UNAMIR, peacekeeping, and the role of the UN bureaucracy in it. Looking at the institutional leadership of DPA as a unit, as Part I has done, is thus insufficient and the contributions of the individuals involved in that department also need to be assessed. A leadership change before a major crisis is particularly useful to ascertain what impact, if any, individual agency had on that crisis.

(i) Jonah, the UN Bureaucracy, and Rwanda

Within the Secretariat, Jonah filled several roles. He was a veteran international civil servant committed to the independence of the SG's office and to what he saw as his high functions.[68] Jonah had written passionately about the

---

[65] MIG-TD-IX, 3-Mar-1994.   [66] MIG-TD-XII, 13-Jun-1995.
[67] MIG-TD-XII, 25-Oct-1995.
[68] James Jonah, 'Differing State Perspectives on the United Nations in the Post-Cold War World', J. W. Holmes Memorial Lecture, *ACUNS Reports*, No.4 (1993).

importance of having an impartial Secretariat—he was keen on emphasizing 'the role of integrity in the international civil service'[69]—and was adamantly opposed to what he saw as meddling from powerful countries (his autobiography offers examples of Cold War attempts to influence the SG by both the USA and the USSR).[70] Jonah was also an African as well as an Africanist and was committed to aiding 'his continent' through the work of the UN—as he saw it, it was his duty to help his 'African brothers' stamp out poverty and corruption.[71] But Jonah was also a consummate bureaucrat attached to his department's prerogatives and hostile to 'interferences' by other parts of the UN Secretariat, especially those he saw as being controlled by the Great Powers.[72] 'It is of utmost importance', he had written in the depths of the Cold War, 'that efforts be made to minimize, if not completely end, the politicization of the international Secretariat.'[73] In the context of the early 1990s, of Boutros-Ghali's interventionism in peacekeeping, and of a divisive Secretariat where both DPA and DPKO were vying to be in charge of the 'political' aspects of peacekeeping, this put Jonah on a collision course with Annan, with Albright, and to a lesser extent also with Goulding. According to Jonah, when Boutros-Ghali became SG, DPKO was to deal with no 'political' issue—it was not, so to speak, supposed to be a 'political' department.[74] Yet bureaucratic friction, for Jonah's DPA, became an opportunity as well as a threat—Goulding ascribes to Jonah and to Jean-Claude Aimé, Boutros-Ghali's Chief of Staff, the distinction between 'political' and 'operational' roles in the Secretariat (although, as mentioned in Chapter 6, Goulding had also contributed to it).[75] Perhaps unsurprisingly given the officials involved in that separation of roles, its biggest beneficiary was DPA.

Jonah's identity as a staunch Boutros-Ghali supporter, an Africanist, and a bureaucrat converged in 1993, when the possibility of setting up a Rwandan mission emerged. The Sierra Leonean diplomat had been horrified by what he saw as Washington's exploitation of the UN in Somalia, among other places, not to mention the Pentagon's influence over peacekeeping through DPKO.[76] Unlike Annan, who saw himself as a universalist, and like Boutros-Ghali, Jonah often spoke *for* the developing world *to* the developed one, with the result that he was not always appreciated by Western capitals. 'On several occasions', Jonah wrote, 'senior officials in the mission of the United States intervened to promote the interests of DPKO and to ensure that the office was given greater authority in the conduct of peacekeeping'[77]—a claim that is incidentally confirmed by Goulding. For Jonah, whose ideal SG was

[69] James Jonah, 'Independence and Integrity of the International Civil Service: The Role of Executive Heads and the Role of States', *International Law and Politics*, Vol.14 (1982), p.848.
[70] Jonah, *What Price*, esp. chs 1 and 3.   [71] Jonah, *What Price*, esp. ch.6.
[72] Jonah, *What Price*, esp. ch.2.   [73] Jonah, 'Independence and Integrity', p.858.
[74] Interview with Jonah, 20 July 2011.   [75] MIG-PD-B, 14-Mar-1993.
[76] Jonah, *What Price*, p.106.   [77] Jonah, *What Price*, p.106.

Hammarskjöld, the head of the Secretariat needed to be firm—even ruthless—with those states *and* officials that favoured one capital over another. In his memoirs, for instance, Jonah criticizes Pérez de Cuéllar for lacking 'the killer instinct one must have to run an operation as complex as the Secretariat',[78] and for leaving 'departments to do as they pleased for the most part'.[79] Jonah admired Boutros-Ghali for doing precisely the opposite, whereas he berated Annan as the epitome of a civil servant who sides with the mighty. 'The organization does not deserve to have yet again a Secretary-General who is installed by one powerful member state',[80] Jonah wrote at the end of Annan's term. Yet Jonah was also determined to retain control of his African 'sphere of influence', which meant guarding it from others, including Goulding and Annan. Together with Boutros-Ghali's attempts to reinvigorate DPA, this not only explains Jonah's involvement with UNAMIR, but it also sheds light on three of Jonah's contributions during the earliest stages of the Rwanda mission.

The first was his lack of success in influencing the Arusha negotiations and their unrealistic timetable.[81] Given that it was the Rwandans who had asked the SG to establish UNAMIR, Jonah was arguably in a good position to influence the timeline of that agreement. It is true that the leeway of Secretariat officials is very limited, since progress during the negotiations is partly determined by events in the field. Still, a problematic document with an overambitious deadline was signed, something that prevented UNAMIR from establishing its firm grip on Rwanda. DPA also appeared willing to prevent DPKO from gathering information of a 'political' nature, but as Chapter 6 has shown, Jonah's—and Boutros-Ghali's—distinction between 'technical' and 'political' was not clearly spelled out and contributed to worsening the friction both at Headquarters and in the field. Jonah's recurring clashes with DPKO and the confusion over who was in charge of reconnaissance suggest that he saw UNAMIR's political functions as a *chasse gardée* of DPA, rather than something in which the UN as a whole had a stake.[82] Last but not least, Jonah's reluctance to directly share with DPKO the intelligence he had received from Boutros-Ghali in December 1993 is also noteworthy. Although Jonah reportedly invited Dallaire and Booh Booh to the meeting with Habyarimana during which such information was discussed, the fact that the head of DPA did not directly consult or notify his colleagues at DPKO about such a serious warning reflected his—and, importantly, Boutros-Ghali's—view that this was a 'political' issue from which DPKO should have been excluded,[83] as the October memo requested. 'DPKO was opposed to the policy of the Secretary-General

---

[78] Jonah, *What Price*, p.92.   [79] Jonah, *What Price*, p.92.
[80] Jonah, *What Price*, p.519.
[81] Jacques Castonguay, *Les Casques Bleus au Rwanda* (Paris: L'Harmattan, 1998), p.44.
[82] Interview with Jonah, 20 July 2011.   [83] Interview with Jonah, 20 July 2011.

which required DPA to have oversight over Security Council reports on field operations', Jonah wrote in his memoirs, pointing out that '... once Kofi Annan was appointed Secretary-General, his first instruction was to reverse the instruction of the Secretary-General, giving oversight to DPKO'.[84] Personal and professional loyalties also played a part: 'Before I left the Secretariat in February 1994', Jonah noted, 'it was clear to me that Ambassador Albright had found her candidate to replace Boutros-Ghali [as SG].'[85]

(ii) Goulding, the UN Bureaucracy, and Rwanda

Goulding was a different UN official from Jonah and Annan, both of whom were career civil servants. A national diplomat by training, Goulding defined himself as 'almost an upstart, inserted by a major power at a young age into a prestigious post which the bureaucracy would have preferred to see occupied by one of its own'.[86] Yet if Lady Thatcher had installed Goulding at UN Headquarters to gain a competitive advantage, she soon learned that the British official paid allegiance to his SG in New York, rather than to his British Prime Minister in London. Professionally, Goulding was almost as controlling as Jonah, but directed his micro-managing tendencies at his department rather than at the Secretariat: 'Goulding was a brilliant, highly competent workaholic', stated Shashi Tharoor, who worked with Goulding when the latter was at the helm of DPKO. 'He was hands on. Everybody reported to Goulding, not to the deputy [Kofi Annan]'.[87] As his diaries show, Goulding was also obsessed with detail: 'He wouldn't sign a cable unless he checked every comma and improved the drafting. This went on for a year, and it was crazy. Goulding was working every night until 11pm. He was beginning to collapse under this'.[88] Although Goulding had brought Annan into DPKO as his deputy, the two had very different leadership styles—one charming but blunt, the other consensual and gentle: 'Annan never pressed his doubts about policy nearly as vociferously as Goulding',[89] one author noted. 'It wouldn't come naturally to [Annan] to express strongly dissenting views about what the Security Council wanted to do.'[90] The same can hardly be said of the famously outspoken Goulding: 'Kofi Annan (who was for a year my deputy in the Peacekeeping Department) [is] a creature of the United Nations', the Briton wrote in his diary, 'imbued with its strengths (conciliation, consensus-building,

[84] Jonah, *What Price*, p.566. See also Boutros Boutros-Ghali, Secretary-General's Memorandum: Reporting Channels, 9 March 1993; Boutros Boutros-Ghali, Secretary-General's Memorandum: The Establishment and Conduct of United Nations Field Operations, 2 October 1993 (MIG-PA).

[85] Jonah, *What Price*, pp.105–6.   [86] Meisler, p.58.   [87] Meisler, p.64.

[88] Meisler, p.64.   [89] Meisler, p.63.   [90] Meisler, p.63.

avoidance of conflict) but also with its weaknesses (slow decision-making, fuzzy compromises, lack of intellectual rigour).'[91]

Because Goulding's heart had always been in peacekeeping, the SG's decision to transfer him from DPKO to DPA and to replace him with Annan saddened the British official, who was also uneasy about sharing the Political Affairs department with Jonah. 'I was sorry to be moved from DPKO and wounded by Kofi Annan's statement to the *New York Times* that the age of the gifted amateur was over',[92] Goulding wrote in his diary. There has long been speculation that Goulding's removal had to do with Boutros-Ghali's relationship with Clinton. According to one author, 'When Washington pressed for UN troops to be sent into Somalia, Boutros-Ghali opposed the mission. Annan took the American line. His superior, Marrack Goulding, was duly removed, and Annan put in charge of all peacekeeping operations... in February 1993.'[93] Although Goulding's diaries suggest that he doubted whether Clinton and Albright were behind the move to replace him, the Briton does believe that Washington was pleased with the outcome because—in his words—they saw Annan as '...a malleable kind of guy. They recognized that he would be amenable to American ideas of peacekeeping.'[94] With remarkable candour, however, Goulding also acknowledges that part of his disappointment came down to professional envy: 'I have been—unforgivably—jealous of the public attention [Kofi] receives from delegations and the media', Goulding wrote in his diary in mid-1993, 'and distressed by my own eclipse'.[95] In Goulding, therefore, we have a relatively atypical UN employee and a rather unusual DPA official, one that remained committed to the work of the UN but who was also increasingly alarmed both at the magnitude of the problems of UN peacekeeping in the early 1990s, and at the US role and influence in peace missions.[96]

Despite his self-confessed jealousy, Goulding's relations with Annan remained courteous, one of the reasons being that Goulding—at least later in his career—agreed with Annan about the need for DPKO to acquire analytical capacity and to handle the so-called 'political' aspects of peacekeeping. This made Goulding unpopular with what he saw as the 'firebrands'[97] of his own DPA and often led him to oppose Boutros-Ghali's activism on the basis that the UN was overstretched and the Great Powers (especially the USA) could not be trusted. 'Peacekeeping is a carefully nurtured resource of which the SG is the trustee/guardian and which should be mobilized only when the conditions are right', Goulding wrote. 'SG and SecCo [Security Council] must be very careful to establish the conditions are right before deciding to

---

[91] Marrack Goulding, 'Peacemonger: Book Proposal', 15 June 1998 (MIG-PA).
[92] MIG-PD-B, 22-Mar-1993.   [93] Anderson, 'Our Man'.
[94] Goulding quoted in Meisler, p.65.   [95] MIG-TD-X, 31-Jul-1993.
[96] Marrack Goulding, *Peacemonger* (London: John Murray, 2002), esp. chs 2 and 15.
[97] MIG-PD-V, 1993.

set up a new pko [peacekeeping operation].'[98] For Goulding, such conditions included the 'holy trinity', namely, the consent of the parties to a dispute, UN impartiality, and the use of force in self-defence only.[99] Boutros-Ghali, on the other hand, wanted peacekeepers despatched more easily in the developing world: 'Boutros-Ghali had an *idée fixe*: Africa had been short-changed',[100] Goulding wrote, '[and] when I did ask questions about the feasibility or wisdom of what was proposed, the question often fell on ears made deaf by the new Secretary-General's determination to do more for Africa.'[101] Despite these differences, the SG respected Goulding for his independence—which is why when Jonah retired in March 1994, the SG made Goulding the sole 'king' of DPA.[102] Ironically, in doing so he also handed Goulding a disaster-in-waiting of historic proportions.

How did the British diplomat handle this? He was clearly not responsible for setting up UNAMIR and for overseeing its earlier phases—Jonah was protective of African operations. Indeed, had it been up to the British official, UNAMIR would probably not have been established in the first place, for Goulding had pioneered the concerns of many in New York about the dangers of mission creep, with the result that he disagreed with both Jonah and Boutros-Ghali about the wisdom of establishing a new operation.[103] '[W]e are drowning', Goulding had written as early as in mid-1991. 'The member states are piling on the Secretariat tasks which we do not have the capability to carry out; and there is no leadership.'[104] This, however, does not mean that Goulding was cynical about peacekeeping as a tool to end conflict; while respectful of national sovereignty, the British official had previously shown enthusiasm for UN activism in international affairs. As early as in 1992, at the beginning of Boutros-Ghali's term, this attitude had led him to warn, in a speech, that 'it would be dangerous to start tinkering with Article 2(7) of the Charter and giving the United Nations a licence to involve itself in the internal affairs of member states'.[105] Yet he had also fretted to add that 'For anyone working in the Secretariat, it's immensely exciting to see this organization at last being used in the way it was intended to be used....'[106] In other words, Goulding was not at all shy to engage the UN wherever he believed it could succeed. In fact, the Briton is rightly credited with a number of regulative ideas about peacekeeping, including the proposition that 'peacekeepers can legitim-ately engage in civilian tasks'[107] and that 'the objective of peacekeeping can

---

[98] MIG-TD-IX, 5-Mar-1993.   [99] Bode, p.158.
[100] MIG-TD-IX, 5-Mar-1993.   [101] MIG-TD-IX, 5-Mar-1993.
[102] MIG-TD-IX, 5-Mar-1993.   [103] MIG-TD-VI (1993) and MIG-TD-VII (1994).
[104] Goulding, 'Peacemonger: Book Proposal'.
[105] Marrack Goulding, 'The Evolving Role of the United Nations in International Peace and Security', *Irish Studies in International Affairs*, Vol.3, No.4 (1992), p.5.
[106] Goulding, 'The Evolving Role', p.8.   [107] Bode, p.159.

and should extend beyond conflict management to establishing conditions for conflict resolution'.[108]

For Goulding, however, peacekeeping was an eminently 'political' activity—though the British official never clearly spelled out what this meant—and should include long-term solutions addressing the root causes of a dispute, rather than short-term measures to stop the fighting. Given the right conditions and proper resources, it is thus likely that both Annan and Goulding would have welcomed a Rwanda mission; under the circumstances of the early 1990s, however, Goulding found UNAMIR unwise at best and risky at worst. Yet Goulding's 'sin', if there was one, lay with his reluctance to advise the SG on any course of action once the massacres started. Not only did the British official fail to encourage the SG to be more proactive, including through the use of the media; under the circumstances he thought it better for the UN to withdraw altogether.[109] Given Goulding's influence over and proximity to the SG, he was in a stronger position than Annan to advocate for decisive action. Several reasons prevented him from doing so, including his considerable disillusionment with Washington and a crowded private life that had been distracting him for some time, but which became public precisely at the time of the Rwanda crisis.[110] 'As befitted a diplomat', one acquaintance of his noted, '[Goulding] had an establishment side but he also had a wild, unconventional one: he was determined to secure his objectives, and became impatient at resistance and delay.'[111] However, Goulding's own performance in Rwanda can hardly be associated with dynamism and action.

The results were both tragic and anti-climactic. Feeling vindicated in his long-held view that the USA and the other Great Powers could not be trusted, Goulding saw Rwanda as merely the latest incarnation of the failures of the 'New World Order'. His diaries convey a mixture of anger and sarcasm, suggesting that the British official saw himself and the SG as unable to contain—let alone solve—the crisis. Yet rage did turn into detachment, a personality trait which Goulding's critics had noted well before the events of 1994, but that in the case of Rwanda assumed alarming levels. Describing his official visit in April 1996 on behalf of the UN to a genocide site in Ntarama, Rwanda, where 'about 5,000 women and children, all Tutsis, had been systematically massacred', Goulding records in forensic detail the process of decomposition and the fact that the corpses remained where they fell, 'mostly skeletons now but with some flesh still adhering to their bones and with a dreadful smell which lingered in my nostrils for hours'.[112] He then adds a passage that can only be regarded as disturbing:

[108] Bode, p.159.   [109] MIG-TD-VI (1993) and MIG-TD-VII (1994).
[110] MIG-TD-VI (1993) and MIG-TD-VII (1994).   [111] Bode, p.151.
[112] MIG-PD-C, 23-Apr-1996.

All this awfulness aroused no spontaneous sentiments in me. The everyday things—pots and pans, combs, children's shoes—which lay among the corpses were pathetic but they produced no tears. I just felt uncomfortable and uncertain what a visiting VIP should do in such circumstances, especially in front of television cameras. My discomfort was aggravated by the fact that the trees around the church were alive with tantalizing passerines but respect for the dead precluded any attempt to identify them [Goulding was a keen ornithologist]. On the way back we stopped briefly by the bridge over the River Nya . . . and I got a black-crowned waxbill, which I think is a lifer. But the TV crews stopped also and I had to suspend birding for fear of 'USG en promenade' coverage.[113]

It is important to note that these comments refer to a visit paid by Goulding to Rwanda two years after the genocide. Goulding was hardly unsympathetic to the fate of Rwandans while the crisis raged (his diaries, for instance, show anguish at Boutros-Ghali's unsuccessful attempts to convince states to supply peacekeepers). Also, 1994 was Goulding's *annus horribilis* and it would thus be utterly unfair to assess his decade at the UN on the basis of it, all the more so since the British official had been instrumental in supporting the concept of 'liberal peace', one of the themes of Goulding's tenure. As one author noted, 'Multi-functional peacekeeping as promoted by Goulding . . . began to promote political, social, and institutional reconstruction within states along liberal democratic lines and perceived illiberal governance within states as a potential threat to international peace and security.'[114] These were hardly the hallmarks of a bureaucrat indifferent to the fate of the world's people. Yet the passage mentioned above suggests that the rage felt by Goulding at the failure of the 'New World Order' did turn into cynicism. Confronted with the sheer horror of Rwanda and the other humanitarian tragedies of the early 1990s—and feeling unable to do much about them—it is almost as if Goulding had become 'immunized' to those tragedies. This is not unusual in high-pressure environments where exposure to humanitarian crises is a daily occurrence. Asked about what might have gone wrong in Rwanda, Mark (now Lord) Malloch Brown, Annan's Deputy SG in 2006, noted:

What really struck me about my years at the top of the UN is how we acclimatized to crises, how they became the new ordinary. Because how many months in a row can you go to work with the world going up in flames? So your power of imagination as an official living in New York, watching Darfur, or Congo, or Rwanda, through bits and pieces of the cables or through the networks, CNN etc. Then days go by and there is a risk that crisis becomes the new normal—and you get too comfortable with it. That your antennae come down and you miss the danger signals in distant events on the other side of the world. And I felt that more to be honest about Srebrenica than Rwanda. I was not at the UN for either, but I talked to people like Samantha Power, and I listened to my own colleagues.

---

[113] MIG-PD-C, 23-Apr-1996.   [114] Bode, p.162.

And the really dangerous thing in UN officials' conscience is to sink into this complacency and miss the alarm signals when they come.[115]

Goulding's coping mechanism befitted his complex personality, one that could be exceptionally charming but also chillingly detached. 'The prospects for the people of B-H [Bosnia-Herzegovina] are grim', he wrote in another entry. 'But I refuse to feel guilty about this. The UN Secretariat, under-funded and poorly managed for five decades, cannot be expected to prevent and stop every conflict in the world.'[116] Whether the same can be said of genocide is a different story, but by this time Goulding had all but lost hope in a UN membership that, in his view, was more attached to national interests than human life. 'The British government', he wrote about the role of his country in Bosnia, '. . . do not see chaos and bloodshed there as presenting a serious threat to their national interests'.[117] In this context it was appropriate—and even desirable—for the UN and for the SG to 'inflict maximum pain on the Member States, especially the USA', as he put it in another diary entry.[118]

Goulding's overall contribution to UN peacekeeping was considerable, long-lasting, and deserves separate treatment. He was one of the first officials to warn against intra-Secretariat rivalries and tried to soothe relations between New York's most important departments. As head of DPA, he also (unsuccessfully) questioned Boutros-Ghali's distinction between 'technical' and 'political' functions of peacekeeping, and was prescient in pointing out that such a distinction was unworkable. Goulding was similarly vocal in warning of UN overstretch and in urging the SG to separate peacekeeping and peace-enforcement, a position that the Somalia debacle vindicated. Last but not least, Goulding acknowledged the multi-dimensional character of peacekeeping as early as in 1992, something that—as Chapter 10 will show—is widely accepted today. Yet Goulding's record during the Rwandan crisis is hardly stellar. Although later critical of Boutros-Ghali's determination to turn DPKO into an 'operational' department, Goulding accepted—and early on endorsed—the distinction between 'political' and 'operational' functions without clarifying what he or the UN Secretariat meant by it. He also allowed himself to be used in the struggle between DPA and DPKO, confessing to his diary that more than once he gave in to Boutros-Ghali in trying to keep Annan 'at bay' and DPKO as 'operational' as possible, while writing of Boutros-Ghali's 'continuing wish to use me to curb Kofi's action and influence'.[119] Neither can Goulding be said to have been proactive in pushing the SG to tackle the Rwanda crisis. The fact that Goulding's long-term and distinguished contribution to UN peacekeeping

---

[115] My interview with Mark Malloch Brown, London, UK, 28 September 2011 (and by email on 16 June 2016).

[116] MIG-TD-XII, 26-Jul-1995.

[117] Marrack Goulding, Note to the SG: Report on Visit to the United Kingdom, 9 February 1993 (MIG-PA).

[118] MIG-TD-XII, 2-Oct-1995.   [119] MIG-TD-XI, 25-Nov-1994.

compares poorly with his lack of leadership in Rwanda is arguably a tragedy in its own right.

JACQUES-ROGER BOOH BOOH AND ROMÉO DALLAIRE

Of all the Secretariat units involved in Rwanda, UNAMIR was the most divided and thus the most dysfunctional. As Part I has explained, theoretically the Head of Mission was the SRSG, Jacques-Roger Booh Booh. He was also nominally in charge of 'political' negotiations among the Rwandan parties which the Arusha Accords required for establishing the country's transitional institutions.[120] In practice, however, Booh Booh played a marginal role and the *de facto* Head of Mission—both 'politically' and 'militarily', to use New York's wording—was Dallaire. The reasons for this situation are as fascinating for students of the UN as they are tragic, for while it is true that UNAMIR was confronted with the exceptional fact of genocide, problems with the mission's leadership were apparent well before the massacres began.

The fact that Booh Booh was never able to take charge of UNAMIR was the result of three factors: bad timing, poor management, and his own professional shortcomings. Booh Booh had been asked by Boutros-Ghali to lead the Rwanda operation and, on paper, he ticked most of the boxes for the SRSG post.[121] A former Foreign Minister with extensive experience of the UN, Booh Booh was also a francophone African intimately familiar with Rwandan politics. His first handicap, his late appointment and arrival in Kigali, was clearly beyond his control[122] but mattered in that it forced Dallaire—a soldier without experience of diplomatic negotiations—to take charge of both the substantive and operational components of UNAMIR from the outset. This situation made it virtually impossible to separate these already ill-defined spheres of competence both before and after Booh Booh eventually reached Kigali; it also strained relations between DPA and DPKO in New York, since the former department—under Jonah—complained vociferously that DPKO and Dallaire had effectively assumed 'political' functions.[123] Given the comprehensive tasks that UNAMIR in particular and UN missions in general were and are still supposed to perform, this should not come as a surprise.[124]

---

[120] Arusha Peace Agreement, available at http://www.incore.ulst.ac.uk/services/cds/agreements/pdf/rwan1.pdf (accessed 11 July 2015).

[121] Jacques-Roger Booh Booh, *Le Patron de Dallaire Parle* (Paris: Éditions Duboiris, 2005).

[122] Castonguay, ch.3.   [123] Interview with Jonah, 20 July 2011.

[124] Chapter 10 will return to this.

Compounding these institutional problems was Booh Booh's leadership style. According to Dallaire, the Cameroonian diplomat was fond of his ambassadorial rank, basked in his friendship with Boutros-Ghali, and prioritized high-level contacts to close working relations with his military commander, whom he clearly disliked (though as we have seen the feeling was—and remains—mutual).[125] Far from being an eccentricity, Booh Booh's top-down approach was noticed by others in Kigali and arguably had a number of implications for UNAMIR. To begin with, it meant that the Cameroonian appeared to cultivate closer ties to Habyarimana than to Kagame and the RPF, a relationship that Booh Booh largely left to Dallaire. The need for SRSGs to engage with a country's leadership, the distinction between 'political' and 'technical' functions, and the fact that Dallaire and Kagame were fellow soldiers, might have contributed to this situation.[126] Yet the fact that the SRSG reportedly spent the Easter weekend before the beginning of the genocide as a guest at Habyarimana's residence did not endear the Cameroonian diplomat to Kagame, who refused to work with Booh Booh. Although accusations of bias against SRSGs are fairly common, Goulding's archive suggests that Booh Booh's performance was criticized not only in Kigali but also in New York.[127] While all this is hardly a recipe for great leadership, the most problematic aspects of Booh Booh's role in Rwanda arguably come down to his reporting to New York, his minimization of the situation on the ground, and his insistence on negotiating a cease-fire. Even allowing for the exceptional circumstances of 1994—a confusing job description, bureaucratic competition in New York, and genocide in the field—it is therefore questionable whether Booh Booh ever became the driving force for negotiation that SRSGs are supposed to be. He did not seem to have displayed the 'excellent political, negotiation, leadership and management skills'[128] required of one.

Both in terms of personality and style, Dallaire could hardly have been more different from Booh Booh. There is no doubt that the Canadian General was committed to UNAMIR and saw the operation as 'his own'.[129] His courage, determination, and temerity in the face of brutality have been extensively commented upon as well as rightly praised.[130] Dallaire's problems were in some respects opposite to those experienced by the Duke of Wellington and mentioned at the beginning of this chapter, for, as Part I has shown, his most direct UN 'master'—DPKO—gave him too little, rather than too much,

[125] Booh Booh, chs 10 and 11; Roméo Dallaire, *Shake Hands with the Devil* (London: Arrow Books, 2005).
[126] Dallaire, *Shake Hands*, ch.2.   [127] MIG-TD-VI (1994).
[128] Connie Peck, 'Special Representatives of the Secretary-General', in David Malone, ed., *The UN Security Council* (Boulder: Lynne Rienner, 2004), p.325.
[129] Dallaire, *Shake Hands*, ch.1.
[130] Agathe Plauchut and Patrice Pourtal, *L'ONU Face au Génocide Rwandais* (Paris: L'Harmattan, 2012).

guidance.[131] Yet Dallaire, too, made mistakes, some of which were more consequential than others. His kowtowing to DPKO's suggestion not to ask for more than 2,500 troops meant that UNAMIR was under-staffed before it even reached Kigali.[132] The post-Somalia atmosphere of budgetary cuts and US scepticism toward peacekeeping in Africa means that Dallaire clearly cannot be blamed for UNAMIR's lack of resources, especially since he spent an inordinate amount of time pleading for them.[133] Yet a field commander who recommends troop numbers which he knows are insufficient is heading for serious trouble.[134] Similarly, Dallaire's reconnaissance in August 1993 was fraught on multiple levels, not least the fact that he engaged with the wrong actors. As a soldier with no previous experience of top-level negotiations, the Force Commander, again, cannot be blamed for failing to understand Rwanda's complex background, particularly given that the Secretariat did not grasp it either. This is especially so if one considers that Dallaire hardly kept New York in the dark; on the contrary, his assiduous reporting to DPKO became renowned.[135] If anything, Dallaire's reaction to the genocide proves that crises can boost leadership and moral stature.[136]

Although Dallaire made both strategic and substantive mistakes in Rwanda, ultimately it was the UN system that failed him rather than the reverse— something that becomes apparent if one considers his fraught relationship with Booh Booh. Both men clearly wanted to be in charge—Dallaire because he thought Booh Booh was ineffectual, Booh Booh because that was how he saw the assignment (by the UN) of his and Dallaire's functions. Both conducted diplomatic negotiations but neither efficiently shared what they knew with each other (the SRSG accused Dallaire of withholding 'technical' information, whereas the Force Commander blamed the Cameroonian for biased 'political' reporting to New York).[137] At its core, however, theirs was far more than a personal animosity; it was a professional rivalry that originated thousands of kilometres away and found its *raison d'être* in the flawed separation of roles reigning at the time in New York. Not only did Booh Booh and Dallaire largely report to different parts of the Secretariat (the former to the SG and DPA, the latter to DPKO), the separation between 'operational' and 'political' roles negatively affected UNAMIR's ability to perform two of its most critical functions, namely, information-gathering and 'political' analysis. As mentioned in Chapter 6, the former was supposedly Dallaire's and DPKO's responsibility, whereas the latter was theoretically the purview of Booh Booh, DPA, and EOSG—both activities being aimed at generating intelligence. What

[131] Dallaire, *Shake Hands*, ch.2.   [132] Dallaire, *Shake Hands*, ch.3.
[133] Dallaire, *Shake Hands*, ch.4.
[134] Lawrence Freedman, *Strategy* (Oxford: Oxford University Press, 2013); John Stone, *Military Strategy* (London: Continuum, 2011).
[135] Linda Melvern, *A People Betrayed* (London: Zed, 2009).
[136] Bobby Jindal, *Leadership and Crisis* (London: Regnery, 2010).   [137] Booh Booh, ch.2.

UN officials failed to realize, however, is that the distinction between information-gathering and 'political' analysis—not to mention the flawed separation of bureaucratic roles that existed in April 1994—is troublesome if (as was the case in Rwanda) the two most important departments in New York fail to liaise with each other and if (as was the case for Boutros-Ghali) the SG privileges one department and sees the other as an existential threat. The bifurcation of leadership in Kigali ultimately reflected the confused division of roles in New York.

MADELEINE ALBRIGHT AND IBRAHIM GAMBARI

The concept of leadership within the SC is particularly controversial. For one thing, the Council is not a part of the Secretariat and its members represent sovereign states rather than UN departments tied to each other by links of hierarchy and bureaucracy.[138] This has implications for the Council's decision-making process insofar as its masters do not reside in New York but in the world's capitals. For another, leadership within a body as distinctive, diverse, and disputed as the SC is especially hard to identify.[139] Compounding this is the secrecy of the SC's deliberations, something that makes assessments of intra-SC leadership difficult. The minutes of the informal consultations on Rwanda partly change that, while the roles of two of the Council's members in 1994—Madeleine Albright and Ibrahim Gambari, who incidentally supported different positions—suggest that individuals do matter and can make a difference.

Let us consider the US Permanent Representative first. The instructions that Albright had received from Washington were clear: the UN peacekeeping budget had to be reduced and the best way of doing so was by containing the costs of 'non-strategic' missions, of which UNAMIR was one. This is why, when the genocide began, Albright was explicitly instructed to request UNAMIR's withdrawal.[140] According to the UK Representative to the UN, David Hannay, 'The day of our first discussion, immediately after the [presidential] plane had been shot down and when obviously appalling things were starting to happen, Madeleine came to me and said: "I've got some appalling instructions, we've got to pull the whole lot out". It was on the basis of Somalia and Mogadishu [that] the American military had said "pull them out".'[141]

---

[138] Edward Luck, *The UN Security Council* (Abingdon: Routledge, 2006).

[139] David Ambrosetti and Mélanie Cathelin, 'Les Enjeux du Leadership au Conseil de Sécurité: Responsabiliser ou Contrôler les Opérations de Paix de l'ONU?', *Revue Internationale et Strategique*, No.68 (2007–08).

[140] Madeleine Albright, *Madam Secretary* (New York: HarperCollins, 2004).

[141] Interview with Hannay, 26 April 2010.

Hannay also recalls how Albright then phoned Washington to have her instructions changed: 'It was true that she was instructed to pull them out, but she never carried out those instructions.'[142] Why would a Permanent Representative, after receiving unambiguous instructions from her capital which she knew were based on a policy originating from the US President through his PDD-25 directive, insist on them being reversed? Defying the powerful military apparatus of the Pentagon and a veteran Secretary of State like Christopher, not to speak of the White House, was not necessarily the wisest career move for somebody who clearly had ambitions to accede to the top job of US diplomacy.

Although in her autobiography Albright argues that the USA was simply 'on the wrong side of the issue',[143] a more nuanced explanation focuses on the nature of multilateral negotiations. As Part I has shown and despite picturesque scenes of diplomats sitting around the Horseshoe Table and raising their hands to yield much-cherished vetoes, Council members—including the P-5—prefer to decide by 'consensus' and go to considerable lengths to do so.[144] This is true for multilateral negotiations in general; as a French diplomat put it, 'The real expertise one gains from the practice—but not necessarily from the academic study—of multilateral diplomacy is the art of compromise'.[145] In April 1994, Albright realized that the position of the USA was not only removed from the realities of Rwanda but also—and far more consequential for US diplomacy—from the collective inclination of the Council.[146] As another diplomat notes, when this happens it is the ambassador's job to do something about it: 'Instructions are never really adapted to the reality on the ground, so it is a matter of interpreting them ... and then presenting them to [other diplomats].'[147] It is partly because the USA ran the risk of being *seen* as isolated on a matter of principle—and because this would have had damaging effects for Washington's effectiveness and reputation—that Albright decided to be vocal with her capital. On the Council, dissent and vetoes can be costly, even for the world's superpower.[148] Red lines—issues which Permanent Representatives cannot cross—do exist,[149] but as Albright's successful petition shows, for Washington Rwanda was not one of them. Seen in this light, her position in 1994 was simultaneously proactive (because she

---

[142] Interview with Hannay, 26 April 2016. [143] Albright, p.213.

[144] David Ambrosetti, *Normes et Rivalités Diplomatiques à l'ONU* (Brussels: Peter Lang, 2009), esp. ch.3.

[145] Yves Buchet de Neuilly, 'Devenir Diplomate Multilatéral: Le Sens Pratique des Calculs Appropriés', in David Ambrosetti et al., eds, *Crises et Organisations Internationales* (Paris: L'Harmattan, 2009), p.89.

[146] Buchet de Neuilly, ch.3. [147] Buchet de Neuilly, p.91.

[148] David Ambrosetti, 'Influence et Légitimité: La Negotiation au Conseil de Sécurité et ses Normes', in Ambrosetti, *Normes*, pp.137–97.

[149] Buchet de Neuilly, p.90.

contributed to a different policy outcome) and pragmatic (because she juggled the various actors of US foreign policy). That the US Embassy in Kigali was clearly in the know about the events in Rwanda weakens Albright's already shaky claim that she was not really aware of events on the ground. It does not, however, fundamentally alter the appraisal of her (as opposed to her country's) role in the crisis.

Another example of a certain readiness to challenge authority—though a far more constrained and less successful one in terms of outcome—is that of Nigerian ambassador Ibrahim Gambari. A supporter of UN intervention in Africa and of UNAMIR, Gambari was uncomfortable with the idea of down-sizing the mission, as Chapter 5 has shown, especially when the situation deteriorated, for he saw that outcome as an abdication of responsibility by the UN and a terrible message that the organization was blind to Africa's needs. Hence his repeated criticism, during the informals, for what he saw as the indecisiveness of the Council and the 'moral bankruptcy' of abandoning Rwandans to their destiny. 'These countries', Gambari wrote about those who wished to 'hit and run' in April 1994, 'ignored the moral and overriding duty to help save hapless and defenceless civilians, including innocent women and children, who were being massacred.'[150] How to explain, then, his vote *in favour* of Resolution 912 reducing UNAMIR from 2,500 to 250? As Gambari concedes, 'Nigeria was not entirely happy with the Council's resolution.'[151] Like Albright's, Gambari's decision to go along with the rest of the Council was pragmatic in the sense that no country was either willing or able to send reinforcements to Rwanda, and that such a strengthening of the numbers would have required the use of force under Chapter VII—an almost unthink-able proposition in the shadow of Somalia.[152] Still, Gambari had never been afraid of criticizing Western countries for abdicating their responsibilities and for withdrawing UN missions from regions which they perceived to be stra-tegically unimportant.[153]

There were therefore other reasons behind Gambari's decision to go along with his colleagues, reasons that clearly transcend Rwanda. One of them was a strong drive towards compromise: 'In the post-Cold War environment', the Nigerian diplomat noted, 'there was considerable pressure on all members to have Security Council resolutions adopted by consensus, and in almost all the cases in 1994-1995 this was indeed the case.'[154] This expectation to come to an agreement was strengthened by the fact that, unlike Albright's home country, Gambari's Nigeria was a *non-permanent* member and did not have a veto. 'Without a doubt it was the Security Council, especially its most powerful members, as well as the international community as a whole, that failed the

---

[150] Ibrahim Gambari, 'Rwanda: An African Perspective', in Malone, *The UN Security Council*, p.515.
[151] Gambari, p.517.
[152] Though not so unthinkable, it turned out, in the Former Yugoslavia.
[153] Gambari, p.517.   [154] Gambari, p.517.

people of Rwanda in their gravest hour of need',[155] Gambari wrote, defensively. It is difficult to disagree, but the fact that all Rwanda resolutions were passed unanimously suggests that even the E-10 were ready to sacrifice what they thought was right on the altar of consensus.[156] Gambari's leadership was thus subject to very considerable constraints, yet his repeated attempts to push the Council to strengthen UNAMIR during the informal meetings are noteworthy, particularly in light of the fact that they took place behind the closed doors of the Consultations Room and away from the media. One should also remember that, unlike Albright, Gambari was not trying to influence a national bureaucracy but an inter-governmental body in which national 'interests' and global norms mingle to form an unpredictable mix.[157] Although his chances to alter the Council's direction were always infinitely slimmer than Albright's ability to change Washington's, Gambari did try to do so.

Given the above constraints, can we speak of 'leadership' at all within the Council? On the one hand, ambassadors represent their countries' positions rather than their own, something that significantly constrains their scope for action. On the other, their willingness—and in Albright's case, her ability—to change other people's stances shows that in 1994 diplomats did have some margin of manoeuvre and that some of them used it.[158] As one author noted, when this happens, ambassadors move from a 'logic of consequences' to a 'logic of appropriateness', a complex process of socialization that makes the most of the ever-evolving—and contradictory—positions of their nation's foreign policies and of their desire to compromise.[159] The Rwanda debate, especially the informal consultations, suggests that while no ambassador 'dominated' the discussions, Albright and Gambari pushed their colleagues towards a different policy solution and, regardless of the outcome, showed some degree of leadership in doing so.

LEADERS OR MANAGERS?

In *War and Peace* (1869), Tolstoy portrays leaders as bow waves of moving boats, always in front and theoretically leading, but in fact merely being pushed along by the boat (a metaphor for the organization they belong to).[160] Is this an accurate portrayal of UN officials in 1994? Did they have a plan—a vision—and did they stick to it? More importantly, were they *permitted* to have a plan, or were they simply expected to execute orders from above?

---

[155] Gambari, p.513.
[156] John Langmore and Jeremy Farrall, 'Can Elected Members Make a Difference in the UN Security Council?', *Global Governance*, Vol.22, No.1 (2016), pp.59–77.
[157] Clive Archer, *International Organizations* (Abingdon: Routledge, 2015), esp. ch.4.
[158] Buchet de Neuilly, p.80.   [159] Buchet de Neuilly, p.13.
[160] Leo Tolstoy, *War and Peace* (London: Penguin, 2006).

Speaking of leadership and international leadership within the UN Secretariat remains highly problematic. Its large size (over 6,000 employees), peculiar composition (with personnel coming from disparate bureaucratic traditions), complex relationship with the SC, and an SG with an ambiguous job description all combine to pose considerable challenges in terms of defining what the organization's policy is, let alone executing it.[161] If one adds to this the peculiarities of the UN bureaucracy in the early 1990s, when different departments seemed to have different supporters with conflicting ideas about what peacekeeping involved and how it should be carried out, it is easy to see why scholars are reluctant to associate the idea of leadership with the UN Secretariat.[162] Although the variability of political leadership at the national level is problematic and explains the myriad of definitions currently in existence, it increases exponentially in an international context where leaders are seen as diminished figures whose scope for action, followers, responsibilities, and accountability becomes even more imprecise.[163] As one author noted, 'Under normal conditions, the operation and study of leadership are influenced by the situation in which leaders attempt to generate and exert some measure of direction. But in [the international context] there is considerable doubt over the nature and boundaries of what could be termed the international situation'.[164] If one adds to this the idiosyncrasies of the UN system, it becomes clear why the idea of individual leadership *within* it—perhaps even more than institutional leadership *by* it—is not seen as providing a useful analytical framework.

An in-depth analysis of the contributions of UN officials during the Rwanda crisis only partly supports this view. Some of the international civil servants involved in UNAMIR had a considerable margin of manoeuvre, not only within their departments but also *vis-à-vis* the SG and SC. The bureaucratic conflict existing in New York in the early 1990s between DPA and DPKO, in particular—coupled with the power-political factor of an SG who was increasingly determined to oppose the Western powers on a range of operations from Somalia, to Haiti, to the Former Yugoslavia—simultaneously hindered and helped intra-UN leadership. If on the one hand such friction created considerable difficulties in terms of coordination and information-sharing within the Secretariat, on the other it contributed to cementing the '*esprit-de-corps*' within each department and gave their heads a chance to translate individual leadership into institutional leadership. This meant that UN officials sometimes went against the express wishes of their bosses and were able to shape

---

[161] Thant Myint-U and Amy Scott, *The UN Secretariat* (New York: International Peace Academy, 2007).
[162] Chesterman, esp. ch.9; Kent Kille, ed., *The UN Secretary-General and Moral Authority* (Washington, DC: Georgetown University Press, 2007).
[163] Foley, p.267.   [164] Foley, p.267.

policy in the way that *they*—rather than the top UN leadership—saw fit. The Rwanda crisis thus suggests that leadership—rather than agency—existed at different levels in 1994, and that international civil servants can do more than states (and the SG) want (and mandate) them to do, especially in times of crisis[165] when national policies are more negotiable and adaptable to the circumstances.[166] According to Goulding, being supported by a Great Power helps too: 'The SG, who takes less and less trouble to conceal his dislike and distrust of Kofi, claimed that the latter had written the report at the dictation of Madeleine Albright',[167] the British diplomat wrote in his diary towards the end of Boutros-Ghali's reign.

DPKO officials are another example of where leadership can exist at the UN: understaffed, worried about the logistics of peacekeeping, and unenthusiastic about UNAMIR from the start, they did not feel the need to actively consult the SG, the SC, EOSG, or DPA when they ordered Dallaire to abort attempts to seize weapons. That decision was undoubtedly complex and a plausible argument can be made that it was the most appropriate under the circumstances. However, it was hardly 'technical' and reflected a policy course taken by DPKO independently of the rest of the Secretariat, one that interpreted UNAMIR's mandate in a traditionalist way rather than in a can-do fashion *because* that was the outcome DPKO leaders wished to achieve. The UNAMIR leadership, too, carved out a space for itself during the crisis, at times deciding (in the case of Dallaire) to disobey orders coming from DPKO *because* its leaders thought that was the proper course of action, at other times selectively choosing (in the case of Booh Booh) to report to New York only what it wanted Headquarters to know. Given the extent of the control exercised on both departments by Boutros-Ghali, DPA and EOSG were arguably in a more constrained position than other departments—but its officials, too, made consequential choices and reportedly influenced—or consciously failed to, in the case of Goulding—UN decision-making processes. The fact that Jonah and Goulding held different views about UNAMIR also suggests a certain degree of autonomy *vis-à-vis* the SG, although as a department DPA appears to have stuck to the Boutros-Ghali 'gospel' both before and after the handover from Jonah to Goulding (in this respect, the British official was largely unable to influence his department's position). As a result, scope for individual leadership—understood as the ability to shape, rather than simply execute, a certain policy—did exist in the Secretariat of 1994. This was especially the case for Boutros-Ghali as the top UN official; he was able to count on a unique—though highly contested—asset, namely, moral authority. The next chapter asks if and how he used it.

---

[165] Joel Oestreich, ed., *International Organizations as Self-Directed Actors* (Abingdon: Routledge, 2012).
[166] Malone, *The UN Security Council.*   [167] MIG-PD-C, 23-May-1996.

9

Morality

'Notwithstanding the persistence of national egoism [and] isolationism among the most powerful states...the world begins to perceive war as a crime and inequality as an injustice. We are thus witnessing the undeniable rise of a universal moral conscience [and] the United Nations...has become, for all states and all peoples, the irreplaceable instrument of international solidarity.'[1] This statement by Boutros Boutros-Ghali sums up his vision of the UN and of the SG's role in it.[2] From 1992 to 1996, the Egyptian diplomat appeared committed to making the UN more relevant on the world stage, attracting considerable criticism for his activism both inside and outside the Secretariat: 'He had an exaggerated vision of his role', David Hannay stated, 'and in particular, he did not understand the difference between power and influence. He thought he had power.'[3] For Boutros-Ghali, his 'power' as SG derived from two sources: one was intangible and lay with the values enshrined in the UN Charter, the other was tangible and coincided with his control over the UN bureaucracy. His programme of reform, like his term in office, was defined by a statist as well as a cosmopolitan stream that simultaneously paid tribute to national sovereignty, while trying to limit the influence of states over the Secretariat. Importantly for our purposes, peacekeeping and peacebuilding were the tools that Boutros-Ghali intended to use in his effort to turn the UN into a 'universal moral conscience'. For this, he needed tangible instruments— such as a supportive bureaucracy free of state 'interferences'—as well as intangible ones, including the only asset which, in Boutros-Ghali's view, the UN had but that states lacked: moral authority.

Few events dented such authority as badly as the Rwandan genocide. Although some of the reasons for this—including Boutros-Ghali's own

---

[1] Boutros Boutros-Ghali, 'Le Secrétaire-Général des Nations Unies: Entre l'Urgence et la Durée', *Politique Etrangère*, No.2 (Summer 1996), p.414.

[2] Kent Kille, ed., *The UN Secretary-General and Moral Authority* (Washington, DC: Georgetown University Press, 2007), ch.8.

[3] My interview with David Hannay, London, UK, 26 April 2011 (and by email on 12 May 2016).

performance during the crisis[4]—have been mentioned in Part I, a lesser known factor involves the compatibility between Boutros-Ghali's 'moral' view of the UN and his involvement with Rwanda prior to becoming SG. This chapter argues that these two streams of his role in Rwanda—the idealist and the pragmatic—are emblematic both of his term in office and of the UN organization as a whole. As we shall see, there is a link between the muscular approach to peacekeeping advocated by Boutros-Ghali early on, the 'moral' purpose he attached to the SG's role, his predilection for DPA over DPKO, and his performance in Rwanda. Following a broad chronological trajectory from 1990 to 1994, this chapter explores such a link, first by exploring the idea of UN 'moral authority' and the reasons behind Boutros-Ghali's—and most SGs'—support for it; then by contrasting that idea with Boutros-Ghali's relations with Presidents Mitterrand of France, Habyarimana of Rwanda, and Mubarak of Egypt. Three questions arise: did Boutros-Ghali's proximity to one side of Rwanda's ethnic divide (the Hutus) prior to becoming SG affect his relations with the other (the Tutsis)? Did such proximity compromise his independence, neutrality, and impartiality—three sources of the SG's moral authority? And was his conduct compatible with his 'moral' view of the UN?

THE UNITED NATIONS AND 'MORAL AUTHORITY'

'The United Nations stands outside all confessions but is nevertheless an instrument of faith.'[5] So Dag Hammarskjöld defined one of the most contested traits of the world body: its moral force. According to him, the organization was more than a place where the world's powerful met to negotiate and solve disputes. To be sure, this function of being the diplomatic crossroads was one of the reasons that had pushed the Allies to establish the United Nations—in its Glasshouse on the East River in New York—in 1945.[6] But it was not the only one, and for Hammarskjöld—like for most SGs—a strong idealistic component was built into the UN. 'Secular Pope' is how he described the role of SG.[7]

This view, however, is contested. For one thing, critics note that Hammarskjöld was unrepresentative as an SG in his attachment to what he saw as the 'moral' principles of the UN Charter—ironically so, since the Swede had

---

[4] Stephen Burgess, *The United Nations Under Boutros-Ghali, 1992–1997* (London: Scarecrow, 2001).

[5] Dag Hammarskjöld, *To Speak for the World* (Stockholm: Atlantis, 2005), p.59.

[6] Stephen Schlesinger, *Act of Creation* (Boulder: Westview, 2003).

[7] Manuel Fröhlich, *Political Ethics and the United Nations* (Abingdon: Routledge, 2007).

been chosen by the P-5 as 'a cautious, safe, and non-political technocrat...
who would avoid controversial political actions'.[8] For another, the UN was
born from the ashes of one of the world's most devastating conflicts: in 1945,
practical considerations of power and empire trumpeted idealistic visions of
equality and human rights, supporters of this argument claim, and the priority
was the re-building of a devastated Europe, a task that could only be accomplished by sovereign (as opposed to colonized) states.[9] According to this
version of events, by pointing out that 'Nothing contained in the present
Charter shall authorize the United Nations to intervene in matters which are
essentially within the domestic jurisdiction of any state...', Article 2 (7) of the
UN Charter makes it clear that the organization is first and foremost an intergovernmental body established upon the principle of national sovereignty,
rather than a metaphysical construction with moral aims. In 1945 the goal was
pragmatic, namely, cementing the new post-Second World War order and
establishing a channel of communication by binding states—especially the
Great Powers of the time—to some common rules, the most important of
which was the P-5's right to a veto. It was arguably for sovereign states—not
for their citizens—that the UN was set up.

While there is some truth in this explanation, it fails to recognize that the
reconstruction of 1945 involved norms and concepts as well as buildings and
bridges. Since the fight against Hitler had been portrayed by the Allies and by
the USSR as a moral struggle involving values as well as military power,[10] the
necessity to reconstruct the international system after the Second World War
was 'moral' as much as 'material'. After two devastating world wars there was a
need for new ideas, a new conception of international politics, and a new way
of solving *and* preventing conflict. 'The new Charter should not be a mere
legalistic document for the prevention of war', one of the most senior delegates
to the San Francisco conference wrote in 1945. In his view, it should also
contain language mirroring the fact that the war against Hitler had been waged
'for the eternal values which sustain the spirit of man in its upward struggle
toward light'.[11] Since 1945 this 'idealistic' component of the UN has arguably
become as important as the statist approaches that were so familiar to the
organization's founders.[12] Several authors noted that the intellectual contribution of the UN includes ideas such as global health, human development,
and climate change, all of which are relatively well-established in the twenty-
first century despite not being prominent in the Charter. Importantly for our

---

[8] Brian Urquhart, *A Life in Peace and War* (New York: Norton, 1987), p.124.
[9] Robert Hilderbrand, *Dumbarton Oaks* (Chapel Hill: University of North Carolina Press,
1990).
[10] Dan Plesch, *America, Hitler and the UN* (London: I.B. Tauris, 2011).
[11] Mark Mazower, *No Enchanted Palace* (Princeton: Princeton University Press, 2009), p.29.
[12] Richard Jolly et al., *The Power of UN Ideas* (New York: United Nations Intellectual History
Project Series, 2005), available at www.UNhistory.org (accessed 3 June 2016).

purposes, two of those ideas are peacekeeping and peacebuilding: like other UN concepts, they have practical implications but are also emblematic of the UN's vocation to look beyond states, towards humanity as a whole.

Although the above interpretation is also contentious, it goes some way towards explaining why the organization and its chief are seen by many—including Boutros-Ghali—as having more 'moral authority' than member states. It also explains why SGs have used this reading of UN functions to legitimize their action and to rationalize their authority: 'I have moral rather than material power',[13] Trygve Lie wrote, while Hammarskjöld was fond of repeating that 'The Secretariat and the Secretary-General are representatives of a secular church of ideas and principles in international affairs'[14]. Kurt Waldheim agreed: 'All I have is moral power. I have nothing else by my side. I do not have any power to compel anybody to do anything',[15] while Kofi Annan[16] and Ban Ki-moon[17] shared this view. The UN itself writes—grandly but tellingly—of 'a silent march towards the universalisation of values, a march that is generated, consolidated and widened by the work of the United Nations'.[18] This is an intellectual enterprise of considerable scope and ambition, one that could only be attempted by simultaneously supporting and undermining the principle on which the UN and international law are based, namely, national sovereignty. Since states are often the first violators of their peoples' rights—and since the worst of such violations, genocide, usually needs the material and legal resources of a state to take place—this 'moral' march of the UN was bound to be controversial and to create tension between SG and membership. This is especially so since states, too, claim 'moral' foundations and routinely legitimize their policies—including their foreign policies—in 'moral' terms.[19]

BOUTROS-GHALI AND 'MORAL AUTHORITY'

Boutros-Ghali's self-described 'moral crusade' as SG included his *Agenda for Peace* (1992), *Agenda for Development* (1994), and *Agenda for Democratization*

[13] Trygve Lie, *In the Cause of Peace* (New York: Macmillan, 1954), p.42.
[14] Hammarskjöld, p.148.
[15] Shirley Hazzard, *Countenance of Truth* (New York: Viking, 1990), p.97.
[16] Kille, *The UN Secretary-General and Moral Authority*, p.15.
[17] Ban Ki-moon, *My Priorities as Secretary-General*, available at https://www.un.org/sg/en/formersg/ban.shtml (accessed 1 May 2017).
[18] Oficina del Comisionado Para los Derechos Humanos, *El Aporte de las Naciones Unidas a la Globalización de la Ética* (Santiago: División de Desarrollo Social de las Naciones Unidas, 2001), p.5.
[19] David Ambrosetti, *La France au Rwanda* (Paris: Karthala, 2001), esp. Part 2.

(1996). In his view, four principles inform the UN Charter and must serve as the guiding lights of any SG, namely, peace, independence, human rights, and development.[20] For Boutros-Ghali, they converged into the ideas of peacekeeping and especially peacebuilding, and he saw it as his job to work towards their implementation. It is true that the first Security Council meeting at the level of Heads of State, in early 1992, had given the new SG an unprecedented mandate to reshape the organization, particularly in the areas of peacekeeping, peacebuilding, and preventive diplomacy. Nevertheless, an argument can be made that Boutros-Ghali went beyond what the SC and the P-5 had originally envisaged. 'The Security Council [represents states and] conveys the general interest in the realist form of a political compromise', he wrote, 'whereas the Secretary-General [represents the organization and] tries to give that compromise a content that is more impartial and, I am tempted to say, also sometimes more moral'.[21]

What did 'moral' mean in this context? Boutros-Ghali understood the term in its original connotation, the Latin term *moralitas* indicating the precepts separating right from wrong and good from bad. But *moralitas* also implies that such precepts be respected *in practice*; for this reason, this expression is commonly used to single out the principles of a proper conduct, what one should do and what one should avoid. In this sense, the term 'morality' refers to rules of conduct that are identified on the basis of certain values—and for Boutros-Ghali, such values are enshrined in the UN Charter. The latter was for him similar to a sacred text which found in the SG its 'guardian'. As one observer noted, SGs 'often used the Charter with a reverence that is almost mystical and that can be likened to a religious text, and they see themselves as the embodiment of the Charter and of its ethical code'.[22] For Boutros-Ghali, one 'believes' or 'does not believe' in the UN ideals as one believes or does not believe in the precepts of a religion. Far from being a weakness, he saw this as the UN's greatest asset.

This does not mean that for Boutros-Ghali states could or should be bypassed; as a former professor of international law and as an admirer of its founder, Hugo Grotius, the SG was well aware that sovereignty was the bedrock of the UN and international system.[23] However, he was also clear about the difference between what he saw as a potentially 'immoral' membership and an SG whose job it was to guide states towards a more principled approach to global affairs. For him, *An Agenda for Peace* provided such a guide in that it not only strengthened UN peacekeeping—by the early 1990s a

---

[20] Boutros-Ghali, *Mes Années à la Maison de Verre* (Paris: Fayard, 1999), chs 1, 4, 5, and 12.

[21] Boutros-Ghali, 'Le Sécrétaire Général', p.410.

[22] Kent Kille, 'Reconsidering the Power of the Secretary-General', Annual Meeting of the American Association of Political Science, 30 August 2006, p.20.

[23] Boutros Boutros-Ghali, 'A Grotian Moment', *Fordham International Law Journal*, Vol.18 (1994–95), p.1611.

well-established idea accepted by states in principle if not always in practice—but also included an arguably utopian idea, namely, averting conflicts *before* they emerge through peacebuilding, preventive diplomacy, and the SG's good offices.[24] As he saw them, these were 'moral' enterprises which he nevertheless intended to pursue through pragmatic means by expanding the profile of the SG, by cementing his hold on the UN bureaucracy, and by strengthening what he saw as his 'political' departments, notably DPA and the EOSG, including through the October 1993 directive mentioned in Chapter 6. 'The Secretary-General has to . . . push states to fulfil their responsibilities and make those decisions which he or she believes are in accordance with the greater interest of the international community',[25] he wrote. In this vision, DPKO was important in managing peace operations on a day-to-day basis and in executing the SG's goals, but lacked a truly moral function and should not have a policy-making role. This does not mean that Boutros-Ghali saw peacekeeping as 'apolitical': indeed, it was precisely because he regarded it as a long-term process and so critical to the UN that he thought that the SG—rather than a single department, especially one controlled by 'immoral' states—should provide 'political' guidance to it, while leaving its operational aspects to DPKO.[26] For Boutros-Ghali, the 'political' functions of the SG, DPA, and EOSG, and the 'moral' ones of the UN, coincided.

This partly explains why Boutros-Ghali adopted an idealistic approach to the UN Charter, for the main objective of his *Agendas*—and of his 'political' role as SG—was to reinforce 'the trust, and with it, the moral authority of the Charter'[27] for the betterment of an organization that 'must be bigger than the sum of its parts'.[28] Although the *Agendas* were couched in pragmatic language, Boutros-Ghali claimed that their spirit was anchored in the UN's 'moral' force—the only one the organization had. 'I insist that the international community mobilize itself against social injustice, exclusion and poverty', he wrote introducing his *Agenda for Development*, 'for it is intolerable that a society which is advancing by leaps and bounds leaves aside, in a state of utter despair, more than 1,5 billion people'.[29] This was consistent with Boutros-Ghali's perception of the SG's role, which was not limited to 'alerting all the time member states of this unbearable cleavage ('*déchirure*') in the world and of all the risks that it implies', but also to 'suggest some forms of action [to member states]'.[30] Since for him SGs should express humanity's hopes, they

---

[24] Bertrand Ramcharan, *Preventive Diplomacy at the UN* (Bloomington: Indiana University Press, 2008), ch.4.

[25] Boutros-Ghali, 'Le Sécrétaire-Général', p.408.

[26] See Jean-Marie Guéhenno, *The Fog of Peace* (Washington: Brookings Institution Press, 2015), p.xvii.

[27] Boutros Boutros-Ghali, 'Un Programa de Paz' (undated), available at http://www.ceppacr.org/3_un_programa_de_paz.pdf (accessed 1 March 2017), p.5.

[28] Boutros-Ghali, 'Un Programa', p.5.

[29] Boutros-Ghali, 'Le Sécrétaire-Général', p.413.

[30] Boutros Boutros-Ghali, 'Beyond Peacekeeping', *New York University Journal of International Law and Politics*, Vol.25, No.113 (1992–93), p.121.

cannot limit themselves to 'facilitate the multilateral activities of states'.[31] Interestingly, Boutros-Ghali claims to have found some of the strongest opposition to this vision among his colleagues in the Secretariat, often perceived as the cradle of die-hard idealists: 'They told me that my project of democratization of the international system was fragile and faulty...and that the Organization did not have the power to do anything beyond what member states wanted it to do',[32] he wrote of some of his aides' reaction to *Agenda for Democratization*. For those aides, the SG was simply an employee of member states.

BOUTROS-GHALI, RWANDA, AND THE FRENCH CONNECTION

Boutros-Ghali's approach to the UN largely stemmed from his academic background. His interest in Rwanda also pre-dated his secretary-generalship and developed during his time in the Egyptian government. Since Boutros-Ghali's involvement in Rwanda came early in his career and contributed to shaping his understanding of the country's ethnic problems, it is helpful to situate it within the context of Egyptian and French foreign policy. This will provide a better picture of Boutros-Ghali's links with Rwanda's politicians and will make it possible to ascertain whether his 'moral' vision of the UN was compatible with his role in Rwanda.

As a member of one of the most prominent patrician families of Egypt—his grandfather, who was assassinated in office, had been the country's only Coptic Prime Minister—Boutros-Ghali played several roles. He was a strong supporter of President Sadat's rapprochement with Israel, advocated a peace agreement between the Israelis and the Palestinians, and was a committed pan-Africanist.[33] The most important of these allegiances was nevertheless his Francophilia: with a doctorate from the Sorbonne, a close friendship with President Mitterrand, a residence in Paris, and an impeccable grasp of the French language, Boutros-Ghali had long been an *habitué* of Paris's élites. 'His experience in Paris made him a lifelong lover of all things French', an observer wrote, 'a trait that some critics believed would later add to his difficulties in getting along with the Americans because of his tendency to see things from a French perspective'.[34] After resigning his professorship in international law at

---

[31] Boutros-Ghali, 'Beyond Peacekeeping', p.121.

[32] Anthony Lang, 'A Realist in the Utopian City', in Kille, *The UN Secretary-General*, p.287.

[33] Boutros-Ghali, *Mes Années*.

[34] 'Boutros Boutros-Ghali, U.N. Secretary General who Clashed with the U.S., Dies', *The Washington Post*, 16 February 2016.

the University of Cairo and serving the Egyptian Government in various capacities, in 1977 Boutros-Ghali became Minister of State for Foreign Affairs. It was a job that allowed him to focus on what he saw as his twin priorities: consolidating his country's presence in Africa—for him, Egypt was first and foremost an African nation—and advocating Cairo's accession to *la franco-phonie*, an association of French-speaking states that included most of Paris's former colonies as well as those countries with a cultural, social, and political bond to France.[35] Given Egypt's tumultuous history this was no easy task, but in the early 1990s Boutros-Ghali succeeded in convincing his sceptical boss, President Hosni Mubarak, that tying Egypt's interests to those of France would result in significant geopolitical assets, including enhanced business opportunities in Africa. 'Egypt can hope to obtain at least three advantages from joining the Francophone zone', Boutros-Ghali wrote in his (published) diary: 'Strengthening its relationship with France, developing its links with Francophone African countries, [and] counterbalancing the cultural and political influence of the American superpower. It is on the basis of these three arguments that I have convinced Egyptian MPs to vote in favour of Egypt's accession to the Francophone area, which is seen by fundamentalists as an opening to French cultural imperialism.'[36]

It is within this peculiar historical context that in October 1990 one of Paris's allies, Hutu President Juvénal Habyarimana of Rwanda, came under military attack from Tutsi rebels.[37] As mentioned in Part I, when Habyarimana took power in Kigali with a coup in the 1950s, many Tutsis fled Rwanda and sought refuge in neighbouring Uganda, vowing to regroup and launch an attack against Kigali. There is an important geopolitical and linguistic dimension here: as a former Belgian colony and French protectorate, the majority of Rwanda's population is Francophone, whereas Ugandans are English-speaking.[38] In the early 1990s, Rwanda and Uganda were thus not only hostile neighbours but also key players in the post-colonial linguistic and cultural fault line separating Francophone and Anglophone Africa.[39] From Kampala, President Museveni allowed the Tutsi refugees to settle but made no secret of the fact that they should eventually go back to Rwanda.[40] As a result, in 1987

---

[35] Boutros Boutros-Ghali, *Émanciper la Francophonie* (Paris: L'Harmattan, 2003).

[36] Boutros Boutros-Ghali, *Entre le Nil et Jérusalem* (Paris: Éditions du Rocher, 2011), p.208.

[37] Ministère Français des Affaires Etrangères, Mission d'Information Parlementaire sur le Rwanda, 4.A.8.; TD Kigali, Message de M. Barateau Relatif à l'Attaque au Rwanda, 4 October 1990; and Présidence de la République Française, Note de l'Admiral Lanxade à l'Attention du Monsieur le Président de la République, 8 October 1990, available at www.assemblee-nationale.fr/dossiers/rwanda/r1271.asp (accessed 18 July 2015) (MIPR).

[38] Claire Griffiths, *Contrasting Historical Divides in Francophone Africa* (Chester: Chester University Press, 2013).

[39] Samuel Gardiner, *A History of the Commonwealth* (London: Forgotten Books, 2012), Vol.1.

[40] André Guichaoua, *Les Crises Politiques au Burundi et au Rwanda* (Lille: Presses Universitaires de Lille, 1995), p.220.

the RPF—a movement composed of English-speaking Tutsi refugees from Uganda—was formed. Although in the 1980s its aim—the removal of the Hutu regime in Kigali—was unlikely to succeed,[41] on 1 October 1990 the RPF launched a military offensive against the Rwandan army in the north-east, prompting Habyarimana's army to retreat. It was the start of a bloody civil war that only ended with the genocide of 1994 and which Museveni actively supported.[42] Uganda, he stated, wanted 'to help the RPF materially, so that they are not defeated because that would have been detrimental to the Tutsi people of Rwanda and would not have been good for Uganda's stability [either]'.[43]

Although the Rwandan military was trained by the French and Paris promptly intervened in support of Habyarimana,[44] Kigali needed something that France was less and less willing to provide: a long-term, steady supply of affordable weapons to fight the RPF, ideally from a regional country so as to minimize transportation costs. As a well-known exporter of heavy weapons Egypt fitted the bill, but Mubarak was not convinced that a deal with Kigali would be profitable, especially since the Rwandan government had a bad credit record due to the country's economic recession and the collapse of the price of coffee, Rwanda's main export. It was at this stage that—with the encouragement of President Mitterrand—Boutros-Ghali's involvement with Habyarimana's Hutus began and deepened.[45] Paris had excellent geopolitical reasons to help Kigali find a military supplier, because the French-speaking economic and political zone in Africa would have been severely damaged by the 'loss' of another state to the English-speaking Commonwealth.[46] On the other hand, for France it was increasingly expensive—logistically and in terms of reputation—to be seen to be providing weapons to Habyarimana's auto-cratic regime at a time of mounting opposition to neo-colonialism.[47] Egypt was thus the ideal provider: it was relatively close to Rwanda, its leadership in the form of Mubarak was friendly and Boutros-Ghali was very friendly towards France, and Egypt itself (through Boutros-Ghali's leadership) was taking steps to join the French-speaking network. 'The Francophone area must allow us to reinforce our presence in Africa',[48] Boutros-Ghali wrote in October 1990, as Rwandan–Egyptian relations reached new highs.

France's desire—and motivation—to discreetly disengage from Rwanda emerges from a declassified letter sent by the head of the French Navy to President Mitterrand, a letter that acquires sinister undertones in light of the

---

[41] Guichaoua, p.220.   [42] Guichaoua, p.220.
[43] Mamdani Mahmood, *When Victims Become Killers* (Princeton: Princeton University Press, 2002), p.183.
[44] Télégramme Diplomatique, 7 October 1990, Situation au Rwanda (MIPR).
[45] Boutros-Ghali, *Entre le Nil et Jérusalem*, p.406.   [46] Mahmood, ch.2.
[47] Présidence de la République, Note de M. Claude Arnaud, 30 March 1990 (MIPR).
[48] Boutros-Ghali, *Entre le Nil et Jérusalem*, p.417.

subsequent genocide: 'Such a diminution of our support for President Habyarimana would also prevent us from appearing to the outside world as too implicated in supporting the Rwandan army if it were to emerge that serious crimes were committed against the population as a result of the current conflict',[49] the Navy Chief wrote, chillingly but presciently. It is in this complex geopolitical context that Boutros-Ghali played a key role, as Egypt's Minister of State for Foreign Affairs, in convincing Cairo to sign a series of contracts for the supply of weapons to Kigali,[50] with a value in the region of USD26 million.[51]

The timeline is critical. The RPF offensive only began on 1 October 1990, but by mid-October Kigali was already in trouble and urgently needed more weapons. 'President Habyarimana called me at 14 hrs local time close to a state of panic to ask for updates about his request of aerial support',[52] the French Ambassador in Kigali wrote in a diplomatic cable to Paris. Through his French connection, Habyarimana's officials then contacted Boutros-Ghali: 'The Rwandan government would like to ask you to use your influence within your own government to obtain assistance as soon as possible', Kigali's ambassador to Egypt wrote to Boutros-Ghali in a 'top secret' letter dated 15 October 1990, adding that this military assistance was all the more urgent 'considering the situation in the North-East of the country following the [RPF] aggression of which Rwanda is a victim'.[53] Despite his self-proclaimed admiration for the idea of disarmament,[54] Boutros-Ghali welcomed Kigali's request and convinced Mubarak that the Hutus were a reliable business and strategic partner. Conversely, so important was *la Françafrique* to Paris and Mitterrand that a dedicated cell was set up at the Elysée Palace which was managed directly by the President's son, Jean-Christophe Mitterrand, rather than by the Foreign Ministry at the Quai d'Orsay, as was customary.[55] France also presented Habyarimana with a private jet because—according to the French ambassador to Rwanda—'this allowed [Paris] to know the President's movements'.[56]

---

[49] Présidence de la République Française, Note de l'Admiral Lanxade au Président de la République Relatif a la Situation au Rwanda, 11 October 1990 (MIPR).

[50] Accord d'Amitié et de Coopération Entre la France et le Rwanda, 20 October 1962. Unless otherwise stated, the documents in this chapter were accessed through—and are available for public consultation at—the Linda Melvern Rwanda Genocide Archive in the Hugh Owen Library, Aberystwyth University, UK (hereinafter, LMRGA). All translations are mine.

[51] Linda Melvern, *A People Betrayed* (London: Zed Books, 2007); Boutros-Ghali, *Entre le Nil et Jérusalem*, p.406.

[52] Télégramme Diplomatique, Appel Pressant du Président Habyarimana, 7 October 1990 (MIPR).

[53] Ambassade Rwandaise au Caire, Lettre de l'Ambassadeur Célestin Kabanda à Son Excellence Boutros Boutros-Ghali, 15 October 1990.

[54] Boutros-Ghali, *Entre le Nil et Jérusalem*, p.293.

[55] François-Xavier Verschave, *La Françafrique* (Paris: Stock, 1998).

[56] Assemblée Nationale, Audition de M. Georges Martres, 22 April 1998 (MIPR); Présidence de la République, Note de M. Claude Arnaud, 30 March 1990 (MIPR).

Nevertheless, it was far more than technical assistance that Boutros-Ghali facilitated. A number of documents show that his intercession allowed Flight ZA600 by Egyptian cargo company ZAS to deliver, on 28 October 1990, 35,570 kilos of weapons and munitions, including 1,000 120mm bombs, 1,000 88mm bombs, as well as a total of 100,000 7.62×51mm and 7.62×39mm (Kalashnikov) cartridges.[57] Only three days later, on 31 October 1990, another flight left Cairo for Kigali to deliver the first batch of 36,211 kilos of weapons,[58] a shipment that took a total of nine Cairo–Kigali flights with a Boeing 707,[59] and this is confirmed in a letter of the Rwandan Embassy in Egypt.[60] This was only the beginning of a long list of supplies by Egypt to Rwanda's Hutus through Boutros-Ghali, specifically to help them defeat the RPF.[61]

Such weapons quickly became Habyarimana's lifeline in that they allowed him to fend off the first RPF offensive and thus remain in power, a fact that was readily and gratefully acknowledged by Kigali: 'The relations between Rwanda and Egypt have improved considerably in the last few weeks thanks to the supply of military materials which have been of great help during the difficult moments we have lived', the Rwandan Ambassador in Cairo wrote to his Foreign Minister in a confidential letter dated 19 December 1990. 'This has allowed our Armed Forces to stop the enemy, something that they would have probably not been able to do if they had relied on their traditional suppliers.'[62] This document also notes that it was thanks to the intervention of a specific person—somebody who knew the Rwanda context extremely well—rather than of the Egyptian government as a whole, that Habyarimana's Hutus had been saved from almost certain defeat by RPF's Tutsis. 'The personal intervention of Minister Boutros Boutros-Ghali with his Defence Ministry colleague has been crucial ["*déterminante*"] to finalize the purchase, for he was following very closely the situation at our borders', wrote the Ambassador, before suggesting that his boss should 'send him a personal message of gratitude that I could deliver to him when I return to the Embassy.'[63]

---

[57] Ambassade Rwandaise au Caire, Sécret: Chargement sur le Vol Spécial du 28 Octobre 1990, 28 October 1990.

[58] Ambassade Rwandaise au Caire, Chargement sur le Vol du 31/10/1990, 31 October 1990.

[59] Ambassade Rwandaise au Caire, Secret: Fax n.082/(C)4I to ZAS (undated).

[60] Ambassade Rwandaise au Caire, Confidentiel: Lettre au Ministère des Affaires Etrangères du Rwanda à Kigali avec copies au Bureau du Président de la République du Rwanda et au Ministère de la Défense du Rwanda, 26 October 1990.

[61] Ministère de la Défense du Rwanda, Acquisition de Matériel Militaire en Egypte, 22 October 1990.

[62] Ambassade Rwandaise au Caire, Confidentiel: Lettre au Ministre des Affaires Etrangères et de la Coopération Internationale, 19 December 1990.

[63] Ambassade Rwandaise au Caire, Confidentiel, 19 December 1990 (emphasis added).

BOUTROS-GHALI AND THE RWANDAN CIVIL WAR

Although Egypt's assistance to Habyarimana proved crucial to fend off the first RPF attack of October 1990, after their initial defeat the RPF was reorganized by an ambitious General who had trained in the USA and who was determined to march on Kigali: Paul Kagame.[64] As a result, throughout 1991 Habyarimana needed more weapons from Egypt: 'As usual, we rely on your cooperation',[65] the Rwandan ambassador in Cairo wrote to speed up the delivery of new military materials.[66] 'We trust that you will process our order urgently', another document noted a few weeks later, 'because we have a pressing need for it.'[67] Yet in 1991 Mubarak's government did not only provide weapons: in July, vehicles were sent from Cairo to Kigali[68] and a battalion-sized barrack for more than 700 soldiers was built for Rwanda's army.[69] Importantly, the rationale for Kigali's request had not changed: 'Since October 1990 Rwanda has been resisting an external aggression', the Rwandan Ambassador in Cairo wrote with reference to the RPF. 'For this reason our armed forces have tripled, hence our enormous difficulties in lodging them.'[70] It was thus specifically to support the fight of the Hutus against the Tutsis that Egypt's—and Boutros-Ghali's—aid was both needed and provided. A memo marked 'EXTREMELY URGENT' by Rwanda's Foreign Minister explained to Habyarimana that while '[u]ntil 1990 our military cooperation with Egypt... was stagnant, it is now flourishing. The recent acquisition of military materials, coupled with the indefectible and appreciable support of the Egyptian government to our country, is testimony to this.'[71] It was also testimony to the personal friendship between Boutros-Ghali, Mitterrand, and Habyarimana.

In May 1991, Boutros-Ghali was appointed Deputy Prime Minister, the highest position a Christian Copt could attain in Egypt's sectarian politics. The new post brought him renewed influence, a circumstance that the Rwandan authorities promptly acknowledged: 'I have the pleasure of conveying to you my brotherly congratulations and wishes for the best of success in your new functions', Kigali's Foreign Minister wrote to Boutros-Ghali in a telegram.

---

[64] Colin Waugh, *Paul Kagame and Rwanda* (Jefferson, NC: McFarland Books, 2004).

[65] Ambassade Rwandaise au Caire, Fax n.142(C)4M à l'Attention du Colonel Adel du Ministère de la Défense de la République Arabe d'Egypte, 26 September 1991.

[66] Ambassade Rwandaise au Caire, Confidentiel: Fax n.72433 SGCA au Ministère de la Défense d'Egypte, 6 November 1991.

[67] Ambassade Rwandaise au Caire. Besoins Exprimés à la Partie Egyptienne à Titre d'Aide dans le Cadre de la Coopération Militaire, 14 December 1991.

[68] Ambassade Rwandaise au Caire, Lettre n.206/16.11.18(C)2J, 7 August 1991.

[69] Ambassade Rwandaise au Caire, Besoins Exprimés à la Partie Egyptienne à Titre d'Aide dans le Cadre de la Coopération Militaire, 14 December 1991.

[70] Ambassade Rwandaise au Caire, Besoins Exprimés à la Partie Egyptienne, 14 December 1991, §1.

[71] Ministère des Affaires Etrangères et de la Coopération Internationale du Rwanda, Très Urgent: Au Président de la République Rwandaise, 23 February 1991.

'I also take this opportunity to rejoice at the excellent links of friendship and cooperation binding Egypt and Rwanda, while expressing my wish that such links will become even stronger in the interest of our two brotherly nations.'[72] Boutros-Ghali's ambitions, however, transcended Egyptian politics and by mid-1991 he had already started campaigning for the UN secretary-generalship. Given his background and connections in both the East and the West, his constituency was vast and included—in addition to Mubarak and Mitterrand—most of the Arab world and a majority of African states (after three Europeans, an Asian, and a South American, it was felt to be 'Africa's turn' to provide an SG).[73] At the same time, Habyarimana was coming under pressure from the international community to democratize precisely when France was becoming frustrated by his frequent and expensive requests for assistance.[74] Eager not to be seen as overly supportive of the Hutus, Paris favoured a peaceful outcome to the Rwanda crisis so long as Habyarimana's francophone Hutu government remained in power.[75] As for Kagame, he was left in no doubt that the West would look unfavourably at another attempted coup in Africa, especially one that resulted in a minority ethnic group ruling over the majority. 'There are reasons to fear that this conflict will end up degenerating in an ethnic war',[76] the French attaché presciently wrote. By the end of 1991, both Habyarimana and Kagame were thus pressured into signing the Arusha Peace Agreement, not least because the military deadlock made it impossible for one side to militarily prevail over the other.

Far from interrupting the flow of Egyptian weapons into Rwanda, however, the military stalemate increased it. Again with the intercession of Boutros-Ghali, this supply continued throughout 1991 and a fax marked 'SECRET' even described it as 'regular' ['*habituelle*'].[77] Yet so expensive had such military assistance become that at one point funds in Kigali dried up, thus re-awakening Mubarak's fears about Habyarimana's credit worthiness. 'Despite the fact that from tomorrow 20-9-1991 the Egyptian Foreign Ministry could try to cash our cheque', a concerned Rwandan Ambassador wrote to President Habyarimana, 'we still have not received the money... something that, were it to become known to the upper echelons [here in Egypt], could end the

[72] Ministère des Affaires Etrangères et de la Coopération Internationale du Rwanda, Télégramme Officiel: À Monsieur Boutros Boutros-Ghali, Vice-Premier Ministre de la République Arabe d'Egypte, 24 May 1991.

[73] Thant Myint-U and Amy Scott, *The UN Secretariat* (New York: International Peace Academy, 2007).

[74] Ambassade de France à Kigali, Extrait du Message de l'Attaché de Défense à Kigali: Analyse de la Situation Politique, 12 October 1990.

[75] Présidence de la République Française, Note à l'Attention du Monsieur le Président de la République au Sujet de l'Entretien Avec M. Juvénal Habyarimana, 23 April 1991 (MIPR).

[76] Ambassade de France à Kigali, Extrait du Message de l'Attaché de Défense à Kigali: Analyse de la Situation Politique, 12 October 1990.

[77] Ambassade Rwandaise au Caire, Secret: Message Fax 119(C)4M au Ministère de la Défense du Rwanda, 28 August 1991.

privileges we have so far received.'[78] This may explain why a scheduled visit from Habyarimana to Mubarak was abruptly cancelled: 'We can conclude that this is a diplomatic refusal!', the Rwandan Ambassador reported to his boss, before inviting him to contact 'their man' in Egypt: 'For all purposes...I give you the details (in Cairo) of Dr Boutros-Ghali, who is currently visiting India and other Asian countries until the 28th of this month....'[79]

BOUTROS-GHALI AND THE RWANDAN PEACE PROCESS

If 1991 was a year of stalemate for the Rwandan civil war, 1992 was one of change—and again the fates of Boutros-Ghali and Rwanda intersected. Reflecting the 'make-it-or-break-it' approach adopted by Habyarimana early in the conflict, 1992 saw the signature of the largest military contracts ever between Egypt and Rwanda, the effects of which went beyond 1992 and in fact continued until the end of the genocide. 'In a spirit of mutual support and assistance', one of those contracts read, 'the Arab Republic of Egypt...undertakes to deliver to the Rwandan Republic...the military material with the price and details explained in Annex A for a total of 6,722,400 US$[80] [and with] the buyer and seller promising not to show this contract to a third party'.[81] By 1992 Egypt had become Rwanda's largest military provider, something that unsettled Kigali's neighbours: 'Reliable sources suggest that Burundi is jealous of our excellent relations with Egypt since the start of the war that was forced upon us', the Foreign Minister wrote. 'Burundi would like to spoil our relations and convince Egypt to stop supplying us with weapons.'[82] In only a few years, Rwanda, one of the world's poorest countries, had become Africa's third largest importer of weapons.

Meanwhile, two events involved Boutros-Ghali directly. In January 1992 the Egyptian took office as the sixth SG of the UN, while in July 1992 the Arusha peace talks between Habyarimana and Kagame began under the auspices of the new SG.[83] The multi-million dollar contract of March 1992 falls in

---

[78] Ambassade Rwandaise au Caire, Urgent: Fax n.135(C)4M, 19 September 1991.

[79] Ambassade Rwandaise au Caire, Confidentiel: Fax n.114(C)182, 16 August 1991.

[80] Contrat n.1/92 Entre le Gouvernement de la République Rwandaise et le Gouvernement de la République Arabe d'Egypte sur la Fourniture par l'Egypte d'un Crédit d'Assistance Militaire, 30 March 1992, p.1.

[81] Contrat n.1/92, 30 March 1992, Article 7.

[82] Ministère des Affaires Etrangères du Rwanda, Très Urgent: Destinataire AMBARWANDA Caire, 15 July 1992.

[83] James Jonah, *What Price the Survival of the United Nations?* (Ibadan: Evans Brothers, 2006), pp.374–83.

between these two events, that is to say, *after* Boutros-Ghali's elevation but *before* the Arusha talks, which means that Boutros-Ghali was no longer in the Egyptian government when these contracts were signed and is not known to have facilitated them (although the tight timing and the fact that the SC elected him in late 1991 make it likely that he was aware of—if not directly involved with—them). In any case, the supply of Egyptian weapons to Habyarimana continued throughout the Arusha negotiations, for while the Rwandan parties were talking peace, at least three deliveries of arms were made, one on 13 July for $456,320,[84] another on 17 July for $555,000,[85] and a third one on 19 July for $620,000.[86]

Kagame, too, was bent on war rather than peace, for the Arusha negoti-ations were briefly interrupted in early 1993 when the RPF launched a surprise attack on Habyarimana that almost managed to overthrow him.[87] Although a mixture of Egyptian weapons and French assistance once again saved the Hutu government from a certain defeat,[88] in 1993 Mitterrand let Habyari-mana know in no uncertain terms that Paris would no longer play the role of bodyguard,[89] forcing Kigali once and for all to reach a power-sharing agree-ment with the RPF.[90] Although the Arusha Accords were signed in August 1993 and UNAMIR was set up in October,[91] the influx of Egyptian weapons continued apace throughout this time. Since 1,000 rockets, 8,000 bombs, 1,600,000 cartridges, 10,000 grenades, and 10,000 mines were delivered by Egypt to Habyarimana *after* the Arusha agreement,[92] the fact that the Accords were fragile should not have come as a surprise. It certainly should not have surprised the SG of the United Nations.

By then Boutros-Ghali was in an awkward position. As the head of an organization with a peacekeeping mission in—and an arms embargo against—Rwanda, the SG was supposed to prevent an influx of weapons to which he had himself contributed. The peculiarity of this situation—one that, as the previous chapters have shown, also involved different Secretariat departments working in the same country without coordination or even knowledge of each other's actions—is best conveyed by Jacques-Roger Booh Booh, Boutros-Ghali's

---

[84] Ministry of Defence of Egypt, Delivery Sheet, 11 July 1992.
[85] Ministry of Defence of Egypt, Delivery Sheet, 13 July 1992.
[86] Ministry of Defence of Egypt, Delivery Sheet, 19 July 1992.
[87] Guichaoua, p.232.
[88] Gérard Prunier, *The Rwanda Crisis* (London: Hurst, 1998), ch.3; Linda Melvern, *Conspir-acy to Murder* (London: Verso, 2006), ch.1; Jacques Semelin, *Purify and Destroy* (New York: Columbia University Press, 2007), Part III.
[89] Telegramme Diplomatique, Retrait des Troupes Françaises du Rwanda, 9 March 1993 (MIPR).
[90] Melvern, *A People Betrayed*, p.24.   [91] Guichaoua, p.232.
[92] Ambassade Rwandaise au Caire, Fax n.21/(C)4M to MINDEF Egypt, 16 February 1993.

Special Representative in Rwanda, in relation to UNAMIR's task of seizing illegal weapons:

> At the very time when we were trying to create the institutional foundations [agreed by Arusha], a C130 military aircraft packed with 80 tons of light and heavy weapons belonging to the Rwandan government landed at the Kigali international airport. These weapons were bought in Egypt through a bank guarantee from the *Crédit Lyonnais* of France covering 100% of the value of the weapons bought by the Rwandan government.[93]

The SRSG also noted that 'the contents of this plane were seized by UNAMIR and remained under its control'.[94] While this specific shipment was therefore blocked by Dallaire, the DPKO's conservative interpretation of UNAMIR's rules of engagement mentioned in Part I meant that such seizures were the exception rather than the rule. Tragically, this allowed Egyptian weapons to reach Kigali *during* the genocide: a Rwandan Embassy letter dated 13 April 1994—a week after the massacres began—makes 'reference to contract n.1/94 signed on 7 February 1994 between the Egyptian Ministry of Defense and Rwanda',[95] and requires 'the urgent delivery of the following military materials: 7,500 rockets, 50,000 cartridges 12.7, 300,000 cartridges 7.62, and 70,000 cartridges 0.5 of the Nato-mixed kind'.[96] 'The total amount of this order will be paid by cheque by the Rwandan Embassy to the International Commercial Bank in Egypt', the document reads, before noting that these materials are needed 'with the greatest urgency'.[97] Another offer from the Egyptian Defence Ministry mentions even larger amounts of weapons.[98] For the Hutu *génocidaires*, Egypt's assistance continued unabated until July 1994, that is to say, until the end of a genocide that caused almost a million violent deaths.

'Everywhere in the world I see a proliferation of weapons which is frankly out of control',[99] Boutros-Ghali wrote in his (public) diary, without acknowledging that he had actively contributed to it. So close were relations between Paris, Cairo, and Kigali during the Rwandan genocide that the Hutus even sought Egypt's help to evacuate to France Habyarimana's widow, who was thought to be involved in the genocide through her *Clan de Madame*.[100] 'The Embassy of Rwanda...has the honor of informing you of the travel plans of Madame Agathe and her three children', a letter dated 24 June and addressed to

[93] Booh Booh, p.70.   [94] Booh Booh, p.70.
[95] Ambassade Rwandaise au Caire, Letter to the Minister of Defense of Egypt, 13 April 1994. See also Banque Nationale du Rwanda, Lettre à la Banque Belgolaise de Bruxelles, 13 April 1994.
[96] Ambassade Rwandaise au Caire, Letter to the Minister of Defense of Egypt, 13 April 1994.
[97] Ambassade Rwandaise au Caire, Letter to the Minister of Defense of Egypt, 13 April 1994, p.2. See Ambassade de la République Rwandaise, Décompte des Fonds Transférés par le Ministère de la Défense à l'Ambassade du Caire, 25 May 1994.
[98] Ministry of Defence of Egypt, Offer No.7 to Ministry of Defence of Rwanda (undated).
[99] Boutros-Ghali, *Entre le Nil et Jérusalem*, p.91.
[100] Boutros-Ghali, *Entre le Nil et Jérusalem*, p.207.

Egypt's foreign minister noted. 'Their departure is scheduled for 25 June 1994 at 8am on Air France flight 8091 to Paris.'[101]

IMPLICATIONS FOR BOUTROS-GHALI'S MORAL AUTHORITY: INDEPENDENCE, NEUTRALITY, IMPARTIALITY

What are the implications of these events? Did Boutros-Ghali's dealings with the Hutus prior to becoming SG affect his conduct at the helm of the UN in the run-up to 1994? And did they impact on what he saw as his—and the UN's—'moral authority'? I propose to address these questions by linking them to the idea—advocated by Boutros-Ghali and by a growing body of IR and UN literature[102]—that the head of the world's largest global institution, unlike heads of states or governments, has an intangible power of moral suasion.

Although this is contested by those who claim that the realities of world politics require international actors to compromise the moral ends which they would otherwise be expected to pursue in a national context,[103] it is significant that neither Boutros-Ghali, nor his predecessors, nor the UN as an organization, refer to the values enshrined in the UN Charter as 'ethical' but rather as 'moral'. This is because the Charter is increasingly perceived as having a human—in addition to an institutional—dimension and is credited with setting standards that, while applicable to states, are also meant to benefit humanity as a whole. Of course, the UN also has its own ethical regulations—increasingly so after corruption was exposed in procurement, sexual abuse was unearthed in peacekeeping, and appropriation of funds was discovered in the 'Oil-for-Food' programme. While the organization has set up an Ethics Office to prevent such abuses, it is on an altogether different scale than the principles of the UN Charter.[104] Under discussion in this section are thus the *moral* values that the UN and its chief administrative officer are supposed to pursue, rather than the *ethical* conduct of UN staff.

---

[101] Ambassade de la République Rwandaise, Lettre n.159/16.11.18/P1 au Ministère des Affaires Etrangères de la République Arabe d'Egypte, 24 June 1994. See also 'Intrigue and Uncertainty Follows Arrest of "Lady Genocide"', *National Post*, 3 March 2010.

[102] Kille, *The UN Secretary-General*, ch.1; Fröhlich, ch.3; Toni Erskine, 'Blood on the UN's Hands? Assigning Responsibilities and Apportioning Blame to an Intergovernmental Organisation', *Global Society*, Vol.18, No.1 (Jan. 2004), pp.21–42; Herman Salton, 'L'Autorité Morale du Secrétaire-Général des Nations Unies', in Blandine Chélini-Pont, ed., *Annuaire Droit et Religions* (Aix-en-Provence: Presses Universitaires d'Aix–Marseille, 2013), pp.663–86.

[103] Richard Price, ed., *Moral Limit and Possibility in World Politics* (Cambridge: Cambridge University Press, 2008), p.1.

[104] See http://www.un.org/en/ethics/ (accessed 19 July 2015).

With this in mind and in addition to the provisions of the UN Charter, three ingredients are seen as making up the 'moral authority' of SGs (a) their independence from any state, person or organization; (b) their neutrality, or the prohibition to favour one side over another; and (c) their impartiality, or the prohibition on taking sides in a dispute between states. Asking whether Boutros-Ghali's involvement with Habyarimana and the Hutus early in his career affected any of these three factors provides a standard of evaluation that assesses what the SG saw as his moral authority against the principles which *he* claimed to cherish. It also allows for a more comprehensive assessment of his performance in Rwanda and recognizes that empirical analysis ought to complement theoretical considerations on the power or influence of SGs.[105]

(i) Independence

A distinctive trait of the role of SGs is their duty of independence from states, individuals, and organizations. SGs are supposed to come to their decisions autonomously, without regard to the pressures that will inevitably arise during their terms of office from both inside and outside their organization.[106] This is a necessity if SGs are to be 'honest brokers', something that Article 100 of the UN Charter envisions as a duty rather than as a right.[107]

Boutros-Ghali's difficult personality—he was aware of his 'terrible temperament'[108] and an adviser described senior staff meetings as 'nuclear'—routinely antagonized New York ambassadors and bureaucrats alike, but also gained him a reputation for independence. 'Boutros-Ghali', an author noted, 'was not popular in the UN. He was very strict, very private (he never went to any reception). And very aloof'.[109] Yet even his critics acknowledge that he was 'his own man' and could be refreshingly insubordinate. Ask people to jump and they will jump, one former aide stated; ask Boutros-Ghali to jump, and he will ask you why.[110] Goulding saw him as an 'intellectual powerhouse'[111] and even Madeleine Albright portrayed him as 'impressive, blessed with brain, confidence and style'.[112] As is well-known, the criteria required for somebody to be appointed SG in New York are almost as nebulous as those involving the selection of a pope in Rome, but it is safe to say that the veto power held by the

---

[105] Price, p.18.   [106] Kille, *The UN Secretary-General*, p.12.

[107] Javier Pérez de Cuéllar, *Pilgrimage for Peace* (New York: St Martin's Press, 1997), p.27.

[108] 'The Unmaking of a Secretary-General', *The New York Times*, 13 June 1999.

[109] Roberto Savio, 'Boutros Boutros-Ghali, a Turning Point in the History of the United Nations', *Human Wrongs Watch*, 16 February 2016.

[110] Jonah, *What Price*, p.98.   [111] MIG-PD-B, 24-Dec-1991.

[112] Madeleine Albright, *Madam Secretary* (Pan Books, 2004), p.136.

P-5 hardly rewards maverick candidates.[113] Since nobody can become SG if they are opposed by one of the P-5, successful candidates do not have a record of 'speaking out' on issues about which the Great Powers feel strongly (Israel in the case of the USA and Tibet in the case of China are known examples). Back in 1991, Boutros-Ghali's long-standing advocacy for the rights of Palestinians did alarm Washington but was offset by his support for President Sadat's rapprochement with Israel, a position that delighted the USA but that attracted hostility from parts of the Arab world.[114] Neither did Boutros-Ghali hesitate to reject positions which he believed would bring the UN into disrepute, as Washington discovered on issues as diverse as Somalia, Bosnia, and Haiti. As the previous chapters have suggested, the SG was also not shy about using the UN bureaucracy—especially DPA—to achieve the moral aims which he thought the UN Charter required him to pursue, including through his October 1993 memo on the 'superiority' of DPA over DPKO. Nor did Boutros-Ghali think twice about criticizing—indeed, patronizing—the UN's most powerful ambassador, with whom he had a progressively catastrophic relationship that culminated in Albright vetoing his reappointment in a rare 14-to-1 vote.[115] 'Coming from the developing world, international law and diplomacy were the bedrocks of my education', he stated, 'and I mistakenly thought that the Great Powers, especially the United States, also trained their ambassadors about the importance of diplomacy and accepted its principles. But the Roman Empire had no need for diplomacy. Neither do the United States.'[116] Goulding routinely cautioned Boutros-Ghali to be more diplomatic, and continued to do so well after the end of the Egyptian's secretary-generalship: 'I still worry about the consequences of making this [Boutros-Ghali's memoirs *UNvanquished*] a tale of confrontation between you and the United States', Goulding wrote in a private letter to Boutros-Ghali in 1998. 'I therefore remain uneasy about the title and about what seem to me to be unresearched side-swipes at the Americans in the preface.'[117]

As for Boutros-Ghali's relations with the rest of the UN membership, SGs often come from national public services and retain links with their country of origin (which will also have campaigned for them during the election process).[118] This was indeed the case for Boutros-Ghali, who had relied heavily on Mubarak's support to become SG. There is nevertheless no indication that

---

[113] United Nations Security Council, The 'Wisnumurti Guidelines' for Selecting a Candidate for Secretary-General, November 1996 (MIG-PA).

[114] Boutros Boutros-Ghali and Shimon Peres, *60 Ans de Conflit Israélo-Arabe* (Brussels: Éditions Complexe, 2006).

[115] Edward Luck, *Mixed Messages* (Washington: Brookings, 1999).

[116] 'The Unmaking of a Secretary-General', *The New York Times*, 13 June 1999.

[117] Marrack Goulding, Letter to Boutros Boutros-Ghali, 23 July 1998 (MIG-PA).

[118] Houshang Ameri, *The Politics of Staffing the United Nations Secretariat* (New York: Peter Lang, 1996).

Mubarak was treated favourably by Boutros-Ghali as SG, for the latter saw himself as the candidate of Africa and the Arab world, rather than Egypt. Given Paris's post-colonial reach in Africa and beyond, his relationship with Mitterrand and France was far more complex. As mentioned, Boutros-Ghali did have deep and long-standing personal as well as professional ties with President Mitterrand. In Rwanda, he also strongly supported France's *Opération Turquoise*, which was approved by the SC in June 1994 in order to create a humanitarian corridor. But as Part I has indicated, the SG did not share France's support for a muscular intervention early in the crisis—indeed, Goulding suggests that he favoured disengagement *against* the wishes of Paris and the Non-Aligned Movement.[119] During his term, Boutros-Ghali was also critical of French positions on the Former Yugoslavia[120] and saw Western powers (including Paris) as duplicitous and unreliable.[121] His insistence as Egyptian Foreign Minister that his country join the *francophonie* stemmed from a desire to ensure that Egypt gained a powerful ally, rather than for reasons of self-interest.[122] As one author noted, 'The Holy Writ [he] was wont to cite was...Article 100 [on the independence of the SG]. The watchword of the SG, Boutros-Ghali said, must be "independence".'[123] Goulding's papers contain plenty of disagreements between the SG and France: 'The SG, with Madame and party, arrived from Paris at 2215hrs', Goulding wrote on 12 January 1994, the day after Dallaire's 'genocide cable'. 'He was very tired and very agitated by a difficult meeting he had *à trois* with Balladur (PM) and Juppé (FM) immediately before leaving Paris.'[124]

The events mentioned in this chapter do not fundamentally alter this picture. Boutros-Ghali was no apologist and was in fact the first world leader to speak of genocide in Rwanda.[125] However, those events do raise a number of concerns about whether his close relations with some of Rwanda's politicians coloured (at best) or delayed (at worst) his realization of what was happening in the field. By virtue of his long-standing involvement with it, Boutros-Ghali did know the country and its ethnic context extremely well—better than any of his UN officials (including Booh Booh and Dallaire) and better than most of the SC ambassadors. Among other things, this raises the issue of what the SG *should* have known in the run up to 1994: 'I was not able to understand from the beginning the importance of what was going on',

---

[119] MIG-TD-X, 15-Apr-1994.

[120] Boutros-Ghali, *Entre le Nil et Jérusalem*, p.74. See also MIG-TD-IX, 12-Jan-1994; MIG-TD-X, 24-Aug-1994; and MIG-TD-XII, 19-Jun-1995.

[121] MIG-TD-IX, 30-Jan-1994.

[122] Vaughan Lowe et al., *The United Nations Security Council and War* (Oxford: Oxford University Press, 2008).

[123] James Traub, *The Best Intentions* (London: Bloomsbury, 2007), p.62.

[124] MIG-TD-IX, 12-Jan-1994. See also MIG-TD-IX, 23-Jan-1994.

[125] United Nations, Press Briefing by Office of Legal Counsel, 4 May 1994 (LMRGA).

Boutros-Ghali said in an interview, '[and] it took me weeks before suddenly we discovered that it was genocide'.[126] It is true that even an observer as close to the events as Dallaire did not immediately grasp the extent of the killings and initially spoke of 'massacres' rather than 'genocide'.[127] The DPA–DPKO feud in New York, faulty reporting lines in the field, and the confusing advice Boutros-Ghali was receiving from Booh Booh and his EOSG further compounded the issue and indicates that Boutros-Ghali was hardly the only UN official to react slowly and inadequately to the crisis. Nevertheless, his long-standing involvement with Habyarimana, his familiarity with the Rwandan civil war, and the intelligence the SG had received in December 1993, do raise serious questions about his ability to connect the dots. His seniority, access to the world's powerful, and encyclopaedic phone book meant that he had a variety of sources—of the highest order—to rely upon. Although there is no indication that Boutros-Ghali 'covered up' for the activities of the Hutu regime as SG, his long-standing links with Habyarimana and the fact that it is easier to find faults with one's enemies than with one's friends led him only to see the civil war—which he was well acquainted with as a result of his interactions with the Hutus during his time as an Egyptian minister—rather than the ensuing genocide.

(ii) Neutrality

The independence of SGs is linked to their neutrality, the second component of their 'moral authority'. The need to avoid taking sides is essential to the role of SG and involves the prohibition of associating oneself too closely with anybody.[128] This, however, can be problematic in that the neutrality principle may be seen as—and can easily become an excuse for—timidity, lack of courage, and opportunistic disengagement.[129] In the context of the UN, this can have nefarious consequences both for populations in danger and for the organization's moral standing.[130] It also risks putting the UN's head in an impossible position: if the SG takes neutrality to the letter, the UN would be unable to implement the Charter on issues as diverse as human rights, democratization, and development. Yet if SGs do take sides between states which they are supposed to 'serve', accusations of bias will inevitably follow. The principle of neutrality came under fire in the mid-1990s precisely as a reaction to the UN's lack of response to tragedies such as Rwanda, Yugoslavia,

---

[126] Boutros Boutros-Ghali, *PBS Frontline Interview*, 12 November 2008.

[127] Roméo Dallaire, *Shake Hands with the Devil* (London: Arrow Books, 2005).

[128] Kille, *The UN Secretary-General*, pp.10–13.

[129] Michael Barnett, *Eyewitness to a Genocide* (Ithaca & London: Cornell University Press, 2003), ch.4.

[130] Kent Kille, *From Manager to Visionary* (Basingstoke: Palgrave Macmillan, 2006); Kofi Annan, *Interventions* (London: Penguin, 2012), chs 2 and 3.

and elsewhere.[131] It is partly out of these crises that the Responsibility to Protect (R2P) emerged, one of its principles being that the UN should *not* be neutral in the face of genocide, crimes against humanity, and war crimes.[132]

The question of whether Boutros-Ghali remained neutral in Rwanda, therefore, ought to be considered alongside the question of whether he *should* have so been. A pessimistic view would suggest that he failed and ended up on the wrong side of both neutrality and impartiality. After the massacres began, the SG clung to the principle of strict neutrality and saw the Rwandan events as a civil war between two long-term enemies, which in his view the organization had neither the power nor the authority to stop. Although for both Boutros-Ghali and the UN Rwanda was a sideshow to Yugoslavia, the SG concentrated his efforts on getting the parties to sign a cease-fire, a move that was bound to fail since one side of Rwanda's ethnic divide (the Hutus) was bent on physically exterminating the other (the Tutsis). Boutros-Ghali's early uncertainty and his disinclination to have the UN stay in Rwanda may have been pragmatic, but it hardly squares with his idealistic views of the UN's 'moral' role. Indeed, it reflects a rigid application of the neutrality principle that drove the reasoning as follows: a civil war is an internal matter; in Rwanda there is no longer a peace to keep; the Great Powers have no interest in the country; so the UN no longer has a role there. Whether this was a matter-of-fact or a defeatist view is disputed, especially in light of what we now know was Boutros-Ghali's intimate knowledge of Rwandan politics. For many observers, however, it was the application of UN neutrality at its worst, not least because it clashed with the activist view of the SG's role which Boutros-Ghali claimed to cherish.

Since one of Boutros-Ghali's aims was the democratization of international relations,[133] this is also paradoxical. For him, 'democratizing' world politics meant limiting the influence of Western countries on the UN, on the Secretariat, and on DPKO, but also ensuring that the organization's work focussed on those regions of the world where it was most needed. 'Certain conflicts run the risk of being forgotten... because they take place in regions that are farther from the world's radar than others', he wrote. 'I thus believe that it is my main responsibility [as SG] to constantly focus the attention of the SC upon those which I call "orphan conflicts", these conflicts left in the shadow and of which the UN has nevertheless the duty to take charge.'[134] It is questionable whether Boutros-Ghali's indecision and his unwillingness to push the SC to act—at least early in the crisis—was the best way to handle such 'orphan conflicts'.

---

[131] Ralph Zacklin, *The United Nations Secretariat and the Use of Force in a Unipolar World* (Cambridge: Cambridge University Press, 2012).
[132] Alex Bellamy, *The Responsibility to Protect* (Cambridge: Polity Press, 2009), esp. chs 1 and 4; Aidan Hehir, *The Responsibility to Protect* (Basingstoke: Palgrave Macmillan, 2012), esp. ch.2.
[133] Boutros Boutros-Ghali, *Démocratiser la Mondialisation* (Paris: Éditions du Rocher, 2002).
[134] Boutros-Ghali, 'Le Sécrétaire-Général', pp.409–10.

(iii) Impartiality

Boutros-Ghali's insistence on strict neutrality is especially problematic in light of his dealings with Habyarimana prior to becoming SG. His role in facilitating contracts with the Hutus raises the question of whether, regardless of his actions as head of the UN, it was even possible for him to be impartial on Rwanda, since prior to becoming SG Boutros-Ghali had not only sided with one party to the dispute (Habyarimana) against the other (Kagame), but had actively contributed to keeping the former in power and the latter out of it. In this respect, *the reason* why weapons were supplied is arguably more problematic than *the fact* of supplying them. One should also bear in mind that impartiality is not the only factor to consider in assessing whether the SG's—and the UN's—moral authority was compromised, for the *perception* of impartiality matters too. As one author wrote, 'IOs become uniquely legitimate actors in world politics. They can do things that individual states cannot legitimately do...' and '...there is a perception that IOs will somehow be impartial, at least more impartial than any state...'[135] While only some of Rwanda's players knew of Boutros-Ghali's dealings with the Hutus, the perception of his independence as SG was affected. Boutros-Ghali's silence on the issue and his statement, when pushed, that 'a few thousand guns would not have changed the situation',[136] did not help.

An argument can be made that the timeline is critical and that as an Egyptian diplomat, Boutros-Ghali was simply doing his job by assisting his country and president. Since there is no indication that Boutros-Ghali facilitated either the Hutus or Habyarimana *after* becoming SG, it can be said that he behaved appropriately and that he served different patrons (Mubarak as a minister, the UN membership as SG) with the passion and dedication for which he was known. A distinction could also be drawn between the domestic and the international sphere in that 'moral' rules which apply to private life are not necessarily valid at the super-national level, where such rules often depend on the distribution of power rather than on the inclinations of leaders.[137] If one adopts this perspective, it was entirely legitimate for Boutros-Ghali to help his country sell weapons to whoever wanted to buy them (at the time, Egypt was also arming Saddam Hussein) because that was in his country's national interest. On this interpretation, it was similarly legitimate for Boutros-Ghali to preach the virtues of demilitarization after—rather than before—becoming

---

[135] Martha Finnemore, 'Paradoxes of Humanitarian Intervention', in Price, p.215.

[136] 'Rwanda: Former UN Secretary-General Hunted by Genocide', *Genocide Watch*, 16 February 2016, available at http://genocidewatch.net/2016/03/14/rwanda-former-un-secretary-general-hunted-by-the-genocide (accessed 17 November 2016).

[137] Duncan Bell, *Ethics and World Politics* (Oxford: Oxford University Press, 2010), p.81.

SG, since this was part of his job description. The fact that his 'moral' vision as SG clashed with his initiatives as an Egyptian Minister is thus in this view acceptable and even inevitable, given that SGs are drawn from national environments where they are expected to defend values that are not necessarily compatible with those of the UN Charter. Different jobs may require the public advocacy of different values.

Yet there are a number of problems with this interpretation, including the fact that Boutros-Ghali's roles as Egyptian Minister and UN Secretary-General were not easily distinguishable. 'Remind you that [Egypt] had asked support of Rwanda at time of [his] election [as SG] STOP',[138] Kigali's Ambassador to Cairo wrote to Habyarimana's Foreign Minister *after* Boutros-Ghali's elevation to the secretary-generalship. Two days later, another letter pointed to Habyarimana's close relations with Boutros-Ghali both before *and* after his appointment as SG: 'We have welcomed the news [of your election] with great joy and enormous pride', the Rwandan ambassador wrote, 'and I would like to personally thank you for the understanding and assistance that this Embassy has always found in Your Excellency.'[139]

On the other side of Rwanda's ethnic equation, Tutsi leader Paul Kagame was not nearly as impressed with Boutros-Ghali and his elevation to SG. Early on, Kagame accused the organization and its chief of being pro-Hutu, later refusing to work with Boutros-Ghali's Representative altogether. This is per se problematic since without the trust of one of the parties to a dispute, the UN has no peacekeeping role to play. Officially, Kagame never raised the issue of Boutros-Ghali's impartiality and indeed in mid-1993 the RPF had sent a delegation to New York to plea for the establishment of a UN mission to Rwanda. A skilled military commander like Kagame, however, would likely have known who was supplying weapons to—and keeping in power—his arch-enemy, especially since the Tutsi leader was a gifted strategist and had prepared his attack against Habyarimana for years. Unsurprisingly, relations between Kagame and Boutros-Ghali remained strained throughout the latter's term of office. 'Kagame is an extraordinary person, almost from another world', Goulding wrote in his diary, describing a tense meeting in December 1994 between Boutros-Ghali and the then Vice-President of Rwanda. 'He is humorless and tough—and resentful of the international community preaching at him. The SG said afterwards that Kagame was bent on revenge and there would be another war within six months. He may be right.'[140] As for Boutros-Ghali, he never publicly recognized that his long association with Habyarimana hardly made him the best broker between the two sides of Rwanda's ethnic divide. UN officials, the media, the public, and the SC had a right to know.

[138] Ambassade Rwandaise au Caire, Fax n.172(C)4B, 23 November 1991.
[139] Rwanda Embassy in Cairo, Letter to Boutros Boutros-Ghali, 25 November 1991.
[140] MIG-TD-XI, 15-Dec-1994.

BOUTROS-GHALI, THE UN BUREAUCRACY, AND 'MORAL AUTHORITY'

Arguably the key ingredient of the SG's 'moral authority' is his or her adherence to the values of the UN Charter. There is controversy over such values, reflecting the division between those who see the UN as an inter-*governmental* organization established on 'minimalistic' principles of sovereignty, national independence, and territorial integrity; and the 'expansionists' (or idealists) who perceive the organization as more than the sum of its members and who highlight 'supra-national' concepts such as human rights, development, and democratization.[141]

Since the birth of the UN and mirroring the expansion of international norms, it is the latter approach that has arguably gained momentum, and the biggest beneficiaries have been SGs. As one author wrote, 'The office of UN secretary-general has been described as a needed voice in an international arena where moral principles are often seen as subservient to concerns over power and interest'.[142] The most distinctive trait of the SG's job is the fact that it involves no hard power; what the post does have is the 'moral' connotation of a good portion of the UN Charter.[143] It is because of this 'moral' dimension—one that was fully embraced and even celebrated by Boutros-Ghali—that the SG is often perceived as a world 'leader' rather than a 'manager', the two being different in that leadership involves adherence to values which are perceived as higher than those sought by managers (i.e. efficiency).[144] As one author explains, 'Leadership... is irrevocably tied to morality, for it implies an ability to transform reality and... to morally elevate one's followers.'[145] Clearly one cannot expect SGs to be 'angels'— Kurt Waldheim's long-hidden affiliation with the Nazi Party is a reminder of this—but it was at least partly to offer 'global leadership' based on the Charter's values that the UN was set up.[146]

Boutros-Ghali claimed to share this 'moral' vision of the UN and had an expansive view of his (and the UN's) remit. Indeed, his *Agendas* were criticized—including from within the Secretariat—for their interventionism and for their arguably 'utopian' approach to global affairs, particularly when it came to democratization, development, and—intriguingly in light of this

---

[141] Jeremy Dunham et al., *Idealism* (London: Acumen, 2011).

[142] Kille, *The UN Secretary-General*, p.1.

[143] Salton, p.663.   [144] Martin Albrow, *Bureaucracy* (London: Pall Mall Press, 1970).

[145] Adel Safty, 'Moral Leadership: Beyond Management and Governance', *Harvard International Review*, 6 May 2006, available at http://hir.harvard.edu/article/?a=1165 (accessed 28 April 2017).

[146] Kille, *From Manager to Visionary*, p.60; Richard Jolly et al., *UN Ideas that Changed the World* (Bloomington: Indiana University Press, 2009). See also Mazower, *No Enchanted Palace*; Hilderbrand, *Dumbarton Oaks*.

chapter—disarmament.[147] Although this made him popular with certain parts of his expansive constituency, it progressively alienated him from some of the Great Powers, particularly the USA. His involvement with Habyarimana prior to becoming SG was also largely incompatible with what he preached as SG; that his business dealings with the Hutus happened *before* his accession to the secretary-generalship is important and needs to be put into its proper historical context, but it does not alter the fact that he was the most enthusiastic promoter of Cairo's assistance to Habyarimana's Hutus—a circumstance that resulted in Egyptian weapons supporting a *génocidaire* government while a genocide was taking place. 'Unless the Charter's principles are applied uniformly rather than selectively, confidence [in the UN] will suffer and, with it, the moral authority of this tool', Boutros-Ghali wrote in 1992, presenting *An Agenda for Peace*. 'In order to acquire confidence, it is indispensable that people have faith that the world organization will react speedily, firmly, and impartially, and that its actions will not be hampered by reasons of either political expediency or bureaucratic failure.'[148]

Therein lies one of the many ironies surrounding Boutros-Ghali's role in Rwanda, as well as the link between 'morality' and UN bureaucracy as he saw it. On the one hand, Boutros-Ghali was an active SG with a proclaimed attachment to the 'idealistic' values of the UN Charter. The courage of his *Agendas* and his proposals for a UN standing army and rapid reaction force attest to his attempts to strengthen the UN's 'moral authority'.[149] For Boutros-Ghali, the latter involved pushing states to implement the values of the Charter against the realist and (as he saw it) cynical impulses of the world's most powerful capitals. Yet as Chapter 6 has explained, this could only be accomplished through pragmatic means, that is to say, by gaining as much control as possible over the UN bureaucracy. For Boutros-Ghali, DPKO embodied the 'realism' (if not cynicism) of the UN membership, whereas DPA assisted the SG in implementing the Charter's highest moral values. Perhaps most important, in Boutros-Ghali's view peacekeeping and peacebuilding were not really on the same 'moral' level: he saw peacekeeping in pragmatic terms since it was necessary for the UN to deal with *existing* conflicts. Yet the SG's and DPA's functions were broader, more ambitious, and included the prevention of conflict *before* it emerges—an 'idealistic', if not utopian, objective that Boutros-Ghali's memo of October 1993 tried to cement. If the price of this was bureaucratic infighting in New York, so be it. 'I continue to believe that peacebuilding, both preventive and post-conflict, is one of the most valuable contributions that the United Nations can make', the SG stated towards the end of his term. 'I have asked the Department of Political Affairs to give

[147] Boutros-Ghali, *Entre le Nil et Jérusalem*, p.93.
[148] Boutros-Ghali, 'Un Programa', p.5.   [149] Boutros-Ghali, *Mes Années*, p.49.

priority to the formulation of proposals for a better coordination of the United Nations system's peacebuilding efforts.'[150]

'The egoism and cynicism of states far outdo those of humans',[151] the former SG wrote in his (public) diary. Nevertheless, it seems that international organizations and their leaders are not exempt from them either. Far from being an aberration, the strange case of Boutros-Ghali in Rwanda can be seen as emblematic of the UN at large in that, in New York, pragmatism and idealism are constantly intertwined.[152] 'Paradoxes of diplomacy: this morning I was preaching the cause of disarmament, while this afternoon I was cracking jokes with one of the world's largest producers of weapons',[153] Boutros-Ghali wrote. The fact that his idealistic view of the UN clashed with the pragmatism of his business dealings in Rwanda should thus not surprise. 'Back in the Middle Ages, the Muslim philosopher El-Farabi dreamt of a "Virtuous City" and of a group of "Virtuous Cities" which would one day form a "Virtuous Planet", the biggest of all dreams',[154] the former SG wrote. 'I express the wish that one day this dream will come true thanks to the United Nations.'[155] While his years in New York suggest that he did try to build that 'Virtuous Planet', his role in Rwanda shows how far he remained from it in practice.

[150] Boutros Boutros-Ghali, Talking Points for the Secretary-General at ACC Meeting, 12 October 1995 (MIG-PA).

[151] Boutros-Ghali, *Entre le Nil et Jérusalem*, p.167.

[152] Paolo Mastrolilli, *Lo Specchio del Mondo* (Rome: Laterza, 2005).

[153] Boutros-Ghali, *Entre le Nil et Jérusalem*, p.148.

[154] Boutros-Ghali, *Entre le Nil et Jérusalem*, p.148.

[155] Boutros-Ghali, *Entre le Nil et Jérusalem*, p.191.

10

Peacebuilding

I was on a plane with [Boutros-Ghali] during an internal trip in Brazil. We were discussing the first draft of his *Agenda for Peace*, where there was a section on peacemaking, another on peacekeeping, and another on preventive diplomacy. Suddenly he turned serious and said: 'Where does El Salvador fit in here? We have a mission there, but it's not peacemaking because the peace has already been made. It's not preventive diplomacy because it was war, over twelve years of fighting; and it is not peacekeeping as I know it because in a matter of months, maybe a year, the monitors of the ceasefire will go. What you have is a structure with a lot of civilians, human rights issues, building institutions, the judiciary, etc. This is completely different, it's more like'—he was thinking aloud, talking to me—'it's more like post-conflict peacebuilding'. So right there, on the spot, he developed this concept and invented a name for it. And in *An Agenda for Peace* you will see that he added a separate section [for post-conflict peacebuilding] which he said was going to be a very large chunk of UN activity in the future.[1]

These were the extraordinary circumstances in which, according to Álvaro de Soto, the intellectual framework guiding the UN to this day was developed.[2] The above passage is emblematic of the excitement that accompanied the early 1990s and which followed the unprecedented mandate given by the SC to the SG in January 1992 to strengthen the capacity of the UN. If de Soto's words give a sense of the intellectual acumen of Boutros-Ghali, however, they also point to a circumstance which matters not only for the Rwanda events, but also for grasping a fundamental trait of the UN of that time (and, arguably, of all times): improvisation. Peacekeeping, peacebuilding, and the other concepts of the UN lexicon[3]—none of which is explicitly mentioned in the UN

---

[1] My Interview with Álvaro de Soto, 20 July 2011, New York, USA (and via email on 4 June 2016).

[2] Boutros Boutros-Ghali, *An Agenda for Peace* (New York: Department of Public Information, 1992).

[3] Although *An Agenda for Peace* makes a threefold distinction between preventive diplomacy, peacemaking, and peacekeeping, the bureaucratic discussions in New York have largely concentrated on peacekeeping, on the one hand, and peacebuilding and peacemaking, on the other. This chapter reflects such a distinction.

Charter—were born out of necessity rather than from any sort of abstract or theoretical construction. There were no blueprints for these concepts, no instructions on what they meant and how they should be applied, no theoretical models to rely upon, no legal guidelines to follow. Discussing UN peace missions in the late 1980s, Goulding wrote that 'the UN displayed in equal measure the vice of failing to plan and the virtue of an extraordinary capacity to improvise'.[4] The latter was not limited to logistics, for ideas such as peacekeeping and peacebuilding were developed by UN officials on Manhattan Island and in the field—even on airplanes—out of practical necessity, in difficult circumstances, and in great urgency.

This improvising attribute of the UN's peace and security architecture emerges most clearly if one considers the interplay between the two main parts of the New York bureaucracy involved in Rwanda, on the one hand, and the concepts of peacekeeping and peacebuilding, on the other. Doing so suggests that it was more than turf jealousy that, in the early 1990s, caused DPA and DPKO to acquire blurred responsibilities and overlapping mandates. In particular, three conceptual issues came to have very practical implications for the UN Secretariat both at Headquarters and on the ground. First, despite Boutros-Ghali's repeated attempts to do so, separating the 'political' from the 'operational' aspects of peacekeeping proved much harder than expected. The nonchalant use of the term 'political' was especially unhelpful since few (if any) activities carried out by UN departments in the early 1990s can unambiguously be defined as 'technical', even by New York's vocabulary. Second, the conceptual borders between peacebuilding and peacekeeping are far more fluid than is often recognized, a situation that in Rwanda worsened the competition, mistrust, and unclear delineation of responsibilities between DPA and DPKO both at Headquarters and in the field. Third, and as a result of the second issue, the periodic attempts to separate the responsibility for *keeping* the peace from the responsibility for *building* it—including the effort I briefly witnessed in 2008—have had limited success partly because in peace operations, bureaucratic and conceptual issues are inextricably linked. Since structures like DPKO and DPA were set up at Headquarters before processes like peacekeeping and peacebuilding were tested in the field, looking at those structures before considering the processes that underpin them—as this book does—is not only more faithful historically, it is also more effective in identifying the factors that hampered peace missions such as UNAMIR.

This chapter continues to do this by bringing the story of DPA–DPKO relations up to the present and by looking at how they have changed since the early 1990s. Although it took tragedies like Rwanda for the Secretariat to

---

[4] Marrack Goulding, 'Peacemonger: Book Proposal', 15 June 1998 (MIG-PA).

internally recognize the existence of some of the issues mentioned in this volume, neither the bureaucratic nor the conceptual problems faced by UNAMIR have been openly addressed, let alone solved. To understand why, we need to pick up the DPA–DPKO confrontation where Chapter 6 left it— that is, at the time of Kofi Annan's appointment as SG—and consider the changes that he (from 1997) and Ban Ki-moon (from 2007) introduced to tackle the relations between DPA and DPKO. Annan's response to this historic rivalry was the 'Lead Department' concept, whereas Ban—following a trend in post-9/11 international relations—prioritized peacebuilding and DPA over peacekeeping and DPKO. Yet far from solving the issues mentioned in this book, the strengthening of DPA in 2008–09—well intentioned as it was—arguably aggravated them. Since the story of the UN Secretariat is one of trial and error—and since the existence of conceptual issues in New York only became apparent after difficulties emerged in the field—closing this book on a long-term evolution of the UN bureaucracy seems an appropriate way to highlight the trends that began in the early 1990s, that contributed to the Secretariat's failure in Rwanda, and that are still partly with us today.

KOFI ANNAN, THE 'LEAD DEPARTMENT', AND THE RISE OF DPKO

'Our job is to intervene: to prevent conflict where we can, to put a stop to it when it has broken out, or—when neither of those things is possible—at least to contain it and prevent it from spreading'.[5] So spoke Kofi Annan mid-way into his first term as SG (1997–2006), thus seemingly articulating a far more proactive attitude than the one adopted by his office in Rwanda. Part of the difference lies precisely with the events of 1994, after which a career bureaucrat became a champion of interventionism and was awarded the Nobel Peace Prize.[6] Clearly this transformation did not happen overnight and was in fact hardly apparent in 1997, when Annan introduced his own bureaucratic 'revolution' in New York. Although this was a far gentler restructuring than the upheavals dictated by Boutros-Ghali in 1992 and 1993, it had implications for both UN structures and processes. At first sight the two SGs adopted radically divergent approaches to the UN bureaucracy, held dissimilar views on the limits and scope of peacekeeping, and handled their relations with Washington quite differently. What is interesting for our purposes is that such

---

[5] Kofi Annan, *The Question of Intervention* (New York: Department of Public Information, 1999), p.4.
[6] James Traub, *The Best Intentions* (London: Bloomsbury, 2007).

differences emerged precisely in the run up to 1994, grew deeper as a result of the Rwanda crisis, and continue to divide the UN Secretariat today.

(i) Revoking Boutros-Ghali's Memo

One of the first executive decisions taken by Annan as SG was to revoke Boutros-Ghali's memo of October 1993 making DPA responsible for the 'political' aspects of peacekeeping. I already mentioned the difficulties created by that dispensation in terms of bureaucratic duplication in New York, as well as the lack of cooperation and poor intelligence within UNAMIR. Annan's move partly rested with the Rwanda experience and with the acknowledge-ment that Boutros-Ghali's directive had failed to work. As the first SG from within the ranks of the organization and as a former USG for Management, Annan was determined to tackle the Secretariat's dysfunctions, of which the DPA–DPKO interface had historically been the most troublesome. As Gould-ing put it in the handover notes to his successor, Annan had an advantage in that 'the [new] SG... unlike his predecessor, knows "the secrets" himself'.[7] Several post-mortem reports on UNAMIR and other missions, while not directly referring to Boutros-Ghali's memo, also highlighted the chronic lack of coordination between different parts of the UN.[8]

Annan's decision to overrule Boutros-Ghali's memo is easy to defend in light of the Rwanda experience, for in 1994 the unity of the so-called 'peace-keeping sequence' had undoubtedly been disrupted by the SG's decision to put DPA in charge of UNAMIR's 'political' functions.[9] Although that was hardly the only reason for the mission's woes, Boutros-Ghali's memo contributed to making matters worse. For Annan, one of the explanations for the confusion in Kigali—over mandate, over rules of engagement, and over intelligence—lay with the fact that peacekeeping was a complex process involving substantive issues such as diplomatic negotiations, mandate interpretation, the establish-ment of state institutions (including, in the case of Rwanda, a transitional government), and free elections. All these functions Annan saw as essentially 'political' in nature, although, as we shall see, the meaning of this term remained as elusive under Annan as it had been under Boutros-Ghali. While the new SG had good reasons to reject Boutros-Ghali's dispensation, therefore, doing so hardly addressed the key question that his predecessor had been trying to answer since 1992: how to create a cohesive bureaucracy capable of handling multi-dimensional peace operations?

---

[7] Marrack Goulding, Handover Notes for Sir Kieran Prendergast, 22 February 1997, §7 (MIG-PA).

[8] See e.g. Lakhdar Brahimi, Report of the Panel on United Nations Peace Operations, 21 August 2000 (A/55/305–S/2000/809) (hereinafter, Brahimi Report).

[9] Marrack Goulding, *Peacemonger* (London: Murray, 2002), p.333.

(ii) Annan Rejects a DPA–DPKO Merger

One obvious solution was to merge DPA and DPKO. Since peacekeeping and peacebuilding cannot easily be ring-fenced, combining the bureaucracies responsible for those functions seems sensible. Yet this was a no-go area for the new SG—Annan was reportedly clear about retaining Boutros-Ghali's architecture, particularly DPKO. In his farewell address to DPA's staff, Goulding confirmed that the SG was 'not in favour of [a] merger of DPA and DPKO'.[10]

Several explanations can be given for this stance, including the acknow-ledgement that a 'bureaucratic monster' of considerable proportions would be created which would account for most of the UN activities (Boutros-Ghali's decision to establish DPA and DPKO in 1992 partly stemmed from the fact that the Office for Special Political Affairs was overburdened). Also important for Annan was the attachment felt by member states towards DPKO. Because of their ability to staff the department with gratis personnel—upon which it came to depend heavily at a time of financial stringency—and partly because of DPKO's strong military–civilian interface, the peacekeeping troubles of the early 1990s had failed to dent such an affection, with states finding DPKO by far the most amenable part of the UN bureaucracy. Its Situation Centre, together with DPKO's carefully nurtured image as an 'operational' office that 'got things done', made the Peacekeeping Department all the more attractive to national capitals, especially the most powerful ones. When, in August 1995, Boutros-Ghali mentioned to Goulding the possibility of return-ing to DPKO while transferring Annan to Zagreb, the British official rejected the offer on the ground that the department was controlled by member states: 'I urged him not to move me to DPKO', Goulding wrote in his diary. 'From my point of view, I would be going back to a Department with whose current set up and *modus operandi* I strongly disagree; reform of it would be difficult and involve me being in constant fights with major Western powers (there are apparently 96 (!) officers paid for by their Governments).'[11] This was in stark contrast to what states (and Goulding) saw as the stuffy DPA, which was consequently marginalized, starved of resources, and happily left to the SG. For Goulding,

> The establishment of a Department of Political Affairs with a mandate to collect and analyze information about all countries where a conflict could occur has meant, in effect, the establishment of a mini-Foreign Office in the Secretariat. Not all Member States see this is as a good thing. For some it seems to threaten

---

[10] Marrack Goulding, Notes for Farewell Speech to DPA, 28 February 1997 (MIG-PA).
[11] MIG-TD-XII, 14-Aug-1995.

unwanted United Nations interference in their internal affairs or in their relations with other countries.[12]

Whatever the reason for Annan's aversion to a DPA–DPKO merger, in December 1996—just before assuming office as SG—he asked all USGs appointed by Boutros-Ghali to resign but wrote to Goulding that he wanted to 'retain [his] experience... in the service of the United Nations'.[13] Given that Goulding had supported Boutros-Ghali's reappointment and had opposed Annan's bid to become SG, this was a generous gesture: 'I wanted Boutros-Ghali to win and, in so far as was proper, helped him in his campaign', Goulding wrote, noting that 'This was not out of personal hostility to Annan. It reflected my conviction that Boutros-Ghali's intellectual power, his commitment to the independence of the office of Secretary-General and his energetic, if sometimes clumsily combative, leadership would better serve the UN's needs than Annan's mellifluous and malleable style.'[14] Goulding received a valedictory assignment: 'Drawing upon the activities of the Organization in peace-keeping operations and peace-making missions, especially since 1990', Annan wrote, 'you should prepare a study analyzing these experiences and the lessons that can be drawn from them.'[15]

Annan knew where Goulding—a peacekeeper at heart—stood on peace operations. Despite having been at the helm of DPA, the Briton had by and large (though inconsistently so) opposed Boutros-Ghali's idea of an 'operational' DPKO and had often sided with Annan on this point. 'I continued to believe in the integrity of peacekeeping and the impossibility of dividing it into "political" and "operational" aspects',[16] Goulding wrote. Yet precisely for this reason Goulding favoured a DPA–DPKO merger. According to Álvaro de Soto, 'Goulding was perfectly clear that the two departments should be merged and that there should be a single department. As a result of this, his report was shelved. [Yet] a lot of the issues for the UN as a political actor in peacemaking arise out of the fact that there is this division and this kind of squabbling.'[17] Two years later, a public report on 'lessons learned' by Lakhdar Brahimi (the Brahimi Report) reportedly met a similar fate: 'Brahimi was told at the start that the idea of a merger between DPA and DPKO was off the table, that he should not even bother to entertain it', de Soto stated. 'So the parameters were clear.'[18] In New York, the 'anticipatory veto' mentioned in Chapter 1 seems to be alive and well—not only in the context of the relations between Security Council and Secretariat, but also within the Secretariat itself.

---

[12] Marrack Goulding, 'Recent Developments in Peace-Making', Presentation by Marrack Goulding to the International Peace Academy, New York, 31 January 1994 (MIG-PA).
[13] Kofi Annan, Letter to Marrack Goulding, 19 December 1996 (MIG-PA).
[14] Goulding, 'Peacemonger: Book Proposal', 15 June 1998.
[15] Annan, Letter to Goulding, 19 December 1996.   [16] Goulding, *Peacemonger*, p.333.
[17] Interview with de Soto, 20 July 2011.   [18] Interview with de Soto, 20 July 2011.

(iii) Goulding's Report and Annan's 'Lead Department' Concept

Goulding's report to Annan is interesting nonetheless, for it partly draws on what the British diplomat saw as the 'lessons' of Rwanda and UNAMIR. Among other recommendations, the document argued that 'an integrated effort is required by the United Nations system as a whole';[19] criticized the 'overlap'[20] of the Secretariat and its 'institutional jealousies';[21] wrote of 'over-confidence'[22] in the UN Secretariat of mid-1993 (an indirect reference to Boutros-Ghali's memo); and recommended, partly on the basis of UNAMIR, a set of 'common services'[23] for those Secretariat units (mainly DPA and DPKO) that were tasked with preventing, managing, and resolving conflict. Such services included 'a common flow of information from the field',[24] an 'early warning system',[25] and a 'policy analysis group'[26]—all features that had been missing in Rwanda. Additionally, the report addressed some of the intelligence and communications problems encountered by UNAMIR, especially the sharing of critical messages containing 'political' intelligence such as Dallaire's 'genocide cable'.[27] Goulding ended his document by noting that 'the UN system must... adopt an integrated approach to the prevention, management, and resolution of conflict in which all dimensions—humanitarian, developmental and, above all, *political*—are addressed in a mutually reinforcing manner'.[28] Although once again there was no mention of what the term 'political' meant in this context, in a letter to an acquaintance Goulding observed that his study had said 'rather bluntly that there is a lot that needs to be put right, especially as regards... cooperation within the UN system'.[29] Goulding's personal correspondence also clarifies why he thought that his report was unlikely to be given much currency in Annan's Secretariat: 'It also contains proposals that have created dissention between the departments primarily concerned, notably a recommendation for the establishment of "common services" [between] DPA and DPKO...DPKO understandably felt that this would oblige them to surrender several of the jewels in their crown.... It is unlikely therefore', Goulding concluded, 'that the recommendation will be accepted (though I still advocate it strongly).'[30] The British official also felt that

---

[19] Marrack Goulding, Practical Measures to Enhance the United Nations' Effectiveness in the Field of Peace and Security: A Report Submitted to the Secretary-General of the United Nations, 30 June 1997, §1.3 (MIG-PA).
[20] Goulding, Practical Measures, §1.5.   [21] Goulding, Practical Measures, §5.12.
[22] Goulding, Practical Measures, §6.37.   [23] Goulding, Practical Measures, II(1).
[24] Goulding, Practical Measures, §2.2.(1)(a).
[25] Goulding, Practical Measures, §2.2.(1)(b).
[26] Goulding, Practical Measures, §2.2.(1)(c).   [27] Goulding, Practical Measures, §3.5.(a).
[28] Goulding, Practical Measures, §7.16 (emphasis added).
[29] Goulding, Letter, 18 September 1997 (MIG-PA).
[30] Goulding, Letter, 18 September 1997 (MIG-PA).

the criticism he levelled against the existing arrangements sat ill with the upbeat tone of the SG's initial reports on UN reform.[31]

Goulding's interpretation is debatable, for Annan only partly disregarded his suggestions. While the SG did retain DPA and DPKO, he introduced the 'Lead Department' concept precisely to facilitate relations between headquarters and the field, including clarifying the chain of command and avoid the kind of duplication that Goulding had noted in UNAMIR. According to the 'Lead Department'—a framework that still partially stands—DPKO is in charge when a peace agreement has been signed and a peacekeeping operation has been set up, though the department is expected to cooperate with—and take into account the advice of—DPA on 'political' matters, a term that the SG once again failed to define. As the 'Lead Department', however, DPKO retains primacy in compiling reports to the SG whenever a peacekeeping mission is despatched. Conversely, when there is no peacekeeping operation on the ground, the 'lead' remains with DPA, which is supposed to consult DPKO on 'operational' matters (again undefined) but retains the power of initiative and report-writing. Annan's dispensation of January 1997 thus differed considerably from Boutros-Ghali's memo of March 1993: conceptually, it recognized that it was unwise to break the unity of the 'peacekeeping sequence', while operationally it acknowledged that the best department to carry through such a sequence was DPKO, which saw its prestige augmented and its role at Headquarters strengthened (Annan's term as SG became known in New York as 'DPKO's reign'). Yet not only did Annan's dispensation continue to rely on Boutros-Ghali's blurry distinction between 'political' and 'operational' matters; it raised a number of additional problems which came to a head in the early months of the new millennium and that are still with us today.

CRISIS OF THE 'LEAD DEPARTMENT' AND DPA–DPKO EXCHANGE

In his farewell address to DPA of February 1997, Goulding apologized to his staff for his managerial shortcomings ('I know what you think of me as a Head of Department'[32]) but also pointed to several 'causes for optimism'[33] for the UN and DPA. To him, they included the fact that 'KA [Kofi Annan] has brought a new style [and that] Mrs A [Albright] is a multilateralist'.[34] '[We] have come a long way together since 1993', Goulding stated, noting that 'KA wants to strengthen the role of DPA, especially in the preventive field and as

[31] Goulding, Email Message, 18 May 2000 (MIG-PA).
[32] Goulding, 'Notes for Farewell Speech to DPA', §8.
[33] Goulding, 'Notes for Farewell Speech to DPA', §6.
[34] Goulding, 'Notes for Farewell Speech to DPA', §6.

the interface with SecCo [Security Council]. Don't feel threatened by [the] concept of the lead department', Goulding told his staff; he had had a 'frank talk with Miyet [DPKO's head]' and came to the conclusion that 'If DPA, DPKO and DHA [Department of Humanitarian Affairs] can forge an alliance, we will be a powerful force within the Secretariat. This is [an] aspect which I will develop in [my] SG assignment. [I will concentrate] also on peace-building [and the] growing acceptance that SG/DPA have a political leader-ship role in the field.'[35]

Although Goulding came across as conciliatory and optimistic to his DPA colleagues—an attempt, perhaps, to instil an *esprit de corps* within his unit—in private the Briton was increasingly concerned about the Lead Department concept and the rise of DPKO under Annan. Goulding had reasons to worry, for at the beginning of the new millennium Annan's 'Lead Department' had visibly failed to improve working relations within the Secretariat. Indeed, in the early months of 2000 the DPA–DPKO confrontation reached its zenith. On the face of it, the reasons for this friction were bureaucratic in nature and resulted in a series of confidential memos written by the heads of the two departments to the SG. These documents lamented the state of the DPA–DPKO interface and noted that, ten years after their creation, the functions of these two departments remained largely undefined. Although by this time Goulding had left the UN, some of this correspondence was sent to him—presumably to solicit his advice—and is available among his papers. For the purposes of this book, two aspects of this exchange between DPA and DPKO matter: first, beyond classical reasons of bureaucratic turf lay genuine doubts about the conceptual limits of peacekeeping and its relations with peacebuild-ing; and second, the origins of the DPA–DPKO confrontation were seen as going back to UNAMIR.

(i) DPA: 'Departmental Roles Remain Unclear'

On 24 January 2000 Kieran Prendergast, the Under-Secretary-General for DPA, wrote a confidential note to the Deputy-Secretary-General expressing a number of concerns about the DPA–DPKO interface. 'A more precise delineation of the responsibilities of each Department as regards the conduct of field operations would bring helpful clarity to our respective roles, reduce the scope for the recurrent turf disputes, and thereby promote the team approach which the Secretary-General wants',[36] Prendergast wrote. The

---

[35] Goulding, 'Notes for Farewell Speech to DPA', §7. This passage was written on a scribbled piece of paper that Goulding used during the speech, hence its fragmentary nature.

[36] Kieran Prendergast, Note to the Deputy Secretary-General: DPKO-DPA Interface, 24 January 2000, §2 (MIG-PA).

head of DPA also worried about the reputational damage that the UN organization was incurring as a result of the DPA–DPKO confrontation: 'There is a perception in the Secretariat (and, unfortunately, outside, including among the media) that relations have been worse than usual for quite a while. True or not, it is hard to argue that our relations are as productive and positive as is desirable.'[37]

Prendergast then plunged into what he saw as the heart of the 'Lead Department' problem: '...DPA is in the lead for preventive diplomacy, peacemaking, and peacebuilding while DPKO is in the lead for peacekeeping. But in reality activities in these fields cannot be so neatly compartmentalized. Ambiguities and duplications are inevitable.'[38] Prendergast noted four examples of how Annan's 'Lead Department' concept created problems. Specifically in light of Rwanda and UNAMIR, the first difficulty involved intelligence and 'political' analysis: both fell within DPA's remit, he noted, yet both suffered as a result of friction at Headquarters and in the field. The second example concerned regional expertise—another supposed function of DPA that in Prendergast's opinion sat ill with DPKO's 'lead' in peacekeeping operations[39]—while electoral assistance and post-conflict peacebuilding were also seen by the head of DPA as dysfunctional in the context of the 'Lead Department'. 'In some cases it is unclear how these focal point responsibilities [of DPA] should be carried out in the context of operations for which DPKO has the lead',[40] Prendergast wrote.

Peace negotiations were the fourth example of how difficult it was to define and separate the two departments' tasks: 'Particular problems arise when political negotiations for a settlement take place in the context of a peacekeeping mission', Prendergast noted. 'In our view, DPA should take the lead in such negotiations, given that we are the Department designated with the responsibility for peacemaking and peacebuilding.'[41] For the head of DPA, the 'political' department was in charge of peace negotiations whenever a peacekeeping presence existed (such as in Rwanda), while DPKO was responsible for implementing the peace agreements once they were finalized (such as in Cyprus, Georgia, and Tajikistan).[42] 'DPA's global coverage and its expertise on a number of key issues place it in the best position to take charge of this dimension of field operations', Prendergast wrote, adding that 'much greater clarity is needed on what is the precise allocation of responsibilities in such circumstances.'[43]

It is easy to dismiss Prendergast's complaints as symptomatic of bureaucratic empire-building, and to the extent that they claimed the 'right' for DPA to handle critical phases of UN peace processes, they are. Yet they also

---

[37] Prendergast, Note, §2.   [38] Prendergast, Note, §3.   [39] Prendergast, Note, §11.
[40] Prendergast, Note, §13.   [41] Prendergast, Note, §6.   [42] Prendergast, Note, §7.
[43] Prendergast, Note, §12.

expressed genuine frustration at the nebulous conceptual borders of peace-building and they were not the comments of a disgruntled bureaucrat, for Prendergast was close to Annan and his views were widely shared within DPA.

> One could argue that none of the above matters very much; that turf wars tend to be unavoidable in any large bureaucracy; that the price of clarity would be cumbersome procedures; and that the system has performed adequately in deploying and managing peace-keeping operations at the same time as conduct-ing or observing complicated peace processes that involve many external actors. My view, on the other hand, is that the current status is profoundly damaging to the Organization—its political reputation, staff morale and operational effectiveness.[44]

Significantly for our purposes, Prendergast concluded by singling out UNAMIR as an example of a situation that had become untenable:[45] 'The Carlsson Report criticized the UN for inadequate analysis and information sharing in 1994. Two recent SRSGs (Messrs. Merrem and Martin) both commented in their end-of-mission reports that the quantity and quality of dialogue between the field and Headquarters dropped sharply once the "lead" passed from DPA.... In short, there is a serious problem of lack of clarity over what the two departments should be doing, and of procedures to ensure proper consultation. The result is duplication and friction.'[46]

(ii) DPKO: 'A Clarification is Needed'

Predictably, the DPKO leadership was not pleased with Prendergast's memo. 'I was initially inclined not to reply to the note addressed to you by Mr. Prendergast', Bernard Miyet—the USG for Peacekeeping—wrote to the DSG. 'However, given its vaguely apocalyptic tone and the fact that it raises some fundamental problems, I feel obliged [to do so].'[47] Miyet did so reluc-tantly: for him, only DPA had problems with the 'Lead Department' concept, but 'such arrangements are again being questioned [and]...the very act of questioning can give rise to tensions'.[48]

For the head of DPKO, the department's functions were straightforward. 'DPKO was established in 1992 as the *operational* arm of the Secretary-General for all peacekeeping operations', Miyet wrote, '[and] its mandate and responsibilities were confirmed in 1997 in the context of the reform report of the Secretary-General.'[49] This meant that DPKO's relations with

---

[44] Prendergast, Note, §14.   [45] Prendergast, Note, §14.
[46] Prendergast, Note, §16–17.
[47] Bernard Miyet, Note to the Deputy Secretary-General: DPKO-DPA Interface, 22 February 2000, §1 (MIG-PA).
[48] Miyet, Note, §2.   [49] Miyet, Note, §26 (emphasis added).

DPA should not cause any friction: 'The current division of labour between DPA and DPKO is clear: when a peacekeeping operation is established, DPKO takes the lead for the implementation of the mandate entrusted to the operation by the Security Council. When the peacekeeping operation ends, the lead reverts to DPA. The only way to achieve clarity and to avoid confusion is to adhere to this simple principle.'[50] For Miyet, departing from Annan's rule would take the UN back to the competition and duplication that had characterized the Secretariat in the early 1990s, especially in Rwanda. It would also mean reverting to Boutros-Ghali's memo of October 1993 and to its flawed division of 'political' and 'operational' functions: '...Mr Prendergast suggests that in cases where a peacekeeping operation is deployed, DPA should take the lead in peace negotiations. Such a division of labour was attempted in 1993 under the previous Secretary-General and was found to be highly unsatisfactory.'[51]

What is most striking about Miyet's response is that, for the head of DPKO, the creation of a department dedicated to the management of peacekeeping missions was a decision to entrust 'political' responsibilities to DPKO—a curious comment in light of Boutros-Ghali's memo of October 1993 saying precisely the opposite.[52]

> The truth, whether we like it or not, is that peacekeeping is an eminently political activity and that it is part and parcel of the peace process. The two activities cannot be arbitrarily divided and the chain of command must not be split. Any attempt to do so would create confusion for SRSGs [Special Representatives of the SG] in the field, who will be unsure to whom they should report on a wide range of issues and will end up receiving contradictory instructions. The SRSGs concerned made that abundantly clear in 1993.[53]

While Miyet saw DPKO as the 'operational' arm of the SG, therefore, he also thought that it should be in charge of all 'political' aspects of a peacekeeping mission. Once again, however, the meaning of those terms remained undefined and, far from being rejected, Boutros-Ghali's distinction between 'technical' and 'political' was adopted at face value.

Miyet ended his letter by noting that the UN membership was satisfied with DPKO's primacy over the 'political' aspects of peacekeeping, and would oppose changes to this arrangement: '[M]ember States, especially Members of the Security Council and other interested parties,... obviously feel more comfortable with the "one stop shopping" system inherent in the lead department concept and would not welcome having to go to different entities to discuss the related parts of a single issue.'[54] What Miyet failed to mention,

---

[50] Miyet, Note, §5.   [51] Miyet, Note, §6 (emphasis added).

[52] Boutros Boutros-Ghali, Memorandum: The Establishment and Conduct of United Nations Field Operations, 2 October 1993, §2 (MIG-PA).

[53] Miyet, Note, §6.   [54] Miyet, Note, §6.

however, was that the membership felt more comfortable with DPKO than DPA partly because it could control the former more easily than the latter. Recalling Boutros-Ghali's late attempt, towards the end of his reign, to address the issue, Goulding noted in his diary that the SG was ultimately unable to do so because Boutros-Ghali 'would run into heavy opposition from member states if he merged DPA and DPKO. The two departments would therefore remain distinct', Goulding had noted in August 1996, 'under their separate USGs…'.[55]

Significantly, Miyet's memo also rejected Prendergast's claim that DPKO had failed to cooperate with DPA in Rwanda: 'Mr Prendergast cites the "Carlsson Report" as having criticized the United Nations for inadequate analysis and information-sharing concerning the tragic events of 1994 in Rwanda. I would like to state, however, that those of my colleagues who were here at the time do not remember that DPA offered *any* political analysis or advice to DPKO during the period leading up to the 1994 genocide in Rwanda.'[56] A point on which Prendergast and Miyet agreed, however, was the need for clarity from the top floor of the UN Secretariat: '[T]he Organization is engaged in work that is far too important to be distracted by a constant discussion of organizational arrangements',[57] Miyet wrote. '[Since] DPA continues… to periodically question DPKO's role, if not its very existence, I believe that it may be necessary, once again, to reaffirm DPKO's mandate, at the highest level.'[58] Annan's intervention was by this time inevitable.

PEACEBUILDING AND PEACEKEEPING
AS CONTESTED CONCEPTS

In mid-2000, Annan discussed the 'Lead Department' concept with the heads of DPA and DPKO. For the SG, the formal division of responsibilities outlined in the UN departmental Bulletins was clear and there was no need to revise it. Annan also confirmed his faith in the 'Lead Department' and asked DPA as well as DPKO to endorse a number of principles for its application, which nevertheless simply reproduced the original distinction between the two departments and largely reiterated the points made by DPKO in Miyet's memo. If anything, such principles added a layer of complexity by suggesting that while DPA was in the lead for preventive diplomacy, peacemaking, and peacebuilding—and DPKO was in the lead when a peacekeeping mission was deployed—peacekeeping may also include some elements of peacemaking and

[55] MIG-PD-C, 7-Aug-1996.   [56] Miyet, Note, §20 (emphasis added).
[57] Miyet, Note, §26.   [58] Miyet, Note, §26.

peacebuilding. As the nature of UN involvement in conflict zones changed, the 'lead' should shift between DPA and DPKO. For the SG, this was the end of the matter.

Except that the situation was far more complex than Annan suggested. First, any reference to the SG's 'bulletins' setting out departmental functions could hardly be conclusive since those documents are broad in nature and concise in form. The SG's Bulletin for DPA, for instance, generically identifies that department's functions as 'provid[ing] advice and support to the Secretary-General in the discharge of his global responsibilities related to the prevention, control and resolution of conflicts, including post-conflict peacebuilding, in accordance with the relevant provisions of the Charter of the United Nations and under the mandates given to him by the General Assembly and the Security Council'.[59] It also states that DPA 'provides the SG with advice and support in the *political* aspects of his relations with Member States and intergovernmental organizations';[60] 'provides *political* guidance and instructions to special envoys/SRSGs';[61] prepares 'reports and notes on *political* and managerial issues';[62] and 'advises the SG in giving overall *political* direction to post-conflict peacebuilding efforts'.[63] However, the term 'political' is never explained—and no wonder; as I discovered in New York, SG Bulletins merely establish a general framework and UN departments are encouraged—in line with the Secretariat's tendency to 'improvise' noted at the outset of this chapter—to keep them as concise as possible so as to enable them to incorporate new administrative functions in the future. Second and with reference to the DPA–DPKO exchange mentioned above, it should be noted that both departments were making fairly reasonable claims: while Miyet was right to reject the unworkable DPA proposal—one that had clearly failed in Rwanda—Prendergast's complaints about the unclear delineation of roles between the two departments, especially DPA, were also well-taken. This leads to the third objection to Annan's response in the DPA–DPKO crisis: at its heart the problem was not bureaucratic but conceptual, for the main reason why a clear division of roles between the two departments has never been achieved despite multiple attempts since 1992 is that the conceptual separation between peacekeeping and peacebuilding is much more problematic than is usually thought. As this book has shown, a deceivingly straightforward

[59] ST/SGB/2000/10, §2.1(a). See also Note by the Secretary-General on the Restructuring of the Secretariat, 21 February 1992, A/46/882, in Charles Hill, ed., *The Papers of United Nations Secretary-General Boutros Boutros-Ghali* (New Haven: Yale University Press, 2003), p.31.

[60] United Nations, Secretary-General's Bulletin: Organization of the Department of Political Affairs, 15 May 2000, §2.1(b), in Jean Krasno, ed., *The Collected Papers of Kofi Annan* (Boulder, CO: Lynne Rienner, 2012), p.1092 (emphasis added).

[61] United Nations, Secretary-General's Bulletin, 15 May 2000, §3.2 (emphasis added).

[62] United Nations, Secretary-General's Bulletin, §4.1(c) (emphasis added).

[63] United Nations, Secretary-General's Bulletin, §6.2(d) (emphasis added).

vocabulary—including the term 'political' and the distinction between 'political' and 'operational' peacekeeping—has further compounded the matter.

(i) Peacebuilding as a Contested Concept

The concept of peacebuilding—a core function of DPA—is an example of such ambiguity. Although hundreds of definitions exist, one author described it as 'preventing the outbreak or recurrence of widespread and systematic violence in the short run, while pursuing longer-term actions to construct the social, economic, and political foundations of lasting peace'.[64]

This, however, is exceptionally difficult. To begin with, peace is not a naturally recurring phenomenon, but one that must be patiently advocated and persistently pursued.[65] This book has shown how difficult it is—and how sophisticated an acumen is needed—to facilitate and implement a peace agreement such as Arusha's. In the case of Rwanda, it is important to recall that the UN role there started as a peace*building* rather than a peace*keeping* operation under the responsibility of DPA. That such a young and dysfunctional department was put in charge of an ethnic cauldron like Rwanda shows not only how under-resourced the UN was at the time, but also how large the divide between hopes and realities was in the early 1990s. It also indicates the extent of Boutros-Ghali's determination to empower DPA at the expense of DPKO, both for reasons of expediency (i.e. to better control 'his' Secretariat) and as a matter of policy (i.e. to allow the UN to fulfil its 'moral' mandate of conflict prevention). Having noted that 'peacebuilding, both preventive and post-conflict, is one of the most valuable contributions that the United Nations can make',[66] Boutros-Ghali had also identified DPA as the ideal home for it. This was consistent with the post-Cold War attitude towards sovereignty and the human rights 'revolution' that affected the UN from the 1970s; preventing wars from happening and turning conflict into peace was part of that 'moral'—almost alchemic—UN mission. As one author noted, this approach—one that, as Chapter 9 has shown, was fully endorsed by Boutros-Ghali—'...became the instrument of a new civilizing mission that...relied heavily on the language of international law and the appeal to universal moral values for its legitimization'.[67]

[64] Robert Jenkins, *Peacebuilding* (Abingdon: Routledge, 2013), p.2.
[65] Department of Political Affairs, 'Peacemaking', in Department of Political Affairs, *United Nations Department of Political Affairs* (New York: Department of Public Information, 2007).
[66] Marrack Goulding, Talking Points for the SG at the ACC Meeting, 12 October 1995, p.2 (MIG-PA).
[67] Mark Mazower, *Governing the World: The History of an Idea* (London: Penguin, 2012), p.379.

Second, peacebuilding does not merely aim at preventing wars but is committed to tackling their root causes, which are usually the result of weak institutions and slow 'development' (itself a contested term). As two authors note, 'stable participatory polities usually reflect and rely upon a shared national identity, well-functioning institutions, a wide middle class, and a growing economy. Both in part and often in whole, these are just what are missing in the typical post-civil war environment where there is often more than one ethnic identity, national identity is weak or contested, [and] state institutions have been corrupted or destroyed altogether...'.[68] Third, there is considerable disagreement—both within and outside the UN—as to *what* is needed to build peace, *when* such a process should be initiated, *which* cases are 'ripe' for a solution, and *how* to assess whether peacebuilding has been successful.[69] This has led another observer to write that 'Peacebulding, then, is like a flag, a symbol for rallying around, even as each constituency is permitted its own interpretation of the symbol's meaning.'[70] Fourth and last, the countries that are considered suitable for peacebuilding measures regularly face problems caused by different understandings of what it means to build peace[71]—does 'building peace' mean to end hostilities, to have a solid economy, to build a democratic polity, or to develop a functioning civil society? A peacebuilding process would be set up very differently by different parts of the UN system depending on which of these functions are prioritized.

Due to this uncertainty and to its over-ambitious targets, successful peacebuilding is the exception rather than the rule.[72] To say that DPA is responsible for peacebuilding, therefore, as both Boutros-Ghali and Annan did, hardly amounts to a clear delineation of roles, especially in the complex bureaucratic ecosystem of the Secretariat in which the wider the function, the larger the room for duplication, and the stronger the turf. Goulding summarized the conceptual nebulosity of peace operations by scribbling these words at the back of Miyet's memo:

(i) Some pkos [peacekeeping operations] exist to create a propitious environment for peacemaking: [they are] mainly military;

(ii) others exist to help implement when peacemakers have successfully negotiated: [they are] as much political as mil [military]?

[68] Michael Doyle and Nicholas Sambanis, *Making War and Building Peace* (Princeton: Princeton University Press, 2006), p.19.

[69] Doyle and Sambanis, ch.1.   [70] Jenkins, p.35.

[71] Erin McCandless and Vanessa Wyeth, 'Seeking the Forest through the Trees: Institutional Arrangements and Tools for Peacebuilding', *Journal of Peacebuilding and Development*, Vol.4, No.2 (2008), pp.1–6.

[72] Doyle and Sambanis, p.19.

(iii) pko [peacekeeping] *is* essentially a political activity, but especially so in multid [multi-dimensional] peacekeeping (and leads into peacebuilding).[73]

After almost ten years of attempting a delineation of roles between DPA and DPKO, however, Goulding—like Annan and Boutros-Ghali—failed to grasp the fact that the distinction between 'technical' and 'political' functions of peacekeeping is problematic to the extent that few (if any) decisions taken in New York can be seen as purely 'operational' in nature. In this respect, Prendergast's note fits within the historic DPA–DPKO turf dispute which has been present within the UN since the two departments were created and that has been highlighted throughout this book. With hindsight, however, it is more than that: reflecting the tendency—often the necessity—of the UN to 'think after acting', Prendergast was highlighting a practical problem—the competition between DPA and DPKO—but was really referring to a larger conceptual issue, namely, the difficulty of delimiting the borders between peacekeeping and peacebuilding. He was also raising the issue that while most UN departments had specific functions which were readily recognized as such by the other parts of the bureaucracy, DPA did—and does—not, as the Rwanda case shows. Preventive diplomacy, peacemaking, and post-conflict peacebuilding cover most of the functions of the UN organization *as a whole*— too much for one department to handle. Goulding saw three options out of this dilemma, none of which satisfied him:

(A) muddle on as now;
(B) draft a detailed division of labour (me [in the] summer of 1993);
(C) merge [the] two departments.[74]

Having attempted options (A) and (B)—and having been told that option (C) was off the table—the Briton found himself in a quandary. Either because he was too close to the events or for reasons of professional pragmatism, Goulding failed to realize that his department had been given a virtually impossible task, particularly in light of member states' long-held opposition to a stronger peacebuilding mandate for the SG.

(ii) Peacekeeping versus Peacebuilding

On the surface, peacekeeping is a simpler term to define than peacebuilding, which is why DPKO was seen as 'operational' by Boutros-Ghali. His *Agenda*

---

[73] Marrack Goulding, Hand-written note at the back of Bernard Miyet, Note to the Deputy Secretary-General, 22 February 2000, §1–3 (emphasis in the original, MIG-PA). Parts of this passage are not easy to decipher; the above represents my best attempt at doing so.
[74] Marrack Goulding, Hand-written note, §4.

for Peace defined peacekeeping as 'a United Nations presence in the field, hitherto with the consent of all the parties concerned, as a confidence building measure to monitor a truce between the parties'.[75] The emphasis was on *military* operations because, for Boutros-Ghali, peacekeeping at its core came down to the process of despatching a military force to monitor a cease-fire or a peace agreement.[76] As a concept, however, peacekeeping is only apparently simple: as the lively exchanges between DPA and DPKO discussed in this book repeatedly (though not entirely disinterestedly) suggest, peacekeeping for the DPKO leadership was—and remains—a complex and multi-dimensional process comprising of functions such as the monitoring of elections, the strengthening of civil society, the interpretation of mandates, and the enforcement of resolutions. Indeed, DPKO's current mission state-ment notes that it may be necessary for peacekeeping missions to 'deploy to *prevent* the outbreak of conflict or the spill-over of conflict across borders'[77]— thus making a separation of roles with DPA virtually impossible—while a former DPKO head defined peacekeeping as 'a highly moral enterprise'.[78] The problem is compounded by the fact that peace*building* is broader than—and can be said to include—peace*keeping*.[79] As Tom Quiggin wrote of UN mis-sions in the 1990s, 'On the ground we would not have used the terms "peacekeeping" and "peacebuilding" in any meaningful way.'[80] Both are part of the UN 'peace implementation' process, yet as one author underlines, 'peacebuilding...draws on a much wider range of instruments, beyond mili-tary action, including humanitarian relief, the restoration of public services, economic development initiatives, inter-ethnic reconciliation programs, tran-sitional justice mechanisms, and so forth'.[81] This is partly the reason why the functions given to DPA have remained undefined for such a long time. It is also why, in Rwanda, DPA wished to engage in a comprehensive way that transcended military operations (and why DPKO contested this). According to Jonah, once UNAMIR was deployed, DPKO claimed the right to carry out 'political' work—a position that DPA opposed on the (familiar) ground that peacekeeping must be seen as a continuum.[82]

Although DPA was partly protecting its turf here, it was also defending the perfectly reasonable idea that UN operations are broader than their military components. As the opening section to this chapter suggests, contested and overlapping concepts such as peacebuilding and peacekeeping were

---

[75] Boutros-Ghali, *An Agenda for Peace*, §20–1 and §55–99.

[76] Boutros-Ghali, *An Agenda for Peace*, §20–1 and §55–99.

[77] Department of Peacekeeping Operations, *Mission Statement*, available at https://unngls. org/index.php/engage-with-the-un/un-civil-society-contact-points/23-department-of-peacekeeping-operations-dpko (accessed 1 May 2017) (emphasis added).

[78] Jean-Marie Guehenno, *The Fog of Peace* (Washington, DC: Brookings Institution Press, 2015), p.xvii.

[79] Jenkins, ch.1.   [80] My interview with Tom Quiggin, 4 May 2016 (by email).

[81] Jenkins, p.21.   [82] My interview with James Jonah, 20 July 2011, New York, USA.

developed by UN officials under difficult—even tragic—circumstances and out of practical necessity.[83] As a result, bureaucratic structures in New York (including DPA and DPKO) were built *before* officials had the chance to test whether those structures and their delineation of responsibilities actually worked. This is especially so for DPA, a department that was meant by its creator (Boutros-Ghali) to handle an exceptionally broad range of contested functions, but the expansion of which has consistently been obstructed by member states unwilling to recognize any substantive policy role to the SG.[84] In this respect, the partial strengthening of DPA in 2008—one that I briefly witnessed—is worth mentioning not only because it links the Rwanda story to the Secretariat of today, but also because it shows that the latter's pathologies have yet to be addressed, let alone solved.

BAN KI-MOON, THE USA, AND THE QUEST FOR 'OPERATIONAL PEACEBUILDING'

The election of Ban Ki-moon as SG in late 2006 only partly challenged Annan's 'Lead Department' concept. The role of DPA has come a long way from the sorry state of the early 1990s, when Goulding dismissed it as a 'lightweight'.[85] Yet a number of issues remain, starting with the department's unclear functions and problematic relations with DPKO. The theatres of confrontation may have moved from Rwanda, Cambodia, and Yugoslavia to Mali, Ivory Coast, and Libya, but a fundamental problem lingers: the concept of 'Lead Department' is seen as perpetuating an artificial division of roles—especially when it comes to the so-called 'political' functions of peacekeeping, which remain undefined—while DPKO's ability to provide 'political' analysis is still resented by DPA. As a result, in 2017 as in 1994, 2000, and 2008, DPA–DPKO relations remain tense. The broader problem, too, continues to be a lack of conceptual clarity over what exactly separates a peacekeeping mission from a larger peace operation. The peace processes the UN is supposed to maintain are by definition fragile (which is why the UN is needed) as well as prone to relapse into conflict. As a result, peacekeeping too involves some degree of preventive diplomacy (understood as negotiations aimed at the prevention of conflict), as shown by the fact that several operations currently managed by DPKO are seen by Headquarters as 'political' rather than as 'peacekeeping' missions.[86]

---

[83] Ingvild Bode, *Individual Agency and Policy Change at the United Nations* (Abingdon: Routledge, 2015), p.152.

[84] MIG-PD-C, 7-Aug-1996.   [85] MIG-PD-B, 14-Mar-1993.

[86] 'DPA in the Field', in *United Nations Department of Political Affairs*, p.4.

(i) UN Audit on DPA and DPKO

Several UN audits have acknowledged these issues and have identified the DPA–DPKO friction and the wide tasks of DPA as obstacles to the organization's—not only the Secretariat's—effectiveness. 'The political nature of [DPA's] work is often intangible and difficult to measure',[87] the Office of Internal Oversight Services (OIOS) wrote in 2007 in a confidential report published by *Wikileaks*. 'DPA is mandated to provide political coverage for countries (global portfolio) and is expected to address conflict prevention and peaceful resolution of conflicts by supporting the SG, which is a daunting challenge and involves a broad range of activities.'[88] Issued early in Ban Ki-moon's term, this report also noted that while DPA had been neglected under Annan, Ban wished to enhance its capacity and move away from peacekeeping towards peacebuilding and preventive diplomacy. 'It was a general consensus that the previous senior management of the UN had not often relied on DPA for highly valued political decision making', OIOS wrote, thus substantiating Goulding's fears of a DPA eclipse under Annan—'but frequently used DPA for less value added tasks such as note taking'.[89]

Although Ban wished to reverse this trend, doing so involved tackling some of the fundamental problems mentioned in this book, including the fact that— as the OIOS report noted—'the delineation of roles for certain functions at working level of DPA and DPKO/DFS [are] unclear...'[90] The UN's Audit Office further agreed that the arrangements for peace missions remains flawed: 'The OIOS audit found that the "lead department policy" of the SG for assigning the management responsibility for SPMs [Special Political Missions] to either DPA or DPKO lacked clear criteria and was not consistently applied'.[91] Last but not least, OIOS acknowledged that the Secretariat lacked not only a well-defined strategy on peacebuilding, but also some basic clarity over what the UN's key departments were already expected to accomplish. Writing specifically about DPA's tasks, OIOS noted that:

> There is often no consensus on what conflict prevention practically means on the ground and how it differs in policy and operational terms from 'normal' development interventions that aim to address vulnerability, exclusion, and participation among various United Nations partners.[92]

---

[87] Office of Internal Oversight Services (OIOS), Risk Assessment: Department of Political Affairs, 23 October 2007, p.7, available at https://file.wikileaks.org/file/un-oios/OIOS-20071023-01.pdf (accessed 6 August 2015). Page numbers reflect the pagination indicated in the OIOS document, not that of the entire PDF file.

[88] OIOS, Risk Assessment, p.1.   [89] OIOS, Risk Assessment, p.3.

[90] OIOS, Risk Assessment, p.20.   [91] OIOS, Risk Assessment, p.19.

[92] OIOS, Risk Assessment, p.16.

Twenty-five years after the birth of DPA and DPKO, the UN auditing office was thus making a remarkable acknowledgement, namely, that it is still not clear what the precise functions of the UN's two key departments actually include. What even this report failed to acknowledge, however, is that one of the reasons for the long-standing DPA–DPKO confrontation in New York lies with the fact that those departments have historically had different supporters, and that both the SG and the UN membership—the so-called 'two UNs'—have used those departments to expand their roles. In this respect, it is striking that the three reasons identified by this book as causing friction between DPA and DPKO— bureaucratic competition, power politics, and conceptual confusion—are also some of the reasons behind the failure of the UN Secretariat in Rwanda.

(ii) Ban Ki-moon and 'Operational' Peacebuilding

In this context, Ban Ki-moon launched not so much a clarification of functions but a strengthening of DPA by trying to turn it into an 'operational' department and by advocating its expansion through the establishment of regional DPA offices around the world.[93] During my short time in New York, DPA was thus meant to acquire 'operational' capacity through a field presence in key regions, including regional hubs in Asia, Africa, and South America.[94] The rationale for such a wide-ranging plan was—and in my view remains— compelling, and lay with the recognition that the processes of peacemaking, peacebuilding, and peacekeeping are inseparable from each other and that the UN Secretariat must be able to carry them through the conflict cycle. Yet had it been approved, this approach would have meant questioning the 'Lead Department' concept, a development that remains anathema to DPKO. As one author wrote, in 2008–09 'resistance from DPKO was instrumental'[95] in preventing DPA from receiving the full mandate as the lead UN actor for peacebuilding that Ban wanted it to have. 'DPKO, though weakened by perennial divisions between its Offices of Operations and of Mission Support, was at the time sufficiently strong to veto any such radical changes'.[96] Ban's proposal was also partly blocked by the UN membership, which preferred to create a states-controlled Peacebuilding Commission (PBC). As this book has shown, however, Ban's plan was only the latest development in a long-standing pattern of SGs trying to carve out a role for themselves, a trend that started with Boutros-Ghali in 1992 and that continued with Annan well into

[93] Department of Political Affairs, 'A Critical Investment in Preventing and Resolving Conflicts', *Politically Speaking—Bulletin of the United Nations Department of Political Affairs* (Winter 2007–08), pp.1–2.

[94] 'Boost in Resources for Conflict Prevention', *Politically Speaking—Bulletin of the United Nations Department of Political Affairs* (Spring 2009), pp.1–5.

[95] Jenkins, p.55.   [96] Jenkins, p.55.

the late 1990s and early 2000s. DPA occupied a critical position in this: several influential reports had called for a stronger peacebuilding role for the UN through the 'political' department, and while Goulding's valedictory study had gathered dust in the late 1990s, it was picked up in the new millennium by successive waves of 'reformers' (always a healthy breed in New York). A General Assembly paper had also recommended that DPA become the primary vehicle for post-conflict peacebuilding,[97] while the influential Brahimi Report had advocated a much stronger role for that department—not only in pre-conflict prevention but also in its post-conflict peacebuilding.[98] This is what Boutros-Ghali had originally envisioned for DPA.

Yet by far the most important tool in Ban's attempt to strengthen DPA at the expense of DPKO was Washington's shift of priorities from peacekeeping to peacebuilding. Sceptical if not openly hostile to DPA throughout the 1990s, by the mid 2000s the USA had fully converted to the department's mission. The reasons for this 'epiphany' arguably lie with three major security shocks for Washington, namely, the US Embassy bombings in East Africa in 1998, the assault on the USS *Cole* off the coast of Yemen in 2000, and the terrorist attacks in Washington and New York in 2001. Particularly after the start of its wars in Afghanistan and Iraq, the USA was prepared to invest unprecedented amounts of money into the processes of democratization, stabilization, and peacebuilding (or 'nation-building', as George W. Bush called it).[99] As Rob Jenkins wrote, 'Advocates pleading for increased resources to rebuild states at risk of collapse found themselves being listened to.'[100] The Monterrey Financing for Development Summit of 2002 was only one of the many signs that the so-called 'international community'—or at least an influential part of it—had shifted its interest from the expensive and risky business of peacekeeping to the supposedly 'cheaper' one of peacebuilding. The UN system adapted to, Ban complied with, DPKO mourned, and DPA revelled in this new eco-system, and the fact that the Political Affairs department has since been led by an American is emblematic of this shift of priorities in both Washington and New York. As a senior UN official put it to me, the 'Lead Department' tends to be the one where the Americans are.

THE PEACEBUILDING DILEMMA

Peacebuilding is an important but contested concept. On the one hand, the question of what should be done when the dust of conflict settles is unavoidable for an organization that has made the promotion of international peace

---

[97] General Assembly, *Renewing the United Nations*, 14 July 1997 (A/51/950).
[98] Brahimi Report.   [99] Jenkins, p.21.   [100] Jenkins, p.11.

and security its primary objective.[101] For Boutros-Ghali, peacebuilding had a strong moral component since the UN had an obligation to establish the foundations of peace where it did not exist, and to cement it where it was already present. Intriguingly, a former head of DPKO has written about peacekeeping in strikingly similar terms, noting that it 'can be successful only if it is understood as a highly moral enterprise'[102] requiring the UN to make choices between various goods and evils.[103] Although the UN failures of the 1990s make it easy to dismiss this statement as self-important, by and large the Secretariat has been more successful than is commonly thought in offering solutions to a complex array of problems resulting from civil wars, ethnic strife, and conflict-torn societies. As Thomas Weiss noted, 'even the RAND Corporation has demonstrated that the UN is better able to re-knit societies than the US military and government'.[104] Given the debacles of Afghanistan and Iraq this is admittedly not a very high standard, but the fact that the UN is regularly asked to step in where even the USA has failed suggests that despite inheriting the most intractable issues, the UN is often better positioned at dealing with them than any of its members.

Partly because of its moral connotation, however, peacebuilding remains an essentially contested concept—'a magnet for politically charged ideas',[105] as one author put it. Since 9/11 peacebuilding—not to mention the even more ambitious process of state-building[106]—has assumed a variety of meanings and has been criticized for resting on a number of Western-centric assumptions like free market, human rights, and democracy.[107] Although this is not the place to delve into the 'liberal peacebuilding' controversy,[108] the latter shows how blurred the term has become and how difficult it is to separate it from wide-ranging questions such as what is the best form of government, how peace is durably achieved, whether international actors should be involved in this process and, if so, when and how.[109] Indeed, the conceptual confusion mentioned in this chapter raises an even more basic quandary: what actually constitutes 'peace'? The UN and its members have come a long way from the time when they simply saw it as the absence of war. As the Rwanda case shows, a peace agreement means little without 'human security'—itself a contested term subject to myriads of interpretations.[110] For these reasons,

---

[101] Thomas Weiss, *Foreword*, in Jenkins, p.vii.   [102] Guéhenno, p.xvi.
[103] See also the review of Guéhenno's book in Yvonne Dutton, *Global Governance*, Vol.22 (2016), p.173.
[104] Weiss, p.vii.   [105] Jenkins, p.4.
[106] Timothy Sisk, *Statebuilding* (Cambridge: Polity Press, 2013), p.64.
[107] Charles Call and Susan Cook, 'On Democratization and Peacebuilding', *Global Governance*, Vol.9, No.2 (2003), pp.233–46.
[108] Jenkins, p.26.
[109] Ramesh Thakur, *The United Nations, Peace and Security* (Cambridge: Cambridge University Press, 2006), p.280.
[110] Stephen MacFarlane, *Human Security and the UN* (Bloomington: Indiana University Press, 2006).

assertions that 'a sound understanding seems to have emerged of where UN operations can be deployed, what they can and cannot do, and what kind of institutional foundation they need',[111] appear optimistic. Disagreements over what it means to keep the peace do exist and, according to another author, 'have politicized peacekeeping'.[112] Nevertheless, the fact that, as this chapter has suggested, even different parts of the same bureaucracy cannot agree on what peace operations involve and how they should be carried out, shows that peacekeeping has *always* been 'political'. The above-mentioned DPA–DPKO exchanges are more than symbols of bureaucratic competition and turf; they lay bare the conceptual confusion that has accompanied UN missions since the early 1990s.

The contested nature of—and the blurred borders between—peacekeeping and peacebuilding, including the fact that the latter can be said to include the former, was one reason for the DPA–DPKO rift in Rwanda.[113] Faced with intractable crises, a divided membership, and insufficient resources, the Secretariat rarely has time to engage in philosophical disquisitions. It has to act quickly, is subject to immense public scrutiny, is rarely given credit for its successes whereas its failures are dissected in forensic detail—a charge of which this book may also be guilty. 'The United Nations perfectly embodies in institutional form the tragic paradox of our age', Herbert Nicholas observed, 'it has become indispensable before it has become effective'.[114] The case of UNAMIR shows that problems in the field reflected structural issues at Headquarters, which were in turn the product of conceptual confusion and an unclear delineation of roles between inimical UN departments that were struggling to identify their own functions, let alone those of other parts of the Secretariat. Bureaucratic politics alone, therefore, cannot explain the tensions between DPA and DPKO. The fact that, at different times and for different reasons, these departments had different patrons contributed to their pathologies. UNAMIR was the first victim of this situation and was asked to do the impossible. Bringing operational clarity out of conceptual confusion was a part of it.

---

[111] Silke Weinlich, *The UN Secretariat's Influence on the Evolution of Peacekeeping* (Basingstoke: Palgrave Macmillan, 2014), p.18.

[112] Emily Paddon Rhoads, *Taking Sides in Peacekeeping* (Oxford: Oxford University Press, 2016), abstract.

[113] Barnett et al., 'Peacebuilding: What is in a Name?', *Global Governance*, Vol.13, No.1 (2007), pp.35–58.

[114] Charles Freeman, ed., *Diplomat's Dictionary* (Washington, DC: US Institute of Peace Press, 2009), p.234.

Conclusion

The UN Secretariat, Yesterday and Today

Twenty-five years after the creation of the 'political' and peacekeeping departments—and more than seventy after the birth of the United Nations—the roles of the two largest departments in New York remain elusive not only to them but also to the top UN leadership. Although further research is needed to ascertain whether, and to what extent, the pathologies identified in this book in relation to UNAMIR were replicated in other peace operations around the world, a cursory look at some of the confidential end-of-mission reports contained in the Goulding Archive suggests that this may indeed have been the case. 'There is bewilderment at the apparently conflicting or parallel roles of the Department of Peace-Keeping Operations and the Department of Political Affairs', the head of the United Nations Mission in Bosnia and Herzegovina (UNMBH) wrote for instance in 2000, 'and disappointment that dialogue on policy, implementation of policy, and planning is rare...'[1] The Deputy Special Representative of the SG for Humanitarian Affairs at the United Nations Mission in Kosovo (UNMIK) similarly reported a 'lack of *political* support and clarity for mission... e.g. UNMIK left to muddle through inherent contradictions of SC mandate',[2] while the leadership of the UN Verification Mission in Guatemala (MINUGUA) had similar complaints.[3] 'The answer to this lacuna is relatively simple', one report suggested, and lies with '...a much closer relationship between the Department of Peace-Keeping Operations and the Department of Political Affairs'.[4] Significantly and to some extent ironically, these reports were also copied to Prendergast at DPA and Miyet at DPKO. The pathologies described in this book thus do

---

[1] Jacques Klein, Outgoing Code Cable: Panel on UN Peace Operations, 9 May 2000, §7 (MIG-PA).

[2] Dennis McNamara, Outgoing Code Cable: Panel on United Nations Peace Operations, 3 May 2000, §6 (MIG-PA) (emphasis added).

[3] Jean Arnault, Outgoing Code Cable: Panel on United Nations Peace Operations, 27 April 2000 (MIG-PA).

[4] Klein, §8.

seem to linger and, as mentioned in Chapter 10, have been highlighted by several UN audits, both internal and external. While the partial strengthening of DPA in 2008–09 has given the department a bigger budget, more staff, regional offices, and a heightened influence,[5] it has hardly solved the issues raised in the previous pages.

A reasonable argument can be made that bureaucratic friction is inevitable in any organization, especially one as complex as the UN with its multiple roles, hundreds of offices around the world, and thousands of employees in New York and in the field. Most of the problems associated with peace operations are hardly unique to the UN: waste, mismanagement, interagency competition, and corruption have for instance been acknowledged in US peace operations from Iraq to Afghanistan. Stuart Bower, the Former US Inspector General for the Iraq Reconstruction, wrote that 'Scattered pieces of the current inchoate system needed to be pulled together',[6] and noted that even after this process was completed, 'The Iraq experience exposed the truth that the United States is not well structured to carry out overseas contingency rebuilding operations'.[7] Likewise, competition between different agencies is so widespread in most national bureaucracies that antagonisms between ministries of defence (MODs) and ministries of foreign affairs (MOFAs) are a regular occurrence worldwide.

While retaining some of the pathologies of national bureaucracies, several factors make the DPA–DPKO relationship peculiar. Government ministers are subject to the ultimate authority of a leader—the Prime Minister—who is responsible to the electorate and who has the power to hire and fire them. By contrast, most of the SG's 'cabinet' is composed of officials who have been 'recommended'—if not directly installed, like Goulding—by the Great Powers, so rarely can SGs choose (or even fully trust) their 'ministers'. The UN chief certainly does not have the option to fire them, a circumstance that would be fiercely resented by the UN membership. The largest departments have long been the preserve of the P-5, which are known to negotiate vigorously to install their nationals to key positions.[8] 'Each member of the P-5 can expect to have one major policy USG at Headquarters or in Geneva', Goulding wrote, 'and... they (especially the Americans) sometimes get one or more additional USG or USG-equivalent post'.[9] Tit-for-tat is common: when, in late 1996, Washington vetoed the reappointment of Boutros-Ghali in an successful attempt to replace

---

[5] Robert Jenkins, *Peacebuilding* (Abingdon: Routledge, 2013), p.55.

[6] Álvaro de Soto and Graciana del Castillo, 'Obstacles to Peacebuilding: The Historical Record Revisited', unpublished paper, available at www.acuns.org (accessed 12 November 2015), p.7.

[7] De Soto and del Castillo, p.7. See also Stuart Bowen, 'No More Adhocracies: Reforming the Management of Stabilization and Reconstruction Operations', *Prism*, March 2012.

[8] Houshang Ameri, *Politics of Staffing in the United Nations Secretariat* (New York: Peter Lang, 1996), p.461.

[9] Marrack Goulding, Letter to N.B., 28 May 2001 (MIG-PA).

him with Kofi Annan, France retaliated by vetoing the US candidate and by pledging to stand firm against the USA 'superpower'—until President Chirac was 'promised' that a French official would lead DPKO (the department has since been run by a French national).[10] According to Goulding, 'The price paid to the French [by the USA to have Annan elected] was DPKO which they want to merge with DPA...whereas the Americans are steadfastly opposed to any such merges but are nevertheless insisting that the number of depts [departments] be reduced to five or six'.[11] It is true that Prime Ministers have far more control over ministers than over bureaucrats, yet national administrations have well-established, hierarchical structures that make insubordination both costly and difficult. The same cannot be said of SGs who, as one author wrote, head 'not only a bureaucracy without a government, but also a bureaucracy without a country'.[12] They are also expected to get their proposals—including the all-important UN budget—'voted by a Parliament where everyone belong[s] to the Opposition'.[13]

DPA AND DPKO: WHAT FUNCTIONS EXACTLY?

Other differences are no less significant, especially the division of roles between DPA and DPKO. Most national bureaucracies have well-defined areas of expertise, and while overlapping and competition are to some extent inevitable—again, the ones between MODs and MOFs spring to mind—the existence of accepted procedures, the presence of an unquestioned source of authority, and the fact that ministers depend on their boss for survival, make it both easier and imperative for Prime Ministers to assign roles and monitor their departments. Dysfunctions and pathologies still occur, of course, for national and international bureaucracies share an interest in expanding their functions, a penchant for appropriating budgets, and an opportunistic tendency to grow. Yet the fact that authority comes from an elected leader who has an agenda and is responsible for implementing it before the electorate makes tasks easier to assign and ministers easier to cajole.

Compare this with the situation of DPA and DPKO in the early 1990s, when the two departments were split not only by bureaucratic friction and turf wars, but also by serious conceptual confusion which resulted in a problematic—if not unfeasible—separation of their core competencies. For

---

[10] Marrack Goulding, 'Peacemonger: Book Proposal', 15 June 1998 (MIG-PA).
[11] MIG-PD-B, 16-Dec-1996.
[12] Inis Claude, *Swords into Ploughshares* (New York: Random House, 1971), p.192.
[13] Claude, p.192. See also Marrak Goulding, 'Power Politics at the United Nations', Remarks at the O'Neill/Roberts Seminar, All Souls' College, 5 December 1997, p.3 (MIG-PA).

when and where exactly did peacekeeping and peacebuilding—and thus the roles of DPKO and DPA—begin and end? Answering this question—one that, as this book has shown, had troubled Goulding since 1992—is arguably *more* difficult today than in the 1990s, and this is for two reasons. On the one hand, the scope of peacekeeping has expanded dramatically in recent years: the emergence of non-state actors such as the so-called Islamic State (also known as IS, ISIL, ISIS, or Daesh) and Al-Shabaab, together with the impossibility of signing peace agreements with such actors, mean that the latest peacekeeping mandates approved by the SC in Mali, Somalia, and the DRC have become far more robust than in the past. As a result, peacekeepers are currently asked to engage in offensive rather than defensive operations which are increasingly removed from the traditional approach associated with neutrality, impartiality, and the consent of the parties.[14] 'This is the first time in the history of UN peacekeeping that the Security Council has created a list of enemies that UN peacekeepers are supposed to neutralize',[15] one author wrote, noting that we are witnessing a 'new era of enforcement peacekeeping'.[16] On the other hand and as mentioned in the previous chapter, the scope of peacebuilding has also expanded considerably—including into the difficult terrain of 'state-' and 'nation-building'—thus putting additional stress on already strained and under-financed UN structures. This is partly due to the magnitude of the tasks and partly the effect of the tense relations which these kinds of aggressive operations produce between Secretariat and membership—especially the USA, as the cases of Libya, Afghanistan, and Iraq illustrate. As the Advisory Group of Experts wrote in 2015 in their *Review of the UN Peacebuilding Architecture*, 'When peace operations are deployed, they must, from the beginning, see their purpose as to maximize the creation of space and opportunity for peacebuilding efforts to advance'.[17] In a context where the already overlapping concepts of peacekeeping and peacebuilding are ever expanding, it is no wonder that the bureaucratic roles of DPA and DPKO have become *more* rather than less ambiguous.[18] The fact that the new Peacebuilding Architecture set up fresh structures (the Peacebuilding Commission, the Peacebuilding Fund, and the Peacebuilding Office) without eliminating the old ones (such as DPA and

---

[14] Emily Paddon Rhoads, *Taking Sides in Peacekeeping* (Oxford: Oxford University Press, 2016).

[15] Mateja Peter, 'Between Doctrine and Practice: The UN Peacekeeping Dilemma', *Global Governance*, Vol.21 (2015), p.354.

[16] Peter, p.353.

[17] United Nations, *The Challenge of Sustaining Peace: Report of the Advisory Group of Experts for the 2015 Review of the UN Peacebuilding Architecture* (New York: Department of Public Information, 2015), p.46.

[18] Office of Internal Oversight Services (OIOS), Risk Assessment: Department of Political Affairs, 23 October 2007, p.4, available at https://file.wikileaks.org/file/un-oios/OIOS-20071023-01.pdf (accessed 24 May 2016).

DPKO) has arguably further increased fragmentation and friction. As a former Assistant Secretary-General has warned, the result is that 'the United Nations bureaucracy is getting in the way of its peacekeeping efforts'.[19]

Boutros-Ghali's design of DPA as 'political'—and thus in his view superior—to the merely 'technical' DPKO is another factor that sets the two departments apart from national bureaucracies. Some of the reasons for that distinction were clearly opportunistic, since the former SG believed that limiting DPKO and keeping Washington at bay was the only tool at his disposal to implement his grand strategy. Other reasons were more mundane and consisted in the fact that DPKO was headed by an official whom Boutros-Ghali disliked and saw as a dangerous competitor. 'When ... Boutros-Ghali wanted to clip the wings of Kofi Annan after the latter's intention to challenge him for the Secretary-Generalship had become apparent', Goulding wrote, 'I was instructed, as head of the Political Department ... to insist on my department's responsibility for all "political aspects" of peacekeeping.'[20] Nevertheless, these were contingent factors that administrative changes, shifts in UN leadership, and the passage of time should have addressed. The fact that they have not been addressed suggests that more insidious issues exist in New York which transcend Rwanda, Boutros-Ghali, and the 1990s, and are still largely present at Headquarters. Two such factors linking 1994 to the present are the unclear use of the term 'political', and resulting doubts over the very role and functions of DPA. It is on these doubts that this volume will close.

'POLITICAL': WHAT IS IN A NAME?

This book has suggested that in the early 1990s considerable confusion surrounded the use of the word 'political'. For Boutros-Ghali, it referred to the ability of a department to devise and implement substantive policy-making initiatives, as opposed to merely handling the day-to-day aspects of UN peace operations. As mentioned, the reasons for this distinction were at least partly self-serving, since it was hardly coincidental that he bestowed 'political' functions upon the department which he felt he could more easily control. Towards the end of his mandate, the SG did advocate an integrated approach to human security by arguing that 'political', humanitarian, economic, military, and social problems had to be addressed jointly.[21] In early 1996, this led Boutros-Ghali and Goulding—the very people who had created DPA and DPKO—to conclude that these departments should be merged and to come

---

[19] Anthony Banbury, 'I Love the UN, but it is Failing', *The New York Times*, 18 March 2016.
[20] Goulding, 'Peacemonger: Book Proposal'.   [21] De Soto and del Castillo, p.3.

up with what Goulding defined as a 'secret plan'[22] for such integration, a position that drew the instant wrath of some states and that was quickly abandoned.[23] After Somalia, Rwanda, and Yugoslavia, Boutros-Ghali also recognized in his *Supplement* to *An Agenda for Peace* that intra-state conflicts presented the UN with a challenge—the collapse of state institutions—which the organization had not confronted since the Congo years.[24] Yet at no time did Boutros-Ghali or Goulding spell out what 'political' meant.[25] An intelligence analyst who served the UN in the 1990s defined the 'technical' versus 'political' divide as 'a distinction without a difference. To those on the ground who thought about such issues, there was little real difference'.[26]

Yet as Chapter 10 has shown, the term 'political' and the distinction between 'political' and 'operational' roles—if not departments—remain popular in New York, despite the fact that Boutros-Ghali's successors scored no better in defining it. 'I have tried several times to define the "political" and "operational" aspects of pko's [peacekeeping operations] in a way that would produce a workable division of labour between the two Depts [departments]', Goulding wrote in his handover notes. 'But', he warned his successor, 'I have come to the conclusion that it cannot be done; DPKO *has* to have the capacity for political analysis and direction...'[27]—although Goulding also advised Prendergast to 'watch like a lynx'[28] other departments, especially DPKO, in their attempts to encroach upon DPA's roles. Today, Goulding's conclusions have largely been accepted at UN Headquarters, as has the fact that the distinction between 'technical' and 'political' activities presents peculiar challenges to an organization in which the role of SGs—one that is also controversially termed 'political'[29]—is routinely contested by the UN membership. In November 2014, the High Level Panel on UN Peacekeeping Operations concluded that 'all conflicts are political and a political strategy should guide a more flexible approach to the UN toolbox for dealing with conflicts, instead of a binary choice between special political missions and peacekeeping operations'.[30] Prevention rather than cure was thus preferable to post-conflict action, the Panel noted, while urging states to develop a 'political strategy when dealing with conflicts'.[31] Likewise, in 2015 the Advisory Group of

[22] MIG-PD-C, 1-Mar-1996.   [23] MIG-TD-XII and MIG-TD-XIII.
[24] Boutros Boutros-Ghali, *Supplement to 'An Agenda for Peace': Position Paper of the Secretary-General on the Fiftieth Anniversary of the United Nations* (New York: Department of Public Information, 1995).
[25] MIG-TD-IX, 31-Jul-1993, p.33.
[26] My interview with Tom Quiggin, 4 May 2016 (by email).
[27] Marrack Goulding, Handover Notes for Sir Kieran Prendergast, 22 February 1997, §14 (MIG-PA).
[28] Goulding, Handover Notes, §35.   [29] Claude, p.206.
[30] John Karlsrud, 'Peaceekeeping Pivot? Exploring a More Flexible Approach to Dealing with Conflicts', *Academic Council on the UN System Newsletter*, No.3 (2015), p.4.
[31] Karlsrud, p.4

Experts reviewing the UN Peacebuilding Architecture acknowledged that 'peacebuilding must be understood as an inherently political process'[32] that should accompany the entire UN peace cycle. Two long-time UN insiders who worked closely with Boutros-Ghali have also recognized the 'fundamentally "political" nature of peacebuilding',[33] writing that it justifies 'the leading role that the UN—through its "political" department—had to play [in it] ...,'[34] whereas another author has noted tentatively that the very role of the Secretariat is 'vague but political'.[35] Nevertheless, today as in 1994, there is very little debate—let alone consensus—over what distinguishes 'political' and 'non-political' roles. Goulding himself hardly solved the riddle; to say that DPKO must carry out 'political' work is not very helpful given the ambiguous nature of that term.[36]

The frequency and vagueness with which this vocabulary is used both in general discourse and in UN documents make the lack of debate over its meaning(s) especially surprising. As one author noted, 'it is difficult to say what, if anything, "political" signifies in its various applications and how it signifies what it does'.[37] As is well known, the term derives from the Greek word *polis* ('πόλις'), a community that was present from Archaic and Classical Greece up to Hellenistic times, but which has since disappeared. Attempts to translate *polis* with 'state' are frustrated by the fact that contemporary notions of 'state' and 'city-state' do not reflect the 'moral' ties that bound the inhabitants of Ancient Greece both to the *polis* and to each other. Aristotle notes that the purpose of the *polis* was the 'good or happy life for man';[38] since for him this was also the aim of all sentient beings, Aristotle defines man as a 'political animal' or *zōon politikón* ('ζῷον πολιτικόν'). Seneca and Aquinas agree: 'Man is by nature political, that is, social',[39] they wrote. Since everything human is also 'political', the word is elusive—all the more so in relation to our modern, secular understandings of national and international institutions.

The amorphous nature of the term 'political' is especially problematic in relation to the concepts of peacekeeping and peacebuilding. As this book has shown, in the Secretariat of the early 1990s this word was used—frequently but inconsistently—in two ways, both of which remain common in UN parlance. First, 'political' issues were seen as being linked to—but also distinct

---

[32] United Nations, *The Challenge of Sustaining Peace*, p.21.
[33] De Soto and del Castillo, p.18.   [34] De Soto and del Castillo, pp.12–13.
[35] Silke Weinlich, *The UN Secretariat's Influence on the Evolution of Peacekeeping* (Basingstoke: Palgrave Macmillan, 2014), p.74.
[36] MIG-PD-C, 14-Jun-1996.
[37] Eugene Miller, 'What Does "Political" Mean?', *The Review of Politics*, Vol.42, No.1 (1980), p.56.
[38] Miller, p.63.
[39] 'Homo est naturaliter politicus, id est, socialis', quoted in Hannah Arendt, *The Human Condition* (Chicago: University of Chicago Press, 1998), p.23.

from—economic, humanitarian, and social problems. Boutros-Ghali's integrated approach to human security, for instance, distinguished between 'political', military, humanitarian, social, and economic issues,[40] and even today the path to peace is said to include 'often simultaneous security, political, social, *and* economic transitions'.[41] Since issues related to security, society, and the economy are often part and parcel *with*—not merely linked *to*—'political' processes, separating them is tricky and often impossible. From an organizational perspective, it is perfectly understandable that the UN would want to assign different administrative functions to different departments, as any efficient bureaucracy would do. Since almost every human activity is to some extent 'political', however, the creation of a dedicated department to deal specifically with 'political' issues was bound to increase functional overlap. Distinguishing between 'political', social, and economic aspects of war, poverty, and development is thus as difficult conceptually as it is practically—a point that both of E. H. Carr's 'Intellectual' and 'Bureaucrat', mentioned in this book's introduction, ought to ponder.

The second way of using the term 'political' at the UN is no less problematic and refers to the division between substantive and administrative functions, so that 'political' and 'administrative' were under Boutros-Ghali—and partly remain today—juxtaposed. This usage has a distinguished history at Headquarters: although the first UN peacekeeping mission—the Emergency Force between Israel and Egypt—was supposed to 'refrain from any activity of a political character in a Host State',[42] in September 1960 the USSR proposed the abolition of the SG's office and its replacement with a 'troika' of officials from Western, Soviet, and Non-Aligned countries precisely because Hammarskjöld had in Khrushchev's view pursued a 'political' rather than an administrative role in the Congo.[43] 'While there are neutral countries there are no neutral men',[44] the USSR chairman famously stated in support of the Soviet proposal: 'There can be no such thing as an impartial civil servant in this deeply divided world, and the kind of political celibacy which the British theory of the civil servant calls for is in international affairs a fiction.'[45] Whether the SG is more than an employee of member states remains highly contentious in the UN Headquarters and points to widely different interpretations of the SG's role in world politics. Yet there can be no doubt that since 1945, SGs and their Secretariats have been associated with functions that are

---

[40] De Soto and del Castillo, p.5.   [41] De Soto and del Castillo, p.5 (emphasis added).

[42] Ronald Paris, *At War's End* (Cambridge: Cambridge University Press, 2004), p.14. See also Department of Peacekeeping Operations, 'Establishment of UNEF I', available at http://www.un.org/en/peacekeeping/missions/past/unef1backgr2.html (accessed 24 May 2016).

[43] Alvin Rubinstein, *Soviets in International Organizations* (Princeton: Princeton University Press, 2015), p.275.

[44] Andrew Cordier and Wilder Foote, *Public Papers of the Secretaries General of the United Nations* (New York: Columbia University Press, 2013), p.471.

[45] Cordier and Foote, p.471.

hardly administrative in nature. 'The political role of the Secretary-General of the United Nations is something new to the world', Trygve Lie—the first SG—had stated at San Francisco. 'The concept of a spokesman for the world interest is in many ways far ahead of our times.'[46] Article 99 of the UN Charter—giving to the SG, as it does, the opportunity to 'bring to the attention of the Security Council any matter which in his opinion may threaten the maintenance of international peace and security'[47]—is seen as a source of 'political' rather than administrative authority for the SG. What that authority actually involves, however, is far more difficult to spell out than describing the administrative functions of the SG as a Chief Administrative Officer. As for states, only selectively do they oppose bureaucratic encroachment since, as one author wrote, 'interested partisans alternately welcome and deplore the intrusions of administrative officials into the policy field, depending upon their approval or disapproval of the bureaucratic position on specific issues. One welcomes the support of "disinterested expert" and denounces the opposition of "unrepresentative bureaucrats"'.[48]

WHAT ROLE FOR DPA?

The lack of clarity over what 'political' means and over what the SG's 'political' role entails is arguably most visible in relation to DPA and its title: what kind of 'political' affairs is the department exactly supposed to handle? As this book has shown, this question has been asked in New York since DPA was set up by Boutros-Ghali in 1992. Prior to that, peacekeeping missions were referred to as 'Special Political Affairs' precisely in order to avoid recognizing *any* standard 'political' role to the SG, a circumstance that would have upset many capitals. Yet the confusion over the limits of what the SG can actually do pre-dates 1992 and was only made apparent by the creation of DPA—predictably so, since the department is supposed to assist the SG in discharging 'political' functions which have remained largely undefined. DPA has also been given one of the most ambitious and far-reaching mandates of the UN bureaucracy: to prevent conflicts around the world *before* they happen—or, to put it in 'alchemic' terms, to turn the 'metal' of war into the 'gold' of peace. As DPA claims in a leaflet, this includes as broad a range of functions as 'prevent[ing] political and armed conflicts from escalating';[49] 'peacemaking and preventive

---

[46] Claude, p.211.

[47] United Nations, 'Charter of the United Nations: Chapter XV—The Secretariat', available at http://www.un.org/en/sections/un-charter/chapter-xv/index.html (accessed 21 February 2016).

[48] Claude, p.206.

[49] Department of Political Affairs, *DPA at a Glance* (New York: Department of Public Information, 2007).

diplomacy';[50] 'providing support and guidance to political missions in the field';[51] 'monitoring global political developments';[52] offering the SG 'strategic political analysis';[53] and 'establish[ing] an overarching political framework within which political, developmental and humanitarian action can go forth'.[54] While it is difficult to overestimate the importance of these tasks, they are aims of the UN system *at large*—a system that is inherently 'political'. As OIOS noted, 'the political and diplomatic nature of [DPA's] tasks ... makes it difficult to openly demonstrate DPA's successes and accomplishments, e.g. compared to those of DPKO'.[55] Since what is 'political' continues to be unclear both in DPA and the Secretariat, this is unsurprising.

As I found out at the UN Headquarters in New York, this situation is hardly the fault of DPA officials. On the one hand, there is genuine confusion over the department's mission, with the result that DPA's bureaucratic problems cannot be solved unless the underlying conceptual confusion is addressed first. On the other hand, none of the grounds for distinguishing the functions of DPA and DPKO employed by Boutros-Ghali—that is, the distinction between 'political' and 'technical' tasks, or the separation between 'peace-building' and 'peacekeeping'—offer promising indications about the roles of these two departments, precisely because the underlying issue is conceptual rather than bureaucratic. The Advisory Group of Experts noted that 'the short-comings in efforts to fill the "gaping hole" in the UN's institutional machinery for building peace are systemic in nature. They result from a generalized misunderstanding of the nature of peacebuilding and, even more, from the fragmentation of the UN into separate "silos".'[56] I respectfully disagree: structural problems can be fixed only *if* a department's core mission is clear. Since the very purpose of DPA (i.e. sustaining international peace) coincides with that of the UN (i.e. 'saving succeeding generations from the scourge of war'), it is inevitable that the department would try to project its influence over a wide array of matters. To be sure, there is an element of empire-building here, for DPA remains a bureaucracy and, as such, it is eager to expand, particularly given the amorphous state of the Secretariat. Yet it is unrealistic to expect the department to solve an issue which goes beyond DPA's role and affects the UN Secretariat—indeed, the UN organization—as a whole. As two authors noted in relation to the peacebuilding architecture of 2005, 'The

---

[50] Department of Political Affairs, *Peacemaking and Preventive Diplomacy* (New York: Department of Public Information, 2007).

[51] Department of Political Affairs, *DPA at a Glance*.

[52] Department of Political Affairs, *Conflict Prevention* (New York: Department of Public Information, 2007).

[53] Department of Political Affairs, *Peacebuilding* (New York: Department of Public Information, 2007).

[54] Department of Political Affairs, *DPA at a Glance*.   [55] OIOS, Risk Assessment, p.4.

[56] United Nations, *The Challenge of Sustaining Peace*, p.7.

problem here cannot be solved by moving or creating boxes, or otherwise tinkering with the architecture; to solve it requires an understanding of the nature of the problem. The conceptual penny needs to drop in the minds of those responsible.'[57] That the problems mentioned in this book still linger despite the fact that the Secretariat keeps being 'reformed' suggests that the proverbial penny has yet to drop. António Guterres, the SG who took office in January 2017, indicated a preference for preventing conflict rather than dealing with its aftermath[58] and, like his predecessors, is likely to consolidate the current UN bureaucratic structures, possibly even merging DPA and DPKO. Nevertheless, only bringing conceptual clarity and a clear delineation of roles can address the above-mentioned issues.

Another formidable obstacle—one that is both frequent and inevitable in the context of the UN—stands in the way of defining what different Secretariat units should do. It is not impossible to untangle conceptual confusion *if* there is a desire to do so by the organization's three main actors, namely, the Secretariat, the SG, and member states. This book has explained why DPA and DPKO have shown little desire to do so. For obvious reasons, SGs have been more proactive—but by no means successful—in tackling this relation- ship, and the book has mentioned at length Boutros-Ghali's travails in trying to take charge of the Secretariat by limiting the influence of member states over it. Yet even an arguably less proactive SG such as Ban Ki-moon ran into trouble with the UN membership as soon as he tried to tamper with the existing peacebuilding architecture. When, early in his mandate, the South Korean diplomat attempted to merge Disarmament Affairs and Peacebuilding into DPA's structure, for instance, part of the membership revolted, prompt- ing him to leave the Peacebuilding Support Office largely untouched. Al- though Ban's plan to strengthen DPA was marginally more successful, it was equally resented not only by a certain portion of the UN membership, but also by the managers and bureaucrats of some of 'his' other departments—most notably DPKO—who reportedly lobbied states against the change.[59]

The effects of this complex mixture of conceptual, bureaucratic, and power- political obstacles are nothing short of tragic for the UN's ability to fulfil its mission, that is, the prevention of international conflict. Most of the countries involved in the so-called 'Arab Spring'—Tunisia, Egypt, Libya, Yemen—were not only 'missed' by the UN 'radar', but had in fact been vetted by UN officials as secure and relatively well-governed only a few months before the uprisings began. As the UN High Commissioner for Human Rights said,

[57] De Soto and del Castillo, p.24.
[58] 'Peace is Top Priority for Next Secretary-General, Antonio Guterres', *The Globe and Mail*, 13 October 2016.
[59] Jenkins, p.55. See also Richard Gowan, 'Floating Down the River of History: Ban Ki-moon and Peacekeeping, 2007–2011', *Global Governance*, Vol.17, No.4 (2011), p.405.

Even as the events were unfolding, we read, for example, that Tunisia showed 'remarkable progress on equitable growth, fighting poverty, and achieving good social indicators', that it was 'on track to achieve the MDGs', was 'far ahead in terms of governance, effectiveness, rule of law, control of corruption and regulatory quality', was 'one of the most equitable societies', 'a top reformer', and that 'the development model that Tunisia has pursued over the past two decades has served the country well'.[60]

Just a few months later, however, the suicide of a street vendor was enough to set off a series of protests that forced long-time Tunisian president Ben Ali to flee. These events in turn ignited a chain reaction around the region, affecting those very countries which the UN system was seeing as stable and on a path to economic development. There clearly remains something wrong with the way the UN organization processes information, weighs options, and considers courses of action. Although the contexts of 1994 and 2011 are quite different, they share the UN's inability to predict what its officials would call 'political' crises partly because those crises are as much social, economic, and humanitarian as they are 'political'. Unfortunately, this does not inspire great confidence in the organization's ability to recognize, let alone prevent, conflict.

Studying the contribution of the UN Secretariat to the events of 1994 tells an intriguing, important, and tragic story—not only about the organization of the early 1990s, but also about that of today. This story suggests that the Rwanda events did not happen in a vacuum but within a bureaucratic structure that reflected the conceptual confusion upon which many of the Secretariat's decisions were based, and which percolated from the First Avenue of New York to the streets of Kigali. Such a story also shows that while, in Rwanda, parts of the UN bureaucracy were semi-independent actors making consequential decisions, they were also prized tools in the hands of influential players of the global game. While the Secretariat is often perceived as stolid, this book has suggested that this is hardly the case, has highlighted the bureaucratic origins as well as the human costs of the Rwanda tragedy, and has warned that the latter runs the risk of repeating itself, unless the issues affecting the Secretariat of 1994 are acknowledged and addressed. In this respect, this project is only the first step towards a better understanding of the relations between peacekeeping, peacebuilding, and the UN bureaucracy—an exciting ground for further research.

---

[60] Navy Pillay, 'Statement by the United Nations High Commissioner for Human Rights to the Introduction of the Annual Report', 3 March 2011, available at http://www.ohchr.org (accessed 28 February 2016).

Bibliography

A. Primary Sources

Marrack Irvine Goulding—Meeting Diary [MIG-MD]

MIG-MD-1 (7-10-88 to 17-1-89); MIG-MD-2 (23-1-89 to 13-3-89); MIG-MD-3 (21-1-86 to 30-5-86); MIG-MD-3 (14-3-89 to 3-4-89); MIG-MD-4 (4-4-89 to 13-4-89); MIG-MD-5 (24-4-89 to 28-4-89); MIG-MD-6 (28-4-89 to 20-6-89); MIG-MD-7 (20-6-89 to 7-7-89); MIG-MD-8 (10-7-89 to 12-9-89); MIG-MD-9 (13-9-89 to 10-10-89); MIG-MD-10 (11-10-89 to 6-12-89); MIG-MD-11 (11-12-89 to 2-3-90), MIG-MD-12 (3-3-90 to 19-4-90); MIG-MD-13 (24-4-90 to 19-6-90); MIG-MD-14 (11-7-90 to 7-11-90); MIG-MD-15 (15-11-90 to 15-1-91); MIG-MD-16 (17-1-91 to 22-3-91); MIG-MD-17 (25-3-91 to 6-5-91); MIG-MD-18 (7-5-91 to 7-7-91); MIG-MD-19 (7-7-91 to 12-9-91); MIG-MD-20 (9-9-91 to 2-11-91); MIG-MD-21 (2-11-91 to 25-11-91); MIG-MD-22 (26-11-91 to 16-1-92); MIG-MD-23 (17-1-92 to 13-3-92); MIG-MD-24 (17-3-92 to 14-5-92); MIG-MD-25 (14-5-92 to 14-7-92); MIG-MD-26 (17-7-92 to 31-8-92); MIG-MD-27 (1-9-92 to 24-9-92); MIG-MD-28 (29-9-92 to 26-10-92); MIG-MD-29 (27-10-92 to 2-12-92); MIG-MD-30 (3-12-92 to 24-1-93); MIG-MD-31 (25-1-93 to 17-3-93); MIG-MD-32 (19-3-93 to 5-6-93); MIG-MD-33 (4-6-93 to 3-8-93); MIG-MD-34 (3-8-93 to 15-9-93); MIG-MD-35 (17-9-93 to 1-11-93); MIG-MD-36 (2-11-93 to 25-12-93); MIG-MD-37 (25-12-93 to 7-2-94); MIG-MD-38 (7-2-94 to 15-3-94); MIG-MD-39 (15-3-94 to 10-4-94); MIG-MD-40 (19-4-94 to 9-6-94); MIG-MD-41 (14-6-94 to 9-8-94); MIG-MD-42 (10-8-94 to 9-9-94); MIG-MD-43 (30-9-94 to 14-11-94); MIG-MD-44 (15-11-94 to 18-1-95); MIG-MD-45 (18-1-95 to 22-3-95); MIG-MD-46 (23-3-95 to 27-5-95); MIG-MD-47 (31-5-95 to 20-7-95); MIG-MD-48 (20-7-95 to 22-9-95); MIG-MD-49 (22-9-95 to 5-11-95); MIG-MD-50 (6-11-95 to 18-1-96); MIG-MD-51 (18-1-96 to 12-4-96); MIG-MD-52 (12-4-96 to 12-6-96); MIG-MD-53 (13-6-96 to 23-8-96); MIG-MD-54 (24-8-96 to 23-10-96); MIG-MD-55 (21-10-96 to 10-1-97); MIG-MD-56 (17-1-97 to 13-5-97); MIG-MD-57 (14-5-97 to 15-9-97).

Marrack Irvine Goulding—Personal Diary [MIG-PD]

6 June 1991; 7 June 1991; 8 June 1991; 9 June 1991; 10 June 1991; 11 June 1991; 12 June 1991; 13 June 1991; 14 June 1991; 29 June 1991; 30 June 1991; 1 July 1991; 2 July 1991; 3 July 1991; 4 July 1991; 5 July 1991; 6 July 1991; 7 July 1991; 23 July 1991; 24 July 1991; 25 July 1991; 26 July 1991; 27 July 1991; 28 July 1991; 29 July 1991; 30 July 1991; 31 July 1991; 3 August 1991; 4 August 1991; 8 August 1991; 9 August 1991; 10 August 1991; 11 August 1991; 12 August 1991; 13 August 1991; 14 August 1991; 15 August 1991; 18 August 1991; 31 August 1991; 8 September 1991; 9 September 1991; 10 September 1991; 11 September 1991; 12 September 1991; 13 September 1991; 14 September 1991; 15 September 1991; 16 September 1991; 17 September 1991; 18 September 1991; 19 September 1991; 20 September 1991; 21 September 1991; 22 September 1991; 23 September 1991; 24 September 1991; 25 September 1991; 27 September 1991;

28 September 1991; 29 September 1991; 30 September 1991; 1 October 1991; 2 October 1991; 3 October 1991; 4 October 1991; 5 October 1991; 6 October 1991; 7 October 1991; 8 October 1991; 9 October 1991; 10 October 1991; 11 October 1991; 25 October 1991; 26 October 1991; 27 October 1991; 28 October 1991; 29 October 1991; 30 October 1991; 11 November 1991; 25 November 1991; 26 November 1991; 27 November 1991; 28 November 1991; 29 November 1991; 10 December 1991; 11 December 1991; 12 December 1991; 13 December 1991; 14 December 1991; 15 December 1991; 16 December 1991; 23 December 1991; 24 December 1991; 25 December 1991; 26 December 1991; 31 December 1991; 1 January 1992; 2 January 1992; 3 January 1992; 4 January 1992; 5 January 1992; 26 April 1992; 18 July 1992; 25 July 1992; 26 July 1992; 1 August 1992; 2 August 1992; 9 August 1992; 11 August 1992; 13 September 1992; 4 October 1992; 18 October 1992; 19 October 1992; 20 October 1992; 25 October 1992; 28 October 1992; 21 November 1992; 27 December 1992; 28 December 1992; 29 December 1992; 30 December 1992; 31 December 1992; 1 January 1993; 2 January 1993; 3 January 1993; 4 January 1993; 5 January 1993; 6 January 1993; 7 January 1993; 8 January 1993; 9 January 1993; 10 January 1993; 11 January 1993; 12 January 1993; 13 January 1993; 14 January 1993; 15 January 1993; 16 January 1993; 17 January 1993; 18 January 1993; 14 March 1993; 21 March 1993; 22 March 1993; 28 March 1993; 1 August 1993; 2 August 1993; 3 August 1993; 8 August 1993; 6 September 1993; 7 September 1993; 8 September 1993; 9 September 1993; 10 September 1993; 11 September 1993; 1 October 1993; 2 October 1993; 3 October 1993; 4 October 1993; 5 October 1993; 6 October 1993; 7 October 1993; 8 October 1993; 9 October 1993; 10 October 1993; 11 October 1993; 12 October 1993; 13 October 1993; 14 October 1993; 15 October 1993; 16 October 1993; 17 October 1993; 18 October 1993; 19 October 1993; 20 October 1993; 21 October 1993; 22 October 1993; 23 October 1993; 11 November 1995; 12 November 1995; 13 November 1995; 14 November 1995; 15 November 1995; 16 November 1995; 17 November 1995; 18 November 1995; 19 November 1995; 20 November 1995; 21 November 1995; 22 November 1995; 23 November 1995; 24 November 1995; 25 November 1995; 26 November 1995; 27 November 1995; 28 November 1995; 29 November 1995; 11 December 1995; 12 December 1995; 13 December 1995; 14 December 1995; 15 December 1995; 16 December 1995; 17 December 1995; 18 December 1995; 19 December 1995; 20 December 1995; 2 January 1996; 3 January 1996; 4 January 1996; 5 January 1996; 6 January 1996; 7 January 1996; 8 January 1996; 9 January 1996; 10 January 1996; 11 January 1996; 12 January 1996; 13 January 1996; 14 January 1996; 15 January 1996; 16 January 1996; 17 January 1996; 18 January 1996; 19 January 1996; 20 January 1996; 21 January 1996; 22 January 1996; 30 January 1996; 31 January 1996.

Marrack Irvine Goulding—Travelling Diary [MIG-TD]

TD-I

8 May 1974; 10 May 1974; 20 May 1974; 28 May 1974; 8 December 1988; 9 December 1988; 11 December 1988; 13 December 1988; 10 January 1989; 14 January 1989; 15 January 1989; 17 January 1989; 18 January 1989; 22 January 1989; 17 March 1989; 19 March 1989; 20 March 1989; 20 March 1989; 21 March 1989; 23 March 1989; 25

March 1989; 27 March 1989; 28 March 1989; 30 March 1989; 2 April 1989; 4 April 1989; 6 April 1989; 9 April 1989; 10 April 1989; 11 April 1989.

TD-II

12 April 1989; 13 April 1989; 15 April 1989; 16 April 1989; 18 April 1989; 19 April 1989; 20 April 1989; 21 April 1989; 25 April 1989; 27 April 1989; 29 April 1989; 30 April 1989; 7 May 1989; 8 May 1989; 9 May 1989; 13 May 1989; 15 May 1989; 17 May 1989; 23 May 1989; 2 August 1989; 6 August 1989; 7 August 1989; 11 August 1989; 12 August 1989; 13 August 1989; 14 August 1989; 16 August 1989; 19 August 1989; 23 August 1989; 26 August 1989; 27 August 1989; 30 August 1989; 1 September 1989; 3 September 1989; 5 September 1989; 9 September 1989; 13 September 1989; 16 September 1989; 17 September 1989; 19 September 1989.

TD-III

20 September 1989; 22 September 1989; 21 December 1989; 29 December 1989; 7 January 1990; 8 January 1990; 14 January 1990; 17 January 1990; 24 January 1990; 26 January 1990; 3 February 1990; 7 February 1990; 10 February 1990; 11 February 1990; 14 February 1990; 24 February 1990; 25 February 1990; 1 March 1990.

TD-IV

18 May 1990; 20 May 1990; 14 July 1990; 15 July 1990; 18 July 1990; 23 July 1990; 24 July 1990; 25 July 1990; 29 July 1990; 1 August 1990; 5 August 1990; 7 August 1990; 9 August 1990; 12 August 1990; 16 August 1990; 19 August 1990; 22 August 1990; 25 August 1990; 6 September 1990; 9 September 1990; 6 November 1990; 7 November 1990; 8 November 1990; 9 November 1990; 10 November 1990; 13 November 1990; 17 November 1990; 18 November 1990; 21 November 1990; 9 December 1990; 18 December 1990; 19 December 1990; 8 January 1991; 11 January 1991; 12 January 1991; 13 January 1991; 15 January 1991; 16 January 1991; 24 January 1991; 26 January 1991; 10 February 1991; 12 February 1991; 12 March 1991; 14 March 1991; 17 March 1991; 19 March 1991; 21 March 1991; 23 March 1991; 24 March 1991.

TD-V

25 March 1991; 27 March 1991; 29 March 1991; 31 March 1991; 1 April 1991; 2 April 1991; 3 April 1991; 7 April 1991; 8 April 1991; 11 April 1991; 12 April 1991; 16 April 1991; 19 April 1991; 20 April 1991; 24 April 1991; 25 April 1991; 26 April 1991; 28 April 1991; 29 April 1991; 1 May 1991; 2 May 1991; 4 May 1991; 5 May 1991; 7 May 1991; 8 May 1991; 9 May 1991; 10 May 1991; 12 May 1991; 24 May 1991; 25 May 1991; 26 May 1991; 28 May 1991.

TD-VI

1 June 1991; 16 June 1991; 20 June 1991; 23 June 1991; 26 June 1991; 28 June 1991; 29 June 1991; 10 July 1991; 14 July 1991; 17 July 1991; 20 July 1991; 23 July 1991; 6 August 1991; 7 August 1991; 17 August 1991; 18 August 1991; 22 August 1991; 24 August 1991; 29 August 1991; 30 August 1991.

TD-VII

1 October 1991; 3 October 1991; 6 October 1991; 7 October 1991; 13 October 1991; 16 October 1991; 17 October 1991; 18 October 1991; 19 October 1991; 20 October 1991; 21 October 1991; 24 October 1991; 1 November 1991; 2 November 1991; 5 November 1991; 8 November 1991; 10 November 1991; 17 November 1991; 24 November 1991; 25 November 1991; 1 December 1991; 3 December 1991; 4 December 1991; 8 December 1991; 9 December 1991; 10 December 1991.

TD-VIII

19 June 1992; 22 June 1992; 26 June 1992; 6 July 1992; 7 July 1992; 11 July 1992; 15 July 1992; 17 August 1992; 24 August 1992; 30 August 1992; 1 September 1992; 3 September 1992; 6 September 1992; 2 October 1992; 30 October 1992; 2 November 1992; 4 November 1992; 6 November 1992; 7 November 1992; 8 November 1992; 9 November 1992; 12 November 1992.

TD-IX

12 November 1992; 20 November 1992; 23 November 1992; 24 November 1992; 26 November 1992; 27 November 1992; 28 November 1992; 29 November 1992; 30 November 1992; 4 February 1993; 9 February 1993; 13 February 1993; 20 February 1993; 21 February 1993; 27 February 1993; 28 February 1993; 2 March 1993; 5 March 1993; 8 March 1993; 9 March 1993; 10 March 1993; 31 July 1993; 30 August 1993; 4 September 1993; 7 December 1993; 11 December 1993; 20 December 1993; 22 December 1993; 26 December 1993; 29 December 1993; 31 December 1993; 1 January 1994; 2 January 1994; 7 January 1994; 9 January 1994; 11 January 1994; 12 January 1994; 19 January 1994; 23 January 1994; 24 January 1994; 30 January 1994; 6 February 1994; 12 February 1994; 13 February 1994; 21 February 1994; 3 March 1994; 5 March 1994; 6 March 1994; 7 March 1994; 12 March 1994; 13 March 1994; 28 March 1994; 30 March 1994; 31 March 1994; 1 April 1994; 3 April 1994; 4 April 1994.

TD-X

5 April 1994; 7 April 1994; 8 April 1994; 9 April 1994; 10 April 1994; 15 April 1994; 16 April 1994; 27 April 1994; 1 May 1994; 2 May 1994; 3 May 1994; 4 May 1994; 5 May 1994; 6 May 1994; 7 May 1994; 8 May 1994; 9 May 1994; 10 May 1994; 11 May 1994; 12 May 1994; 13 May 1994; 14 May 1994; 15 May 1994; 16 May 1994; 21 May 1994; 23 May 1994; 24 May 1994; 25 May 1994; 29 May 1994; 30 May 1994; 31 May 1994; 4 June 1994; 5 June 1994; 6 June 1994; 7 June 1994; 8 June 1994; 9 June 1994; 12 June 1994; 13 June 1994; 14 June 1994; 15 June 1994; 16 June 1994; 17 June 1994; 18 June 1994; 25 June 1994; 28 June 1994; 3 July 1994; 4 July 1994; 5 July 1994; 6 July 1994; 7 July 1994; 8 July 1994; 9 July 1994; 10 July 1994; 11 July 1994; 12 July 1994; 13 July 1994; 14 July 1994; 15 July 1994; 16 July 1994; 17 July 1994; 24 July 1994; 25 July 1994; 31 July 1994; 1 August 1994; 2 August 1994; 3 August 1994; 4 August 1994; 5 August 1994; 6 August 1994; 7 August 1994; 14 August 1994; 24 August 1994; 25 August 1994; 30 August 1994; 31 August 1994; 3 September 1994; 5 September 1994; 8 September 1994; 11 September 1994; 12 September 1994; 13 September 1994; 14 September 1994; 15 September 1994; 16 September 1994; 17 September 1994; 18 September 1994; 19

September 1994; 20 September 1994; 21 September 1994; 22 September 1994; 24 September 1994; 25 September 1994; 26 September 1994; 27 September 1994.

TD-XI

11 October 1994; 12 October 1994; 13 October 1994; 14 October 1994; 15 October 1994; 16 October 1994; 17 October 1994; 18 October 1994; 19 October 1994; 20 October 1994; 21 October 1994; 22 October 1994; 23 October 1994; 24 October 1994; 25 October 1994; 26 October 1994; 27 October 1994; 28 October 1994; 29 October 1994; 30 October 1994; 31 October 1994; 1 November 1994; 2 November 1994; 3 November 1994; 4 November 1994; 6 November 1994; 9 November 1994; 10 November 1994; 11 November 1994; 12 November 1994; 13 November 1994; 14 November 1994; 15 November 1994; 16 November 1994; 17 November 1994; 18 November 1994; 19 November 1994; 20 November 1994; 21 November 1994; 22 November 1994; 23 November 1994; 24 November 1994; 25 November 1994; 26 November 1994; 27 November 1994; 29 November 1994; 30 November 1994; 1 December 1994; 2 December 1994; 3 December 1994; 4 December 1994; 5 December 1994; 6 December 1994; 7 December 1994; 8 December 1994; 9 December 1994; 10 December 1994; 11 December 1994; 12 December 1994; 13 December 1994; 14 December 1994; 15 December 1994; 16 December 1994; 17 December 1994; 18 December 1994; 19 December 1994; 20 December 1994; 21 December 1994; 22 December 1994; 23 December 1994; 24 December 1994; 25 December 1994; 26 December 1994; 27 December 1994; 28 December 1994; 29 December 1994; 30 December 1994; 31 December 1994.

Marrack Irvine Goulding—Personal Archive [MIG-PA] (selection)

Aimé, Jean-Claude. Sécret: Répartition des Compétences au Cabinet du Secrétaire Général, 11 January 1994.

Annan, Kofi. Letter to Marrack Goulding, 19 December 1996.

Boutros-Ghali, Boutros. Memorandum: The Establishment and Conduct of United Nations Field Operations, 2 October 1993.

Goulding, Marrack. Command and Control of UN Peace-Keeping Operations, Irish Military College, Dublin, 8 November 1991.

Goulding, Marrack. Email Message, 18 May 2000.

Goulding, Marrack. Handover Notes for Sir Kieran Prendergast, 22 February 1997.

Goulding, Marrack. Letter to Boutros Boutros-Ghali, 23 July 1998.

Goulding, Marrack. Letter to G.M., 14 September 2000.

Goulding, Marrack. Letter to N.B., 28 May 2001.

Goulding, Marrack. Note to Mr Aimé: The Establishment and Conduct of UN Field Operations, 19 July 1993.

Goulding, Marrack. Note to Secretary-General: Report on Visit to the United Kingdom, 9 February 1993.

Goulding, Marrack. Notes for Farewell Speech to DPA, 28 February 1997.

Goulding, Marrack. 'Peacemonger: Book Proposal', 15 June 1998.

Goulding, Marrack. 'Power Politics at the United Nations', Remarks to the O'Neill/ Roberts Seminar, All Souls' College, Oxford, 5 December 1997.

Goulding, Marrack. Practical Measures to Enhance the UN's Effectiveness in the Field of Peace and Security: A Report Submitted to the Secretary-General of the United Nations, 30 June 1997.

Goulding, Marrack. Private Letter, 18 September 1997.

Goulding, Marrack. Recent Development in Peace-Making, International Peace Academy Talk, 31 January 1994.

Goulding, Marrack. Relationship between Office for Special Political Affairs (OSPA) and the Field Operations Department (FOD) (undated).

Goulding, Marrack. Rise and Fall of United Nations Peacekeeping after the End of the Cold War: A Personal Memoir by Marrack Goulding, 8 January 1997.

Goulding, Marrack. Statement Attributable to the Secretary-General, 1 February 1994.

Goulding, Marrack. Talking Points for the Secretary-General at the ACC Meeting, 12 October 1995.

Miyet, Bernard. Note to the Deputy Secretary-General: DPKO–DPA Interface, 22 February 2000.

Pérez de Cuéllar, Javier. Letter to the Permanent Representative of the Union of Soviet Socialist Republics to the United Nations, Yuliy Vorontsov, 21 May 1991.

Prendergast, Kieran. Note to the Deputy Secretary-General: DPKO–DPA Interface, 24 January 2000.

Security Council, The 'Wisnumurti Guidelines' for Selecting a Candidate for SG, November 1996.

Wallroth, C. et al. Report to the Secretary-General on the Review of the Planning and Management of Peacekeeping Operations and Other Special Missions, 6 September 1991.

White House, Presidential Decision Directive No.25 Establishing U.S. Policy on Reforming Multilateral Peace Operations, available at http://fas.org/irp/offdocs/pdd/pdd-25.pdf.

Linda Melvern Rwanda Genocide Archive [LMRGA] (selection)

Ambassade de France à Kigali. Extrait du Message de l'Attaché de Défense à Kigali: Analyse de la Situation Politique, 12 October 1990.

Ambassade Rwandaise au Caire. Secret: Fax n.082/(C)4I to ZAS (undated).

Ambassade Rwandaise au Caire. Lettre à M. Boutros Boutros-Ghali, 15 October 1990.

Ambassade Rwandaise au Caire. Confidentiel: Lettre au Ministère des Affaires Etrangères du Rwanda à Kigali avec copies au Bureau du Président de la République du Rwanda et au Ministère de la Défense du Rwanda, 26 October 1990.

Ambassade Rwandaise au Caire. Fax n.085/(C)4 I to Rwanda Foreign Ministry, 26 October 1990.

Ambassade Rwandaise au Caire. 'Chargement sur le Vol Spécial du 28 Octobre 1990', 28 October 1990.

Ambassade Rwandaise au Caire. Letter to Rwanda Ministry of Defence, 28 October 1990.

Ambassade Rwandaise au Caire. 'Reçu', 31 October 1990.

Ambassade Rwandaise au Caire. Confidentiel: Lettre au Ministre des Affaires Etrangères et de la Coopération Internationale, 19 December 1990.

Ambassade Rwandaise au Caire. Lettre n.206/16.11.18(C)2J, 7 August 1991.

Ambassade Rwandaise au Caire. Confidentiel: Fax n.114(C)182, 16 August 1991.

Ambassade Rwandaise au Caire. Secret: Message Fax n.119(C)4M au Ministère de la Défense du Rwanda, 28 August 1991.

Ambassade Rwandaise au Caire. Urgent: Fax n.135(C)4M, 19 September 1991.

Ambassade Rwandaise au Caire. Fax n.142(C)4M à l'Attention du Colonel Adel du Ministère de la Défense de la République Arabe d'Egypte, 26 September 1991.

Ambassade Rwandaise au Caire. Confidentiel: Fax n.72433 SGCA au Ministère de la Défense d'Egypte, 6 November 1991.

Ambassade Rwandaise au Caire. Lettre à M. Boutros Boutros-Ghali, 25 November 1991.

Ambassade Rwandaise au Caire. Besoins Exprimés à la Partie Egyptienne à Titre d'Aide dans le Cadre de la Coopération Militaire, 14 December 1991.

Ambassade Rwandaise au Caire. Fax n.21/(C)4M to MINDEF Egypt, 16 February 1993.

Ambassade Rwandaise au Caire. Lettre au Ministère de la Défense de la République Arabe d'Egypte, 13 April 1994.

Ambassade Rwandaise au Caire. Fax 35/(C)2F, 13 July 1994.

Ambassade de la République Rwandaise. Décompte des Fonds Transférés par le Ministère de la Défense à l'Ambassade du Caire, 25 May 1994.

Ambassade de la République Rwandaise. Lettre n.159/16.11.18/P1 au Ministère des Affaires Etrangères de la République Arabe d'Egypte, 24 June 1994.

Egyptian Ministry of Defence. 'Offer', December 1991.

Egyptian Ministry of Defence. 'Offer Letter' by Col Sami Said, undated document.

Ministère de la Défense du Rwanda. Acquisition de Matériel Militaire en Egypte, 22 October 1990.

Ministère de la Défense du Rwanda, Fax 01145/02.1.9, 6 November 1991.

Ministère de la Défense du Rwanda. Contrat n.1/92 Entre le Gouvernement de la République Rwandaise et le Gouvernement de la République Arabe d'Egypte sur la Fourniture par l'Egypte d'un Crédit d'Assistance Militaire, 30 March 1992.

Ministère des Affaires Etrangères et de la Coopération Internationale du Rwanda. Très Urgent: Au Président de la République Rwandaise, 23 February 1991.

Ministère des Affaires Etrangères et de la Coopération Internationale du Rwanda. Télégramme Officiel: À M. Boutros Boutros-Ghali, Vice-Premier Ministre de la République Arabe d'Egypte, 24 May 1991.

Ministère des Affaires Etrangères du Rwanda. Très Urgent: AMBARWANDA Caire, 15 July 1992.

Ministry of Defence of Egypt. Delivery Sheet, 11 July 1992.

Ministry of Defence of Egypt. Delivery Sheet, 13 July 1992.

Ministry of Defence of Egypt. Delivery Sheet, 19 July 1992.

Ministry of Defence of Egypt. Offer n.7 to Ministry of Defence of Rwanda (undated).

Minutes of the Informal Consultations of the UN Security Council on Rwanda: 4 April 1994; 5 April 1994; 6 April 1994; 8 April 1994; 9 April 1994; 11 April 1994; 12 April 1994; 13 April 1994; 14 April 1994; 15 April 1994; 18 April 1994; 19 April 1994; 21 April 1994, 22 April 1994; 26 April 1994; 28 April 1994; 3 May 1994; 4 May 1994.

Permanent Mission of Rwanda to the United Nations. Letter to the President of the Security Council Requesting Deployment of UN Military Observers to Rwanda–Uganda Border, 22 February 1993.

Bibliography

Permanent Mission of Rwanda to the UN. Letter from the Permanent Representative of Rwanda to the UN, 15 June 1993.

Présidence de la République. Requête Conjointe du Gouvernement Rwandais et du Front Patriotique Rwandais au Secrétaire-Général Relative à la Mise en Place d'une Force Neutre au Rwanda, 11 June 1993.

Présidence de la République Française. Note à l'Attention du M. le Président de la République au Sujet de l'Entretien avec M. Juvénal Habyarimana, 23 April 1991.

United States Department of State. *The Clinton Administration's Policy on Reforming Multilateral Peace Operations* (Washington, DC: State Department Release, 1994).

United States Department of State. Code Cable from SECSTATE WASHDC to USUN, 13 May 1994.

Mission d'Information Parlamentaire sur le Rwanda [MIPR]
(selection, chronological order)

1962–75

Accord d'Amitié et de Coopération entre la France et le Rwanda, 20 October 1962.
Accord Particulier d'Assistance Militaire, 18 July 1975.
Audition de M. Balladur et de M. Juppé, 21 April 1998.

1982–85

Lettre du Conseiller Technique Guy Penne au Président de la République, 11 June 1982.

Déclaration du Président François Mitterrand à l'Aéroport de Kigali, 7 October 1982.

Conférence de Presse du Président François Mitterrand à Kigali, 7 October 1982.

Allocution du Président François Mitterrand au cours du Déjeuner Offert par le Président du Rwanda, Juvénal Habyarimana, 7 October 1982.

Lettre du Ministre Rwandais des Affaires Etrangères à l'Ambassadeur de France, 22 March 1983.

Modification de l'Article 3 de l'Accord Particulier d'Assistance Militaire, 20 April 1983.

Projet de Lettre de l'Ambassade de France au Rwanda, April 1983.

Lettre du Conseiller Guy Penne au Président de la République, 8 June 1983.

Allocution du Président Mitterrand devant la Communauté Française au Rwanda, 10 December 1984.

Discours du Président François Mitterrand après le déjeuner Offert par J. Habyarimana, 10 December 1984.

Lettre du Conseiller Guy Penne au Président de la République, 11 July 1985.

1990

Télégramme de M. Martre au Ministère de la Défense, 23 January 1990.
Télégramme de M. Martre au Ministère de la Défense, 24 January 1990.
Télégramme de M. Martre au Ministère de la Coopération, 11 March 1990.
Télégramme de M. Martre au Ministère de la Coopération, 12 March 1990.
Préparation du Voyage Officiel en France du Président Habyarimana, 14 March 1990.

Note de l'Ambassadeur de France au Président de la République, 30 March 1990.

Présidence de la République, Note de M. Claude Arnaud, 30 March 1990.

Lettre du Président Juvénal Habyarimana au Président François Mitterrand, 25 May 1990.

Télégramme de M. Barateau au Ministère des Affaires Etrangères, 4 October 1990.

Telegramme Diplomatique, Situation au Rwanda, 7 October 1990.

Lettre de l'Amiral Lanxade au Président de la République, 8 October 1990.

Lettre de l'Amiral Lanxade au Président de la République, 11 October 1990.

Extrait du Message de l'Attaché de Défense à Kigali, 12 October 1990.

Télégramme de M. Martre au Ministère de la Défense, 13 October 1990.

Télégramme de M. Martre au Ministère de la Défense, 14 October 1990.

Analyse de la Situation par la Population d'Origine Tutsi, 15 October 1990.

Télégramme de M. Martre au Ministère de la Défense, 16 October 1990.

Note à l'Attention de Monsieur le Président de la République sur le Rwanda, de la Part du Conseiller à la Présidence de la République, Jean-Christophe Mitterrand, 16 October 1990.

Note de l'Ambassadeur de France pour le Président de la République, 18 October 1990.

Note à l'Attention de Monsieur le Président de la République sur le Rwanda, de la Part du Conseiller à la Présidence de la République, Jean-Christophe Mitterrand, 19 October 1990.

Lettre du Président Juvénal Habyarimana au Président François Mitterrand, 22 October 1990.

Télégramme de M. Martre au Ministère de la Défense, 24 October 1990.

Extrait du Message de l'Attaché de Défense à Kigali, 24 October 1990.

Télégramme de M. Martre au Ministère de la Défense, 25 October 1990.

Note de M. Leveque au Conseiller du Président Mitterrand, 27 October 1990.

Compte Rendu du Conseil des Ministres, 14 November 1990.

Télégramme de M. Martre au Ministère de la Défense, 14 December 1990.

Télégramme de M. Martre au Ministère de la Défense, 19 December 1990.

1991

Note de l'Amiral Lanxade au Président de la République, 2 January 1991.

Télégramme de M. Pagnier sur le Rwanda, 10 January 1991.

Verbatim de la Réunion de Mercredi 23 Janvier à 18H00 au Palais de l'Elysée, 23 January 1991.

Lettre du Chargé de Mission auprès du Président de la République, 30 January 1991.

Lettre du Président Mitterrand au Président Habyarimana, 30 January 1991.

Note de M. Leveque pour le Ministre d'Etat au sujet du Rwanda, 31 January 1991.

Note de l'Amiral Lanxade au Président de la République, 3 February 1991.

Note de Roland Dumas au Président de la République, 12 March 1991.

Lettre du Président Habyarimana au Président Mitterrand, undated.

Note de Gilles Vidal au Président de la République, 22 April 1991.

Note de l'Amiral Lanxade au Président de la République, 22 April 1991.

Note de Gilles Vidal au Président de la République, 23 April 1991.

Note du Général Quesnot au Président de la République, 23 May 1991.

270

Bibliography

Note du Général Quesnot au Président de la République, 20 June 1991.
Message de l'Attaché de Défense à Kigali, 12 August 1991.
Note de Catherine Boivineau au Ministère des Affaires Etrangères, 14 November 1991.
Note de l'Etat Major Particulier auprès de la Présidence de la République, 20 November 1991.

1992

Note de Paul Dijoud au Ministre d'Etat, 11 March 1992.
Lettre du Président Habyarimana au Président Mitterrand, 6 May 1992.
Télégramme de M. Martre au Ministère de la Défense, 5 June 1992.
Télégramme de M. Martre au Ministère de la Défense, 7 June 1992.
Note du Chargé de Mission au Président de la République, 16 June 1992.
Note du Général Quesnot au Président de la République, 1 July 1992.
Note du Général Quesnot au Président de la République, 13 July 1992.
Note de M. Lodiot—Rwanda: Accord Gouvernement, 15 July 1992.
Note de Bruno Delaye au Président de la République, 21 July 1992.
Note du Général Quesnot au Président de la République, 23 July 1992.
Proposition de Modification de l'Accord d'Assistance Militaire, 31 July 1992.
Note du Ministre de la Défense au Président de la République, 6 August 1992.
Courrier du Ministère de la Défense au Ministère des Affaires Etrangères, 6 August 1992.
Avenant du 26 Août 1992 à l'Accord Particulier d'Assistance Militaire, 26 August 1992.
Lettre du Conseilleur du Président, M. Delaye, à l'Ambassadeur de France, 20 October 1992.
Lettre du Président Mitterrand au Président Habyarimana, 20 October 1992.
Lettre du Président Habyarimana au Président Mitterrand, 5 December 1992.

1993

Note du Ministre de la Défense au Président de la République, 26 February 1993.
Lettre du Sénateur Belge Willy Kuijpers au Président Habyarimana, 2 October 1993.
Synthese du Commandant de l'Opération Amaryllis, 12 October 1993.

1994

Minaberry, Jean-Pierre. Lettre du Pilote du Falcon Présidentiel: Missiles Menaçant la Sécurité des Vols du Falcon, 28 January 1994.
Liste des Personnalités Rwandaises Evacuée de l'Ambassade de France vers Bujumbura, 13 April 1994.
Télégramme Diplomatique, Réduction des Effectifs de MINUAR, 22 April 1994.
Compte Rendu de l'Opération Amaryllis, 27 April 1994.
Note du Conseiller de la Présidence au Président de la République, 28 April 1994.
Note du Général Quesnot au Président de la République, 6 May 1994.
Note du Conseiller de la Présidence au Président de la République, 16 May 1994.
Note du Président Sindikubwabo au Président Mitterrand, 22 May 1994.
Note du Général Quesnot au Président de la République, 24 May 1994.
Correspondance entre M. Kouchner et M. Mitterrand, 21 June 1994.

Note du Conseiller de la Présidence au Président de la République, 21 June 1994.
Note du Général Quesnot au Président de la République, 24 June 1994.
Note du Chef d'Etat Major des Armées au Président de la République, 2 July 1994.
Note de l'Admiral Jacques Lanxade, 2 July 1994.

Interviews

Afzal, Ezaz. Chittagong, Bangladesh, 20 April 2016 (and via email on 29 April 2016).
Bolton, John. Washington, DC, USA, 24 June 2011 (and by email on 28 April 2016).
De Soto, Álvaro. New York, USA, 20 July 2011 (and by email on 4 June 2016).
Hannay, David. London, UK, 26 April 2011 (and by email on 12 May 2016).
Jonah, James. New York, USA, 20 July 2011.
Malloch Brown, Mark. London, UK, 28 September 2011 (and by email on 16 June 2016).
Quiggin, Tom. 4 May 2016 (by email).
UN Official. New York, USA, 14 July 2011.

Code Cables (selection, alphabetical order)

Code Cable from Booh Booh/UNAMIR to Annan/DPKO, 12 January 1994.
Code Cable from Booh Booh/UNAMIR to Annan/NEWYORK, 21 April 1994.
Code Cable from Dallaire/UNAMIR to Annan/NEWYORK, 29 April 1994.
Code Cable from Dallaire/UNAMIR to Baril/DPKO, 6 January 1994.
Code Cable from Dallaire/UNAMIR to Baril/DPKO, 11 January 1994.
Code Cable from Dallaire/UNAMIR to Baril/DPKO, 2 February 1994.
Code Cable from Dallaire/UNAMIR to Baril/NEWYORK, 8 April 1994.
Code Cable from Dallaire/UNAMIR to Baril/NEWYORK, 17 April 1994.
Code Cable from Dallaire/UNAMIR to Baril/NEWYORK, 20 July 1994.
Code Cable from Dallaire/UNAMIR to Emery Brusset/NAIROBI, 22 April 1994.
Code Cable from SECSTATE/WASHDC to USUN/NEWYORK, 15 April 1994.
Code Cable from USUN to SECSTATE/WASHDC, 5 May 1994.

Official Briefings by the Spokesman for the UN Secretary-General

7 April 1994; 8 April 1994; 11 April 1994; 12 April 1994; 13 April 1994; 15 April
1994; 18 April 1994; 22 April 1994; 25 April 1994; 26 April 1994; 27 April 1994; 29
April 1994; 2 May 1994; 4 May 1994; 9 May 1994; 11 May 1994; 13 May 1994; 16
May 1994.

Official Statements by the President of the UN Security Council

17 February 1994; 20 February 1994; 21 March 1994; 7 April 1994; 8 April 1994; 10
April 1994; 19 April 1994; 22 April 1994; 26 April 1994; 10 May 1994; 12 May 1994;
14 May 1994.

UN Reports (selection)

Brahimi, Lakhdar. Report of the Panel on UN Peace Operations (A-55-305–S/2000/
809), 21 August 2000.
Department of Political Affairs. *Conflict Prevention* (New York: Department of Public
Information, 2007).

Department of Political Affairs. *DPA at a Glance* (New York: Department of Public Information, 2007).

Department of Political Affairs. *Peacemaking and Preventive Diplomacy* (New York: Department of Public Information, 2007).

DPKO. *Secretary-General's Bulletin for DPKO* (New York: Department of Public Information, 1998).

DPKO. *United Nations Peacekeeping Operations: Principles and Guidelines* (New York: Department of Peacekeeping Operations/Department of Field Support, 2008).

DPKO. *Lessons Learned from the Strategic Assessment for Somalia* (New York: Department of Peacekeeping Operations, undated).

DPKO. *Report of the UN Reconnaissance Mission in Rwanda* (New York: Department of Peacekeeping Operations, undated).

DPKO. *The United Nations Operation in Somalia: Lessons Learned—Report by Mj Gen M Nyambuya* (New York: Department of Peacekeeping Operations, undated).

DPKO/Lessons Learned Unit. *Comprehensive Report on Lessons Learned from United Nations Assistance Mission for Rwanda* (New York: Department of Peacekeeping Operations, 1996).

DPKO/Lessons Learned Unit. *Summary of Lessons Learned from UNOSOM, UNMIH, UNAVEM and UNAMIR* (New York: Department of Peacekeeping Operations, 1996).

DPKO/Lessons Learned Unit. *Report on Status of Implementation of Lessons Learned from Peacekeeping Operations* (New York: Department of Peacekeeping Operations, 1997).

General Assembly. Renewing the United Nations: A Program for Reform, 14 July 1997.

General Assembly. Proposed Program Budget for 2008–2009, 2 November 2007.

Office of Internal Oversight Services, Risk Assessment: Department of Political Affairs, 23 October 2007, p.3, available at https://file.wikileaks.org/file/un-oios/OIOS-20071023-01.pdf (accessed 24 May 2016).

UN Secretary-General. First Report on UNAMIR, 30 December 1993 (S/26927).

United Nations. Further Report of the Secretary-General on Rwanda Concerning the Arusha Peace Agreement and the Possible Role of the United Nations, 24 August 1993 (S/26350).

United Nations. Interim-Report of the Secretary-General on Rwanda, Recommending the Establishment of a UN Observer Mission Uganda-Rwanda, 20 May 1993 (S/1993/25810).

United Nations. Letter Addressed to the UN Secretary-General Transmitting the Peace Agreement Signed at Arusha, 23 December 1993 (A/48/824-S/26915).

United Nations. Peace-Agreement between Government of the Republic of Rwanda and Rwandese Patriotic Front, 4 August 1993.

United Nations. Report on Extrajudicial, Summary, or Arbitrary Executions, 11 August 1993 (E/CN.4/1994/7/Add.1).

United Nations. Report of the Secretary-General on Rwanda, 13 May 1994 (S/1994/565).

United Nations. Report of the Secretary-General on Rwanda, 31 May 1994 (S/1994/640).

United Nations. Report of the United Nations High Commissioner for Human Rights on His Mission to Rwanda of 11–12 May 1994, 19 May 1994 (E/CN.4/S-3/3).

United Nations. Special Report of the Secretary-General on UNAMIR with a Summary of the Developing Crisis and Proposing Three Options for the UN, 20 April 1994 (S/1994/470).

United Nations. Report of the Investigative Team Charged with Investigating Serious Violations of Human Rights and International Humanitarian Law in the DRC, 1998.

United Nations. Report of the Independent Inquiry into the Actions of the United Nations during the 1994 Genocide in Rwanda (S/1999/1257), 1999.

United Nations. *The Challenge of Sustaining Peace: Report of the Advisory Group of Experts for the 2015 Review of the UN Peacebuilding Architecture* (New York: Department of Public Information, 2015).

United Nations. Report of the UN Reconnaissance Mission in Rwanda (undated).

United Nations Assistance Mission for Rwanda (UNAMIR). *Rules of Engagement* (undated).

UNOMUR. Preliminary Report of the Technical Mission to Uganda and Rwanda, 13 April 1993.

UNOMUR. Terms of Reference for UN Technical Mission to Rwanda and Uganda, 31 March 1993.

Urquhart, Brian and Erskine Childers. Reorganization of the UN Secretariat: A Suggested Outline of Needed Reform, UN Report, New York, February 1991.

B. Secondary Sources

Abbott, Kenneth et al. *International Organizations as Orchestrators* (Cambridge: Cambridge University Press, 2015).

Adelman, Howard and Astri Suhrke. 'Rwanda', in David Malone, ed., *The UN Security Council: From the Cold War to the 21st Century* (London: Lynne Rienner, 2004).

African Rights. *Rwanda: Death, Despair, Defiance* (London: African Rights, 1995).

Albright, Madeleine. *Madam Secretary: A Memoir* (London: Pan Books, 2004).

Albright, Madeleine. *PBS Frontline Interview*. 25 February 2004.

Albrow, Martin. *Bureaucracy* (London: Pall Mall Press, 1970).

Alem, Jean-Pierre. *L'Espionage: Histoire et Methodes* (Paris: Lauvauzalle, 1987).

Alex, Gregory. *PBS Frontline Interview*, 18 October 2003.

Ambrosetti, David. *La France au Rwanda: Un Discours de Légitimation Morale* (Paris: Karthala, 2001).

Ambrosetti, David. *Normes et Rivalités Diplomatiques à l'ONU* (Brussels: Peter Lang, 2009).

Ambrosetti, David and Mélanie Cathelin. 'Les Enjeux du Leadership au Conseil de Sécurité: Responsabiliser ou Contrôler les Opérations de Paix de l'ONU?', *Revue Internationale et Stratégique*, No.68 (2007–08).

Ambrosetti, David et al., eds. *Crises et Organisations Internationales* (Paris: L'Harmattan, 2009).

Ameri, Houshang. *Politics of Staffing the United Nations Secretariat* (New York: Peter Lang, 1996).

Anderson, Perry. 'Our Man', *London Review of Books*, 10 May 2007.

Annan, Kofi. *Interventions: A Life in War and Peace* (London: Allen Lane, 2012).

Annan, Kofi. *PBS Frontline Interview*, 17 February 2004.

Annan, Kofi. *The Question of Intervention* (New York: UN Department of Public Information, 1999).

Anyidoho, Henry. *Guns Over Kigali* (Accra: Woeli Publishing, 1997).

Archer, Clive. *International Organizations* (New York: Routledge, 2015).

Archibugi et al. *Cosmopolis. E' Possibile una Democrazia Sovranazionale?* (Rome: ManifestoLibri, 1993).

Arendt, Hannah. *Men in Dark Times* (New York: Harcourt Brace, 1968).

Arendt, Hannah. *The Human Condition* (Chicago: University of Chicago Press, 1998).

Assemblée Nationale, Mission d'Information Parlementaire sur le Rwanda, Auditions, available at http://www.assemblee-nationale.fr/dossiers/rwanda/auditi01.asp (accessed 30 December 2015).

Ban Ki-moon. *My Priorities as Secretary-General*, available at www.un.org/sg/priority.print.htm (accessed 14 July 2015).

Banbury, Anthony. 'I Love the UN, But it is Failing', *The New York Times*, 18 March 2016.

Barkin, Samuel. *International Organization: Theories and Institutions* (Basingstoke: Palgrave, 2013).

Barnett, Michael. *Eyewitness to a Genocide: The United Nations in Rwanda* (Ithaca and London: Cornell University Press, 2002).

Barnett, Michael and Raymond Duvall, eds. *Power in Global Governance* (Cambridge: Cambridge University Press, 2004).

Barnett, Michael. 'The UN Security Council, Indifference, and Genocide in Rwanda', *Cultural Anthropology*, Vol.12, No.4 (1997).

Barnett, Michael and Martha Finnemore. *Rules for the World: International Organizations in World Politics* (Ithaca and London: Cornell University Press, 2004).

Barnett, Michael and Martha Finnemore. 'The Politics, Power and Pathologies of International Organizations', *International Organization*, Vol.53, No.4 (1999).

Barnett, Michael et al. 'Peacebuilding: What is in a Name?', *Global Governance*, Vol.13, No.1 (2007).

Beardsley, Brent. *PBS Frontline Interview*, 15 November 2003.

Beetham, David. *Bureaucracy* (Minneapolis: Minnesota University Press, 1966).

Bell, Duncan. *Ethics and World Politics* (Oxford: Oxford University Press, 2010).

Bellamy, Alex. *The Responsibility to Protect: The Global Effort to End Mass Atrocities* (Cambridge: Polity Press, 2009).

Bellamy, Alex et al. *Understanding Peacekeeping* (Cambridge: Polity Press, 2010).

Bode, Ingvild. *Individual Agency and Policy Change at the UN: The People of the United Nations* (Abingdon: Routledge, 2015).

Bolton, John. *Surrender Is Not An Option: Defending America at the UN and Abroad* (New York: Threshold, 2007).

Bolton, John. 'UN Secretariat Restructuring and Unitary UN' (Speech, Geneva Group Consultative Level Meeting, 19–20 March 1992).

Booh Booh, Jacques-Roger. *Le Patron de Dallaire Parle: Révélations sur les Dérives d'un Général de l'ONU au Rwanda* (Paris: Éditions Duboiris, 2005).

Boswell, James. *The Life of Samuel Johnson* (London: Penguin, 2008).

Boutros-Ghali, Boutros. 'A Grotian Moment', *Fordham International Law Journal*, Vol.18 (1994–95).

Boutros-Ghali, Boutros. *An Agenda for Democratization* (New York: Department of Public Information, 1996).

Boutros-Ghali, Boutros. *An Agenda for Development* (New York: UN Department of Public Information, 1995).

Boutros-Ghali, Boutros. *An Agenda for Peace* (New York: UN Department of Public Information, 1992).

Boutros-Ghali, Boutros. 'Beyond Peacekeeping', *New York University Journal of International Law and Politics*, Vol.25, No.113 (1992–1993).

Boutros-Ghali, Boutros. *Démocratiser la Mondialisation* (Paris: Éditions du Rocher, 2002).

Boutros-Ghali, Boutros. *Émanciper la Francophonie* (Paris: L'Harmattan, 2003).

Boutros-Ghali, Boutros. 'Empowering the United Nations', *Foreign Affairs*, Vol.71, No.5 (Winter 1992).

Boutros-Ghali, Boutros. *En Attendant la Prochaine Lune: Carnets, 1997–2002* (Paris: Fayard, 2004).

Boutros-Ghali, Boutros. *Entre Le Nil et Jérusalem: Chroniques d'un Diplomate Egyptien, 1981–1991* (Paris: Éditions du Rocher, 2011).

Boutros-Ghali, Boutros. 'Le Secrétaire-Général des Nations Unies: Entre l'Urgence et la Durée', *Politique Etrangère*, n.2 (Summer 1996).

Boutros-Ghali, Boutros. *Mes Années à La Maison de Verre* (Paris: Fayard, 1999).

Boutros-Ghali, Boutros. *PBS Frontline Interview*, 21 January 2004.

Boutros-Ghali, Boutros. *Supplement to 'An Agenda for Peace': Position Paper of the Secretary-General on the Fiftieth Anniversary of the United Nations* (New York: Department of Public Information, 1995).

Boutros-Ghali, Boutros. *The United Nations and Rwanda* (New York: United Nations Department of Public Information, 1996).

Boutros-Ghali, Boutros. *Twenty-Twenty Interview*, Transcript of Tape 76 (undated).

Boutros-Ghali, Boutros. 'Un Programa de Paz' (undated), available at http://www.ceppacr.org/3_un_programa_de_paz.pdf (accessed 1 March 2017).

Boutros-Ghali, Boutros. *UNvanquished: A US–UN Saga* (London: I.B. Tauris, 1999).

Boutros-Ghali, Boutros and Shimon Peres. *60 Ans de Conflit Israélo-Arabe* (Brussels: Éditions Complexe, 2006).

Bowen, Stuart. 'No More Adhocracies: Reforming the Management of Stabilization and Reconstruction Operations', *Prism*, March (2012).

Braeckman, Colette. *Rwanda. Histoire d'un Génocide* (Paris: Fayard, 1993).

Burgess, Stephen. *The United Nations Under Boutros-Ghali, 1992–1997* (London: Scarecrow, 2001).

Cahill, Kevin. *Preventive Diplomacy* (Abingdon: Routledge, 2000).

Call, Charles and Susan Cook. 'On Democratization and Peacebuilding', *Global Governance*, Vol.9, No.2 (2003).

Carr, Edward. *The Twenty Years' Crisis: An Introduction to the Study of International Relations* (London: Palgrave Macmillan, 2001).

Carr, Edward. *What is History?* (London: Macmillan, 2001).

Castonguay, Jacques. *Les Casques Bleus au Rwanda* (Paris: L'Harmattan, 1998).

Champagne, Bram. *The UN and Intelligence* (New York: Peace Operations Training Institute, 2006).

Chesterman, Simon. 'Does the UN Have Intelligence?', *Survival*, Vol.48, No.3 (2006).

Chesterman, Simon, ed. *Secretary or General? The UN Secretary-General in World Politics* (Cambridge: Cambridge University Press, 2007).

Chesterman, Simon. 'The Secretary-General We Deserve?', *Global Governance*, Vol.21, No.4 (2015).

Citizens for Global Solutions. 'The Responsibility Not to Veto: A Way Forward' (Washington, DC: CGS, 2010).

Clark, Ian. 'Another "Double Movement": The Great Transformation after the Cold War?', *Review of International Studies*, Vol.25, No.5 (2001), pp.237–55.

Clark, Ian. *Hegemony in International Society* (Oxford: Oxford University Press, 2011).

Clark, Ian. *Legitimacy in International Society* (Oxford: Oxford University Press, 2007).

Clark, Ian. *The Vulnerable in International Society* (Oxford: Oxford University Press, 2013).

Claude, Inis. *Swords into Ploughshares: The Problems and Progress of International Organization* (New York: Random House, 1971).

Clausewitz, Carl. *On War* (Oxford: Oxford University Press, 2008).

Coate, Roger et al. *United Nations Politics: International Organization in a Divided World* (Abingdon: Routledge, 2010).

Cordier, Andrew and Wilder Foote. *Public Papers of the Secretaries General of the United Nations* (New York: Columbia University Press, 2013), 6 volumes.

Cox, Robert and Harold Jacobson. *Anatomy of Influence: Decision Making in International Organization* (New Haven: Yale University Press, 1977).

Curtis, Mark. *The Great Deception: Anglo-American Power and World Order* (London: Pluto, 1998).

Dallaire, Roméo. *PBS Frontline Interview*, 1 April 2004.

Dallaire, Roméo. *Shake Hands with the Devil: The Failure of Humanity in Rwanda* (London: Arrow Books, 2005).

Darnton, Robert. 'The Good Way to Do History', *The New York Review of Books*, 9 January 2014.

De Soto, Àlvaro. 'Confidential: End of Mission Report', May 2007, available at http://image.guardian.co.uk/sys-files/Guardian/documents/2007/06/12/DeSotoReport.pdf (accessed 10 June 2015).

De Soto, Àlvaro and Graciana Del Castillo. 'Obstacles to Peacebuilding: The Historical Record Revisited', *Global Governance*, Vol.22, No.2, April–June (2016).

De Stefani, Paolo. 'Lo Spazio dell'ONU nei Processi di Produzione Normativa Internazionale', *Pace, Diritti dell'Uomo, Diritti dei Popoli*, Vol.7, No.2 (1993).

Deme, Amandou. *Rwanda 1994 and the Failure of the United Nations Mission* (Bloomington: XLibris, 2010).

Department of Political Affairs. 'Peacemaking', in *United Nations Department of Political Affairs* (New York: Department of Public Information, 2007).

Derrida, Jacques. *Archive Fever: A Freudian Impression* (Chicago: University of Chicago Press, 1988).

Derrida, Jacques. *La Voix et le Phénomène* (Paris: Presses Universitaires de France, 1967).

Derrida, Jacques. *Who Is Afraid of Philosophy?* (Stanford: Stanford University Press, 2002).

Des Forges, Alison. *PBS Frontline Interview*, 1 October 2003.

Di Nolfo, Ennio. *Prima Lezione di Storia delle Relazioni Internazionali* (Rome: Laterza, 2006).

Di Nolfo, Ennio. *Storia delle Relazioni Internazionali, 1918–1999* (Rome: Laterza, 2007).

Dorn, Walter. 'The Cloak and the Blue Helmet: Limitations on Intelligence in UN Peacekeeping', *International Journal of Intelligence and Counterintelligence*, Vol.12, No.4 (1999).

Dorn, Walter. 'United Nations Peacekeeping Intelligence', in Linton Johnson, ed., *The Oxford Handbook of National Security Intelligence* (Oxford: Oxford University Press, 2010).

Dorn, Walter and David Bell. 'Intelligence and Peacekeeping', *International Peacekeeping*, Vol.2, No.1, (1995).

Doyle, Mark. *PBS Frontline Interview*, 12 December 2003.

Doyle, Michael. *Keeping the Peace: Multinational UN Operations in Cambodia and El Salvador* (Cambridge: Cambridge University Press, 1997).

Doyle, Michael. *Making War and Building Peace: United Nations Peace Operations* (Princeton: Princeton University Press, 2006).

Doyle, Michael and Nicholas Sambanis. 'International Peacebuilding: A Theoretical and Quantitative Analysis', *American Political Science Review*, Vol.94, No.4 (2000).

Doyle, Michael and Nicholas Sambanis. *Making War and Building Peace* (Princeton: Princeton University Press, 2006).

Dunham, Jeremy et al. *Idealism* (London: Acumen, 2011).

Durch, William, ed. *UN Peacekeeping, American Policy and the Uncivil Wars of the 1990s* (Basingstoke: Palgrave Macmillan, 1996).

Duroselle, Jean-Baptiste. *Introduction à l'Histoire des Relations Internationales* (Paris: Armand Colin, 2007).

Dutton, Yvonne. Book Review, *Global Governance*, Vol.22 (2016).

Economides, Spyros and Mats Berdal, eds. *United Nations Interventionism, 1991–2004* (Cambridge: Cambridge University Press, 2007).

Eriksson, Pär. 'Intelligence in Peacekeeping Operations', *Intelligence and Counterintelligence*, Vol.10, No.1 (1997).

Erskine, Toni. 'Blood on the UN's Hands? Assigning Responsibilities and Apportioning Blame to an Intergovernmental Organisation', *Global Society*, Vol.18, No.1 (January 2004).

Farge, Arlette. *Le Goût de l'Archive* (Paris: Seuil, 1989).

Fasulo, Linda. *An Insider's Guide to the United Nations* (New Haven: Yale University Press, 2004).

Feil, Scott R. 'Could 5,000 Peacekeepers Have Saved 500,000 Rwandans? Early Intervention Reconsidered', E. A. Walsh School of Foreign Service, Georgetown University, Vol.III, No.2 (1997).

Foley, Michael. *Political Leadership* (Oxford: Oxford University Press, 2013).

Foot, Rosemary, Stephen MacFarlane, and Michael Mastanduno. *US Hegemony and International Organizations* (Oxford: Oxford University Press, 2003).

Freedman, Lawrence. *Strategy: A History* (Oxford: Oxford University Press, 2013).

Freeman, Charles, ed. *The Diplomat's Dictionary* (Washington, DC: US Institute of Peace Press, 2009).

Fröhlich, Manuel. *Political Ethics and the United Nations* (Abingdon: Routledge, 2007).

Gaiduk, Ilya. *Divided Together: The United States and the Soviet Union in the United Nations, 1945–65* (Stanford: Stanford University Press, 2012).

Gaillard, Philippe. *PBS Frontline Interview*, 12 December 2003.

Gambari, Ibrahim. *PBS Frontline Interview*, 15 January 2004.

Gambari, Ibrahim. 'Rwanda: An African Perspective' in David M. Malone, ed., *The UN Security Council: From the Cold War to the 21st Century* (London: Lynne Rienner, 2004).

Gardam, Judith. *Necessity, Proportionality and the Use of Force by States* (Cambridge: Cambridge University Press, 2011).

Gardiner, Samuel. *A History of the Commonwealth* (London: Forgotten Books, 2012).

George, Terry, dir. *Hotel Rwanda* (Los Angeles: Lions Gate Entertainment, 2005).

Gharekhan, Chinmaya. *The Horseshoe Table: An Inside View of the UN Security Council* (New Delhi: Longman, 2006).

Ginzburg, Carlo. 'Microhistory: Two or Three Things That I Know About It', *Critical Inquiry*, Vol.20, No.1 (1993).

Goodsell, Charles. *The New Case for Bureaucracy* (Thousand Oaks, CA: CQ Press, 2014).

Goodspeed, Stephen. *The Nature and Function of International Organization* (New York: Oxford University Press, 1967).

Gordenker, Leon. *The UN Secretary-General and Secretariat* (Abingdon: Routledge, 2010).

Gordenker, Leon. *The UN Secretary-General and the Maintenance of Peace* (New York: Columbia University Press, 1967).

Goulding, Marrack. *Peacemonger* (London: John Murray, 2002).

Goulding, Marrack. 'The Evolving Role of the United Nations in International Peace and Security', *Irish Studies in International Affairs*, Vol.3, No.4 (1992).

Gowan, Richard. 'Floating Down the River of History: Ban Ki-moon and Peacekeeping, 2007–2011', *Global Governance*, Vol.17 (2011).

Griffiths, Claire. *Contrasting Historical Divides in Francophone Africa* (Chester: Chester University Press, 2013).

Grint, Keith. *Leadership* (Oxford: Oxford University Press, 2010).

Gromyko, Andrei. *Memoirs* (New York: Hutchinson, 1989).

Guéhenno, Jean-Marie. *The Fog of Peace: A Memoir of International Peacekeeping in the 21st Century* (Washington: Brookings Institution Press, 2015).

Guichaoua, André. *Les Crises Politiques au Burundi et au Rwanda* (Lille: Lille University Press, 1995).

Haas, Peter. 'Introduction: Epistemic Communities and International Policy Coordination', *International Organization*, Vol.46 (1992).

Hammarskjöld, Dag. *To Speak for the World: Speeches and Statements* (Stockholm: Atlantis, 2005).

Hannay, David. 'Intelligence and International Agencies', in Harold Shukman, ed., *Agents for Change: Intelligence Services in the 21st Century* (London: St Ermin's, 2000).

Hannay, David. *New World Disorder: The UN After the Cold War* (London: I.B. Tauris, 2008).

Hazzard, Shirley. *Countenance of Truth* (New York: Viking, 1990).

Hehir, Aidan. *The Responsibility to Protect: Rhetoric, Reality and the Future of Humanitarian Intervention* (Basingstoke: Palgrave Macmillan, 2012).

Hessel, Stéphane. *Danse avec le Siècle* (Paris: Éditions du Seuil, 2011).

Hibbert, Christopher. *Wellington: A Personal History* (New York: HarperCollins, 2010).

Hilderbrand, Robert. *Dumbarton Oaks: The Origins of the United Nations and the Search for Postwar Security* (Chapel Hill: University of North Carolina Press, 1990).

Hill, Charles, ed. *The Papers of the United Nations Secretary-General Boutros Boutros-Ghali* (New Haven: Yale University Press, 2003), 3 volumes.

Holbrooke, Richard. *To End a War: The Conflict in Yugoslavia* (New York: Modern Library, 1999).

Holmes, Richard. *Wellington: The Iron Duke* (New York: HarperCollins, 2003).

Holzner, Burkart and John Marx. *Knowledge Application: The Knowledge System in Society* (Boston: Allyn and Bacon, 1979).

Hopkins, Raymond and Richard Mansbach. *Structure and Process in International Politics* (New York: Harper & Row, 1973).

International Peace Academy. *Peacekeepers Handbook* (New York: Pergamon, 1994).

Jenkins, Robert. *Peacebuilding: From Concept to Commission* (Abingdon: Routledge, 2013).

Jindal, Bobby. *Leadership and Crisis* (London: Regnery, 2010).

Johnston, Paul. 'No Cloak and Dagger Required: Intelligence Support to UN Peacekeeping', *Intelligence and National Security*, Vol.12, No.4 (1997).

Jolly, Richard et al. *The Power of UN Ideas* (New York: UN Intellectual History Project Series, 2005).

Jolly, Richard et al. *UN Ideas that Changed the World* (Bloomington: Indiana University Press, 2009).

Jonah, James. 'Differing State Perspectives on the United Nations in the Post-Cold War World', J. W. Holmes Memorial Lecture, *ACUNS Reports*, No.4 (1993).

Jonah, James. 'Independence and Integrity of the International Civil Service: The Role of Executive Heads and the Role of States', *International Law and Politics*, Vol.14 (1982).

Jonah, James. *What Price the Survival of the United Nations? Memoirs of a Veteran International Civil Servant* (Ibadan: Evans Brothers, 2006).

Kagame, Paul. *PBS Frontline Interview*, 30 January 2004.

Keating, Colin. 'An Insider's Account' in David Malone, ed., *The UN Security Council: From the Cold War to the 21st Century* (London: Lynne Rienner, 2004).

Kennedy, Paul. *The Parliament of Man: The United Nations and the Quest for World Government* (London: Penguin, 2007).

Kille, Kent. *From Manager to Visionary: The Secretary-General of the United Nations* (London: Palgrave, 2006).

Kille, Kent. 'Reconsidering the Power of the Secretary-General: Religious Leadership and Moral Authority in International Affairs', Annual Meeting of the American Association of Political Science, 30 August 2006.

Kille, Kent, ed. *The UN Secretary-General and Moral Authority: Ethics and Religion in International Leadership* (Washington, DC: Georgetown University Press, 2007).

Knott, Jack and Gary Miller. *Reforming Bureaucracy: The Policy of Institutional Choice* (New Jersey: Prentice Hall, 1987).

Krasno, Jean, ed. *The Collected Papers of Kofi Annan: UN Secretary-General, 1997–2006* (Boulder, CO: Lynne Rienner, 2012), 5 volumes.

Lang, Anthony. 'A Realist in the Utopian City: Boutros Boutros-Ghali's Ethical Framework and Its Impact', in Kent Kille, ed., *The UN Secretary-General and Moral Authority: Ethics and Religion in International Leadership* (Washington, DC: Georgetown University Press, 2007).

Langmore, John and Jeremy Farrall. 'Can Elected Members Make a Difference in the UN Security Council? Australia's Experience in 2013–2014', *Global Governance*, Vol.22, No.1 (2016).

Larsson, Pavel. *The United Nations, Intelligence, and Peacekeeping* (Lund: Lund University, 2007).

Levi, Giovanni. 'On Microhistory', in Peter Burke, *New Perspectives on Historical Writing* (Cambridge: Polity Press, 1991).

Lie, Trygve. *In the Cause of Peace* (New York: Macmillan, 1954).

Lowe, Vaughan et al., eds. *The United Nations Security Council and War: The Evolution of Thought and Practice Since 1945* (Oxford: Oxford University Press, 2010).

Luck, Edward. *Mixed Messages: American Politics and International Organization, 1919–1999* (Washington, DC: Brookings Institution Press, 1999).

Luck, Edward. *The UN Security Council: Practice and Promise* (Abingdon: Routledge, 2006).

McCandless, Erin and Vanessa Wyeth. 'Seeking the Forest through the Trees: Institutional Arrangements and Tools for Peacebuilding', *Journal of Peacebuilding and Development*, No.4, no.2 (2008).

McDermott, Anthony. *United Nations Financing Problems and the New Generation of Peacekeeping and Peace Enforcement* (Providence, RI: Watson Institute Press, 1994).

MacFarlane, Neil et al. *Human Security and the UN: A Critical History* (Bloomington: Indiana University Press, 2006).

MacGregor Burns, James. *Leadership* (New York: HarperCollins, 2010).

MacQueen, Norrie. *Peacekeeping and the International System* (Abingdon: Routledge, 2006).

Mahmood, Mamdani. *When Victims Become Killers: Colonialism, Nativism and the Genocide in Rwanda* (Princeton: Princeton University Press, 2002).

Maier, Kenneth. *Politics and the Bureaucracy* (Belmont, CA: Wadsworth Publishing, 2006).

Malone, David. 'Security Council', in Thomas Weiss and Sam Daws, eds, *The Oxford Handbook on the United Nations* (Oxford: Oxford University Press, 2008).

Malone, David, ed. *The UN Security Council: From the Cold War to the 21st Century* (London: Lynne Rienner, 2004).

Malone, David. 'US–UN Relations in the UN Security Council in the Post-Cold War Era', in Foot et al, eds., *US Hegemony and International Organizations* (Oxford: Oxford University Press, 2003).

Marchal, Luc. *Rwanda, La Descente aux Enfers* (Brussels: Éditions Labor, 2001).

Mastrolilli, Paolo. *Lo Specchio del Mondo: Le Ragioni della Crisi dell'ONU* (Rome: Laterza, 2005).

Mayall, James. *The New Interventionism, 1991–94* (Cambridge: Cambridge University Press, 1996).

Mazower, Mark. *Governing the World: The History of an Idea* (London: Penguin, 2012).

Mazower, Mark. *No Enchanted Palace: The End of Empire and the Ideological Origins of the United Nations* (Princeton: Princeton University Press, 2009).

Meisler, Stanley. *Kofi Annan: A Man of Peace in a World of War* (London: J Wiley & Sons, 2007).

Melvern, Linda. *A People Betrayed: The Role of the West in Rwanda's Gencide* (London: Zed Books, 2009).

Melvern, Linda. 'Briefing by Linda Melvern: Question and Answers', United States Holocaust Memorial Museum, see https://www.ushmm.org/confront-genocide/speakers-and-events/all-speakers-and-events/briefing-by-linda-melvern/briefing-by-linda-melvern-questions-and-answers.

Melvern, Linda. *Conspiracy to Murder: The Rwandan Genocide* (London: Verso, 2006).

Miller, Eugene. 'What Does "Political" Mean?', *The Review of Politics*, Vol.42, No.1 (January 1980).

Moose, George. *PBS Frontline Interview*, 21 November 2003.

Morgenthau, Hans. *Politics Among Nations: The Struggle for Power and Peace* (New York: Knopf, 1967).

Northouse, Peter G. *Leadership: Theory and Practice* (London: Sage, 2012).

Ntisoni, Lambertus. *J'ai Traversé des Fleuves de Sang: Le Calvaire d'un Officier des Ex-Forces Armées Rwandaises* (Paris: L'Harmattan, 2007).

Nye, Joseph. *Understanding International Conflict* (New York: Pearson, 2005).

O'Brien, Conor. *To Katanga and Back* (New York: Grosset and Dunlop, 1962).

Oestreich, Joel, ed. *International Organizations as Self-Directed Actors* (Abingdon: Routledge, 2012).

Oficina del Comisionado Para los Derechos Humanos, *El Aporte de las Naciones Unidas a la Globalización de la Ética* (Santiago: División de Desarrollo Social de las Naciones Unidas, 2001).

Ohlin, Jens David. *The Assault on International Law* (Oxford: Oxford University Press, 2015).

Paddon Rhoads, Emily. *Taking Sides in Peacekeeping: Impartiality and the Future of the United Nations* (Oxford: Oxford University Press, 2016).

Paris, Ronald. *At War's End* (Cambridge: Cambridge University Press, 2004).

Peck, Connie. 'Special Representatives of the Secretary-General', in David Malone, ed., *The UN Security Council: From the Cold War to the 21st* Century (London: Lynne Rienner, 2004).

Pérez de Cuéllar, Javier. *Pilgrimage for Peace: A Secretary-General's Memoir* (London: St Martin's Press, 1997).

Peter, Mateja. 'Between Doctrine and Practice: The UN Peacekeeping Dilemma', *Global Governance*, Vol.21 (2015).

Peters, B. Guy. *The Politics of Bureaucracy* (Abingdon: Routledge, 2009).

Piiparinen, Touko. *The Transformation of UN Conflict Management: Producing Images of Genocide from Rwanda to Darfur and Beyond* (Abingdon: Routledge, 2009).

Plauchut, Agathe and Patrice Pourtal. *L'ONU Face au Génocide Rwandais: Le Silence des Machetes* (Paris: L'Harmattan, 2012).

Plesch, Dan. *America, Hitler and the UN: How the Allies Won World War II and Forged Peace* (London: I.B. Tauris, 2011).

Ponomaryov, Boris et al. *History of Soviet Foreign Policy* (London: ILP Press, 2001).

Power, Samantha. *Chasing the Flame: Sergio Vieira de Mello and the Fight to Save the World* (London: Penguin, 2008).

Price, Richard, ed. *Moral Limit and Possibility in World Politics* (Cambridge: Cambridge University Press, 2008).

Prunier, Gérard. *Rwanda, 1959–1996: Histoire d'un Génocide* (Paris: Éditions Dagorno, 1997).

Prunier, Gérard. *The Rwanda Crisis: History of A Genocide* (London: Hurst & Company, 1998).

Quiggin, Tom. 'Intelligence in Support of UN Peacekeeping in Bosnia during the 1990s', *Spy Museum*, podcast available at http://www.spymuseum.org (accessed 11 February 2013).

Quiggin, Tom. 'Response to No Cloak and Dagger Required: Intelligence Support to UN Peacekeeping Missions', *Intelligence and National Security*, Vol.13, No.4 (1998).

Ramcharan, Bertrand. *Preventive Diplomacy at the UN* (Bloomington: Indiana University Press, 2008).

Ramjoué, Melanie. 'Improving United Nations Intelligence: Lessons from the Field', Geneva Centre for Security Policy Papers No.19, August 2011.

Rawson, David. *PBS Frontline Interview*, 5 October 2003.

Recchia, Stefano and Jennifer Welsh. *Just and Unjust Military Intervention* (Cambridge: Cambridge University Press, 2013).

Renouvin, Pierre and Jean-Baptiste Duroselle. *Introduction à l'Histoire des Relations Internationales* (Paris: Armand Colin, 2007).

Rich, Nathaniel. 'James Baldwin & the Fear of a Nation', *The New York Review of Books*, 12 May 2016.

Riza, Iqbal. *PBS Frontline Interview*, March 2003.

Rotberg, Robert and Thomas Weiss. *From Massacres to Genocide: The Media, Public Policy and Humanitarian Crises* (Washington, DC: Brookings Institution, 1996).

Roux, André. 'Intelligence and Peacekeeping: Are We Winning?', *Conflict Trends*, No.3 (2008).

Rubinstein, Alvin. *Soviets in International Organizations: Changing Policy Toward Developing Countries, 1953–1963* (Princeton: Princeton University Press, 2015).

Ruggie, John. 'The UN: Stuck Between Peacekeeping and Enforcement', in *Peacekeeping: The Way Ahead?* (Washington: Institute for National Strategic Studies, 1993).

Safty, Adel. 'Moral Leadership: Beyond Management and Governance', *Harvard International Review*, 6 May 2006.

Saint-Exupéry, Patrick De. *L'Inavouable: La France au Rwanda* (Paris: Les Arènes, 2004).

Salton, Herman. 'L'Autorité Morale du Secrétaire-Général des Nations Unies', in Blandine Chélini-Pont, ed., *Annuaire Droit et Religions* (Aix-en-Provence: Presses Universitaires d'Aix-Marseille, 2013).

Savio, Roberto. 'Boutros Boutros-Ghali: A Turning Point in the History of the United Nations', *Human Wrongs Watch*, 16 February 2016.

Scheid, Don. *The Ethics of Humanitarian Intervention* (Cambridge: Cambridge University Press, 2014).

Schlesinger, Stephen. *Act of Creation: The Funding of the United Nations* (Cambridge, MA: WestView, 2003).

Sciora, Romuald, ed. *À la Maison de Verre: L'ONU et Ses Secrétaires-Généraux* (Paris: Saint-Simon, 2006).

Searle, John. *Expression and Meaning* (Cambridge: Cambridge University Press, 1976).

Semelin, Jacques. *Purify and Destroy: The Political Uses of Massacre and Genocide* (New York: Columbia University Press, 2007).

Sisk, Timothy. *Statebuilding* (Cambridge: Polity Press, 2013).

Steedman, Carolyn. *Dust: The Archive and Cultural History* (Manchester: Manchester University Press, 2001).

Stone, John. *Military Strategy: The Politics and Technique of War* (London: Continuum, 2011).

Strange, Susan. *The Retreat of the State* (Cambridge: Cambridge University Press, 1997).

Tatu, Michel. *Power in the Kremlin* (New York: Viking, 1967).

Tauzin, Didier. *Rwanda: Je Demande Justice pour la France et ses Soldats* (Paris: Jacob-Duvernet, 2011).

Thakur, Ramesh. *The United Nations, Peace and Security: From Collective Security to Responsibility to Protect* (Cambridge: Cambridge University Press, 2006).

Thant Myint-U and Amy Scott. *The UN Secretariat: A Brief History, 1945–2006* (New York: International Peace Academy, 2007).

Thant, U. *View from the UN* (New York: Doubleday, 1978).

Thompson, Allan. *Media and the Rwanda Genocide* (London: Pluto Press, 2007).

Tolstoy, Leo. *War and Peace*, tr. Larissa Volokhonsky and Richard Pevear (London: Penguin, 2006).

Traub, James. *The Best Intentions: Kofi Annan and the UN in the Era of American World Power* (London: Bloomsbury, 2007).

Tzu, Sun. *The Art of War* (London: CreateSpace, 2013).

United Nations. *Charter of the United Nations* (New York: Department of Public Information, 2006).

United Nations. *The Blue Helmets: A Review of UN Peacekeeping* (New York: Department of Public Information, 1996).

United Nations. *The United Nations and Rwanda, 1993–1996* (New York: Department of Public Information, 1996).

United Nations. *The United Nations and Somalia* (New York: Department of Public Information, 1996).

United States Department of State. *The Clinton Administration's Policy on Reforming Multilateral Peace Operations* (Washington, DC: State Department, 1994).

United States Senate. *U.S. Participation in Somalia Peacekeeping: Hearing before the Committee on Foreign Relations* (Washington, DC: United States Senate, 2012).

Urquhart, Brian. *A Life in Peace and War* (New York: Norton, 1987).

Urquhart, Brian. *Hammarskjold* (New York: Harper, 1972).

Urquhart, Brian. *Peacemaking, Peacekeeping and the Future: The John W Holmes Memorial Lecture* (Toronto: GREF Publishing, 1990).

Urquhart, Brian. 'Thoughts on the 20th Anniversary of Dag Hammarskjöld's Death', *Foreign Affairs*, Vol.60 (1981).

Van Kappen, Frank. 'Strategic Intelligence and the United Nations', in *Peacekeeping Intelligence: Emerging Concepts for the Future* (London: OSS, 2003).

Verdirame, Guglielmo. *The UN and Human Rights: Who Guards the Guardians?* (Cambridge: Cambridge University Press, 2011).

Verschave, François-Xavier. *La Françafrique* (Paris: Stock, 1998).

Vreeland, James and Axel Dreher. *The Political Economy of the UN Security Council: Money and Influence* (Cambridge: Cambridge University Press, 2014).

Wallis, Andrew. *Silent Accomplice* (London: I.B. Tauris, 2014).

Waugh, Colin. *Paul Kagame and Rwanda: Power, Genocide and the Rwanda Patriotic Front* (London and Jefferson, NC: McFarland, 2004).

Weber, Max. 'Bureaucracy', in Hans Gerth and Charles Wright Mills, eds, *From Max Weber: Essays in Sociology* (Oxford: Oxford University Press, 1978).

Weber, Max. *Theory of Social and Economic Organization* (Oxford: Oxford University Press, 1947).

Weinlich, Silke. *The UN Secretariat's Influence on the Evolution of Peacekeeping* (Basingstoke: Palgrave Macmillan, 2014).

Weiss, Thomas. *What's Wrong with the United Nations and How to Fix It* (Cambridge: Polity Press, 2009).

Weiss, Thomas and Rorden Wilkinson, eds. *International Organization and Global Governance* (Abingdon: Routledge, 2013).

Weiss, Thomas and Sam Daws, eds. *The Oxford Handbook on the United Nations* (Oxford: Oxford University Press, 2008).

Weiss, Thomas et al. 'The "Third" United Nations', *Global Governance*, Vol.15 (2009), pp.123–42.

Willame, Jean-Claude. *Les Belges au Rwanda. Le Parcours de la Honte* (Brussels: Éditions GRIP/Complexe, 1997).

Willum, Bjørn. 'Legitimizing Inaction Towards Genocide in Rwanda: A Matter of Misperception?' *International Peace-Keeping*, Vol.6, No.3 (Autumn 1999).

Wilson, James. *Bureaucracy* (New York: Basic Books, 1991).

Woods, Ngaire et al. *Effective Leadership in International Organizations* (Geneva: World Economic Forum, 2014)

Yakemtchouk, Romain. *La Politique Étrangère de la Russie* (Paris: L'Harmattan, 2008).

Zacklin, Ralph. *The UN Secretariat and the Use of Force in a Unipolar World* (Cambridge: Cambridge University Press, 2012).

Index